HEALTHCARE IN CHILDREN'S MEDIA

Children's Literature Association Series

HEALTHCARE IN CHILDREN'S MEDIA

Edited by Naomi Lesley and Sarah Layzell

University Press of Mississippi / Jackson

The University Press of Mississippi is the scholarly publishing agency of
the Mississippi Institutions of Higher Learning: Alcorn State University,
Delta State University, Jackson State University, Mississippi State University,
Mississippi University for Women, Mississippi Valley State University,
University of Mississippi, and University of Southern Mississippi.

www.upress.state.ms.us

The University Press of Mississippi is a member
of the Association of University Presses.

Copyright © 2025 by University Press of Mississippi
All rights reserved
Manufactured in the United States of America

∞

Publisher: University Press of Mississippi, Jackson, USA
Authorised GPSR Safety Representative: Easy Access System
Europe - Mustamäe tee 50, 10621 Tallinn,
Estonia, gpsr.requests@easproject.com

Library of Congress Control Number: 2025932625
ISBN 9781496857859 (hardback)
ISBN 9781496857866 (trade paperback)
ISBN 9781496857873 (EPUB single)
ISBN 9781496857880 (EPUB institutional)
ISBN 9781496857897 (PDF single)
ISBN 9781496857903 (PDF institutional)

British Library Cataloging-in-Publication Data available

CONTENTS

Acknowledgments ix

Introduction: A Systemic Overview of Healthcare
(and Its Absence in Media for Children) 3
Naomi Lesley and Sarah Layzell

Interview with Dallas Ducar, CEO of Transhealth, and
Nichole Mayweather-Banks, LCSW, Founder of Changing
FACES Counseling & Wellness, LLC 21
Naomi Lesley, Dallas Ducar, and Nichole Mayweather-Banks

Part 1: Healthcare in Contemporary Realism

Substance Use, Community Healing, and Care Gaps in
Children's Literature 37
Naomi Lesley

Conjoinment as/and Inequality in Sarah Crossan's *One* 59
Joseph Holloway

Mental Health and Masculine Silence in Adib Khorram's
Darius the Great Is Not Okay 85
Jeremy Johnston

Part 2: Bibliotherapy and Health Literacy Books

An Interview with Anna Macdonald, Graphic Medicine Project
Manager for Comics Youth 109
Sarah Layzell and Anna Macdonald

Dealing with Dementia: Patients and Their Caregivers in
German Picturebooks 120
Farriba Schulz and Antje Tannen

Caregiving Children and Absent Medical Professionals:
Hyperemesis Gravidarum in Picturebooks 141
B.J. Woodstein

Moving toward Literature-Based Dentistry to Boost Oral Health
Literacy of Children: Interprofessional Partnerships between
Dentists, Doctors, and Librarians. 162
Valerie A. Ubbes, Madison Miner, and Manjushri Karthikeyan

Part 3: Storytelling Ethics and Speculative Care

An Interview with Sudeshna Shome Ghosh, Publisher for
Talking Cub, about *A Bend in Time: Writings by Children on the
COVID-19 Pandemic*. 199
Sarah Layzell and Sudeshna Shome Ghosh

"Unviling" ALife: Ethical Choices of Healthcare Practitioners
about Future Children. 204
Anna Bugajska

Shifting Stories: Care Ethics and Masculinities in the Television
Series *Teen Wolf* 225
Carrie Spencer

The Metaphor of Madness: Metaphor and Mental Illness in
Contemporary YA Fiction. 246
Melanie Goss

"No One Would Be Moved by Any Feeling Save Pity":
Children, Narrative, and Healthcare in Annie Fellows Johnston's
Little Colonel Series 264
Dawn Sardella-Ayres

Afterword: Women of Color Health Equity Collective Executive
Board Discussion: Health Inequities and COVID-19. 290
Vanessa E. Martínez-Renuncio, Dayna Campbell, and Jenise Katalina

About the Contributors 299

Index 305

ACKNOWLEDGMENTS

We are indebted to many people for bringing this volume to fruition. Thank you to Katie Keene and Katie Turner at the University Press of Mississippi for supporting us through the publication process. We also thank our anonymous reviewers, whose thorough and careful comments were invaluable in improving the volume.

Thank you to everyone who attended the panel on Healthcare in Children's Literature at ChLA 2018, whose thoughtful responses encouraged us to put together a book on this topic. Sarah would also like to acknowledge the Arts and Humanities Research Council UK for providing the funding that enabled them to attend the conference.

Thank you to Gretchen Papazian and Daniel Lesley for their generous and thoughtful readings and suggestions on the introduction. Thank you to Meghanne Flynn for additional library services.

We extend special gratitude to Abbye E. Meyer, who was an integral part of this volume from the beginning. Abbye, we appreciate all the work you contributed in the form of organizational support and editorial suggestions.

Last, we thank our dedicated contributors, who patiently stuck with this project through many delays, and our interviewees, who generously contributed their time and expertise. We are so glad to be able to see your wonderful research and writing go out into the world.

HEALTHCARE IN CHILDREN'S MEDIA

INTRODUCTION

A Systemic Overview of Healthcare (and Its Absence in Media for Children)

NAOMI LESLEY AND SARAH LAYZELL

In Mildred D. Taylor's novel *Let the Circle Be Unbroken*, set in the 1930s, an outbreak of scarlet fever sweeps through the rural Mississippi community that is home to the Logans, a family of Black landowners in the Jim Crow South. Narrator Cassie falls seriously ill and is cared for in isolation from the rest of her family. Several characters die of the disease. Another of Taylor's Logan novels, *The Road to Memphis*, shows a character experiencing a medical emergency and being refused treatment at a whites-only hospital, then being cared for in the community before his death. In the final novel in the series, *All the Days Past, All the Days to Come*, a now-adult Cassie experiences white medical practitioners sexually harassing her and refusing to treat her; meanwhile, her father David refuses to seek formal medical advice at all.[1]

These seemingly minor subplots contain a multitude of detail about illness, recovery, and healthcare systems in the US pre- and post–World War II, covering experiences of epidemics, community care networks, home remedies, and impacts of refusal of access to medical care. These books are not *about* healthcare; nonetheless, Taylor offers representation that informs our understanding of historical and contemporary health inequalities in ways that speak to child readers, literary critics, and medical professionals alike.

Taylor's series is one example of how healthcare issues are subtly built into many children's novels even when they are not the focus of the plot. Moreover, the systemic issues highlighted by her novels are still relevant despite changes in medicine and healthcare delivery. Of course, the past decade has seen enormous upheavals in healthcare systems around the world. The most obvious of these is the COVID-19 pandemic that has stretched healthcare institutions to their breaking points, exacerbated vaccination debates, and forced communities to reconsider their approaches to homelessness and food insecurity. Disruption has not begun and ended with the pandemic, however. Medical research developments in the field of gene therapy and gene editing have also raised questions about bioethics and health equity. Disability communities are increasingly concerned that gene editing may slide into eugenic erasure (Hafner). In the meantime, the cost of sought-after therapies calls attention to inequities in both nationalized and privatized healthcare systems, as these systems struggle to provide basic care to many patients (Robbins and Nolen). Political shifts have also threatened the health of millions internationally, including austerity policies in the UK, a global refugee crisis, and ongoing threats to Medicaid and gender-affirming care in the US.

The editors began work on this collection prior to the pandemic, and much has already changed since our contributors first began to send us their work.[2] Nevertheless, many of the dramatic events in healthcare over the past decade are not new, but rather highlight and heighten long-existing vulnerabilities in care systems. The questions we began with are still relevant. How does children's media represent healthcare systems? Does this media acknowledge issues of accessibility, financial strain, and inequity? What can medical professionals learn from children's media about effective care? How does children's media demonstrate the caretaking work that children do and model communities that care for the caretakers? What new ethical quandaries are raised by advances in medical science? What does "care" mean outside a medical framework?

This collection examines a range of children's media. Our contributors examine how children are confronted with healthcare issues in picturebooks, novels, comic books, e-textbooks, and television shows. Most of our contributors focus on texts from the US and the UK, but we include discussions of children's media from four different nations, because healthcare systems and experiences vary widely by nationality. Some of these international comparisons allow us to see similarities in issues across national boundaries; for example, Farriba Schulz and Antje Tannen's examination of German picturebooks and B.J. Woodstein's analysis of British picturebooks both highlight how picturebooks are used as tools to socialize children into understanding gendered and intergenerational networks of family caregiving. The essays in this collection also reach into the past and the future, to children's literature from the early 1900s and to young adult futuristic dystopias, to contemplate what models of healthcare children might see other than the systems they encounter in their own lives. Finally, in considering texts for this collection, we were expansive in our definition of "healthcare system." While some contributors discuss formal healthcare systems and access to medical treatment, some consider informal caregiving networks. Still other essays explore foundational assumptions of healthcare; Melanie Goss's chapter, for example, considers how metaphors of illness prevalent in our language shape the kinds of treatment and recovery trajectories we imagine. Despite these variations, the essays in this collection all address systemic issues in healthcare and not solely experiences of illness. To the extent that language systems, community support systems, and bioethical systems become important and sometimes invisible components of our more formalized care systems, we felt they were important to address in this volume. We are aware that this volume does not cover many aspects of healthcare in international children's media, including issues of racial bias and toxic stress, healthcare in Indigenous communities, and healthcare within colonized territories. We hope this volume will prompt further inquiries into these important issues of healthcare in children's media.

The global pandemic has shaped this collection of essays. Sadly, several contributors had to withdraw from the project, as disruptions to their lives prevented their participation. Our hope is that this collection is only the beginning of a conversation to which these excellent scholars can contribute at a later date. The pandemic also produced a flood of educational children's media, and we include interviews with publishers and public health workers about the impact of the pandemic on children's media. Finally, the pandemic may shape many readers' responses to the essays in this collection. Although most of the media discussed by these scholars was published prior to 2020, the issues raised by these essays—inequities in the impact of illness, ethical questions about care rationing, and the importance of informal care networks, among others—have taken on more urgency in public discourse despite having been long-standing issues.

CURRENT SCHOLARSHIP

The essays in this volume build upon existing scholarship about health and sickness in children's media. Some of this scholarship focuses on healthcare delivery in classic children's books, examining how representations of healthcare are elided in books about illness. Alexandra Valint, for example, observes an erasure of care work in the unofficial, home-based healthcare setting of *The Secret Garden*, while Helen A. Aveling questions why Pollyanna's experience in the hospital is shielded from the reader's view (25). Meredith Guthrie suggests that the prevalence of white middle-class disabled characters means that many novels for young people take access to treatment for granted (185). Other scholars investigate the generic conventions of children's literature about illness. Julie Elman, for example, focuses on the genre of young adult "sick-lit," noting that the purpose of cancer-kid tearjerkers is not to illuminate the experiences of teens in the oncology system, but to encourage volatile teenaged readers to become emotionally mature adults (179). Gabriel Duckels examines recent queer young adult novels that use conventions of melodrama to help young adult readers navigate the ongoing legacy of the AIDS crisis; he has also worked with Amy Ryder to explore the emerging representation of COVID-19 in texts for children. This scholarship provides insight into what illness novels are meant to do for readers and why they render healthcare systems invisible or irrelevant to the story. Contributors to this volume broaden our understanding of illness narratives for children and youth by attending to this important aspect of illness—even when it may be partially written out of the texts.

A more recent strain of children's literature scholarship focuses on depictions of mental illness in children's media. Some of this work, like Imogen Church's analysis of female mental illness in picturebooks, focuses on how representations of mentally ill characters reflect historical changes in stigma. Other scholars reference rising levels of diagnoses in young people and explore how children's literature can either raise awareness of or misrepresent available treatment for mental illness. Alyssa Chrisman traces representations of treatment for obsessive-compulsive disorder (OCD) and urges scholars to attend to intersectional oppression that influences teen characters' (and teen readers') access to effective treatment. Kia Jane Richmond outlines some of the treatments modeled in a large body of young adult novels that represent mental illness.

Another body of scholarship comes from medical and public health approaches. Pediatricians, child psychologists, and oncologists use children's books to increase health literacy and to help children and their families to work through the implications of diagnosis and treatment. They critique representations of illness and healthcare in children's literature through a different lens. One fairly large-scale US study examined forty-five picturebooks about maternal breast cancer, culled from a wider Amazon search. The authors argue that easy access to emotionally engaging and medically accurate children's books is an important form of family healthcare. Children handle their parent's illness better when given a chance to learn about it and discuss it. Since not all families have access to clinical information and guidance programs, children's books might potentially fill this gap in access (Huang et al. 610). The authors' analysis of the books through a medical framework echoes many critiques offered by disability activists. They, too, find the representations of illness to be overly medicalized, leaving out concerns about financial strain and school disruption that are central to children's experiences of parental illness. Likewise, they find representations of illness to be disproportionately white (Huang et al. 619). Another project, a practitioners' reading group initiated by a UK pediatrician, approaches children's literature from a self-critical standpoint: "We are naturally drawn to our colleagues' and patients' accounts in order to discover, or confirm our perceptions of illness and healthcare. Perhaps we should acknowledge this more, and draw on literature to provide greater insight into our profession.... Can we perhaps learn something from how children are depicted in books?" (Rudolf and Storr 635). This scholarship suggests that medical personnel, too, seek alternate ways to think about healthcare. Valerie A. Ubbes, Madison Miner, and Manjushri Karthikeyan suggest in their contribution to this volume that literature of dental healthcare is also a necessary and often overlooked inclusion to this archive.

Some medical approaches to children's literature are instrumental rather than analytic and focus on individual medical treatments rather than holistic analyses of how health and illness are constructed by unequal conditions.[3] Nevertheless, many medical writers note that doctors desire more knowledge of children's literature in order to make book recommendations (Mendel et al. 535). In some cases, they also wish to facilitate the creation of appealing children's literature for health education. Kendra S. Albright and Karen W. Gavigan, for example, worked with incarcerated youth and library youth groups to create graphic novels that correct common misperceptions about HIV/AIDS. Their interviews with youth creators and readers reflect the power of public health involvement in children's literature, as they pay close attention to what youth found effective in conveying information. While some work has been done to bring children's literature scholarship into conversation with public health scholarship—for example, in the 2015 Fragile Subjects conference and ensuing 2018 essay collection (Ahlbeck et al.)—children's literature scholarship can do more to support scholars working in public health and to learn from their insights. Some of this work will involve creatively mining unexpected texts for what they can tell us about healthcare (or its lack), even when those texts are not overtly "about" formal medical care. We hope this volume will provide a start, as many contributors to this volume spotlight material that is not likely to be reflected in an Amazon search for medically related books.

Two other areas of scholarship provide grounding for the essays in this collection. One is care ethics. Scholars such as Mary Jeanette Moran, Wesley Jacques, and Roberta Seelinger Trites have examined how ethical principles of feminist and antiracist care are central to understanding not only representations of caregiving, but also ethical activism in many children's novels. While this scholarship is often not directly concerned with healthcare systems, it provides groundwork for understanding some of the ethical quandaries that arise in healthcare. For example, Moran analyzes representations of anger in young women pushed into caregiving roles and argues that ethical care requires that caregivers also care for themselves. Jacques focuses on the importance of relationality in care, emphasizing that "supposed theories, epistemologies, and facts about care may... represent the standpoints and interests of their creators, while neglecting those that have been historically delegitimized by, for example, white supremacy and patriarchy" (7). Trites outlines how ethical feminist care work necessitates attention to the material aspect of caring; she notes that "relationships require a physical component" (159). Care ethics is also significant for understanding how children are socialized into family care systems in international children's literature, as Katsura Sako and Sarah Falcus observe in their analysis of reciprocal intergenerational care in Japanese picturebooks. This work on care ethics helps envision how systemic healthcare might become more equitable, including how we might re-envision medical practice and improve the material conditions of both the cared-for and the carers.

Finally, critical work in disability studies is foundational to the project of understanding healthcare in children's literature. Much literary scholarship establishes common tropes in representations of disability that recur in narratives of healthcare. Lois Keith's book *Take Up Thy Bed and Walk: Death, Disability, and Cure in Classic Fiction for Girls* examines the prevalence of the "kill or cure" dichotomy in classic children's texts, and Patricia Dunn examines how disabled characters are shorn of agency in *Disabling Characters: Representations of Disability in Young Adult Literature*. More recently, Abbye E. Meyer examines how narratives about disability have become integrated into the larger genre of young adult realism. Much of this scholarship focuses on the nuances of representational politics, rather than on what the novels say about systems of healthcare. As with illness narratives, scholars must sometimes look for elisions in children's texts in order to question how disabled characters and their caregivers have to navigate formal and informal healthcare systems. Extension of scholarship in this direction is one of the aims of this volume, as experiences with healthcare systems are part of everyday life for disabled children and their families.

One central healthcare issue that emerges from disability studies is the need to distinguish between independence (the ability to perform daily functions without assistance) and autonomy (the right to retain control over decisions about one's body).[4] This collapse of independence and autonomy means that disabled patients and their families are not always granted the right to medical consent, as our contributor Joseph Holloway explains in his essay about conjoined twin narratives. Within networks of informal care, too, family caregivers and children must learn to navigate between support and autonomy, as Farriba Schulz and Antje Tannen discuss in their essay about dementia in picturebooks.

Disability theory's attention to socially constructed barriers—including those of racism, sexism, and classism—is also foundational to understanding inequities of healthcare access. Liz Crow notes that although disabled people may not wish to be "cured," that does not mean they do not wish for access to appropriate medical treatment and community resources. A disability studies lens is essential for analyzing how public resources are funneled toward healthcare as "cure" and away from healthcare as support for public health and livable communities (Crow 8–9). Naomi Lesley's essay in this volume draws from this critique in her analysis of representations of substance use disorder, which often focus on narrow forms of treatment and do not address broader public health supports.

HEALTH, SICKNESS, AND CARE IN DIFFERENT NATIONS: TWO OVERVIEWS

The details of healthcare systems matter, as they form the structures that can either disable or enable those who need care. Healthcare—including medical techniques, definitions of healing, provisions for access, and assumptions about illness and wellness—varies considerably based upon time period and location. The texts tackled by our essayists range in time setting from the early twentieth century to the imagined future, and they are variously set in the United States, the United Kingdom, Germany, India, and future dystopic nations. Some of these are works of contemporary realism and assume that their readers share their own "common sense" knowledge about healthcare; others use future settings in order to challenge their readers' assumptions about healthcare. We cannot provide all of the background information about healthcare that would be useful. Nevertheless, in this introduction we offer a brief history and overview of healthcare in the two nations most prominently discussed in this volume, the United States and the United Kingdom. This overview helps to illuminate some of the specific assumptions and anxieties about healthcare that children's media creators bring to their writing.

The United States

The United States does not have only one healthcare system but many. In this introduction, we focus on civilian healthcare systems that serve US mainland citizens, as these form the backdrop for the US-based essays in the collection. We acknowledge, however, that this is not the only healthcare system in the US.[5]

The US healthcare system changed dramatically in the mid-twentieth century with the development of large-scale health insurance, and so children's media reflects different kinds of systemic concerns depending upon the time periods being portrayed. Nevertheless, two themes remain constant throughout the historical shift from an out-of-pocket payment system to an insurance system. The first theme, which is often centered in children's books about illness, is that medical care differs from healing. The second is that medical care *and* healing are both warped by pressures to measure and place a monetary value on care.

Barbara Ehrenreich and Deirdre English define the difference between medical care and healing as the difference between a "commodity" that can be quantified, valued, and paid for and a complex system of relationships, "kindnesses, encouragements, and stored-up data about the patients' fears and strengths" (50). They note that early US doctors were not generally independently wealthy and needed to charge fees to survive. As a result, they needed to commodify the act of healing. This process intensified throughout the twentieth century as the upper echelon of doctors began to standardize training and drive out lower-cost healers and midwives. Medical critic Elisabeth Rosenthal, herself a doctor, similarly observes how healing devolves into commodified medical care within the US system. As practitioners have come to assume that their patients will be insured, fees have ballooned so that patients' bills are still untenably high even when they pay only a percentage of the cost. Kelly Yang's novel *Front Desk*, set in the 1990s, dramatizes this shift. The protagonist Mia's mother has to go to the emergency room, against her will because the family is uninsured. The hospital supervisor will only offer them a 40 percent discount despite their poverty, which leaves them with a bill of $3,480. Mia's mother becomes so distressed that the doctor overhears and forces the supervisor to waive the fees; in this situation, he inhabits the role of a healer who recognizes that financial stress will damage his patient further (Yang 178–79).

Lack of access and poor treatment is a central problem, and it is exacerbated by systemic inequality in ways that children's media often highlights. Disparities in care based on race are noticeable in books that trace civil rights battles over desegregation, such as Mildred Taylor's Logan Family Saga and Lorenz Graham's Town series. Racial disparities are also evident in more recent books, but more work remains to be done in this area, as contributors from the Women of Color Health Equity Collective (WOCHEC) discuss in their afterword to this volume. Certainly, racial disparities in medical treatment continue in the United States, resulting from a combination of structural inequalities and overt bias. African American and Native American women are three times more likely than white women to die from pregnancy-related causes; the Center for Disease Control concluded that women of color experienced less doctor–patient communication, less access to preventive care, and less access to stable transportation and housing (Rabin). A 2002 study by the Institute of Medicine traced many disparities directly to racial bias in treatment, rather than to systemic factors like inadequate transportation (Stolberg).

Studies on the healthcare of LGBTQ+ individuals and disabled people reveal similar disparities, and for similar reasons. One group of researchers in Wisconsin found that LGBT adults, especially trans adults, were more likely to have a low income and to be underemployed and therefore more likely not to be able to afford their healthcare costs. In addition, they found that LGBT adults experienced discrimination from healthcare providers and often did not get appropriate screenings as a result (Jennings et al.). Dallas Ducar and Nichole Mayweather-Banks explain how they address these inequities as providers in their interview for this volume. People living with disabilities in the US are also likely to be underemployed and underinsured, delaying care because they cannot afford it; they are likely to encounter difficulties finding adequate transportation to medical appointments; and when they do arrive, they often find that clinics do not have accessible weight scales, exam tables, or screening equipment that can accommodate their disabilities (Krahn et al.).

Even as race, class, sexuality, and disability put up barriers to effective medical care, racial minorities and poor women have been integral to the development of medical treatments and the training of doctors. The Tuskegee experiments, in which treatment was withheld from African American men with syphilis, are infamous. The experience of Henrietta Lacks is also well known; as Rebecca Skloot has chronicled, Lacks was a Black woman whose cancer cells were used for research without the full knowledge and consent of her family. Her cells enriched the medical industry as her orphaned children suffered.[6] Anna Bugajska's essay in this volume draws from this medical history, pointing out how children's science fiction about artificial life both critiques a history of racialized medical exploitation and also envisions alternative bioethical frameworks for care.

Moreover, healthcare in the United States cannot be considered outside the context of how the nation cares for the health and well-being of its citizens more generally. Stress physiologist Robert Sapolsky suggests, "Poor health also has something to do with poor jobs in a shrinking economy, . . . or living in a crummy overcrowded apartment close to a toxic waste dump or without enough heat in winter. . . . If we can't consider disease outside the context of the person who is ill, we also can't consider it outside the context of the society in which the person has gotten ill, and that person's place in that society" (353–54).[7] Dawn Sardella-Ayres's essay in this volume offers an account of how the social context of illness is a focus for early Progressive children's literature. This is a broader definition of healthcare, one with links to the scholarship on care ethics discussed earlier. As Naomi Lesley discusses in this volume, this definition is essential for understanding how children's literature that does not specifically reference health insurance is nevertheless entwined with systemic failures of public health in the United States.

Healthcare in the United Kingdom

Healthcare provision in the United Kingdom is often evoked as a counterexample to the US system. In the UK, the vast majority of people use at least part of the National Health Service (NHS). This widespread usage contributes to an enduring affective link between the NHS and childhood, emphasized in the opening ceremony of the London 2012 Olympics, directed by Danny Boyle. One section of the ceremony, titled "Second on the Right and Straight on till Morning," quoting from J. M. Barrie's *Peter Pan*, intertwines the history of the health service with British children's literature, featuring hospital beds in the shape of the Great Ormond Street Hospital (GOSH) logo, nurses reading bedtime stories to young patients, and a multitude of Mary Poppinses flying in to ward off nightmares (Olympics 43:52–55:42).

The history of GOSH—often heralded as a beacon of British healthcare—reveals a crucial role in changing conceptualizations of children. Opening in 1852, GOSH is considered the first hospital to acknowledge that children's medical needs differed from those of adults ("Breakthroughs"). Now an NHS hospital, GOSH also draws support from other funding streams, most famously as the owners of the copyright to *Peter Pan*. Barrie bequeathed the copyright to the hospital; due to a political intervention to protect this revenue source for the hospital, the play and associated publications remain in copyright in perpetuity. Children's healthcare provision in the UK and the recognition of a separate status for children are inseparable here from the images of childhood found in canonical British children's literature.[8]

Prior to the NHS, an institution frequently described in quasi-religious terms,[9] healthcare in the UK was provided by a mix of private doctors, public health initiatives, contribution schemes, and charities. Establishing a publicly funded, universal alternative was a priority of Clement Atlee's post-war Labour government, which founded the NHS in 1948 with the promise of care from the cradle to the grave. Public health historian Virginia Berridge writes, "The principles of unconditional relief of poverty and equality of access were more strongly built into the British health system than elsewhere. The British system was also unusual in being centrally funded out of taxation, which helped to secure the political ideal of a free and equal service for all to a degree unmatched in other Western European countries" (23). Despite its founding principle of universalism, formal healthcare provision throughout the UK excludes many and inequalities persist. For example, a 2017 study found that women and disabled people reported worse access to healthcare and that people with a severe disability are the most likely to have unmet health needs (Sakellariou and Rotarou). There are inequalities in the treatments that a patient can access and in the outcomes they can expect, depending on factors such as ethnicity. There are regular reports of unacceptably long waiting times for emergency treatment. Mental health is a particular concern, with a survey by Charity Mind reporting that one in five people discharged from hospital after a mental health crisis are given no notice of their discharge ("Leaving Hospital" 4). As healthcare policy is devolved to the four nations of the UK and administered locally, gaps and inconsistencies also arise due to national differences and variations in local service provision and funding.

In addition to the gaps in formal healthcare provision, economic and political factors in the UK have a negative impact on health more generally, just as they do in the US and internationally, notoriously in the wide discrepancies in life expectancy between the most and least deprived regions. Numerous reports have highlighted the devastating effects of austerity policies, particularly on disabled people ("Dignity and Opportunity"). On a 2018 visit to the UK, United Nations Special Rapporteur on Extreme Poverty and Human Rights Philip Alston "met many for whom a single crisis, such as an unexpected health condition, a divorce or a disability, led to disaster" (United Nations 4). Economic recession and austerity in the UK have also been linked with increased rates of homelessness, food insecurity, depression, and old-age mortality (Stuckler et al.). An examination of how austerity politics and COVID-19 have affected healthcare workers as well as informal care networks in the UK is outside our scope but would be a fruitful avenue for further inquiry.

Meanwhile, neo-Victorian "deserving" and "undeserving poor" rhetoric characterizes debates about whether free health provision is justified in cases of illness assumed to be related to factors such as weight or addiction. Outpourings of love for "our" NHS are coupled with xenophobic anti-migrant panic about "health tourism," the phenomenon of people traveling to the UK in order to access free healthcare, despite this accounting for just 0.3 percent of the NHS budget (Torjesen). Joseph Holloway's essay in this collection addresses how assessments of the worthiness of patients and rationing of care affect UK residents despite, or perhaps because of, having a universal healthcare system in which all residents are stakeholders. These problems—austerity, care rationing, morality politics, and systemic inequalities—were all exacerbated by COVID-19 and continue to have negative impacts on children, despite the affective link between the NHS and childhood. Tensions between nostalgia, idealism, and reality are often elided in cultural representations of the UK's healthcare system aimed at young audiences. B.J. Woodstein's and Joseph Holloway's contributions to this volume, however, push against some of the nostalgic associations between the NHS and childhood, looking at some of the ethical cracks in provision and how these are depicted in children's media.

ORGANIZATION OF THIS VOLUME

The contributors to this volume approach issues of healthcare in children's media from a variety of disciplines, including literary scholarship, disability studies, medical and dental education, and public health. Essays address a range of genres, from picturebooks to middle grade and young adult realism to speculative fiction to television shows, taking up systemic issues that include inequities of care based on race, class, and gender; informal caregiving networks in the absence of formal health systems; and emerging questions of bioethics and healthcare for artificial life forms. Additionally, we felt it was important to acknowledge other stakeholders in the production of children's media about healthcare and to allow space for other ways to write about healthcare in children's media beyond traditional academic essays.

We divide the volume into three sections based upon three different functions or types of insight that children's media might provide for understanding healthcare systems in a variety of ways. These sections are organized around children's media as a critique of existing systems, children's media as tools for care providers, and children's media as a source of vision for better systems. Our organizational schema is designed to clarify for readers what the volume might have to offer them, whether they are seeking literary analysis of specific texts, resources for bibliotherapy and health literacy, or insight into children's media as an archive of public health discourse. Interviews and statements from practitioners, publishers, and public health advocates are interspersed between sections. These perspectives place the traditional research essays into conversation with direct accounts of how children are experiencing healthcare and are involved in creating their own healing literature.

Our volume opens with an interview with Dallas Ducar and Nichole Mayweather-Banks, healthcare practitioners who address controversies over gender-affirming healthcare for youth. They define care more broadly than medicalization and insist upon the importance of telling fully humanizing narratives by, for, and about trans youth, establishing some of the themes for the essays in part 1: Healthcare in Contemporary Realism. These essays examine media that expose gaps in healthcare as well as media that elides representation of inequities. First, Naomi Lesley's essay "Substance Use, Community Healing, and Care Gaps in Children's Literature" investigates how novels about substance use disorder simultaneously expose existing care gaps and erase discussion of necessary community support. Joseph Holloway's "Conjoinment as/and Inequality in Sarah Crossen's *One*" analyzes a verse novel that brings attention to medical consent and care rationing. Jeremy Johnston's essay "Mental Health and Masculine Silence in Adib Khorram's *Darius the Great Is Not Okay*" highlights a young protagonist who struggles to develop agency within systems not designed to support him.

An interview with Anna Macdonald, the project manager of Graphic Medicine at Comics Youth, introduces the next section, Bibliotherapy and Health Literacy Books. Macdonald explains how the Comics Youth team invites young people to contribute to the process of bibliotherapy through the creation and publication of their own comics. The essays that follow this interview highlight how children's media contributes to healthcare education for families and even providers. The three essays in this section—Farriba Schulz and Antje Tannen's "Dealing with Dementia: Patients and Their Caregivers in German Picturebooks," B.J. Woodstein's "Caregiving Children and Absent Medical Professionals: Hyperemesis Gravidarum in Picturebooks," and Valerie A. Ubbes, Madison Miner, and Manjushri Karthikeyan's "Moving toward Literature-Based Dentistry to Boost Oral Health Literacy of Children: Interprofessional Partnerships between Dentists, Doctors, and Librarians"—each approach a body of picturebooks intended for bibliotherapy and health literacy. Schulz and Tannen discuss German picturebooks that help children come to terms with the dementia of a loved one; Woodstein highlights the under-discussed issue of how children cope with a pregnant parent struggling with hyperemesis gravidum; and Ubbes, Miner, and Karthikeyan argue for more attention to dental health within the field of health literacy. All three essays emphasize the ways that children are asked to participate actively in informal systems of care in both positive and detrimental ways.

Next, publisher Sudeshna Shome Ghosh explains in an interview how the Speaking Tiger Press in India responded to the COVID-19 pandemic with an anthology of child-authored stories and reflections about the pandemic. Ghosh considers the importance of amplifying children's voices in response to public health crises. This interview begins the third section, Storytelling Ethics and Speculative Care, which highlights how children's media provides an archive for envisioning alternative care systems and methods of telling care stories. Next, Anna Bugajska's essay, "'Unviling' ALife: Ethical Choices of Healthcare Practitioners about Future Children," examines how young adult novels intervene in pressing bioethical debates about artificial life and cloning. Carrie Spencer's essay, "Shifting Stories: Care Ethics and Masculinities in the Television Series *Teen Wolf*" considers how a science fiction television series offsets current paradigms of independence and autonomy with care ethics. Melanie Goss's essay, "The Metaphor of Madness: Metaphor and Mental Illness in Contemporary YA Fiction," asks readers to consider how we tell stories. She outlines prevalent metaphors for understanding mental illness and suggests how some young adult novels offer alternative metaphors for young readers to process their experiences with mental illness. Dawn Sardella-Ayres further asks us to consider who can ethically tell care stories and under what circumstances in her essay "'No One Would Be Moved by Any Feeling Save Pity': Children, Narrative, and Healthcare in Annie Fellows Johnston's *Little Colonel* Series." The volume closes with an afterword from Vanessa E. Martínez-Renuncio, Dayna Campbell, and Jenise Katalina, public health advocates on the Executive Board of the Women of Color Health Equity Collective. In "Women of Color Health Equity Collective Executive Board Discussion: Health Inequities and COVID-19," they reflect on the importance of depicting inclusivity and collective action, as well as engaging children in discussions about health equity and the media that represents their lives.

NOTES

1. A new collection of critical and creative responses to Taylor's work, *Song of the Land*, is forthcoming from University Press of Mississippi, edited by Sarah Layzell, Tammy L. Mielke, and Michelle H. Martin.

2. During the first wave of global lockdowns, Sarah Layzell wrote some reflections on the difficulties of writing this introduction, difficulties which have only seemed to intensify since.

3. See, for example, Goddard and Mendel et al.

4. The distinction between the medical model and the social model of disability is central to disability studies. Within the medical model, disability is a result of an individual's impairment; the focus is on what that person is unable to do. Correspondingly, the best solution is to "cure" or mask the impairment. Within the social model, impairment and disability are distinct from one another. Impairments and variations are an expected aspect of existence and do not automatically diminish a person's quality of life. Instead, what disables people are artificially constructed barriers to full participation in society, such as inaccessible architecture and lack of funding for supportive care. Liz Crow, Valerie Novack, and Sunny Taylor provide excellent overviews of the social model. Robert McRuer's foundational work places the social construction of disability within the context of capitalism and heterosexism.

5. Healthcare systems in the US can vary depending on region and state. There are also different care systems for military members and for members of sovereign Indigenous tribes overseen by the Bureau of Indian Affairs. The government provides varying (often inadequate) levels of support for those who are unemployed, previously employed, disabled, or incarcerated.

6. Less well known are the poor and immigrant women in charity hospitals who were used involuntarily as practice subjects for obstetricians in training during the early twentieth century (Ehrenreich and English 104–5). US doctor Cornelius Rhoads used African American and Puerto Rican citizens to test the effects of mustard gas, which he later developed for use in chemotherapy (Immerwahr).

7. Citing research on the potential effects of universal health insurance, Sapolsky concludes that universal health insurance would fix only a tiny fraction of the health

problems that come with inequality. Fixing healthcare in the United States would ultimately require that we address the "stressors caused in a society that tolerates leaving so many of its members behind" (Sapolsky 382).

8. This association is emphasized in, for example, art by children's illustrator Quentin Blake displayed in children's hospitals and maternity units in the UK and France. For more on *Peter Pan* and Great Ormond Street, see Jacqueline Rose's *The Case of Peter Pan*.

9. See, for example, the collection of religious references in the *British Medical Journal's* editorial on the sixtieth birthday of the NHS (Delamothe).

WORKS CITED

Ahlbeck, Jutta, et al., editors. *Childhood, Literature and Science: Fragile Subjects*. Routledge, 2018.

Albright, Kendra S., and Karen W. Gavigan. "Information Vaccine: Using Graphic Novels as an HIV/AIDS Prevention Resource for Young Adults." *Journal of Education for Library and Information Science*, vol. 55, no. 2, 2014, pp. 178–85.

Aveling, Helen A. "Modelling Illness in the Early 20th Century." *Unseen Childhoods: Disabled Characters in 20th-Century Books for Girls*, 2nd ed., edited by Helen A. Aveling, Bettany Press, 2011, pp. 19–47.

Berridge, Virginia. *Health and Society in Britain Since 1939*. Cambridge UP, 1999.

"Breakthroughs." *Great Ormond Street Hospital Charity*, https://www.gosh.nhs.uk/about-us/our-history/breakthroughs.

Chrisman, Alyssa. "Social Justice and Mental Health: Accessibility to Treatment in YA Literature." *Teen Librarian Toolbox*, 2 June 2017, *School Library Journal*, http://www.teenlibrariantoolbox.com/2017/06/social-justice-and-mental-health-accessibility-to-treatment-in-ya-literature-a-guest-post-by-alyssa-chrisman/.

Church, Imogen. "The Picture of Madness—Visual Narratives of Female Mental Illness in Contemporary Children's Literature." *Children's Literature in Education*, vol. 49, no. 2, 2018, p. 119–39.

Crow, Liz. "Including All Our Lives: Renewing the Social Model of Disability." *Encounters with Strangers: Feminism and Disability*, edited by Jenny Morris, Women's Press, 1996, pp. 1–21.

Delamothe, Tony. "A Fairly Happy Birthday." *British Medical Journal*, vol. 337, no. 7660, 2008, pp. 25–29.

"Dignity and Opportunity for All: Securing the Rights of Disabled People in the Austerity Era." *Just Fair*, 2014, http://justfair.org.uk/wp-content/uploads/2018/05/Dignity-and-Opportunity-for-All-Summary-R.

Duckels, Gabriel. "Melodrama and the Memory of AIDS in American Queer Young Adult Literature." *Children's Literature Association Quarterly*, vol. 46, no. 3, 2021, pp. 304–24.

Duckels, Gabriel, and Amy Ryder. "Emergency Children's Literature: Rapidly Representing COVID-19 in Digital Texts for Young People in the United Kingdom." *COVID-19 and Education in the Global North: Storytelling and Alternative Pedagogies*, edited by Ruby Turok-Squire, Palgrave Macmillan, 2022, pp. 137–61.

Dunn, Patricia. *Disabling Characters: Representations of Disability in Young Adult Literature*. Peter Lang, 2015.

Ehrenreich, Barbara, and Deirdre English. *For Her Own Good: Two Centuries of the Experts' Advice to Women*. Anchor Books, 2005.

Elman, Julie. "'Nothing Feels as Real': Teen Sick-Lit, Sadness, and the Condition of Adolescence." *Journal of Literary and Cultural Disability Studies*, vol. 6, no. 2, 2012, pp. 175–91, https://doi.org/10.3828/jlcds.2012.15.

Goddard, Anna. "Children's Books for Use in Bibliotherapy." *Journal of Pediatric Health Care*, vol. 25, no. 1, Jan. 2011, pp. 57–61.

Guthrie, Meredith. "'I Don't Want to Be Different': Diabetes in Contemporary Young Adult Fiction." *Unseen Childhoods: Disabled Characters in 20th-Century Books for Girls*, edited by Helen A. Aveling, Bettany Press, 2011, pp. 179–213.

Hafner, Katie. "Once Science Fiction, Gene Editing Is Now a Looming Reality." *New York Times*, 22 July 2020, https://www.nytimes.com/2020/07/22/style/crispr-gene-editing-ethics.html.

Huang, Xiaoyan, et al. "Talking About Maternal Breast Cancer with Young Children: A Content Analysis of Text in Children's Books." *Journal of Pediatric Psychology*, vol. 40, no. 6, 2015, pp. 609–21, https://doi: 10.1093/jpepsy/jsu110.

Immerwahr, Daniel. *How to Hide an Empire: A History of the Greater United States*. Farrar, Straus and Giroux, 2019.

Jacques, Wesley. "Reading Relational in Mildred D. Taylor: Toward a Black Feminist Care Ethics for Children's Literature." *Research on Diversity in Youth Literature*, vol. 2, no. 2, 2020, https://iopn.library.illinois.edu/journals/rdyl/article/view/1548.

Jennings, Linn, et al. "Inequalities in Lesbian, Gay, Bisexual, and Transgender (LGBT) Health and Health Care Access and Utilization in Wisconsin." *Preventive Medicine Reports*, vol. 14, 2019, https://doi.org/10.1016/j.pmedr.2019.100864.

Keith, Lois. *Take Up Thy Bed and Walk: Death, Disability, and Cure in Classic Fiction for Girls*. Routledge, 2001.

Krahn, Gloria, Deborah Klein Walker, and Rosaly Correa-De-Araujo. "Persons With Disabilities as an Unrecognized Health Disparity Population." *American Journal of Public Health*, vol. 105, no. S2, 2015, pp. S198–S206, https://doi.org/10.2105/AJPH.2014.302182.

Layzell, Sarah [*published as* Sarah Hardstaff]. "Living in the Prequel, Travelling Through Time and Finding Hope in Mildred D. Taylor's Historical Fiction." *Sarah Hardstaff: Writing on Children's Literature (Mostly)*, 21 Oct. 2020, https://shardstaff.wordpress.com/2020/10/21/living-in-the-prequel-travelling-through-time-and-finding-hope-in-mildred-d-taylors-historical-fiction/.

"Leaving Hospital: Briefing on Discharge from Mental Health Inpatient Services." *Mind*, Dec. 2017, https://www.mind.org.uk/media/18839049/leaving-hospital-minds-good-practice-briefing.pdf.

McRuer, Robert. "Compulsory Able-Bodiedness and Queer/Disabled Existence." *Disability Studies: Enabling the Humanities*, edited by Sharon L. Snyder et al., Modern Language Association of America, 2002, pp. 88–99.

Mendel, Marisa R., et al. "Bringing Bibliotherapy for Children to Clinical Practice." *Journal of the American Academy of Child and Adolescent Psychiatry*, vol. 55, no. 7, 2016, pp. 535–37, https://doi.org/10.1016/j.jaac.2016.05.008.

Meyer, Abbye E. *From Wallflowers to Bulletproof Families: The Power of Disability in Young Adult Narratives*. UP of Mississippi, 2022.

Moran, Mary Jeanette. "The Angry Caregiver: Gendered Emotion in the Penderwicks Series and the One Crazy Summer Trilogy." *Emotion in Texts for Children and Young Adults: Moving Stories*, edited by Karen Coats and Gretchen Papazian, Benjamin Press, 2023, pp. 104–29.

Novack, Valerie. "The Future Liberation of Disability Movements." *The Disability Visibility Project*, edited by Alice Wong, 2020, https://disabilityvisibilityproject.com/2020/07/19/the-future-liberation-of-disability-movements/.

Olympics. "The Complete London 2012 Opening Ceremony: London 2012 Olympic Games." *YouTube*, 27 July 2012. https://www.youtube.com/watch?v=4As0e4de-rI#t=43m52s.

Rabin, Roni Caryn. "Huge Racial Disparities Found in Deaths Linked to Pregnancy." *New York Times*, 7 May 2019, https://www.nytimes.com/2019/05/07/health/pregnancy-deaths-.html.

Richmond, Kia Jane. *Mental Illness in Young Adult Literature: Exploring Real Struggles through Fictional Characters*. Libraries Unlimited, 2019.

Robbins, Rebecca, and Stephanie Nolen. "A Dilemma for Governments: How to Pay for Million-Dollar Therapies." *New York Times*, 20 Jan. 2023, https://www.nytimes.com/2023/01/24/health/gene-therapies-cost-zolgensma.html.

Rose, Jacqueline. *The Case of Peter Pan: The Impossibility of Children's Fiction*. U of Pennsylvania P, 1992.

Rosenthal, Elisabeth. *An American Sickness: How Healthcare Became Big Business and how You can Take it Back*. Penguin Books, 2018.

Rudolf, M. C. J., and E. Storr. "Tell Me a Story . . . : What Can Paediatricians Gain from Reading Stories?" *Archives of Disease in Childhood*, vol. 88, no. 7, 2003, pp. 635–37, https://doi.org/10.1136/adc.88.7.635.

Sakellariou, Dikaios, and Elena S. Rotarou. "Access to Healthcare for Men and Women with Disabilities in the UK: Secondary Analysis of Cross-Sectional Data." *BMJ Open*, vol. 7, no. 8, 2017, https://bmjopen.bmj.com/content/7/8/e016614.

Sako, Katsura, and Sarah Falcus. "Care, Generations and Reciprocity in Children's Picturebooks in Japan." *Contemporary Narratives of Ageing, Illness, Care*, edited by Katsura Sako and Sarah Falcus, Routledge, 2022, pp. 177–99.

Sapolsky, Robert M. *Why Zebras Don't Get Ulcers*. Times Books, New Yo2004.

Skloot, Rebecca. *The Immortal Life of Henrietta Lacks*. Crown, 2011.

Stolberg, Sheryl Gay. "Race Gap Seen in Care of Equally Insured Patients." *New York Times*, 21 Mar. 2002, https://www.nytimes.com/2002/03/21/us/race-gap-seen-in-health-care-of-equally-insured-patients.html.

Stuckler, David, et al. "Austerity and Health: The Impact in the UK and Europe." *European Journal of Public Health*, vol. 27, no. 4, 2017, pp. 18–21, https://academic.oup.com/eurpub/article/27/suppl_4/18/4430523.

Taylor, Mildred D. *All the Days Past, All the Days to Come*. Penguin, 2020.

Taylor, Mildred D. *Let the Circle Be Unbroken*. Dial Press, 1981.

Taylor, Mildred D. *The Road to Memphis*. Dial Press, 1990.

Taylor, Sunny. "The Right Not to Work: Power and Disability." *Monthly Review*, 1 Mar. 2004, https://monthlyreview.org/2004/03/01/the-right-not-to-work-power-and-disability/.

Torjesen, Ingrid. "Migrant Charging in the NHS: How Doctors Can Support Patients When Hospital Care Is Denied." *British Medical Journal*, vol. 365, no. 8201, 2019, p. 2281, https://www.bmj.com/content/365/bmj.l2281.

Trites, Roberta Seelinger. *Twenty-First-Century Feminisms in Children's and Adolescent Literature*. UP of Mississippi, 2018.

United Nations, Human Rights Council. Visit to the United Kingdom of Great Britain and Northern Ireland: Report of the Special Rapporteur on Extreme Poverty and Human Rights, 23 Apr. 2019. *United Nations*, https://undocs.org/A/HRC/41/39/Add.1.

Valint, Alexandra. "'Wheel Me Over There!': Disability and Colin's Wheelchair in *The Secret Garden*." *Children's Literature Association Quarterly*, vol. 41 no. 3, 2016, pp. 263–80. *Project MUSE*, https://doi.org/10.1353/chq.2016.0032.

Yang, Kelly. *Front Desk*. Arthur A. Levine Books, 2018.

INTERVIEW WITH DALLAS DUCAR, CEO OF TRANSHEALTH, AND NICHOLE MAYWEATHER-BANKS, LCSW, FOUNDER OF CHANGING FACES COUNSELING & WELLNESS, LLC

NAOMI LESLEY, INTERVIEWER, AND DALLAS DUCAR AND NICHOLE MAYWEATHER-BANKS, INTERVIEWEES

Naomi Lesley (NL): Good afternoon! To start off, can each of you first introduce who you are and what your job is?

Nichole Mayweather-Banks (NMB): My name is Nichole Mayweather-Banks. I am a licensed clinical social worker in the state of Connecticut. I am the owner of a private practice therapy called Changing FACES Counseling & Wellness, LLC. Changing FACES (Freedom of Access to Community Equity and Support) is a queer-owned ally and advocate for the gender-expansive community. The goal is to create a sense of safety and resilience for gender-expansive individuals, both in the therapeutic setting and in the community. My clinical practice specializes in supporting gender-diverse individuals through any type of mental health challenges they may be having, including gender transition or just life transitions. I'm also a public speaker and a trainer. I advocate for the rights of gender-queer individuals. The mission of Changing FACES is "to increase the life expectancy of gender diverse young adults by increasing access to interpersonal connections, housing, employment, education and healthcare." I want to make sure that I point out that I am talking from secondhand experience working with the gender-queer community and not from firsthand experience. It's always important for me to let people know.

Dallas Ducar (DD): My name is Dallas Ducar; my pronouns are she and her. I am an open transgender woman. And I also serve as the chief executive officer and president of Transhealth. We're a pioneering organization that's committed to really transforming healthcare in many different ways. Right now,

Transhealth provides care to over 2,500 trans and gender-diverse individuals, and we employ a staff of over fifty employees, many of whom identify as trans or gender-diverse themselves, with provision of primary care across all ages, mental healthcare across all ages, both psychotherapy and psychiatry and ASD [autism spectrum disorder] evaluations, along with community care. We also have things like farm shares, yoga groups, DBT [dialectical behavior therapy] groups, support groups, meditation groups, all that. And then we do lots of meaningful advocacy and research with the National Research Advisory Board that we've created and education, both in house and externally.

I also serve as a faculty member at the University of Virginia School of Nursing, Columbia University, and the MGH Institute for Health Professions. I'm a fellow of the American Academy of Nursing and co-chair of the LGBTQ Primary Care Alliance, and also member of other boards, and have worked with the state of Massachusetts on the transition team for the new attorney general and also serve on the Northampton Board of Health, too.

NL: Obviously, in the last few years, healthcare for trans and gender-diverse youth has been an especially contested issue. What reverberations of that do you see in your work?

NMB: I can say from the work that I've done, I've seen a lot of increase in feelings of hopelessness for the people that I work with, trying to get a better understanding of what's really happening. Everything is igniting so quickly. It was always there, was always an underlying issue, but with the administration and with all the new bills that have come out, things have started to happen so quickly. So individuals really still are trying to kind of catch up in understanding what's happening. There's really a sense of, "Hey, we are under attack, and we are being persecuted." There's that feeling of "Who's on our side, who's out there fighting with us, not just for us?" So I've seen a lot of hopelessness and fear, really desperation. Individuals are trying to unfortunately get affairs in order based on all of the different laws that are coming out and all of the restrictions that are going on in regards to healthcare and support services.

I'm also seeing a increase in concerns in regards to financial responsibilities for those individuals who want to make medical transitions, and it's leading individuals to have to make decisions before they're actually ready to, from all of the changes that are happening and all the restrictions that are happening. Individuals are scared that they may lose their healthcare or they may lose the option of making those medical transitions that they may have wanted to make in the future with more time, but it's kind of like, "Well, I better do it now, or I may not be able to do it at all."

DD: I would echo all of that. There's definitely been some profound implications for providers, advocates, the broader community and the health and wellbeing of trans and gender-diverse people. In general, we've seen an increased demand for services amidst a heightened awareness and visibility. There's a growing demand for gender-affirming care. But then also in places like Massachusetts with a shield law, we are seeing on a weekly basis now, youth, especially in families who are affluent enough, are relocating to Massachusetts. Now, those are the folks that have the means to do so, right? So there are many, particularly Black and brown trans and gender-diverse individuals at the poverty line in the southern states, that are unable to move. And I think there's so many targeted attacks that also mirror a lot of the work on abortion right now. But it's really amplified because gender-affirming care is a lifelong process, right? It's not a one and done type thing. And so, especially for lab [tests], hormones, blockers, anything, people are moving because telehealth care, even with the shield law, may not be sufficient.

There's also just so many policy and legal challenges. I can't accentuate this enough that we are really at a constitutional moment. I never thought I would know so much about constitutional law from working in this job. And that is because one state's pathway to liberation in a place like Massachusetts or Connecticut is another state's felony, truly. And so it is a very, very tense time for providers, and there are very clear legislative efforts aimed at restricting access for gender-affirming care for youth, and it's created this environment of uncertainty and fear. It's put healthcare providers in difficult positions navigating ethical obligations to patients and new constraints imposed by laws. And then that creates a psychological impact too. I mean, just so much stress, anxiety, fear amongst youth, especially as you see more and more negative media coverage because so many Americans don't know that they know a trans person. And so, the right-wing media especially attempts to seize on this and use this, especially in this election season, for personal gain and votes.

As a result of this, we really have seen more community mobilization, though. We have seen more mobilization in some safer states around the queer community, among allies, more ability to talk about the protection of transgender individuals. There's also been more shifts in healthcare provisions, especially by expanding telehealth and offering supportive resources and more comprehensive resources. And then there's been more focus, I think, on educational efforts trying to train the general public and educators in the way we didn't see in the past ten years, and research. So it's a pretty substantial change that we've seen over the past couple of years, and it's really reverberating on so many fronts.

NL: If I can ask a brief follow-up question, and this is for the benefit of readers of this volume who don't live in Massachusetts, can you briefly explain what the shield law is that you referenced?

DD: In Massachusetts, and it's different in different states, the shield law is the protection of gender-affirming care and reproductive care and really ensuring it's a constitutional right. And so this is basically saying that the state is able to be a refuge state or shield to providers in the state. The primary goal is to protect transgender people, their families, providers from ongoing attacks, and protect access to gender-affirming healthcare. So for example, if a person travels from a state where gender-affirming healthcare is banned and receives that care in another state, the shield law can protect the recipient or provider of the healthcare against civil or criminal charges from the state where the healthcare is. Right now, as of February 12, 2024, there's eleven states plus DC that have actual shield laws on the books, three states that have shield executive orders on the books, and then the rest do not have a shield law, with around twenty-four states banning or restricting best practice medical care for transgender youth.

NL: Thank you very much. So as you mentioned right now with the election coming up, there's a lot of front-and-center, immediate issues. What are some long-standing issues that we're not talking about?

NMB: I feel like we're not talking about the importance of allyship. I don't feel like we're talking about the importance of being visible allies for the community and how important it is to have individuals who do identify be accepted in their totality. We talk about individuals from the standpoint of gender, but we don't really get into the other aspects of who they are, right? The other intersections of their lives? Who are they as professionals, who are they as family members? And I think that is part of where we get into the issues with misunderstanding of the trans community because we're not really looking at who these individuals are. What do their daily lives look like? What do they contribute to society? We're talking about the health concerns; we're talking about the policies and procedures. We're talking about the government aspect of it, but we're rarely talking about who are the individuals? Who are the people behind these identities? I think that's one thing that's really important that's missing. The more education, the more you know about someone, then the hope is the better you do.

DD: Thank you. I totally agree with that. I think one reason that we founded Transhealth in the way that we did is we wanted to really center gender euphoria, gender joy. I mean, this was right before the attacks really started to spike. So we had a lot of hope then, and we still do. But we want to center the fact that trans people are no different and we all have full lives and we are not objects. We are people too. And we are people that, by and large, face more economic inequality and, especially at the intersection of race and ethnicity, more housing insecurity and incarceration and legal system challenges, as well as mental health stigma and access to care. Elder care and aging: we rarely talk about our trans elders, but it's a real long-standing issue, the intersection of identities, as you mentioned.

And then also global perspectives, too, don't really get considered here. I mean, there are many ways to be gender diverse or have varying gender expressions. And when we look at things with a more global cultural context and look at the many different third genders or more than three genders that exist in different, especially Indigenous cultures, one begins to realize how limiting the word "transgender" is because it's just a Western concept. So I think there's a lot of long-standing intersecting issues and really at the end of the day, I think we can frame at least some of this in the overarching perspective of gender and how there's an element of economic justice to gender. If you look in nursing and among physicians, in nursing, where there's a very strong majority of women generally, women still get paid less, right? Men will get paid more in both those professions. That's in healthcare. I don't know where it stands everywhere else. But I just think there are so many ways in which gender interweaves in all of our lives, and the more that we are able to reflect on that and to consider our own positionality in that, the better off, the more relatable and understandable trans folks would be too.

NMB: Thank you. I think that also this plays a role not just in the external society, but what I see a lot with my clients is that individuals will come in and speak to me specifically in regards to gender-related issues. And I actually have to talk to them and let them know, as we're in the sessions, we're not just going to be talking about gender, right? We're going to be talking about your life in its totality because every aspect of gender impacts every aspect of your life. So there's no way to just kind of pull that part out and not talk about family history, not talk about substance issues, not talk about the other parts of your life. So individuals who do identify as gender queer will come in, and they do not identify the other intersections of their identity. I mean, as far as gender identity, they don't put it in the category of other struggles or challenges that they may be having in their life. They pull it out and make it a separate issue.

NL: Thank you. Since this is a book about children's media, what are the biggest current problems or gaps that you notice in children's media representations of trans and gender-diverse identities, including representation of intersectional identity? And have you seen changes in this over time?

NMB: My biggest one is lack of representation. And over the years, there has been an increase in representation, but there still is a disproportionate number of individuals who are not represented as far as being gender diverse in children's media. So the lack of representation is one thing, and then accurate representation, right? When you're looking at specific media or specific literature, how are gender-diverse individuals being depicted in these stories or in these films, right? Are we casting correctly? Are we casting individuals who actually identify as part of the community, or are we casting individuals to play a role that they do not naturally fit into? And then are the individuals that are being cast fitting into a specific category? The way that we work is we're visual people. As soon as we see something that doesn't fit the typical either feminine or masculine role, then we make automatic assumptions in regards to people's identities based on what we see visually. There are some individuals who do have the luxury of either transitioning earlier in life. So they don't have those secondary sex hormones really protruding through or they may have softer features or harder features to where they are able to transition and not go out and live stealth, right? Some people use that term. Those are some of the challenges that I see is that there's not a real depiction of "If I am a trans individual who is visibly trans, then where do I fit into this narrative?"

DD: I echo everything you said. I don't think there's much more I could say about the limited representation. I think you also touched on stereotyping and simplification. I just might also say it's so nice when I, as a trans person, don't have to talk about being a trans person all the time, or working at Transhealth all the time, and I can just be a person. There's just so many narratives where the trans person has to go through the trans process in some way. And that narrative is generally centered on trauma. I would just go back to more narratives that can focus on joy, resilience, everyday life, ensure that there are intersectional identities and that people of color or people who are disabled or from varied socioeconomic backgrounds are represented in the narratives too. And I would just also say that obviously when those positive representations exist, stories can be really limited due to censorship or pushback from different groups, and we're seeing book bans everywhere, right? So there's really a need to fight for the freedom of speech so that people can actually be able to have access to information, and then we also work with industries to help shape those narratives to be more realistic, less centered on trauma, more intersectional, less stereotypical. That also really means having more diverse creators of content in children's media.

NL: You mentioned the book bans. We haven't seen a whole lot of book bans in Western Massachusetts. To what extent do you see your clients being affected by knowledge of those book bans?

NMB: I work with adults. We don't really talk a lot about the book bans, but I feel like it gets lumped into everything else. It's one more thing. They are another thing that they're using to weaponize identity in regards to marginalized communities regarding gender. These book bans are really smaller pieces of a trend towards injustice that are happening everywhere against transgender individuals. So even if we look at Drag Queen storytelling, right? There's a lot of controversy in regards to those types of events happening across the country that are trying to use fear mongering to get individuals to not want to participate or to ban those types of programs for children. And I think that's one of the things that also creates that visibility for children to have someone who is demonstrating nonnormative gender expression. And I do want to be very clear that drag and trans, they're not the same thing, so I'm not putting them in the same category. But when we are looking at it from a systemic view, usually what happens is that the two are put together. So that's another piece of education that can be put out there, that trans identity and drag are two completely different things. But because there is a difference in expression with the drag community, then it's seen as not okay, and it's a form of sexualizing individuals.

DD: I think more than anything too, I see that a lot of these laws and all of these actions have a chilling effect, right? Even if you're not seeing over-enforcement in a way where you might imagine the worst-case scenario, knowing that such bans exist can really create a more chilling effect on open discussions about gender identity and gender expression. And people might just feel more hesitant to explore topics, fearing backlash, misunderstanding, even in more supportive environments. And for so many people in the queer community, part of being able to be yourself is being able to see representations of yourself in spaces. And so it could really create a pretty harmful psychological impact and may lead individuals to feel that they are unwelcome or unsafe in society and really exaggerate feelings of marginalization, isolation. I often say that what we see in the trans community is really an amplified experience of what we see in many ways across the United States. And one way that this plays out is with the loneliness epidemic and the experience that so many people have, being more lonely when on social media, not connected to others, not in community. And one of the great things about the queer community in general is the ability to be in community with others. But if you actively work to destroy that, then the impact of isolation is really harmful, which is one of many reasons why you see such high suicide attempt rates among youth, when you don't have a feeling that you're okay in some way. So you know, there's a cultural and a psychological impact here that really is nefarious and harmful.

NMB: And I think not just on individuals who do identify as trans or gender diverse, but also on individuals who are part of the cis community. And it gives the wrong message. It does not provide visibility for them. It does not give them opportunity to explore other identities or other cultures outside of themselves. In regards to not being represented, that can cause a lot of internalized phobia and discrimination [for a gender-diverse person]. But then there's also the externalized form; if I've never seen someone who identifies as trans or I've constantly seen them be vilified or constantly told that it's wrong, then that's going to be the thought process that I grow up with, if this is the message that I'm continuously receiving, that I'm better than they are.

NL: I know that both of you work with adult clients. What difference do you think it would have made for those adult clients (or to your youthful selves) to have been represented more fully and respectfully in the media during childhood?

NMB: I'm going to divert from the gender piece on this and I'm going to go towards sexuality, me identifying as a lesbian woman. For me, if I had seen more representation of myself in the media as a lesbian Black woman, more representation of myself in a more positive light and more inclusivity and acceptance of sexually diverse individuals, then I feel like there would have been a lot of steps that I would not have taken in life. I did originally marry a man, not that I didn't love him, but I also knew long before that that was not the direction for me. But I never felt like it was okay. I never felt like I would be accepted. So that was something that I kind of held back. I didn't come out until later in life and it made it a lot more difficult for me to come out later in life. I have children. So now, I had to explain that to them. And they're also not seeing that [sexual diversity] represented, and now they have a parent who does not fit into a heteronormative depiction of society. So I think that's the other part to tie in is that we not only have to look at the experiences of the trans individual, but if you're parenting, what are the experiences of your children? And we want for our children to see representation of their own family members in media and in literature as well. When it comes to clients that I've worked with in the past, a lot of individuals have come out later in life, and then I have to work with them through a lot of regret and guilt and shame around, "If I would have just been brave enough to do it previously.... How come I didn't do it before all of these changes came that I'm now not able to reverse?" So if they had more representation and more inclusivity, then maybe they could've felt as though it would have been safe to do it before.

NL: Like putting it on themselves to be the superheroes who had to be brave.

NMB: Yes. "How come I couldn't just stand up? How come I just couldn't be who I am before?" And then I think sometimes I have to take a step back and explain to them, "Let's look at where you were at that time in your life. Let's look at where society was at that time in your life. How would this journey have looked different for you at that point? Sometimes the time that you do transition is the time that's going to be the healthiest for you to transition and sometimes those are decisions that have to be made."

DD: I just think—reflecting on the experiences of adults and youth that I work with and considering my own journey—the impact goes so far beyond being represented in media, but that is really, really important, representations beyond who looks like you on screen or in print. It's about recognizing the parts of your identity, and the experiences you've had reflected in the wider world, and validating your existence and experiences in society. The media often renders nonnormative identities invisible or marginalized. And so for adults who I did work with (I don't actively provide clinical care right now), many of them grew up in times when trans representation was nonexistent or steeped in stereotypes, and that led to lasting effects on self-esteem, mental health, the ability to envision a hopeful future for themselves. The internalization of social rejection leads to a profound sense of isolation, which we talked about, and many adults work continuously to unlearn the shame and the fear associated with their own identities, a process that could be mitigated really early on. And for youth, the landscape is changing a little bit, but it's a long way to go. Being able to see oneself could reduce those feelings of isolation and self-esteem foster community, and get ahead of some of that shame that comes later that's internalized.

I'd say, from my own personal perspective, I wish I could have transitioned at a much earlier age. It just wasn't possible. There weren't words for it. I felt, growing up in a Catholic family that was fairly liberal, that something was really wrong with me and that I was definitely othered in some way. There was an internal struggle of trying to reconcile my own identity with the very invisible depictions of what it meant to be able to be your own authentic self. And in some ways, I'm really glad, though, that I transitioned when I did because I think some of that has motivated me to help cocreate Transhealth. I often think of the different defense mechanisms in psychology, one of them being sublimation, and how we take the difficult experiences we've had and we try to then create a better world out of it. And I do see Transhealth as one result of that, so that others don't have to experience that pain and suffering, so that others have that representation and understanding of who they are. And at the same time, boy, would I have loved to just have a typical young adulthood, right? And that's what I hope for so many other patients in the future, that other people are able to just grow up and be themselves without conflict. A couple months ago, our pediatrician here at Transhealth had someone come in from out of state who flew in here. She had never met a trans CEO before. So he brought her up here to have a chance to meet me. And we talked about her favorite sport, which was soccer, and her favorite subject, which was recess, and we didn't mention being trans at all. We didn't talk about it because it was just human to human. And that's what I want for so many people so that they don't have to struggle with pain later in life as an adult.

NMB: I also want to put in there when I think about the whole acronym, the LGBT, all of the letters that come after that, I feel like that "T" is lost in there. I feel like there is a difference between sexuality and gender identity, and when individuals do not understand that there's a difference, then transgender identifying individuals get lumped into a category that they may not fit in. Their experiences are completely different from individuals who identify as either gay or lesbian or have another [marginalized] sexual identity. So I feel like it's important to understand that there are differences in experiences and feel like that's why it's important for the LGB counterparts to really be allies for the T in that acronym and understand that within our marginalized community population, they are even more marginalized. Even when we look at the bills and the laws today, most of them that target LGBTQ+ individuals are geared towards the trans community.

NL: Do you think that social media is changing the landscape for youth right now and in what ways, if so?

NMB: Absolutely. I think there's always the positives and the negatives of social media. I feel like whatever you're going to look for in social media, that's what you're going to find. But I feel like it's a greater chance to find community. That's what I have been finding in the work that I do—for a lot of individuals that I work with, that's where most of the interactions and connections come from, through social media or social gaming sites or being involved in some sort of virtual connection. Either because there's not a lot of tangible community in their area or they're not comfortable with going out interfacing with the world at this point in time.

So social media has been a positive, but then there's also the negative side, because it gives individuals the ability to bully or shame from wherever they are. So that's why sometimes I have to have conversations with clients, that you have to be intentional about where you are going to look for your information because if you want to look for information that's going to be negative, or given by hate, then you're going to find that. But also understand that there are other places where you can find community and you can find support.

DD: I echo everything you said again, Nichole. I think with social media, there's increased diversity of voices. Social media allows for a broader range of voices to be heard unlike traditional media. There's a lot more peer-led representation. It means that young people are not just passive recipients but active creators of the media, which can be empowering too and create narratives in ways the traditional media doesn't achieve. You can also have rapid response to social issues, especially with inclusion of many different identities. Movements for social justice, especially, can gain more traction more quickly. You have more normalization of just more diversity because there's more experiences that are being shared for young audiences, which really reduces stigma and enhances understanding, along with better access to information.

But I also say there are other sides of this too. There are echo chambers and polarization. There are algorithms that can create and reinforce existing beliefs. And I will say that for the LGBTQ community too. I really do worry about how many people on either side of a political belief actually talk to each other. I think this is part of what's fomenting some of our loneliness epidemic and our political polarization. Also, social media really spreads misinformation. And again, this is not just on one side. We saw lots of blatant misinformation around COVID from very liberal communities in the pandemic and misinformation is a tool that gets weaponized. And then there's also the risk of commercialization as representation, you know, brands and corporations that try to reach youth audiences and try to dilute authenticity of representation efforts, reducing queer people to marketing tactics. And there's also huge mental health concerns. I mean, social media places pressure on young people to conform to idealized standards of identity or lifestyle, and there's clear research that shows it really harms youth, especially younger women. And also, we know that in general, body dissatisfaction can be higher in some ways amongst the trans community. So then seeing certain imagery, especially an idealized transition, people may feel like they can't get there. They may feel emotional distress because of that.

NMB: I've had a lot of clients come to me, and they've used that face app, an app that will show you how you may look as the opposite gender. And I have individuals that will come to me and say "This is how I aspire to look" and it can be very harmful. A lot of times when you see pictures on any type of social media, you don't really know what the person really looks like because there's so many filters that you're able to put out there. So those things can also cause harm.

NL: What are the most hopeful developments that you see right now for gender-diverse youth?

NMB: The fact that we're talking about it. I think that's a big thing is the fact that we're actually having a discussion and we're talking about it. We're talking about what the challenges are, but I think that there's more trying, as Dallas said, to promote trans joy, positivity within trans identities. I think that is a key piece, trying to make connections and not have people isolated.

I tried to form support groups, bringing individuals so that they are able to engage in community. And for me, when I do my support groups, I make sure that I let people in the support group know that this support group is here for you to talk about whatever it is that you want to talk about. But the reason why it's geared towards either transwomen or transfemme or another population is because we can take that part of the conversation out if you would like for it to be. I don't want that to be a barrier to you coming in and engaging, right? So that's something that we all know, that shared identity. But now we can just talk about regular stuff.

DD: I think even if it doesn't really feel like it, there's increased legal protections. Throughout the world, there's increasing recognition of the rights of gender-diverse people. Even if there is politicization over the provision of care. There's still more rights than we saw ten years ago, twenty years ago. I mean, back when Obama was president, HRC (Human Rights Campaign) did not want trans people on the lawn with them at the White House. Back in the

1970s, homosexuality was a diagnosis in the *DSM* [*Diagnostic and Statistical Manual of Mental Disorders*]-*III*. So it's important to consider the larger arc of history here. Not to say it's always going to progress that way. But we have seen more protections, more advancements in care, more educational reform, schools and institutions that have implemented policies and curricula that are inclusive of gender diversity, more community and peer support, more visibility in media and culture, and a lot more activism, too. I mean, ten years ago, I couldn't imagine there being a place called Transhealth or that there would be academic institutions or other institutions around the United States that are working towards gender-affirming care. And that's really great. I think that also leads to more supportive family dynamics at the end of the day. I mean, years ago, I came out as trans. It's very different than right now. And even if it doesn't feel like it all the time from what we see in the media, I believe there's nuanced conversations, and there's more families that are willing to lean in rather than just kick their child out.

NMB: I definitely see more opportunities for events that are more inclusive. I'm not sure if your organization does specific events that are geared towards gender-diverse youth to engage in, but I know out here in Connecticut, we're in the midst of bringing back one of the largest conferences in the US for LGBTQ+ youth, allies, and advocates. The conference is called SOGIEcon (Sexual Orientation, Gender Identity/Expression Conference) and is geared towards motivation and positive visibility of LGBTQ+ folx. There's workshops, there's entertainment and just being able to be together as a community to connect. I see more intentionality about having those community connections and connecting an individual to other community supports.

NL: Is there something that I should have asked you that I didn't ask you or that I didn't give you a chance to talk about?

DD: I might just say that so much of the care that we provide at Transhealth is not revolving around hormones or blockers. First off, we're not doing surgeries, right? It revolves around conversations, having conversations with families and giving parents the chance to better know their child. And that's an amazing opportunity. And so much of the media focuses on hormones, blockers, surgeries, et cetera, but that's just not the reality for so many people who try to receive gender-affirming care and for so many kids. And there's so many different ways of being trans or gender diverse, it does not have to revolve around a healthcare center in any way too. So, the medicalization of trans identity, I think, is really harmful in media. And instead, [we are] really highlighting the joy, the resilience, the lived experiences. All of the life that is outside of that one little visit to a clinic is really, really important. And we don't talk about cisgender people in relation to their diabetes or their hypertension, so I don't think it seems appropriate to talk about trans people in relation to their medical care specifically. To show the whole picture of a person's story is really important. And that starts, importantly, by having more trans creators, writers, people in positions of power, frankly.

NMB: I think that what you're saying, Dallas, about having those conversations and really talking, that's the level that we want to be at because I feel like if we're actually having those conversations, if we're actually validating at that level, then you will see a decrease in the potential mental health support that may be needed out there. Because when it comes down to the diagnosis of dysphoria, for example, that is not the issue. It's the depression and anxiety that goes along with it. If we're having those conversations and then there's a decrease of depression and anxiety, then you will see a difference in the mental health of these individuals. If we're actually able to tackle it at a core when it comes down to family and community, then my job would still be relevant in some way, but maybe not as much in the way that it is now. A lot of the work that I do is not around identity, but it's a lot around helping to build up resilience for individuals, to be able to manage society.

This interview has been edited for clarity and length.

Part 1

Healthcare in Contemporary Realism

SUBSTANCE USE, COMMUNITY HEALING, AND CARE GAPS IN CHILDREN'S LITERATURE

NAOMI LESLEY

Substance use in the United States is situated at the nexus of the criminal justice system, the neoliberal market-based healthcare system, and the public health system. As part of the criminal justice system, substance use is treated as a racialized crime; within the healthcare system, addiction is an individual medical diagnosis that requires insurance coverage and payment for treatment[1]; and within the public health system, it is regarded as an issue of communal responsibility akin to fire safety. Substance use disorder (SUD) is listed as a medical diagnosis, a mental health disorder included in the *Diagnostic and Statistical Manual of Mental Disorders (DSM)*. But because of its overlap with the criminal justice system, SUD has not been medicalized in the same ways as other chronic health conditions. Although disability studies activists have criticized medicalization, substance use disorder is not medicalized largely because people with SUD are framed as moral failures unworthy of resources for treatment (Del Real). As a result, medical treatment, including access to rehabilitation and medication-assisted treatment (MAT), is not sufficiently available in the United States. Indeed, many critics call for drug use to be *more* medicalized and treated as a chronic health issue rather than as a legal or a moral issue. From a broader public health perspective, however, even making medical treatment more available would not fully solve the issue, given that addiction develops within a context that creates risk factors, such as stress and injury. Effective care for this disorder would include access to professional medical treatment, but it would also reach beyond the medical treatment system to encompass a more humane, supportive way to structure community life. For many residents of the United States, access to well-supported, livable communities is even more limited than access to formal medical care.

Many American middle grade and young adult novels about SUD both highlight and replicate these gaps in healthcare. I considered thirty-four novels that involved addiction or substance abuse either as a central problem for the protagonist or as an important component of their relationship with a loved one. The earliest was published in 1967, but most of the books were published in the last twenty years and might therefore be expected to reflect more recent developments in treatment. Instead, many of these novels focus on addiction as a personal psychological illness and track a character's treatment with little acknowledgment of barriers like cost and access; in several novels, characters do not even seek treatment. Out of thirty-four novels, no character ever gets put on a waiting list for rehab. Only two novels mention health insurance or denial of treatment due to insurance policies.[2] For the most part, the addicted character simply needs to commit to rehabilitation treatment. These novels rarely acknowledge that many rehabilitation programs have little data supporting their effectiveness (Glaser).

Because the role of the healthcare system is so conspicuously invisible in these novels, I focus instead on a relatively unusual subset of novels that highlight the role of a resilient community in recovery. Novels like Alice Childress's *A Hero Ain't Nothin' but a Sandwich*, Angie Thomas's *The Hate U Give*, and Susan Patron's *The Higher Power of Lucky* avoid a medicalizing approach to SUD, focusing instead on the ways that communities wracked by substance use can provide supportive environments that include loving connection, childcare, and employment support. In the process, these novels envision small rural towns and inner-city neighborhoods as resources for healing instead of portraying them more stereotypically as toxic for children. Nevertheless, this form of rehabilitation places the full burden of healing on the community's already-stressed residents and does not acknowledge the role that a medical system of treatment might provide. These novels both point toward a vital form of health reform—the building of social capital—and also obscure the medical interventions that would support those social networks.

Of the three novels, Childress's places the most central focus on the issue of addiction. Published in 1973, *A Hero Ain't Nothin' but a Sandwich* follows a thirteen-year-old boy's struggle with addiction during the heroin epidemic of the 1960s and '70s. Benji's battle is also his family's and community's, and the chapters are written as narrative monologues from different characters' points of view—we hear from Benji, but also from his mother, his stepfather, his teachers, and others. These voices establish that Benji's substance use disorder is not only a personal illness, but also a community one. It pains his community both because they care about him and also because it strains their trust, their financial resources, and their sense of safety. Yet Benji's community continues to view him as a child in need of help. Despite reluctance, frustration, and despair, his teachers and family do what they can to treat Benji's addiction. In the 1970s, however, medical treatments for opiate addiction were limited to detoxification and twelve-step abstinence programs. Methadone substitution treatment had only just been approved in 1970, and the opioid blocker buprenorphine had not yet been developed. Thus, the novel ends ambiguously. Even after Benji's family demonstrates their commitment to helping him, and after Benji voices his desire to recover, the final image is of Benji's stepfather waiting in the cold outside Benji's rehab meeting, unsure whether Benji is merely late or has returned to using. Everyone has done their best, but their best may not be enough.

In the other two novels, addiction is a subplot that functions to establish a stigmatized community's potential for nurturing. Susan Patron's 2006 novel *The Higher Power of Lucky* revolves around an orphaned girl's fear that her guardian Brigitte will abandon her due to the town of Hard Pan's economic depression and lack of opportunities. Addiction is part of this initially grim setting. The book's title is drawn from the language of twelve-step programs; Lucky has one of the few paying jobs in town, cleaning up after the many "Anonymous" meetings. She eavesdrops on the meetings and reveals that nearly all the adults in town seem to attend at least one of them. Hard Pan's twelve-step programs are limited to legal substances like alcohol and smoking; however, Patron's novel was published during a period of public concern over methamphetamine use in rural areas. Thus, the twelve-step programs in the novel can be read as stand-ins for a broader concern about youth in depressed rural areas. Similarly, Angie Thomas's *The Hate U Give* focuses primarily on the issues of police brutality and racist lack of justice. Nevertheless, one issue in the novel is whether Khalil, the murdered youth, is an "innocent" victim because he has been dealing drugs. Starr, the narrator, struggles with her feelings about this, as well as her conflicted feelings about living in Garden Heights. The subplot of Khalil's mother Brenda's addiction is important in part because it is placed within a broader context of community issues; addiction treatment is just one example of holistic support the community needs in order to thrive.

All three novels have received considerable attention in the press, in award lists, and on reading lists; thus, they are arguably widely read and influential, even if they are not always read as novels about addiction. Neither scholarly nor popular discussions of the three books have fully analyzed the novels' portrayals of addiction treatment. Indeed, most discussions of Patron's *The Higher Power of Lucky* have focused on the censorship debates surrounding the book rather than the twelve-step programs built into the novel's title.[3] Khalil's drug dealing in Thomas's *The Hate U Give* has been discussed by Marah Gubar and Gabrielle Owen. Brenda's addiction, however, which edges her son into dealing, has not received attention beyond a general objection to drug use being included in the many reasons why some school districts challenge the book.[4] Benji's addiction is so central to Childress's *A Hero Ain't Nothin' but a Sandwich* that it has been discussed by critics. Yet, since Benji does not receive adequate care, critics have tended to focus instead on analyzing the causes of his addiction and on how it reveals divisions of race, class, and gender.[5] I hope to fill a gap in criticism by placing these widely read novels within the context of public discussions about addiction treatment in the United States.

TREATMENT OF SUBSTANCE USE DISORDER IN THE UNITED STATES

In order to understand how these three novels help to highlight gaps in the care of substance abuse in the United States, it is helpful to know the most common medical approaches and understand how they have fallen short. According to many disability activists in the US, the UK, and elsewhere, the medical model of disability has been destructive and stigmatizing, leading to an emphasis on "fixing" people's impairments rather than on spending the equivalent amount of time and money to create inclusive social systems. One common example of this is when medical practitioners insist that disabled people should learn to walk unassisted, however much pain and time it may cost them; they may participate fully in society only if they erase the impairments that make the able-bodied uncomfortable. In contrast, in a social model of disability, the time, energy, and money previously used to "fix" the person's impairments would instead be put toward making assistive devices available and building ramps and elevators, creating a society that enables disability to exist visibly in the world (Crow 10). Nevertheless, disability scholars such as Tom Shakespeare and Liz Crow increasingly call for recognition that disabled people often want medical assistance and relief from physical struggle *in addition to* social change (Shakespeare 18–19; Crow 4). In other words, medical treatment need not result in ignoring social context. The medical treatment of SUD has not been heavily subsidized in the United States, but neither have social structures to reduce the impact of SUD been supported. A dual medical and social approach is what critics of current SUD treatment call for in the United States.[6]

Currently, substance users in the United States avoid being treated as medical "problems" because they are instead treated as criminal or moral problems. Thus, they tend not to be offered appropriate medical treatment in the first place, and they sometimes avoid treatments when they are offered. Even as early as the 1900s, addicts were legally defined as criminals, not patients. Doctors could be held liable for abetting criminal behavior if they prescribed maintenance doses of morphine to prevent withdrawal symptoms. In effect, as there were no other medical treatments available for addiction, these legal changes pushed SUD out of the medical realm (Smith 96). This conscious demedicalization dovetailed with the growth of Alcoholics Anonymous (AA) and faith-based interventions, which depended upon a community of recovering users rather than trained medical personnel. By the 1970s, rehabilitation was becoming a business; it garnered even more profit by utilizing counselors with little training, rather than more highly paid medical personnel. A 2012 Columbia University report found that treatment facilities lacked trained counselors; only six states required substance and alcohol abuse counselors even to have a bachelor's degree, and in fourteen states, nothing more than a high school diploma and an introductory training course was required (Glaser). Furthermore, many treatment centers simply monetized the volunteer-based twelve-step method of treatment, charging money for an approach that had previously been free—without necessarily adding other evidence-based approaches such as cognitive or dialectical behavior therapy. Rehabilitation centers that use the twelve-step approach rarely publish data on their success rates or track their patients once they leave, unlike other medical facilities that are required to do so (Glaser; Guth).

The neoliberal free-market design of the US healthcare system exacerbates gaps in care. Nominally, this system allows consumers to choose the option that works best for their individual circumstances. The U.S. Substance Abuse and Mental Health Services Administration emphasizes that "[n]o single treatment works best. Treatments must address each person's needs and symptoms" ("Behavioral Health Treatments"). Accordingly, the flexibility of a free-market system might be ideal. Overviews of treatment options in the US emphasize the wide range of therapies that consumers can choose, including medication to manage cravings, cognitive behavior therapy, and expressive therapies (see "Drug and Alcohol""; "Treatment"). In practice, however, social workers and psychiatrists observe that the "selection of treatment" is constrained by a number of factors, including cost, types of treatment available in a specific location, and availability of openings at the specific time a person is ready to enter treatment. Because twelve-step treatment is more widely available, it is more likely to be "chosen" ("Treatment" 230; Guth). Furthermore, consumers' choices are also constrained by healthcare providers' lack of knowledge about the effectiveness of MAT (Metcalf qtd. in Guth). One study found that in Massachusetts, only three in ten overdose patients revived by emergency technicians received follow-up MAT, despite research that MAT reduces later fatalities from overdose. In comparison, 98 percent of heart attack patients receive follow-up medication and follow-up visits (Larochelle; Bebinger). This lack of viable choices—or, more likely, of knowledge that different people might need different treatment options—is reflected in young adult novels. In only one of the novels I read (Walter Dean Myers's *The Beast*) did any character mention researching different methods of treatment. Most often, they reference "rehab," "therapy," and "group" as undifferentiated masses—except in the case of attending twelve-step meetings, which are clearly named.

The minimal treatment awareness reflected in these novels seems to feed into Shakespeare's and Crow's arguments that disability activism can include *both* acceptance of medical care *and* reduction of disabling social factors such as stigma, poverty, and regional lack of resources. Since the novels do not reflect actual treatment methods, they cannot address some of the stigmas and barriers attached to these methods. A case in point is medication-assisted treatment. Even when they are offered MAT, patients often refuse it, citing stigma or draconian limitations on autonomy: "'It feels like a jail,' [one patient] says. 'There's literal bars across the gates that don't open 'til a certain time. There's security guards. No one wants to be there. The only reason people go is because they need it'" (Bebinger). Many observers discuss the factors that prevent substance users from receiving MAT. These include a lack of doctors licensed or willing to prescribe, complex application processes that many addicts are ill equipped to complete, prohibitive commute times for rural patients, lack of insurance coverage for MAT, and discrimination against MAT patients because they are not "clean" (Rigg et al. 122; Interlandi; Macy, *Dopesick* 216).[7] As with other disabilities, "cure" is prioritized over long-term management, so that harm reduction is sacrificed for the hope of a full individual "cure."

Indeed, the stigma against giving any medication to an addict extends even to medications for other mental illnesses such as depression and bipolar disorder. These do tend to be medicalized but often remain untreated when a person has "dual diagnosis," or SUD in addition to another mental illness (Glaser). According to the Substance Abuse and Mental Health Services Administration, in 2014 20.2 million Americans had a SUD, and of those, 7.9 million had another major mental illness; that means 39 percent of people with SUD have a dual diagnosis (Center 32). The stigma against medication for dual diagnosis is reflected in children's literature. Many novels feature mental health issues that require medication for treatment. Examples include Brandy Colbert's *Little and Lion* and Erika Sánchez's *I Am Not Your Perfect Mexican Daughter*, in which part of the resolution involves a character accepting medication. In children's books involving addiction, however, the 39 percent of substance users who might need medication for a major mental illness are drastically underrepresented. Only three of the thirty-four novels mention depression as an additional diagnosis that requires treatment. Only two of these mention antidepressant medication as part of a character's holistic care. Only one discusses schizophrenia and a character's decision to self-medicate with opioids and alcohol rather than accept the side effects of antipsychotic medication.[8]

In this respect, novels might reflect a lack of public awareness that lags behind access to medical care, inadequate as that is.

Just as critics of current care for SUD note gaps in medical access to treatment, they also note gaps in how social structures provide care and support for addicts, families, people in recovery, and other community members. Not surprisingly, many scholars of addiction call for as much work in this area as they do in the areas of harm reduction and MAT. Khary Rigg et al. argue that the nation's focus on rural areas as epicenters of the opioid crisis conceals important differences between different rural areas.[9] They suggest that some of these differences can be explained by levels of supportive infrastructure. In states that did not expand Medicaid, for example, rural residents often lack access to primary healthcare. As a result, relatively minor injuries may go untreated and become very painful before the person finally goes to an emergency room. They are then more likely to be prescribed opiates than if they had been able to seek medical care at an earlier stage (Rigg et. al 124). Citing a study by Shannon M. Monnat and David L. Brown, Rigg et al. also emphasize that governments should meet residents' basic needs: "[T]he most important upstream solution may well be a revitalized economy and social safety net. It is no coincidence that overdose rates are highest in places with the most disadvantaged labor markets that have hemorrhaged jobs over the past three decades" (126). Biologist Robert Sapolsky, too, emphasizes that stress management ought to be the responsibility of governments and communities, not merely of individuals. He argues that communities in which people experience high levels of social capital—where they trust their neighbors, they observe that community organizations work for everyone's benefit, they see that resources are invested in public goods—experience lower levels of stress and also globally better health (including less addiction, for which stress is a risk factor) (Sapolsky 318–20). "Treating" SUD fully would thus involve constructing a culture of care that includes, but is not limited to, basic medical care. The novels by Childress, Thomas, and Patron provide valuable insights into how communities can provide this broader level of care but can also be challenged by this responsibility.

AMBIVALENT COMMUNITIES: RISK FACTORS OR SOLUTIONS?

The community's role in treating substance use disorder has the potential to elevate under-resourced, stigmatized communities as valuable sources of healing support. Unfortunately, discussions of social capital in the popular press can have the opposite effect, further stigmatizing rural towns and inner-city communities as places that lack social capital and cause addiction. Jose A. del Real, for example, notes that methadone clinics tend to be shunted toward majority Black and Latino urban neighborhoods and are rarely opened in suburban areas. Because people have to stand outside in line for the clinics and can be publicly identified as having an addiction, suburban users who travel to urban clinics have longer commutes but more anonymity. Thus, even though rural and suburban users may suffer from the lack of accessible clinics, the disparities in clinic placement do not foster a narrative that urban neighborhoods are providing medical infrastructure—they instead feed a narrative that addiction is a racialized urban problem. Similarly, Beth Macy chronicles how suburban Roanoke, Virginia was slow to respond to the opioid crisis with education and services because addiction was viewed as a problem of "jobless hillbillies" or "inner-city blacks." Conversely, she expresses concern that federal disability support in rural areas morphed from a social safety net into a risk factor, providing a pipeline for prescription opiates to enter the community (Macy, *Dopesick* 124–26). Scholars who study twelve-step communities observe that even they are often ambivalent about whether their larger communities are sources of healthy social support or of risk. Adam Rafalovich finds that narratives of Narcotics Anonymous (NA) meetings construct a sense of the world "out there" as being dangerous for recovering addicts; "out there" often means the world outside the NA meeting, which includes stressors and temptations (147). By contrast, Linda Farris Kurtz and Michael Fisher find that committed NA and AA members become active in improving their neighborhoods in a variety of ways. Their involvement in recovery leads them to advocate for the broader health of their communities, supporting homeless residents, healthcare organizations, and youth groups (Kurtz and Fisher 886, 889).

This ambivalence about the role of communities hit hard by substance use is reflected in *A Hero Ain't Nothin' but a Sandwich*, *The Hate U Give,* and *The Higher Power of Lucky*. All three novels acknowledge public concern over inner-city and rural communities, but ultimately showcase them as potential sources of the social capital necessary for addressing addiction.

All three novels evoke common stigmas about either segregated Black urban neighborhoods or white rural towns. Various characters voice concern that their neighborhoods put youth "at risk" of poverty, addiction, and criminal activity. In Childress's *A Hero Ain't Nothin' but a Sandwich,* the white principal of Benji's school fears that his assemblies about addiction will backfire, inviting students to "see drugs as something to use and then bravely give up" (Childress 56). He also worries about the generational poverty of his students (56). While he claims he has come "begrudgingly to respect the poverty-stricken," he is simply going through the motions and waiting for retirement, having given up hope that education can combat the lure of drugs (56–57).

A few generations later, Thomas depicts an intensification of the stigma and risk attached to majority Black urban neighborhoods in *The Hate U Give*.

Whereas Benji's principal worried about his charges becoming addicts, Starr and her neighborhood friends are constantly suspected of being dealers and gang members. Scholars Jay Shelat and Owen have both discussed how Starr manages her self-presentation in the white world; she is acutely aware of the need to manage her predominantly white classmates' view of her as being respectable. In addition, however, Starr's self-presentation reflects her awareness that she is viewed as a risk to white people, even as her own health is at risk. Despite her grief, she initially denies having known Khalil, because she realizes, "The drug dealer. That's how they see him. . . . If it's revealed that I was in the car, what will that make me? The thug ghetto girl with the drug dealer? What will my teachers think of me? My friends? The whole fucking world, possibly?" (Thomas 115). Starr fears she will be not only perceived as being "ghetto," unable to function at her private school, but also as a "thug," a risky person to be around. Benji's principal admits to fearing his actively addicted students, but he also fears *for* them (Childress 56). In contrast, Starr hears police and media talk only about drug deals and gang violence that represent the harm youth might cause, never about the issues of hunger, housing insecurity, asthma, and domestic abuse that Starr either experiences or witnesses. Starr herself never worries that Khalil might drift into using, despite his familial history of SUD—she only worries about why he is dealing.

Indeed, Starr has internalized much of the stigma attached to her and her neighbors. She initially has trouble empathizing with Khalil, blaming him for dealing despite his knowledge of the pain of addiction. Nor can she empathize with Brenda, blaming her for the financial need that drove Khalil into dealing. While Starr's nurse mother Lisa rubs Brenda's back and makes sure she gets fed, Starr is able to see Brenda only as the person who damaged Khalil and not as a person who deserves healing (Thomas 93–94). Starr is also torn between her mother, who sees Garden Heights as a place where her children might be shot, and her father, who tries to grow roses in the yard in defiance of tanks rolling through the streets. In fact, the narrative partially reinforces Garden Heights as a place that poisons youth and puts them at risk; Starr's father finally agrees to move, and his rose bushes do not thrive until they are transplanted in richer suburban soil.

Susan Patron's *The Higher Power of Lucky* taps into a different set of stereotypes about hollowed-out, jobless rural towns ravaged by addiction. Orphaned Lucky, cleaning up after the twelve-step programs, tells the reader that most adults in Hard Pan get their income "out of having a disability or being old or from fathers who didn't like children," and consequently nearly everyone qualifies for free "Government" food (Patron 35–36). The town has a population of only forty-three people, including at least three children, yet it supports at least four different twelve-step groups. As with the other two novels, the characters indicate their awareness of stigma and worry that their environment is unhealthy. Lucky's friend Lincoln paints graffiti on the public sign announcing "SLOW CHILDREN AT PLAY;" his graffiti, however, is merely a colon between "SLOW" and "CHILDREN," intended to defuse drivers' assumptions about the town and its children. Lincoln explains to Lucky that "people see that sign and they think, 'Huh. Slow children. Kids around here aren't too smart'" (23). Lincoln has clearly absorbed an awareness that outsiders assume Hard Pan's children are unintelligent and damaged. Lucky also learns, through eavesdropping on the Smokers Anonymous meeting, that her friend Miles's mother is in prison on drug charges. Miles's grandmother enters the twelve-step program out of guilt, because she feels she has been a bad influence on her daughter and does not want to bring up her grandson in a house with any kind of addiction (72–73). Even though her nicotine use was unlikely to have caused her daughter's heroin addiction, Mrs. Prender taps into the fear that Hard Pan is toxic to its children, offering unhealthy influences with little opportunity to offset them. It is therefore ironic that cleaning up after the twelve-step programs is one of the only paying jobs in town; at the start of the novel, the only source of economic stability is based in profiting from the residents' addictions.

All three novels thus evoke common notions that over-stressed communities are poisonous, risky environments for the young. At the same time, all three narratives attempt to counteract the stigmas attached to depressed communities, emphasizing the networks of caring adults who serve as resources and safety nets. In ethnographer Matthew Desmond's study of eviction, he observes that "[p]oor neighborhoods provided their residents with quite a lot. In the trailer park, residents met people who knew how to pirate cable, when the best food pantries were open, and how to apply for SSI [Supplemental Security Income]. All over the city, people who lived in distressed neighborhoods were more likely to help their neighbors, buy groceries, fix their car, or lend a hand in other ways, compared to their peers in better-off areas" (181). As in Desmond's analysis, social networks in these novels help to ameliorate the stresses of poverty, racism, and classism and to address the residents' overall well-being, not merely to solve addiction.

In Patron's version of a small rural town, for example, the community forms social rituals that soften the humiliation of receiving free surplus food. Short Sammy, one of the recovering alcoholics, routinely conducts culinary experiments on "commodities day," trying to create recipes out of whatever happens to arrive (Patron 49, 57). Although not everyone appreciates Sammy's greasy productions, everyone is clearly welcome, and the town's children love eating Sammy's food and listening to him talk. Brigitte later opens a French café as a destination that helps outsiders see the beauty of Hard Pan; yet she still maintains the tradition of "Commodity Tasting," setting out a complimentary platter of food that creatively uses the free ingredients to which everyone in town has access (134). Lucky and Miles are hurt by parental abandonment, but Miles charms cookies even out of the "bossiest and crabbiest" adult in Hard Pan, and all the town's adults turn out to search when the children go missing in the desert (27). Patron evokes stereotypes only to solve them (somewhat blithely). Nobody goes hungry; the humiliating government aid is transformed into entrepreneurial celebration; and although most of the adults in town are in recovery, not one appears to be falling off the wagon.

The two urban novels are grimmer, but they too emphasize the rich social resources to be found in economically poor neighborhoods. In *The Hate U Give,* Starr points out the various forms of "other mothering" that adults in Garden Heights do for neighborhood youth.[10] Gubar observes the "complexly interwoven web of loving relationships" portrayed in the novel. Mr. Reuben, the owner of the local barbecue restaurant, gives free food to local kids who bring in school report cards and offers the good reports a place of pride on the restaurant wall. We learn that years earlier, Khalil's grandmother insisted upon babysitting for Starr without pay so that Starr's mother Lisa could finish her nursing education; without this childcare, Starr's family might not have achieved the financial stability they have. These relationships ultimately serve to bolster public health in Garden Heights. Because she has been able to get her nursing degree, Lisa can work at a neighborhood clinic where she is in a position to feed Brenda and guide her into rehab. Starr's father Maverick tries to help first Khalil, and then another youth, DeVante, by offering them paying jobs at his store. Even Mr. Lewis, the neighborhood barber who constantly criticizes Maverick, steps in to support him both emotionally and financially when Maverick is targeted by the police and local gang members. While none of this is sufficient to treat Brenda's addiction or to eliminate the poverty that draws Khalil and DeVante into drug dealing, it does establish that many adults in Garden Heights try to ameliorate the stresses of hunger, financial strain, and racism.

Adults in Childress's *A Hero Ain't Nothin' but a Sandwich* are portrayed as far more stressed and morally compromised, and the community's social network appears more frayed. Benji's teacher Mr. Cohen is a defensive white liberal who is primarily concerned about protecting his job against the Black nationalist activism he fears. Mr. Cohen's inclination is to let tricky situations slide because "kid addicts don't bother a soul" (Childress 36). His former teacher Nigeria Greene is a passionate Black nationalist who nevertheless talks *at* Benji's stepfather rather than *to* him, "rappin on harder than ever" about "nation time" as Butler is worrying about how Benji is faring in detox (106). Butler himself leaves the family for a time, too angry to care for Benji after he returns from detox and steals Butler's suit. When Benji asks Butler to let him fall off the roof to his death, Butler realizes his own failure of nurturing: "*I was runnin from him*. . . . If this was my flesh-and-blood child, I wouldn't have run when he stole my suit" (109). The adults' monologues (specifically, the men's) are so damning of their motives and their behavior that much scholarship on the novel has focused on analyzing the varied ways in which those characters are responsible for perpetuating racism and classism, as well as for letting Benji drift into addiction.[11] La Vinia Delois Jennings further notes that the drug dealer's monologue draws readers' attention to how an unseen white power structure is benefiting from the drug trade (95). Even as readers see how many adults in Benji's orbit fail to support him, we also see that those adults are themselves caught in systems that exhaust them.

The portrayal of adults in *A Hero Ain't Nothin' but a Sandwich* highlights the limitations of what a community's social networks can do for healthcare in the absence of concrete resources and viable forms of medical treatment. Benji's teachers and parents are genuinely tired and confused about what they can offer youth besides talk, and their resources are strained by the enormity of the addiction crisis they face. Macy suggests that this is a common pattern; in the absence of accessible medical treatment and support, "relatives become worn out by a user's behavior" and stop investing in rehab treatment ("'I Am Going to Die'"). A similar pattern holds true for the broader-scale food, housing, and basic medical care that underpin long-term recovery and health. Desmond argues that even as poor communities offer valuable social networks, residents sometimes feel so ground down that they feel reluctant to admit to their neighbors that they need help (181). When they do rely on each other, the level of support they must request can feel like "a lot to ask of someone you barely knew" (162). These writers, along with scholars like Sapolsky, emphasize that "social capital" (the kind of support that protects health) does not merely mean sociable relationships among community members. Social capital also requires infrastructure—jobs, clinics, affordable housing and transportation. It requires a stable social contract with trust between community and government.

In the final section, I discuss how the three novels either acknowledge a need for more infrastructure or attempt to substitute social networks for more robust forms of social capital. Moreover, all three demonstrate a need for more medical treatment options.

SOCIAL CAPITAL AND COMMUNITIES UNDER STRESS

Shakespeare notes that activists with HIV/AIDS have helped to shift disability activism toward a more symbiotic relationship with medical science, rather than an oppositional one: "many people with HIV/AIDS have become treatment activists, lobbying for more and better medical research and development, and other disabled people have major personal investments in medical research" (14). Similarly, Crow suggests that prevention of impairment is not always erasure of disability. She writes, "Prevention of impairment through public health measures receives only minimal consideration and resourcing. The isolation of impairment from its social context means the social and economic causes of impairment often go unrecognized" (9). She argues that public health measures should include investments that might improve the lives of disabled people as well as prevent additional stress-linked illnesses. Better access to food, housing, and transportation would reduce pain and risk for everyone. These novels highlight that substance users and their families do not experience pain only from stigma, but also from the life-threatening experience of substance use disorder. All three novels do attempt to reduce the stigmas that damage already struggling communities. But Childress's novel goes further, contributing to the "treatment activism" and public health advocacy that Shakespeare and Crow call for.

A Hero Ain't Nothin' but a Sandwich articulates a sense of helplessness—a sense that whatever the adults can do is not enough to help Benji and others like him. Indeed, its portrayal of adult burnout and indifference only serves to highlight the inadequacy of adult caring as a solution to SUD. Benji wants someone to care for him, and some adult characters do. Teacher Nigeria Greene may struggle with classism, but he cares enough about Benji to inform his parents of his addiction; Benji's mother and grandmother are at a loss for how to help him, but give him time, care, and love;[12] and Butler is the titular "hero" because he commits to loving and supporting Benji despite having no biological tie to him. Yet this caring, which Benji thinks will solve the problem, cannot fix his addiction. Nigeria Greene feels increasingly frustrated that he has nothing to offer but "tired, opportunistic advice" (Childress 98–99). Similarly, Butler is "wonderin what to do besides talk" (110). The voices of the few supportive adults reveal the community's need for broader public health support and actual medical treatment, as well as their consequent burnout when they have neither to fall back upon.

Legal scholar James Forman provides insight into how this sense of community helplessness played out in Black communities during the 1970s, as they tried to combat the heroin crisis. According to Forman, Black leaders and community members at the time were actually calling for more policing in their neighborhoods because they believed officers were not doing enough to combat drug activity; this was an ironic early cause of the current mass incarceration crisis (30). He emphasizes, however, that activists wanted law enforcement as only one of many measures aimed at improving the overall health of Black communities. They also asked for better jobs, housing, and schools and sought redress of the entrenched racism and poverty that were "root causes" of the heroin epidemic. Consistently, however, all they got was more incarceration without more infrastructure (Forman 12–13, 29).

A similar pattern plays out in Childress's novel. Benji reports the punitive measures adopted by the youth court: if he does not report to his social worker, "they will book [him] into a reform detention and charge [his] family with negleck of a minor" (Childress 114). Benji's family is demonstrably *not* neglecting him, so this threat is unfair as well as ineffective; moreover, the assigned social workers are so incompetent and condescending that Butler sometimes wants to "hit them full on" (124). Yet, in light of the historical context outlined by Forman, the fact that Benji was given counseling through a juvenile drug court at all was a form of progress—just not the right form of progress. In the meantime, several characters name the resources they wish the neighborhood kids had. Nigeria Greene wants the Black elite to work against economic inequality in the neighborhood (47). Butler desires environmental health as well as community strength, wanting Benji to retreat to the South for a while to "see sky and run and play where there's no concrete and crowds" (82).[13] Jimmy-Lee Powell, Benji's friend, wants "some place to go without bein in trouble"; he envies the support given to kids who fall into substance use, but doesn't want to have to become addicted in order to have a counselor or a recreation facility (84). We never read a monologue from one of the incompetent social workers, but they would have few options for treatment beyond talk. Childress's novel was published before the existence of MAT or targeted therapies for SUD, and the lack of medical treatments available highlights the crucial need for them. The city is not yet using everything in its toolbox to combat the heroin epidemic—it is not providing safe recreational spaces for youth or relief from poverty—but its toolbox for those already addicted is pitifully empty.

In *The Hate U Give*, published more than four decades later, the public health measures are, if anything, worse than in Childress's novel. As Forman observes, the Black community has gotten punitive law enforcement without supportive infrastructure. Thus, Maverick and Mr. Lewis still see a dearth of stable jobs for youth, and Maverick tries to grow roses because the neighborhood still needs beauty and greenery. Maverick and Starr discuss the lack of infrastructure in their neighborhood, unpacking how racism leads to a lack of investment, leading to joblessness, leading to further disinvestment and the alternate economy of the drug trade (Thomas 168–69). Now, however, their health is also at risk from the daily stressors of over-policing. During an argument between Maverick and Mr. Lewis, police officers pull up and force Maverick to the ground in front of his children. They let him up, physically unharmed, because several neighbors gather as witnesses (189–93). Several studies indicate that Black citizens' constant vigilance against racist incidents causes long-term stress reactions that accumulate over time. Journalist Clint Smith describes how each time he is pulled over as a Black man, he is aware that the interaction can turn violent. His system is flooded with adrenaline and cortisol. Even if the pullover proceeds without incident, these stress hormones take time to subside. Over time, such repeated floods of stress hormones in the body cause terrible damage. Smith reports on one finding that "simply perceiving or anticipating discrimination contributes to chronic stress that can cause an increase in blood-pressure problems, coronary-artery disease, cognitive impairment, and infant mortality. Black Americans do not have to directly experience police brutality to experience the negative health ramifications of its possibility." Similarly, Mav's children observe their father's endangerment and distress. Although they are not targeted by the police in this scene, their health as well as Mav's is literally threatened by such scenes; Starr describes the continued "knotting" of her stomach even after the incident is over (Thomas 194).

These public health issues—over-policing, violence, and neighborhood disinvestment—are the focal points of *The Hate U Give*. Vincent Haddad critiques *The Hate U Give* for invoking the Black Lives Matter movement only to back away from the BLM protests as "unrealistic" solutions (41). He suggests that by condemning the protests, the novel ignores BLM's calls for economic support, which are continuations of the calls for support made by the earlier activists Forman discusses (48). In a similar way, while Thomas's novel powerfully portrays a need for public health infrastructure, its ending seems to ask stressed communities to bear the burden of public infrastructure. It ends with the neighborhood banding together to clean up after the protests and the gang-related arson of Black-owned businesses. The morning after Starr is tear-gassed and her father's store burns down, she thinks, "We did all that stuff last night because we were pissed, and it fucked all of us. Now we have to somehow un-fuck everybody" (Thomas 426). This phrasing suggests that it is the community's task to "un-fuck" themselves, despite the ongoing lack of infrastructure. Starr articulates a sense of responsibility for gentrifying members of the Black community, like her family, to remain in the neighborhood and provide some level of social and economic capital. Yet her family is economically strained, too, and they cannot commit to rebuilding the shop until Mr. Lewis offers to retire and give Mav his property. In the novel's final scene, the community has given up on the city's help, and residents attempt to make social networks stretch as far as they can.

At the same time, the public health issue of addiction is pushed to the side. Despite the novel's indictment of over-policing as a solution for the drug trade, it stops short of portraying addiction as an issue that requires changes in medical treatment as well as more access to healthcare and jobs.[14] Starr's grandmother Nana is a recovering alcoholic, and Starr's narrative grants her a certain amount of complexity. Nana's alcoholism has strained her relationship with her children, and Starr suggests that Nana still drinks (Thomas 249). Nana is still an educated retired teacher with resources to offer, tutoring DeVante when Maverick moves him to the suburbs. Yet Nana's more genteel addiction is treated as an internal family matter, rather than the spiraling community scourge that Brenda's becomes after stealing from a gang leader in order to buy drugs, thus forcing Khalil into dealing in order to pay her debt. In this respect, the novel reflects a sense that substance use is more of a community risk issue in the inner city than it is in the suburbs (a bias Macy also confirms). Moreover, Starr's mother, a trained nurse, makes no mention of MAT or of specific treatment options for Brenda—she simply says that Brenda must "really want" to change, and that she can get her into a rehab facility (Thomas 93). This unspecified treatment might include MAT or professional cognitive-behavioral therapy; however, Lisa makes no mention of the insurance and payment restrictions that generally accompany MAT (see Del Real; Interlandi). Social networks can get Brenda a coveted spot in rehab, but there is no acknowledgment that the available rehab might be medically insufficient even if Brenda "really wants" it.

The Higher Power of Lucky does still less to acknowledge the realities of public health and medical treatment gaps. What the town lacks in medical care and employment, it makes up for in its rural desert setting, which provides its children with beauty, recreation, and opportunities for scientific exploration. Lucky feels, looking at the desert, that it "made your brain feel rested. It made you feel like you could become anything you wanted, like you were filled up with nothing but hope" (Patron 61). This paean to the benefits of beauty and wide-open space glosses over the fact that Lucky has been eavesdropping on multiple twelve-step stories of Hard Pan adults who have not become what they wanted or been filled with hope. Short Sammy tells Lucky to look out at the desert in part so that she will not focus on the "jumble of trailers, sheds, outhouses, shacks, and rusty vehicles" that make up Hard Pan (60). The presence of healthy natural space simply replaces other forms of housing and environmental reform as a solution. The portrayal of addiction is similar. Despite numerous critiques from the medical community about the effectiveness of twelve-step programs,[15] the anonymous programs in Hard Pan all seem to work perfectly. Since the town is too small to support a hospital or clinic, the twelve-step programs seem to have functionally replaced medical care. In Hard Pan, social networks do not agitate for better housing or job training; they instead work to combat government interference when the county board of health tries to shut down Brigitte's café in the sequel *Lucky for Good*.

CONCLUSION: TREATMENT ACTIVISM

When *A Hero Ain't Nothin' but a Sandwich* was published in 1973, communities had few effective medical treatments available for SUD, and the novel evokes the desperate need for such treatment. By the time *The Hate U Give* and *The Higher Power of Lucky* were published decades later, a wider range of treatments had been developed, including not merely long-term MAT for opioids and alcohol, but also techniques like motivational enhancement and cognitive-behavioral therapy (Glaser). Yet these medical treatments do not appear in either of the later novels, nor do they appear in many contemporary books for children; only four of the thirty-four novels I surveyed mentioned any form of MAT, and no novels mentioned targeted therapies.[16] MAT and professional counseling are thus not only inaccessible to many users in real life, but they are also inaccessible even in the solutions we imagine through fiction. Disability activists, as well as substance use experts, point out that addiction is one of many chronic illnesses that must be addressed by improving social capital and infrastructure. Fighting for housing security, jobs, safety, and racial equity is a form of healthcare and a form of disability activism. But sometimes, as these scholars point out, it is not enough. Treatment activism is also necessary.[17] The stigma attached to addiction treatments other than abstinence-based twelve-step approaches contributes to its lack of accessibility. Normalizing MAT and professional counseling programs in fiction for youth would help to address this stigma and perhaps help make treatments more accessible in the future.

NOTES

1. The medical system has also produced substance dependence through overprescription; see David Smith for an overview of this history.

2. In Kate Messner's *The Seventh Wish*, Charlie wishes that insurance will cover four weeks of treatment instead of just two, and acknowledges that might still be insufficient. In *How I Made It to Eighteen*, by Tracy White, one character leaves therapy before she is finished with treatment because insurance will no longer pay.

3. See, for example, Miller; Houdyshell and Martin; and Patron, "Are Some Words Off-Limits."

4. Many critics focus on other aspects of the novel. Vincent Haddad critiques the novel's portrayal of the Black Lives Matter movement, while Gubar defends how the novel troubles empathic identification. Jay Shelat analyzes Starr's sneakers as a metaphor for her mobility between worlds. Owen discusses how the novel questions the politics of respectability.

5. See, for example, Ortiz; Muoneke; Meyer; and Evans. Often, critics will praise one adult while critiquing the rest.

6. See, for example, Zoorob and Salemi; Bebinger; and Rigg et al.

7. Beth Macy observes that these structural barriers feed further stigma against MAT. The difficulty of obtaining buprenorphine leads to its black-market diversion to patients anxious to stay off heroin. Furthermore, patients weaned too quickly off MAT often relapse, contributing to perceptions that MAT is ineffective (Macy, *Dopesick* 222).

8. In *The Art of Losing*, by Lizzie Mason, Raf discusses his chronic depression; in *Clean*, by Amy Reed, and *How I Made It to Eighteen*, by Tracy White, the characters are prescribed antidepressants, which aid their addiction recovery. In Mason's *Between the Bliss and Me*, the protagonist's father refuses antipsychotic medication and instead lives with addiction, paranoia, and delusions. Zach, in Benjamin Alire Sáenz's *Last Night I Sang to the Monster*, experiences trauma. So do Gabi in Walter Dean Myers's *The Beast* and Laurel in Jacqueline Woodson's *Beneath a Meth Moon*. In those novels, no adult suggests that trauma might need to be treated separately from the addiction.

9. They note that rural areas in the upper Midwest and in the Southeast have lower mortality rates from opioids than rural areas in Appalachia, parts of the Southwest, and New England; they also note that higher prevalence of churches and other community organizations correlates with lower overdose fatality rates.

10. Scholars of African American educational history, such as Jacqueline Jordan Irvine, describe "other mothering" as a tradition of Black woman teachers sharing responsibility with other community members for the success of their students (Irvine; Ramsey 37).

11. See, for example, Ortiz; Meyer; and Muoneke.

12. Jennings points out that entrenched sexism is revealed in the monologues and that it interferes with the mother's and grandmother's ability to support Benji (89).

13. Jennings argues that Benji would have interpreted such an intervention as another abandonment by a father figure (96). I agree but focus here on the public health implications of Butler's statement regarding what is missing in Benji's neighborhood.

14. Haddad argues that the novel does not truly condemn over-policing as a solution to the drug trade, noting that the arrest of King and his associates is celebrated, and no alternative to incarceration is proposed (47).

15. See, for example, Glaser; Macy, *Dopesick* (particularly part three); and Forman (123).

16. Two novels—Kate Messner's *The Seventh Wish* and Amy Reed's *Clean*—mention suboxone, specifically as a taper to prevent withdrawal pain and not as a long-term treatment to prevent relapse. Two other novels mention methadone—Walter Dean Myers's *The Beast*, which presents it only as an undesirable choice, and Melvin Burgess's *Smack*, a British book in which methadone prescriptions are plentiful but unaccompanied by counseling or attention to basic needs. This partial treatment is unsuccessful for the characters in the novel.

17. There is no existing MAT for methamphetamine addiction, and the effectiveness of available treatment often depends upon a user's specific addiction.

WORKS CITED

Bebinger, Martha. "After an Overdose, Patients Aren't Getting Treatments That Could Prevent the Next One." *NPR*, 18 June 2018, https://www.npr.org/sections/health-shots/2018/06/18/619620769/after-an-overdose-patients-arent-getting-treatments-that-could-prevent-the-next-.

Burgess, Melvin. *Smack*. Holt, 1998.
Center for Behavioral Health Statistics and Quality. *Behavioral Health Trends in the United States: Results from the 2014 National Survey on Drug Use and Health*. Substance Abuse and Mental Health Services Administration, Sept. 2015, https://www.samhsa.gov/data/sites/default/files/NSDUH-FRR1-2014/NSDUH-FRR1-2014.pdf.
Childress, Alice. *A Hero Ain't Nothin' but a Sandwich*. 1973. Puffin Books, 2000.
Colbert, Brandy. *Little and Lion*. Little, Brown, 2017.
Crow, Liz. "Including All of Our Lives: Renewing the Social Model of Disability." Jan. 1996. *ResearchGate*, 7 May 2018, https://www.researchgate.net/publication/246453360_Including_All_of_Our_Lives_Renewing_the_Social_Model_of_Disability.
Del Real, Jose A. "Opioid Addiction Knows No Color, but Its Treatment Does." *New York Times*, 12 Jan. 2018, https://www.nytimes.com/2018/01/12/nyregion/opioid-addiction-knows-no-color-but-its-treatment-does.html.
Desmond, Matthew. *Evicted: Poverty and Profit in the American City*. Crown Publishers, 2016.
"Drug and Alcohol Addiction Treatment." *Addiction Center*, 2020, https://www.addictioncenter.com/treatment/.
Evans, Don. "Alice (Conversations with Alice Childress)." *Obsidian III*, vol. 1, no. 1, 1999, p. 197–204. *General OneFile*, https://www.proquest.com/docview/206790972?sourcetype=Scholarly%20Journals.
Forman, James. *Locking Up Our Own: Crime and Punishment in Black America*. Farrar, Straus and Giroux, 2017.
Glaser, Gabrielle. "The Irrationality of Alcoholics Anonymous." *Atlantic*, vol. 315, no. 3, 2015, https://www.theatlantic.com/magazine/archive/2015/04/the-irrationality-of-alcoholics-anonymous/386255/.
Gubar, Marah. "Empathy Is Not Enough." *Public Books*, 19 July 2017, https://www.publicbooks.org/empathy-is-not-enough/.
Guth, Kerianne Johnstin. "Reevaluating the 12-Step Model Legacy." *Social Work Today*, vol. 18, no.1, 2020, https://www.socialworktoday.com/archive/JF18p20.shtml.
Haddad, Vincent. "Nobody's Protest Novel: Novelistic Strategies of the Black Lives Matter Movement." *The Comparatist*, vol. 42, 2018, pp. 40–59. *Project MUSE*, https://doi.org/10.1353/com.2018.0002.
Houdyshell, Mara L., and Coleen Meyers Martin. "You Go, Girl! Heroines in Newbery Medal Award Winners." *Children and Libraries*, vol. 8, no. 1, Spring2010, pp. 25–31, https://journals.ala.org/index.php/cal/article/view/46/21.
Interlandi, Jeneen. "48 Million Americans Live with Addiction. Here's How to Get Them Help That Works." *New York Times*, 13 Dec. 2023, https://www.nytimes.com/2023/12/13/opinion/addiction-policy-treatment-opioid.html.
Irvine, Jacqueline Jordan. "'The Education of Children Whose Nightmares Come Both Day and Night.'" *The Journal of Negro Education*, vol. 68, no. 3, 1999, pp. 244–53. *JSTOR*, https://doi.org/10.2307/2668099.
Jennings, La Vinia Delois. *Alice Childress*. Twayne Publishers, 1995.
Kurtz, Linda Farris, and Michael Fisher. "Participation in Community Life by AA and NA Members." *Contemporary Drug Problems*, vol. 30, no. 4, 2003, pp. 875–904, https://doi.org/10.1177/009145090303000407.

Larochelle, Marc R., et al. "Medication for Opioid Use Disorder After Nonfatal Opioid Overdose and Association With Mortality: A Cohort Study." *Annals of Internal Medicine*, vol. 169, no. 3, 2018, pp. 137–45, https://doi:10.7326/M17-3107.

Macy, Beth. *Dopesick: Dealers, Doctors, and the Drug Company that Addicted America*. Little, Brown, 2018.

Macy, Beth. "'I Am Going to Die If I Keep Living the Way I Am.' She Was Right." *New York Times*, 20 July 2018, https://www.nytimes.com/2018/07/20/opinion/sunday/opioid-addiction-treatment.html.

Mason, Lizzy. *The Art of Losing*. Soho Teen, 2020.

Mason, Lizzy. *Between the Bliss and Me*. Soho Teen, 2021.

Messner, Kate. *The Seventh Wish*. Bloomsbury USA Children's, 2017.

Meyer, Adam. "'The Gesture Was Never Enough': Harlem as a Problematic Proving Ground for Jewish Reformers in the Post–World War II Period." *Twentieth-Century Literary Criticism*, edited by Carol A. Schwartz, vol. 385, Gale, 2020. *Gale Literature Resource Center*, https://go.gale.com/ps/i.do?p=LitRC&u=anon~72d4f8b2&id=GALE|H1420127481&v=2.1&it=r&sid=bookmark-LitRC&asid=58481f97.

Miller, Alyson. "Unsuited to Age Group: The Scandals of Children's Literature." *College Literature*, vol. 41, no. 2, 2014, p. 120–40. *ProjectMUSE*, https://doi.org10.1353/lit.2014.0025.

Muoneke, Romanus. "A Call for Change: Liberation as Motif in Alice Childress's *A Hero Ain't Nothing but a Sandwich*." *Twentieth-Century Literary Criticism*, edited by Carol A. Schwartz, vol. 385, Gale, 2020. *Gale Literature Resource Center*, https://go.gale.com/ps/i.do?p=LitRC&u=anon~72d4f8b2&id=GALE|H1420127482&v=2.1&it=r&sid=bookmark-LitRC&asid=ce6b30e6.

Myers, Walter D. *The Beast*. Scholastic, 2003.

Ortiz, Miguel A. "The Politics of Poverty in Young Adult Literature." *Lion and the Unicorn*, vol. 2, no. 2, 1978, pp. 6–15. *Project MUSE*, https://doi.org/10.1353/uni.0.0374.

Owen, Gabrielle. "Adolescence, Blackness, and the Politics of Respectability in *Monster* and *The Hate U Give*." *Lion and the Unicorn*, vol. 43, no. 2, 2019, pp. 236–60. *Project MUSE*, doi:10.1353/uni.2019.0021.

Patron, Susan. "Are Some Words Off-Limits in Children's Books?" *Talk of the Nation*, 28 Feb. 2007, NPR, https://www.npr.org/2007/02/28/7644587/are-some-words-off-limits-in-childrens-books.

Patron, Susan. *Lucky for Good*. Illustrated by Erin McGuire, Atheneum Books for Young Readers, 2011.

Patron, Susan. *The Higher Power of Lucky*. Illustrated by Matt Phelan, Atheneum Books for Young Readers, 2006.

Rafalovich, Adam. "Keep Coming Back! Narcotics Anonymous Narrative and Recovering-Addict Identity." *Contemporary Drug Problems*, vol. 26, no. 1, 1999, pp. 131, https://doi.org/10.1177/009145099902600106.

Ramsey, Sonya. "'We Will Be Ready Whenever They Are': African American Teachers' Responses to the Brown Decision and Public School Integration in Nashville, Tennessee, 1954–1966." *Journal of African American History*, vol. 90, no.1–2, 2005, pp. 29–51. *JSTOR*, http://www. https://www.jstor.org/stable/20063974.

Reed, Amy. *Clean*. Simon and Schuster Books for Young Readers, 2012.

Rigg, Khary K., et al. "Opioid-Related Mortality in Rural America: Geographic Heterogeneity and Intervention Strategies." *International Journal of Drug Policy*, vol. 57, 2018, pp. 119–29, https://doi.org/10.1016/j.drugpo.2018.04.011.

Sáenz, Benjamin A. *Last Night I Sang to the Monster: A Novel*. Cinco Puntos Press, 2009.

Sánchez, Erika L. *I Am Not Your Perfect Mexican Daughter*. Alfred A. Knopf, 2017.

Sapolsky, Robert M. *Why Zebras Don't Get Ulcers*. Times Books, 2004.

Shakespeare, Tom. "Social Models of Disability and Other Life Strategies." *Scandinavian Journal of Disability Research*, vol. 6, no. 1, 2004, pp. 8–21.

Shelat, Jay. "'I swear those things are so fresh': Sneakers, Race, and Mobility in *The Hate U Give*." *CEA Critic*, vol. 81, no. 1, 2019, p. 70–74. *Project MUSE*, https://doi.org/10.1353/cea.2019.0011.

Smith, Clint. "Racism, Stress, and Black Death." *The New Yorker*, 16 July 2016, https://www.newyorker.com/news/news-desk/racism-stress-and-black-death.

Smith, David E. "Medicalizing the Opioid Epidemic in the U.S. in the Era of Health Care Reform." *Journal of Psychoactive Drugs*, vol. 49, no. 2, 2017, pp. 95–101, https://doi.org/10.1080/02791072.2017.1295334.

Thomas, Angie. *The Hate U Give*. Walker Books, 2017.

"Treatment: Outpatient Versus Inpatient Setting." *Encyclopedia of Drugs, Alcohol and Addictive Behavior*, edited by Pamela Korsmeyer and Henry R. Kranzler, 3rd ed., vol. 4, Macmillan Reference USA, 2009, pp. 228–31.

U.S. Department of Health and Human Services. "Behavioral Health Treatments and Services." *SAMHSA: Substance Abuse and Mental Health Services Administration*, 21 Apr. 2020. *Internet Archive*, https://web.archive.org/web/20200424052244/https://www.samhsa.gov/find-help/treatment.

White, Tracy. *How I Made It to Eighteen: A Mostly True Story*. Roaring Brook Press, 2010.

Woodson, Jacqueline. *Beneath a Meth Moon: An Elegy*. Nancy Paulsen Books, 2012.

Zoorob, Michael J., and Jason L. Salemi. "Bowling Alone, Dying Together: The Role of Social Capital in Mitigating the Drug Overdose Epidemic in the United States." *Drug and Alcohol Dependence*, vol. 173, 2017, pp. 1–9.

APPENDIX: LIST OF NOVELS SURVEYED

Alexie, Sherman. *The Absolutely True Diary of a Part-Time Indian*. Illustrated by Ellen Forney, Thorndike Press, 2007.

Anderson, Laurie H. *The Impossible Knife of Memory*. Viking, 2014.

Burgess, Melvin. *Smack*. Holt, 1998.

Childress, Alice. *A Hero Ain't Nothin' but a Sandwich*. 1973. Puffin Books, 2000.

Dessen, Sarah. *Saint Anything: A Novel*. Viking, 2015.

Duyvis, Corinne. *On the Edge of Gone*. Amulet Books, 2016.

Grosso, Alissa. *Ferocity Summer*. Flux, 2012.

Hinton, S. E. *That Was Then, This Is Now*. Viking Press, 1971.

Holm, Jennifer L. *Sunny Side Up*. Illustrated by Matthew Holm, Scholastic, Inc, 2015.

Hopkins, Ellen. *Crank*. Margaret K. McElderry Books, 2013.

Hyde, Catherine R. *The Year of My Miraculous Reappearance*. A. A. Knopf, 2007.
Johnson, Alaya D. *Love is the Drug*. Arthur A. Levine Books, 2014.
Krosoczka, Jarrett. *Hey, Kiddo*. Graphix, 2018; 2018.
Lipsyte, Robert. *The Contender*. Harper & Row, 1967.
Mason, Lizzy. *The Art of Losing*. Soho Teen, 2019.
Mason, Lizzy. *Between the Bliss and Me*. Soho Teen, 2021.
Messner, Kate. *The Seventh Wish*. Bloomsbury, 2016.
Myers, Walter D. *The Beast*. Scholastic, 2003.
Myers, Walter D. *Dope Sick*. HarperTeen / Amistad, 2009.
Nelson, Blake. *Recovery Road*. Scholastic Press, 2011.
Patron, Susan. *The Higher Power of Lucky*. Illustrated by Matt Phelan, Atheneum Books for Young Readers, 2006.
Quintero, Isabel. *Gabi, a Girl in Pieces*. Cinco Puntos Press, 2014.
Reed, Amy L. *Clean*. Simon Pulse, 2011.
Rivera, Lilliam. *The Education of Margot Sanchez*. Simon and Schuster BFYR, 2017.
Sáenz, Benjamin A. *Last Night I Sang to the Monster: A Novel*. Cinco Puntos Press, 2009.
Schmatz, Pat. *Bluefish*. Candlewick Press, 2011.
Sharpe, Tess. *Far from You*. Little, Brown Books for Young Readers, 2014.
Tate, Meredith. *The Last Confession of Autumn Casterly*. G. P. Putnam's Sons, 2020.
Tharp, Tim. *The Spectacular Now*. Alfred A. Knopf, 2008.
Thomas, Angie. *The Hate U Give*. Balzer + Bray, 2017.
White, Tracy. *How I Made It to Eighteen: A Mostly True Story*. Roaring Brook Press, 2010.
Williams, Ismée. *This Train Is Being Held*. Amulet Books, 2020.
Woodson, Jacqueline. *Beneath a Meth Moon: An Elegy*. Nancy Paulsen Books, 2012.
Zentner, Jeff. *In the Wild Light*. Crown, 2021.

CONJOINMENT AS/AND INEQUALITY IN SARAH CROSSAN'S *ONE*

JOSEPH HOLLOWAY

Conjoinment is a form of impairment that is strikingly prevalent in fiction compared to the number of real-world incidents. Fewer than one in 200,000 live births are conjoined (Quigley 71), yet a wide range of authors—most famously, Alexander Pope, Mark Twain, and Irvine Welsh[1]—have written texts featuring conjoined protagonists or using conjoinment as a prominent theme, to say nothing of the ubiquitous genre fiction, horror films, and video games that have conjoined "monsters." This preponderance is partially explained by the many fundamental concepts that interact both with discourses of health and central concerns of literature—such as sovereignty, free will, privacy, and individuality—that are complicated by conjoinment. This is true both from a disability studies perspective and for nondisabled readers, as conjoinment is used to highlight the intercorporeal aspects of nondisabled existence. Similarly, while many readers may not have encountered conjoined twins before, the inequalities in healthcare that they represent in fiction resonate much more broadly.

That young adult literature is well-equipped to engage with these themes is especially evident in Sarah Crossan's evocative and engaging novel *One* (2016). Through its use of teenage conjoined protagonists, Grace and Tippi, *One* carefully highlights and resists harmful tropes related both to conjoinment specifically and disability generally, while also providing positive counternarratives. Like many other young adult novels that explore questions of identity—such as Jacqueline Woodson's *Brown Girl Dreaming* (2014) and Dean Atta's *The Black Flamingo* (2019)—*One* is a verse novel. Mike Cadden argues that free verse functions in young adult texts by facilitating a more "natural expression" of the protagonist narrator(s), that "distances the reader from the frame of mind that formal poetry inspires" (22). This is certainly the case with *One*. The verse form elevates the voice of the teenage protagonist, as the placement of individual line breaks develops the wider themes of the text.

This essay provides a crucial intervention for both disability studies and children's literature studies by contextualizing *One*'s representation of conjoinment within broader fictional tropes related to the portrayal of disability and healthcare, as well as showing how children's literature can develop young readers' understandings of disability, philosophical concepts of sovereignty, and healthcare inequalities. These inequalities are primarily expressed in *One* through the traumatic depiction of a family that has to choose whether to actively kill one conjoined twin in an attempt to save the life of the other, or to do nothing and risk both dying. So-called "sacrifice surgery" is not uncommon in actual cases of conjoinment. The events and the language used by Crossan deliberately recall the 2000 case of the British Attard conjoined twins. Through the responses of her nonconjoined characters—hereafter referred to by the established term "singletons" (Dreger 7)—Crossan evokes this significant episode in medico-legal history, highlighting the ableism that conjoined twins face as they are systematically assumed to have less entitlement to their internal organs than singletons do and, ultimately, less right to be alive.

Crossan draws on this case to challenge the harmful trope of representing conjoined twins as an unequal relationship of "host/parasite." Similarly to Melanie Goss's problematization in this volume of the "mental illness [. . .] as an invader or intruder" metaphor because of the "deeply dehumanizing" implication that people with mental illness no longer have an authentic sense of self (253, 254), Crossan criticizes this phrase because of its connection to widespread ableist tropes such as disability as a burden on society or the embittered "disabled avenger" figure (Okuyama 31; Mitchell and Snyder, "Body Genres" 186). In her rebuttal, Crossan unpicks what is found to be "problematic" about conjoinment, as she evokes singleton concerns relating to conjoinment and the nature of the individual. Through the depiction of shared digestive processes between the twins, *One* reflects the question of individuality back upon singletons, revealing them to be just as interdependent, just as intersubjective, and just as "parasitical" as conjoined twins are feared to be. Accordingly, Crossan problematizes singleton normalization strategies that attempt to "resolve" this disruption to the concept of "individuality." Crossan's depictions of separation surgery and the precursory practices through which singletons conceptually trace the border "between" conjoined twins and reimagine this as a fixed and solid boundary between them—a process I term "mapping"—make clear that these normalization strategies *create* the perceived inequalities in conjoinment. Richly evoking Eli Clare's nuanced consideration of the notion of "cure" in disability and trans studies, it is instead medical procedures that are revealed to be disabling experiences.

INEQUALITIES OF CONJOINMENT: "HOST" AND "PARASITE"

Crossan's depiction of conjoinment is informed by and responds to the overuse of the medical term "parasitic twin," where conjoinment is primarily perceived as a biologically determined inequality. Strictly speaking, this is only accurate if used in reference to a conjoined twin that stopped development during gestation, but it is widely overapplied to conjoined twins in both medical and popular journalism. Generally, this practice relies on and reinforces existing harmful understandings of disability generally as "beggarly fraudsters" or a "drain" on social resources. For example, in Mark Twain's farcical representation of the conjoined Tocci twins *Those Extraordinary Twins* (1892), the singleton characters express envy at the twins' seeming ability to game the system as they "always travel as one person, since we occupy but one seat, so we save half the fare" and "both of us get a bath for one ticket, theater seat for one ticket, pew-rent is on the same basis" (139, 140). In a more recent representation of conjoinment, Chris Abani's thriller *The Secret History of Las Vegas* (2014), the "parasitical" portrayal of conjoinment is more literal: the text concludes with the medical resolution of a modified MRI machine that conclusively reveals one of the twins to have been in a vegetative state since birth; the other has operated him like a ventriloquist's dummy. In *One*, however, this tendency to portray conjoined twins as parasitical (literally or metaphorically) is highlighted and resisted. Crossan deliberately shows her characters engaging with this concept before problematizing it and suggesting counternarratives for how we might instead read conjoinment. Conjoinment is thus valued as a form of Clare's "brilliant imperfection . . . rooted in the nonnegotiable value of body-mind difference" (xvii); in other words, disability is just as valid a mode of existence as being nondisabled, and not a problem requiring a medical resolution. Crossan's conjoined characters resist the various normalization pressures they face and instead evoke what Halberstam calls "the queer art of failure" (87), whereby failure "imagines other goals for life, for love, for art, and for being" (88), as conjoinment is constructively used to illustrate our interdependence as a species and connectivity to each other.

The "parasite/host" binary is primarily challenged in *One* as the plot requires the family to make the agonizing choice outlined in the introduction. As one of the twins develops cardiomyopathy, they face the decision of whether to surgically separate or not. Their doctor tells the family gathered around protagonist Grace that:

"Left as it is,
they'll both die."

Mom starts to cry.
Dad holds her hand.

"With a separation, they have hope,
a fighting chance,
but I can't put a number on it.
If I did, it would be low.
It would be quite low." (259)

The grouping together of the "Mom" and "Dad" responses here hints at the interdependence common to all humans as the singleton characters empathize with and emotionally support each other. The family—but ultimately Grace and Tippi—have to decide whether to undergo the psychological and physical trauma of separation surgery for a "fighting chance" of survival to accept the twins' impending heart failure while conjoined. The twins elect to be surgically separated, as our narrator attempts to sacrifice herself so that the stronger Tippi will survive. However, against expectations, Grace survives and Tippi dies, and the book ends as Grace is left struggling both to contain her grief and adapt to her new singleton existence.

There are striking resemblances between the decision that Grace and Tippi face and an important and controversial UK court case (2000). In *Re A (Conjoined Twins)* the parents of the conjoined Gracie and Rosie Attard (referred to in court by their respective pseudonyms of "Jodie" and "Mary") were told that if left conjoined, there was a high percentage that both would die within six months, whereas if they underwent separation surgery, one twin would certainly die, and the other would have a higher likelihood of survival. In contrast to Crossan's scenario, however, the Attard parents decided not to try to separate the twins, but the attending medical team sued them for the right to operate anyway in an attempt to save Gracie.[2] Controversially, the Court of Appeals granted the medical team permission to perform the operation and—as predicted—Gracie survived while Rosie died.

The most striking resemblance between the two cases is in the determining factor of presenting the twins within a parasite/host framework. Crossan's author's note makes it clear that the parallels are not coincidental—the similarity in names between "Gracie and Rosie" and "Grace and Tippi" highlights this—as she disrupts this widespread representation of conjoinment as an inequality. In the transcript of the court proceedings, the term "parasite" was used several times to describe Rosie, despite the fact that Lord Justice Walker conceded that "Jodie and Mary [Gracie and Rosie] must be regarded as two separate persons" because "they have two brains and two nearly complete bodies" (England and Wales Court of Appeal). The hearing included the expert testimony of Mr. Adrian Whitefield QC that "it has not been and could not be suggested that this case comes anywhere near that category [of parasitic conjoinment]" (England and Wales Court of Appeal), but despite this, the judges portrayed Rosie/Mary as a parasitic growth, summarizing their judgment in this way:

> Mary may have a right to life, but she has little right to be alive. She is alive because and only because, to put it bluntly, but nonetheless accurately, she sucks the lifeblood of Jodie and she sucks the lifeblood out of Jodie.... Mary's parasitic living will be the cause of Jodie's ceasing to live. If Jodie could speak, she would surely protest, "Stop it, Mary, you're killing me." Mary would have no answer to that. Into my scales of fairness and justice between the children goes the fact that nobody but the doctors can help Jodie. Mary is beyond help. (England and Wales Court of Appeal)

The insistence that Rosie/Mary is parasitic is used to justify her separation from Gracie/Jodie. More than just a drain of her resources, Rosie is shown to be feeding off Gracie: "suck[ing] the lifeblood." Severing their common aorta was presented as a passive act, a withdrawal of food supply, and not an active form of euthanasia. Separation surgery was explicitly compared to "switching off a ventilator" by the judges, as this "is also regarded as a withdrawal of treatment (that is, as an omission rather than a positive act) even though it results (and is expected to result) in immediate death" (England and Wales Court of Appeal).

As noted in Alice Dreger's review of this case, the use of "parasite" conceptually transforms Rosie into a harmful growth that needs to be cut away for Gracie's health. Separation surgery becomes sacrifice surgery, as "a mentally functioning person [is used] as a vital-organ donor" (Dreger 95). Conjoinment is reimagined by the judges as fundamentally unequal, ignoring that Rosie had been "using" these organs just as long as Gracie and that she had just as intimate a visceral connection to them—and hence just as much entitlement to them—as Gracie did, or indeed as any singleton does to their own. With little legal precedent available for the three judges to draw on, they relied instead on "an intuitive judgement that the state of being a conjoined twin is a disease and that separation is the indicated treatment" (Dreger 104). The judges approached the case with the ableist "singleton assumption—that a life conjoined is an unjust, unworthy life" (Dreger 104), understanding conjoinment as an inherently parasitical and unequal relationship. The discrete individual bodymind is presented as the only viable model for existence, and this judgment failed to recognize that a deviation from this can nonetheless be a rich and fulfilling life. The judges were enabled to ignore the medical testimony that contradicted this and to authorize the separation surgery against the wishes of the parents.

This repeated inaccurate depiction of a conjoined twin as parasitical draws on the more widespread established perception that disabled people are the parasitical Other of what Robert McRuer calls the "able-bodied worker" (161). In *Spaces of Hope*, David Harvey shows that under capitalism, "sickness (or any kind of pathology) gets defined within this circulation process as inability to go to work" (106). To not "work" (be unemployed) is conceptually blurred with having a body that does not "work" (is disabled). People are valued by the relationship that they are perceived to hold with the wider economy, and as disabled people face increased barriers to employment, they are valued less and seen as unjustly "free-riding" on nondisabled society. This is a hangover of Victorian industrialization, as "those unable to meet industrial workplace standards because of a disability or deformity were increasingly exiled from the capitalist 'norm,' which demanded 'useful' bodies, able to perform predictable and repeated movements" (LaCom 547). The irony of this is clear, as many disabilities in the Victorian era were themselves caused by industrial accidents or the general work conditions as, for example, during the second half of the nineteenth century "a miner was killed every six hours, seriously injured every two hours, and injured badly enough to need a week off work every two or three minutes" (Benson 40). Within capitalist culture disabled people are valued by the extent that they perform a service; those unable to conform to these ableist ideals were instead "forced into less socially desirable positions" and understood as a cost to the social body (Turner and Blackie 5).

The understanding of conjoinment as parasitic evokes this more widespread ableist image of disabled people as beggarly, dependent on handouts and creating more costs to society than nondisabled people. As the UK's National Health Service is publicly funded from tax revenue, in British books and other media, disabled people have consistently been represented as a drain on resources and hence as unproductive and less valuable citizens. As one example of the prevalence of this belief, the hashtag #BenefitsNotBurdens was started on Twitter (now X) by Dr. Amy Kavanagh (@BlondeHistorian) as people with impairments demonstrated their positive interpersonal and societal value. That so many disabled people considered that this needed to be said, and that it received such attention, reveals the extent to which the "beggarly" trope is ingrained into depictions of disabled people and the formative role that this has in perceptions of disability, including internalized ableism.

Relatedly, in *One*, Grace labels herself a "burden" to Tippi when she discovers her cardiomyopathy:

If I were a singleton
I might have dropped dead by now.

Instead
my sister bears the burden of keeping me alive,
of pumping most of the blood around our bodies.

Instead
I freeload.

And she
doesn't complain. (334)

Crossan's character demonstrates how conjoinment as "parasite" continues the understanding of disability as "burden," as the supposed harmful draining of vital (economic) resources from the social body is mirrored in representation of one conjoined twin "suck[ing] the lifeblood" out of the other. Grace has internalized singleton ableism, saying of herself, "I freeload," metaphorically evoking perceptions of disability support. Similarly, the presentation of conjoined twins as inherently unequal—one feeding off the other—reinforces understandings of disabled people as threat, both as the "disabled avenger of horror" and the "threat toward the integrity of the able body" tropes (Mitchell and Snyder, "Body Genres" 186). In countless children's, young adult, and adult media—from J. M. Barrie's Captain Hook to Captain Ahab of *Moby Dick*, from Shere Khan in *The Jungle Book* to Mason Verger in *Hannibal*—the disabled figure is frequently presented as embittered by their impairment, doggedly pursuing those they deem responsible, aiming to similarly disable them. In presenting conjoinment as an unequal and antagonistic relationship where one is "feeding" off the other, the twins are simultaneously understood as pursuer and pursued, one disabled by the other, never able to escape the looming presence of their disabled adversary.

Understandings of conjoinment as inherently unequal and oppositional automatically build toward a medical "resolution" of surgery. In contrast to the social model of disability—where disability is understood as resulting from a combination of impairment and social barriers and prejudice, the medical model of disability understands impairments as inherently pathological, as problems to be fixed. The medical model takes nonnormative bodies and ensures that they are "transformed, and improved" into typical "docile bodies" (Foucault 136). The presentation of one conjoined twin as a harmful, parasitic growth upon the other—used to justify separation surgery—is a clear example of the ways that medical and nonmedical discourse can harmfully reinforce each other. Conjoinment and other disabilities "are structuring culture(s) and at the same time are structured and lived through culture" (Waldschmidt 20), and here we see both mutually inform each other in a closed loop. The cultural overapplication of the medical term "parasitic" in relation to nonparasitic conjoined twins is reabsorbed by the medical sphere, as the additional assumptions surrounding disability as "parasite" are unfairly invoked as justification for separation surgery.

Crossan's exploration of the loaded term "parasite" shows awareness of the sensitive Attard case, of the nuances around representations of disabled people, and of conjoined twins especially. In the author's note she says that her text was "based on amalgamated stories of real-life conjoined twins, both living and dead," particularly citing Dreger's analysis of this case referenced earlier as having "profoundly informed my views on separation surgery" (460). After the twins are told about Grace's cardiomyopathy, the next chapter is even titled "Parasite" and we see the effect that this term has on the twins:

> "You think we're partners, but really
>   I'm a parasite," I whisper.
> "I don't want to suck
>   Your life from you." (265)

Grace's internalized ableism means that their shared venous system has been represented as her "feeding" on Tippi. This language is infused with monstrous vampiric undertones, as the phrase "suck the life from you" deliberately echoes the phrasing of the judges in the Attard case. In her response, however, Tippi states that "all this *you* and *me* is a lie. / There has only ever been *us*." This brief discussion evidences Clare's point that "the ideology of cure" is "a kind of restoration" (14). Such an attitude contains an implicit assumption "that what existed before is superior to what exists currently" and thus "seek[s] to return what is damaged to that former state of being" (14). As Goss's problematization of conventional metaphors for mental illness establishes, however, by their very chronicity, such conditions are not helpfully understood as "a single hurdle to overcome" (260), as the lived experience across time does not neatly fit with expectations "that the hurdle will be cleared and left behind" (247). With Grace and Tippi, such a "hurdle" cannot be cleared and this "return" is impossible, because it "doesn't originate from my visceral history. Rather it arises from an imagination of what I should be like, from some definition of normal and natural" (Clare 14). Whether we view Grace as a "parasite" or not is related to our understanding of the twins' body ownership. If their body is shared, then both are experiencing the cardiomyopathy: both are equally at risk, and Grace is not a parasite. This is how Tippi understands their relationship, richly evoking Audre Lorde's "interdependency of different strengths, acknowledged and equal" (103). If, however, as singletons understand them, they are two separate but intricately linked bodies, then only Grace experiences and is responsible for the cardiomyopathy, and she could be considered a parasite upon Tippi.

WHAT IS "PROBLEMATIC" ABOUT CONJOINMENT?

This "parasite" trope gains traction because it evokes fundamental concerns related to conjoinment and the myth of the discrete and sovereign individual. This myth—whereby we are the self-reliant originators of our desires and not dependent on any others—is integral to Anglo-American culture. It underpins our legal systems, for example, and "economics remains the study of the individual" (Marçal 153). We have seen how the perceived usefulness to the economy informs nondisabled understandings of worth, and it is important to note how this lens is inherently singleton. This fundamental idea of such an "individual," however, with a discrete "diamond mind" that is unaffected by the actions of others (Selisker 51), has been systematically refuted in studies about how people are influenced, as our integrity is continuously compromised by other people, advertisements, and propaganda.

This ideal of "the individual" is thus conceptually connected to agency and the extent to which we are able to resist the influence of others. As disability studies scholars have made clear, however, "freedom in society is constituted by both independence and interdependence" (Bostad and Hanisch 373). Everyone is enmeshed in the processes of globalization, and we are all interdependent on and connected to each other. Further, we have all experienced a form of intrasubjectivity in the womb: "we don't start our lives in a state of independence . . . but when we are supposed to argue for the importance of a society we almost always start here: with an autonomous individual" (Marçal 155). Despite this, or perhaps even as a result of this, "white Western culture goes to extraordinary lengths to deny . . . the utter reliance of human upon human" (Clare 136). The agency that is associated with being an "individual" is sharply contrasted with the idea of disability as "an overwhelming dependency, a terrifying loss of privacy and dignity" (Clare 136). Conjoinment—as well as other "problematic" intrasubjective bodies, such as the pregnant person—is often depicted as threatening due to the disruption it presents to the patriarchal, nondisabled, and singleton fantasy of "the individual" and thus in need of some form of containment.

In *One* these "problematic" elements are made explicit as particular focus is drawn to the mutual vascular and digestive processes of Tippi and Grace. This is then reflected back onto the (presumed singleton) reader, showing that these concerns are baseless as we have all been—and continue to be—intercorporeal. The realities of shared digestion are alluded to as Grace reports that

> I want vanilla yoghurt.
> Tippi chooses coconut cream
> with chocolate chips.
>
> Tippi and I share a lot
> —we always share dinner—. (105–6)

The wordplay within "we always share dinner" reminds the reader of the twins' mingled digestive processes, producing an effect of disgust in many readers because they are socialized into ableist worldviews that lead them to other disabled bodies. All food involves a negotiation of the boundary between "inner/self" and "outer/other" as when we eat, we incorporate external matter into our core, as "the processes of ingestion, digestion, and excretion force us to acknowledge that our bodies are not finite cohesive structures but permeable corporeal organisms constantly in flux with the outside" (Daniel 6). We all breathe air that has been in someone else's lungs, and we all ingest matter that has passed through other bodies in a different form previously. If we reflect upon our porous bodily boundaries, we reveal ourselves to be the disgusting one, as in Kristeva's words, "I expel myself, I spit myself out, I abject myself" (3). Reactions of disgust—nausea—threaten to make us even more permeable, as the instinctive urge to vomit is in itself a further transgression of these fundamental boundaries. The "horror" of the intercorporeality of conjoinment, then, is a return of repressed knowledge about how we have all been parasites, we have all ingested (bits of) others. In a form of what Melanie Klein calls "projective identification," the "bad" intercorporeality (permeability, dependence) is split from the self-image of the singleton and projected onto the figure of conjoined twins.

This form of presentation shows that the feared porosity of conjoinment is experienced by all eating subjects, as the type of food that is described—soft creamy desserts with little tangible texture—point toward foundational and archetypal memories of food. When explaining how "food loathing is perhaps the most elementary and most archaic form of abjection," Kristeva specifically points to "that skim on the surface of milk—harmless, thin as a sheet of cigarette paper, pitiful as a nail pairing" (2). Milk-based and milk-resembling foods such as the "vanilla yoghurt" and "coconut cream" are an excellent vehicle for evoking this abjection. Milk is both the first substance most babies ingest and a product created inside another animal (often another human) then expressed before being ingested by the baby. It is thus already a potential vehicle for evoking abjection; any additional corruption of it (such as "the skim on the surface")—especially the suggestion of mingled digestive processes—simultaneously perverts fundamental assumptions about the purity of food while also evoking latent anxieties about the transgression of boundaries involved in digestion.

That the foodstuffs alluded to by Crossan evoke the primal experience of being breastfed shows that the "parasitical" depiction of conjoinment examined previously is more widely applicable to singletons. In her analysis of representations of eating in children's literature, Daniel argues that "sweet, rich food often metaphorically represents the body of the mother in popular culture and that the desire for such food includes a subconscious yearning for the restoration of the primal relationship with her" (89). Here, the first and foundational relationship that humans typically form is presented as food, and we are introduced into this world as literal consumers of our mother's body. In *The Family in English Literature*, Ann Alston argues that "to feed someone is to exercise power, to penetrate metaphorically the body of another" (105). Conjoinment complicates Alston's power dynamic, however, as the passively "fed" member instead becomes an active "feeder" upon the "host" body. As Rosie was described as "sucking the lifeblood" out of Gracie, there was a presumed inversion of the hierarchy between mother and fetus, where the "parasite" gains the power to penetrate the other back. If, however, conjoined twins can be understood as "parasites" because of their intersubjective corporeality and exchange of nutrients, then so too is every singleton while inside the womb, as well as any that have been breastfed.

Food anxieties are explicitly mapped onto the twins' bodies in *One*, further reinforcing how conjoined twins serve as a target for projective identification from singleton people concerned about their own intercorporeality. As Ischiopagus Tripus twins—twins with four arms and two legs—the twins have a connected digestive system:

> Our intestines begin
>   apart
>   then merge.
>
> And below that we are
>   one. (28)

The crucial line breaks before "apart" and "one"—as well as the shape of the lines—reinforce this understanding of the twins as one person from below the waist, as the words on the page resemble a journey through the gut. Previously,

Grace has listed what they have two of, progressing down the body to rest at "two sets of lungs and kidneys" (28), establishing the stomach as the point by which "we are / one." Ordinarily, when we eat food we lose sight of it until we regain control of it through defecation. As what we ingest enters the black box of the body cavity, it is surrendered to processing by the body. These processes are, of course, crucial to our existence, but at the same time they are a reminder of our mechanical, physical, and fallible corporeality. Even in health, our bodies undergo a myriad of such processes without our conscious awareness. While this makes our attention more available for additional tasks, our inability to divert attention onto such processes—we can't will our digestion to stop, start, or change—is an unsettling reminder that we cannot control our autonomic functions. This activates repressed concerns over the physicality of our bodies and their inevitable decline: we cannot avoid death through pure strength of mind. This description of a shared digestive system reminds us of these automatic processes. Such a transgression of physical boundaries draws back the corporeal curtain and uncovers the hidden workings of this somatic black box, revealing the ordinarily hidden and thus more easily repressed knowledge. In this subtle evocation of intestines that "begin / apart / then merge," Crossan presents her fictional conjoined twins as abjectly embodying a blurring of inner and outer space, reminding the reader of their own (repressed) corporeality. In so doing, the twins' HIV-positive friend, Yasmeen, recognizes herself in them:

> I reek of death,
> of low life expectancy. Like
>   you guys,
> I guess. (95)

Here the higher rate of mortality of both the conjoined Grace and Tippi and the HIV-positive Yasmeen is conceptually blended with the nondisabled singleton re-encountering their own mortality. The position of the words on the page reinforce this, as the decreasing indent for "like," "you," and "I" indicate a downward sliding toward death. As signifiers of bodily functions evoke physicality and thus fallibility, so too disability reminds "those who consider themselves non-disabled [that they] are in fact no more than temporarily able-bodied" (Shildrick 13). This is such a monumental and foundational truth that to dwell on it is difficult and painful; hence, it is often passively repressed and actively avoided by the nondisabled. It is "what I permanently thrust aside in order to live" (Kristeva 3). As Nancy Mairs put it, "most nondisabled people I know are so driven by their own fears of damage and death that they dread contact, let alone interaction, with anyone touched by affliction of any kind" (100). In the eyes of the nondisabled, conjoined people are understood as in some way "death-touched" because their perceived bodily fallibility reminds the nondisabled reader of their own.

In many young adult books featuring mortality—notably, the subgenre of teenage "sick-lit"—there is often an investment in "maintaining an image of always-already sad teenagers in diametric opposition to 'happy' children and emotionally 'stable' adults" (Elman 178). These "tearjerkers" reductively present disability purely as a source of misery and "traffic in the most egregious and patronizing [examples] of cultural stereotypes about disability" (Elman 179), reinforcing perceptions of disability as helpless and pitiable, requiring a medical resolution. In some ways, Crossan's reader is led to think that the novel will play into these tropes: for example, the final separation surgery and unexpected death of Tippi is an emotionally charged conclusion. The recognition of ableist prejudice, however, ("reek[ing] of death") from Crossan's conjoined and HIV-positive characters resists the "emotional habitus" of more typical teenage sick-lit (Gould 27), highlighting the problematic aspects of these depictions. Tippi's death may well be tragic, but Crossan's text presents it as *resulting* from medical intervention, and the text otherwise celebrates her individuality, her agency, and her vibrancy.

The overapplication of the term "parasitical" conjoined twins, then, is medically inaccurate but culturally applicable, because it is useful for singletons as it helps repress concerns that they have about their own intercorporeality, lack of individuality, and mortality. As these concerns become activated by the image of conjoined twins, singletons project them outward onto these twins as the ultimate expression of these anxieties, distracting from and re-repressing them. Through food abjection and a detailed exploration of this "parasite" trope, however, Crossan undermines this practice by deconstructing and making visible these very processes.

PROBLEMATIZING "RESOLUTIONS"

The "parasite" trope that I have analyzed so far is part of a more general mechanism by which singletons unconsciously try to demarcate conjoined twins into two discrete individuals through a process I term "mapping." This mapping limits the extent to which the conjoined twins threaten the ideal of the individual, as the singleton characters visualize the site of conjoinment in increasingly precise levels of detail, like "Russian nesting dolls . . . hiding one inside the other" (Crossan 316). Through this, singletons attempt to conceptually separate the twins and disentangle the two mingled selves. They reimagine the boundary between conjoined twins as fixed and impenetrable, as opposed to the dynamic and permeable reality. In doing so, they provide a metaphorical version of the same "resolution" offered by separation surgery: it is an attempt to conceptually unpick the Gordian knot of conjoinment, rather than to surgically separate it.

This metaphorical process underpins the curiosity of singletons about the degree to which each twin can feel or control different parts of their body/ies, and questions about this frequently appear in interviews.[3] Similarly, experiments that provided a tantalizing view of their physical connection were staple elements of nineteenth-century conjoined performers' routines, such as feeding one twin asparagus and smelling the urine of the other[4] or placing a disk of zinc on the tongue of one and a silver one on the other and observing that both twins experience the sour taste that occurs when the two metals are combined.[5]

In Crossan's text, however, her characters refute such praxis, emphasizing their uniqueness and the inherent limits of this mapping. While conjoined twins may be medically categorized through distinct "types" of configuration—grouped by the site of connection as, for example, Ischiopagus conjoined twins have fused pelvises—Grace nonetheless emphasizes the individual and complex visceral connections that she has to Tippi:

> Although scientists have come up with ways to
> categorise conjoined twins
> each and every pair that ever existed
> is unique—
> the details of all our bodies remain a secret. (27)

While an experimental mapping of their body/ies may provide a low-resolution outline of the connection between them, the details of this connection is "unique" and hidden. Reinforcing this, the overall meaning of Grace's words runs across lines, and the manner by which each is connected to those around—as well as the length and meter—is fittingly unique, emphasizing Grace's point. This contrasts with later sections that tightly control the line length:

> Dad turns away,
> Dragon blushes
> and Mom doesn't speak,
> because
> they all know
> that finding love is
> something
> that will never
>   happen
>   for us. (34–35)

In this example, the collective (incorrect) assumption of their singleton family members—that the twins will never find love—is presented through consistency of form, emphasized by the unnatural spacing used to align "never," "happen" and "for us."

In celebrating their unique and hidden connection, however, Crossan resists the attempts by singletons to salve the anxieties related above. Other depictions of conjoined twins conceptually draw a hard partition between them, preventing the idea of mingled selves and shared identities through professing to locate each twin (solely) in one specific part of their body/ies.[6] Asking the twins whether they always get sick at the same time or showing that what one tastes is affected by what is in the other's mouth serve a similar purpose to surgical separation: they reimagine the visceral interactions between the twins and represent conjoinment as a merely surface level attachment, like two balls of Velcro stuck together, denying a more mixed connection and limiting the challenges to singleton understandings of the "individual."

In these other narratives, shared internal processes that contradict this reinterpretation of conjoinment are presented as inherently harmful for the twins. When other singleton characters/authors map out the connection between conjoined twins, disruptions to the conceptually fixed and impervious internal boundary "between" them is presented as a pollution or a weakness in their defenses. Crossan appears to engage in this process initially but uses it to instead emphasize how intricately connected the twins are. When they discuss ingesting substances that have a physical effect on them—such as coffee and cigarettes—Grace relates that

> I am a peppermint tea sort of person.
> Tippi drinks coffee the colour of coal.
> She guzzles down around five mugs a day
>   —not that I get a say—
> as the caffeine careens around her body
> and has her buzzing like a blender
>   —and me, too
> these days. (96)

Here the somatic response that the twins experience from drinking coffee moves from one to the other. The structure of the lines highlight how each twin's experience is nested within the other, as Grace interjects her own narration of Tippi's actions ("—not that I get a say—") rather than splitting this into separate sentences. Coffee is thus used by Crossan as an authorial means of mapping the connection between the twins—functioning similarly to the asparagus or zinc and silver experiments, like tracing intersecting drains through the use of colored dye—but she uses it to emphasize their intersubjectivity, rather than as a means of teasing apart and outlining two separate individuals.

Similarly, Crossan seems to show this point at which the twins mingle as a site of vulnerability for them, as it allows harmful substances to be shared from one to the other. This reinforces how intimately and viscerally connected the twins are to each other and reflects this back upon singleton "individuality." When Tippi decides to smoke, for example, Grace relates that

> Yasmeen blows a mouthful of smoke into the sky
> then passes me her cigarette.
>
> I shake my head but before I can object,
> Tippi has the smouldering cancer-stick
> between two fingers and is
> inhaling great gulps
> of tobacco and tar.
>
> She stops
> and coughs
> so hard I think she might throw up.
>
> Yasmeen laughs.
> Jon scratches his head.
>
> And I gently pat my sister
> on the back
> when what I really want to do is
> let her choke. (78)

Other authors might here have implied that the twins are uniquely vulnerable to each other by virtue of their conjoinment, but Crossan's depiction of the unique connection between the twins illustrates and illuminates the ways that the actions of nondisabled singletons affect each other. Tippi ignores Grace's indication that she doesn't want to ingest the cigarette smoke and consents for them both. The additional line breaks before "inhaling" and after "stops" and "coughs" emphasize Grace's experience, as readers are forced to pause where we normally wouldn't, as if to take an extra breath. Grace is clearly concerned by the health implications of smoking, and in the recognition that "what I really want to do is / let her choke," Grace acknowledges that she would like to let Tippi make her own decisions but cannot, as her sister's decisions are directly connected to her own physical health. Beyond pregnancy, few readers will have been in such a position literally—where their own consumption directly affects the health of another—but many of us will nonetheless be able to understand this indirectly, as the COVID-19 pandemic forced us to adapt our social behavior to avoid having a negative impact on the health of others. As close as the group is, Grace is surely inhaling secondhand smoke from Tippi and the other friends just as effectively as through her direct connection with Tippi. Later, the twins argue about Tippi's smoking:

> "I think we should have discussed it," I say,
> not needing to remind her
> that
>   this shoddy body
>   never split like it should
>   and that if she dies,
>   so do I.
>
> "Sorry," she says.
>   "So can I smoke?"
>
> I turn my head,
>   curl away from her
> as best I can.
>
> It isn't really a question. (87–88)

The line breaks and additional indentation makes it clear that the "shoddy body" section is the implied and unvoiced subtext, as the varied line length shapes the segment like the smoke through their respiratory systems, paralleling Grace's attempts to "curl" away from Tippi. Tippi is upset because, for her at this moment, conjoinment is a limit to her immediate personal agency: she is being made to feel guilty because her actions directly affect another due to their physical connection. On the other hand, Grace is upset with Tippi because, for her at this moment, conjoinment is a source of vulnerability. She moves away from Tippi "as best I can," trying to put as much distance between them as possible, implicitly reiterating the impossibility of escaping each other. Grace reiterates what she does not need to remind Tippi, that "if she dies / so do I," foreshadowing the conclusion to the text. In this portrayal of mapping the connection between the twins, Crossan activates the concerns that may justify such a process, explicitly showing that conjoinment facilitates the pollution of carcinogens between them. However, what is also clear is that this is not meaningfully distinct from the connections between singletons, as we are all affected by each other's choices, be it the passive inhalation of cigarette smoke or lack of social distancing. Paradoxically, what otherwise may be understood to be a form of mapping the connection between the twins instead emphasizes their connection and the impossibility of installing a neat, conceptual boundary between them. In doing so, Crossan successfully avoids what Goss in this volume warns against—"lean[ing] too far into the metaphor" (250)—by highlighting conventional metaphors (conjoinment as limitation/vulnerability) before problematizing this.

Crossan also challenges the claim that separation surgery is an unproblematic resolution to singleton anxieties surrounding individuality and disability through the resulting unequal outcomes for the twins. Even when it is explained to Grace and Tippi that this is the only way to potentially save their lives, they are fiercely resistant:

> "No. Absolutely not.
> We'll take our chances as we are," Tippi says.
> "You can knock us both out
> and put a new heart in.
> Or do whatever it is you have to do.
> You don't have to separate us first" (256)

The involvement of the twins here with the decision-making process is far from typical, as in real life cases the decision is usually made on behalf of the twins, and so it is worthwhile digging a little deeper. To date, there is only one pair of conjoined twins that have been consensually separated. The craniopagus (joined at the head) Bijani twins (1973–2003) consensually pursued separation surgery, but both died during the procedure. In every other case of conjoinment, either the guardians have consented on behalf of the twins to be separated (due to their being below the age of consent), or they have elected to remain conjoined. The psychological trauma and the physical risk of death or serious disability associated with separation surgery increases as the twins age, and so separation surgery—if it is to be performed at all—is generally done as soon as possible. Apart from the Bijani twins, however, when nonfictional adult twins have been able to decide for themselves between a chance of singleton survival or certain conjoined death, they have always chosen to remain conjoined.

All of their lives, Grace and Tippi have been conjoined, and to suddenly become separate is an abhorrent prospect for them. In documenting the nuances of this, Crossan resists the "ideology of cure" (Clare 7), as the societal norms are not "normal" for the conjoined characters. Under this ideology, impairment is in opposition to overarching norms and hence the supposed cure (separation surgery) is uncomplicatedly presented as worth any risk. Through the twins' reactions, Crossan challenges an unquestioning adherence to the entrenched norm of "one body, one person" (Cousser 52), instead celebrating Clare's concept of "brilliant imperfection" (xvii). While curative practices can hold great value for disabled people, the overapplication of it is revealed to be a form of erasure, as a removal of nonnormative bodies. Through the celebration of Grace and Tippi's resistance to (potentially lifesaving) surgery, Crossan instead reflects the experiences of many conjoined twins and offers a positive means of breaking down our adherence to capitalist individuality. Conjoinment and interdependence become something to be celebrated, not feared, as difference is "not merely tolerated, but seen as a fund of necessary polarities" creating an "interdependency of different strengths, acknowledged and equal" (Lorde 103).

Crucially, we don't witness how Grace persuades Tippi to have the surgery, as Tippi goes from vehemently stating, "I won't do it. / You can't *make* me / have an operation" to the two twins meeting "Dr Derrick to give him our decision [to separate]" in just a few pages (Crossan 261, 276), with no disagreements or discussion presented between the twins. Even the page before the twins meet Dr. Derrick, in the section titled *No Run-throughs* Grace evidences uncertainty. The momentous decision is contrasted with writing multiple drafts in English class, checking their workings in maths, or repeatedly rehearsing the same bit of music. Unlike these situations, Grace tells us that:

> Yet when it matters,
> when it's a life-and-death decision,
> like whether to slice ourselves
>   apart or not,
> we've no way to perfect the path we're taking
> and have only
> one choice. (281–82)

The excess space between "slice ourselves" and "apart or not" embodies the violence of the separation surgery while also testifying to the emotional weight of these words and the uncertainty that Grace still feels. She takes a moment to steel herself, visible to us as a prominent gap, the lines of text imitating the two separated twins. She is unable to fully voice their final choice, and we can only infer what the decision is from Dr. Derrick's response:

> "This is a big project and it won't happen
> overnight.
> But we can't wait too long, either."

> He looks at me directly.
> "Obviously, we can't wait too long." (282–83)

Dr. Derrick's unsubtle allusion to Grace's deteriorating condition—emphasized through the line break after "overnight" as a long, deliberate pause, as well as the previous sections detailing the twins creating "bucket lists" (273), suggests that Grace and Tippi's decision to separate is informed by this. However, Crossan suggests that Tippi's acquiescing to separate, despite her sentiment that "We're meant to be together. / If we separate, we'll die," is a prioritization of her family's needs over her own (265). In the interval between Tippi's marked resistance and the twin's announcement of their decision to Dr. Derrick, the twins come across the raw documentary footage that is being filmed with their family and view an interview with their parents:

> And we see
> Mom and Dad's crinkled faces
> As Caroline softly asks,
> "Do you think Tippi and Grace
> *should* be separated?"
>
> Dad stares into his lap.
>
> "I want to keep them alive," Mom says.
> "No parent should bury a child,
> and definitely not two of them.
> But it's up to them to decide.
> It's up to them."
>
> We watch
> Mom cry into the camera
> and beg Caroline to turn it off,
> and then we stare at each other
> thinking exactly the same thing.
>
> This isn't just about us. (280–81)

Here it is clear that despite Tippi's misgivings, she agrees to be separated out of consideration for her family's feelings, as the care and affection from their singleton family members persuade the twins to try separation surgery—and the potential sacrifice of Grace—in an attempt to save Tippi. The repetition of Mom that "it's up to them" reiterates the importance of Grace and Tippi's sovereignty in this decision; as the twins watch this footage and think "exactly the same thing," it seems that they agree with Mom's sentiment. However, as Grace outlines what they mean—that the decision to try and save Tippi as a singleton or not "isn't just about us"—it becomes clear that the twins are actually in agreement with each other and disagree with their Mom's insistence that it is entirely up to them.

Despite the well-intentioned desire of the family to have at least one of their twins survive, even under these circumstances Crossan continues to question separation surgery as a normalization strategy. After informing Dr. Derrick of their decision to separate, Grace relates,

> I have read reports.
>
> I have read old newspapers.
>
> When conjoined twins are separated,
> it's deemed a success so
> long as one of them lives.
>
> For a while.
>
> And that,
> to me,
> is the saddest thing
> I know about how
> people see us. (258–59)

Here the space around the momentous "for a while" evokes the "land of / so much / space" that is the post-separation surgery existence for surviving twins (342), as even a "successful" procedure is fraught with psychological trauma. Even if both survive the operation untraumatized, there is a very high probability of surgical follow-up procedures. Crossan's reference to this further discredits separation surgery as a satisfactory "resolution" to conjoinment as she explores related fundamental healthcare inequalities. It is only at the surface that the conjoined body can be demarcated into two individuals because of the unique challenges around body ownership outlined previously. Grace introduces this to us as she questions,

> *How* can they reconstruct our lower halves
> so that we end up with two whole bodies?
> We share most of our

> intestines
> but Dr Derrick says this is not a problem.
> We share our privates
> but Dr Derrick says he'll give those pieces
> to Tippi and
> fix me up
> so I'll be like any other girl when he's
> > finished.
>
> But this is a lie.
>
> In any case I don't question him
> and I never
> ask why he's decided to give the originals to
> > Tippi. (322–23)

As Grace makes clear, separation surgery is ultimately a process of unfair division of unequal parts. The mid-clause line breaks after "intestines" and "privates" reiterate how these shared body parts are being divided up between the twins. While stable conjoined twins have sufficient internal organs for continued existence, they rarely have enough organ redundancy for both to exist as independent singletons. If they are joined at the chest, for example, rather than both "having" a functioning heart that can be allocated to each after separation, what is more common is that the twins will share a larger heart, which can adequately pump blood around their whole body/ies but cannot simply be cut in half. Even in rare instances where conjoined twins have enough internal organs for each twin separately, one will often have a more intimate nervous connection to a majority of the organs, making it impossible to make a "fair" division.

As a result, separation surgery is often a disabling experience, and Crossan's depiction of this shows conjoinment to be just as viable and even preferable in some situations. Similarly, Dreger cites an interview with nurses that were part of the team that operated on the conjoined Htut twins. In this interview the nurses say that before the separation "as nurses we were not sure what to do with [these] 'healthy' children but that after the operation they were 'separate but badly deformed. *Now* they seemed handicapped'" (38). The operation, far from medically "fixing" the bodies of the conjoined twins, separated them into two individuals, meaning that both were lacking internal organs and limbs and were disabled by the process. In a striking demonstration of the social model of disability, the disabilities have been literally constructed through social pressures and procedures. Other authors have presented separation surgery as a wondrous gift to conjoined twins, bestowing the gift of "individuality" upon two pitiable conjoined figures as a form of Mitchell and Snyder's "narrative prosthesis"—a narratological desire "to resolve or to correct [. . .] a deviance" (*Narrative Prosthesis* 53). Instead, Crossan shows this to be a mistake, as singleton citizenship is ultimately shown to simply be "alone / in a land of / so much / space" (334).

Overall, then, Crossan's text thoughtfully critiques more widespread portrayals of conjoinment through a focus on healthcare inequalities. The conjoined body is initially shown to be understood by singletons as inherently unequal, but as Crossan draws on and deconstructs the "host/parasite" trope, she shows how this relies on and evokes the more systemic idea of the "disabled as beggarly." In addition, both of the singleton responses to conjoinment—the conceptual "mapping" of their connection and the clinical separation surgery—are shown to also be intrinsically unequal, a fundamentally unfair division of parts, as one functioning collective is divided into two asymmetric, struggling singletons. Through this, Crossan deconstructs nondisabled singleton assumptions surrounding conjoinment in light of underlying anxieties connected to the ideal of the "individual" and bodily fallibility.

This vitally important young adult book challenges the accepted assumptions of both medical professionals and singleton readers with regard to the experience of conjoinment. The sensitivity and complexity of Crossan's representation makes *One* an accessible and valuable text for young people while also revealing important aspects about conjoinment in a way that much material aimed at their older peers does not. By highlighting the perceived injustice of the conjoined body as seen by singletons, Crossan emphasizes the far greater injustice of the unequal division of separation surgery, as well as its inherently disabling element. Faced with this, we are encouraged to consider the motivations behind the singleton's desire to separate conjoined body/ies both physically and metaphorically, as well as to confront prejudices surrounding nonconforming, noncompliant bodies.

As this chapter has shown, while conjoinment is statistically rare in real life, the nuances of intersubjective experience can be profitably used to help singletons understand similarly porous states—such as our primal intrasubjective experience in the womb or in everyday intercorporeal and globalized existence—and to question the over-investiture in (the impossibility of) being a self-reliant individual. As the deconstruction of both the "parasite" trope and the "mapping" process involved in common portrayals of conjoined twins has made clear, conjoined twins are commonly presented as conceptually problematic because they activate repressed concerns about singleton sovereignty and impermeability. The impossibilities of a "fair" separation surgery represent the impossibilities of disentangling any nondisabled singleton from the globalized socioeconomic culture in which they are enmeshed, as—despite the Western infatuation with the myth of the individual—even for these, "dependence, not individual independence, is the rule" (Davis 239). If any of us were to be truly "on our own," we would soon perish.

NOTES

1. See Pope's *Memoirs of the Extraordinary Life, Works, and Discoveries of Martinus Scriblerus*; Twain's *Pudd'nhead Wilson and Those Extraordinary Twins*; and Welsh's *The Sex Lives of Siamese Twins*.

2. In English law parental consent can be overruled by the Court of Protection if the refusal of treatment "may lead to their death or a severe permanent injury" ("Children and Young People").

3. See, for example, an interview with conjoined twins Abby and Brittany Hansel in which the twins are asked, "What happens when you get cold?" and "What about if one of you feels unwell?" ("Abby and Britanny Hensel" 00:53–01:23).

4. Dr. Bolton relates performing this on Chang and Eng Bunker, concluding "that the sanguineous communication between the united twins is very limited" (qtd. in Wallace and Wallace 86).

5. Dr. Roget related performing this experiment on Chang and Eng Bunker (Wallace and Wallace 87).

6. See, for example, Judith Rosner's *Attachments* (1977); Lori Lansen's *The Girls* (2005); Shelley Jackson's *Half Life* (2006); and Irvine Welsh's *The Sex Lives of Siamese Twins* (2014).

WORKS CITED

Abani, Chris. *The Secret History of Las Vegas*. Penguin, 2014.
"Abby and Britanny Hensel: Conjoined Twins—Quick Q & A." *YouTube*, uploaded by OMG Stories, 8 Sep. 2017, https://www.youtube.com/watch?v=1RiFbEA3aOw.
Alston, Ann. *The Family in English Children's Literature*. Routledge, 2008.
Benson, John. *British Coalminers in the Nineteenth Century: A Social History*. Macmillan, 1980.
Bostad, Inga, and Halvor Hanisch. "Freedom and Disability Rights: Dependence, Independence, and Interdependence." *Metaphilosophy*, vol. 47, no. 3, 2016, pp. 371–84.
Cadden, Mike. "The Verse Novel and the Question of Genre." *ALAN Review*, vol. 39, no. 1, 2011, pp. 21–7.
"Children and Young People: Consent to Treatment" *NHS*, www.nhs.uk/conditions/consent-to-treatment/children.
Clare, Eli. *Brilliant Imperfection: Grappling With Cure*. Duke UP, 2017.
Court of Appeals, England and Wales. *Re A (Conjoined Twins)*. EWCA Civ 254, 22 Sep. 2000. *British and Irish Legal Information Institute*, https://www.bailii.org/ew/cases/EWCA/Civ/2000/254.html.

Cousser, G. Thomas. *Signifying Bodies: Disability in Contemporary Life Writing*. U of Michigan P, 2009.

Crossan, Sarah. *One*. Bloomsbury, 2015.

Daniel, Carolyn. *Voracious Children: Who Eats Whom in Children's Literature*. Routledge, 2006.

Davis, Lennard. "The End of Identity Politics and the Beginning of Dismodernism: On Disability as an Unstable Category." *The Disability Studies Reader*, 2nd ed., edited by Lennard J. Davis, Routledge, 2006, pp. 231–43.

Dreger, Alice Domurat. *One of Us: Conjoined Twins and Future of Normal*. Harvard UP, 2004.

Elman, Julie. "'Nothing Feels as Real': Teen Sick-Lit, Sadness, and the Condition of Adolescence." *Journal of Literary & Cultural Disability Studies*, vol. 6, no. 2, 2012, pp. 175–91, https://doi.org/10.3828/jlcds.2012.15.

Foucault, Michel. *Discipline and Punish: The Birth of the Prison*. Translated by Alan Sheridan, Vintage, 1977.

Goss, Melanie. "The Metaphor of Madness: Metaphor and Mental Illness in Contemporary YA Fiction." *Healthcare in Children's Literature*, edited by Naomi Lesley and Sarah Layzell, UP Mississippi, 2025, pp. 246–63.

Gould, Deborah. *Moving Politics: Emotion and ACT UP's Fight against AIDS*. U of Chicago P, 2009.

Halberstam, Jack. *The Queer Art of Failure*. Duke UP, 2011.

Harvey, David. *Spaces of Hope*. U of Edinburgh P, 2000.

Jackson, Shelley. *Half Life*. Harper Collins, 2006.

Klein, Melanie. "Notes on Some Schizoid Mechanisms." *The International Journal of Psychoanalysis*, vol. 27, no. 1, 1946, pp. 99–110.

Kristeva, Julia. *Powers of Horror: An Essay on Abjection*. Translated by Leon S. Roudiez, Columbia UP, 1982.

LaCom, Cindy. "'The Time Is Sick and Out of Joint': Physical Disability in Victorian England." *PMLA*, vol. 120, no. 2, 2005, pp. 547–52.

Lansens, Lori. *The Girls*. Thorndike Press, 2006.

Lorde, Audre. *Sister Outsider*, Penguin, 2019.

Mairs, Nancy. *Waist-High in the World: A Life among the Nondisabled*. Beacon Press, 1996.

Marçal, Katrine. *Who Cooked Adam Smith's Dinner? A Story About Women and Economics*. Translated by Saskia Vogel, Portobello Books, 2015.

McRuer, Robert. *Crip Theory: Cultural Signs of Queerness and Disability*. New York UP, 2006.

Mitchell, David, and Sharon Snyder. "Body Genres: An Anatomy of Disability in Film." *The Problem Body: Projecting Disability on Film*, edited by Sally Chivers and Nicole Markotić, Ohio State UP, 2010, pp. 179–205.

Mitchell, David, and Sharon Snyder. *Narrative Prosthesis: Disability and the Dependencies of Discourse*. U of Michigan P, 2000.

Okuyama, Oshiko. *Reframing Disability in Manga*. U of Hawai'i P, 2020.

Pope, Alexander. *Memoirs of the Extraordinary Life, Works, and Discoveries of Martinus Scriblerus*, edited by Charles Kirby-Miller, Yale UP, 1950.

Quigley, Christine. *Conjoined Twins: An Historical, Biological, and Ethical Issues Encyclopedia*. McFarland, 2006.

Rosner, Judith. *Attachments*. Simon and Schuster, 1977.

Selisker, Scott. *Human Programming: Brainwashing, Automaton, and American Unfreedom.* U of Minnesota P, 2016.

Shildrick, Margrit. "Living On; Not Getting Better." *Feminist Review*, vol. 111, no. 1, 2015, pp. 10–24.

"The Recent Operation on Xiphopagous Twins." *Journal of the American Medical Association*, vol. 38, no. 19, 1902, pp. 1244–5.

Turner, David, and Daniel Blackie. *Disability in the Industrial Revolution: Physical Impairment in British Coalmining, 1780–1880.* Manchester UP, 2018.

Twain, Mark. *Pudd'n'head Wilson and Those Extraordinary Twins*, edited by Sidney Berger, W. W. Norton, 2005.

Waldschmidt, Anne. "Disability Goes Cultural: The Cultural Model of Disability as an Analytical Tool." *Culture—Theory—Disability: Encounters Between Disability Studies and Cultural Studies*, edited by Anne Waldschmidt et al., Transcript Verlag, 2017, pp. 19–28.

Wallace, Amy, and Irving Wallace. *The Two: The Story of the Original Siamese Twins.* Cassell, 1978.

Welsh, Irvine. *The Sex Lives of Siamese Twins.* Doubleday, 2015.

MENTAL HEALTH AND MASCULINE SILENCE IN ADIB KHORRAM'S *DARIUS THE GREAT IS NOT OKAY*

JEREMY JOHNSTON

Contemporary young adult (YA) fiction is currently at the forefront of nuanced and empathetic depictions of mental health. Adolescents experiencing different forms of mental distress have been featured in hundreds of YA novels since 2000, and that trend continues to grow.[1] YA critics, of course, are astutely pointing out how reading these novels offers adolescents a genuine opportunity to learn about the language of mental health and embrace a deeper understanding of the kinds of mental distress that many adolescents continue to navigate. Kelly Jensen notes in her 2018 article for *Book Riot* that "the growth in YA books about mental illness is hard to ignore" and "talking openly about mental health in YA books has seen an increase as the category of books has grown, too." In addition, argues Kia Jane Richmond, YA novels centering on mental health "help high school and college students investigate vocabulary associated with mental illness and explore how characters with psychological problems are treated by peers, bullies, and community members" (24). These comments highlight how YA authors are increasingly attending to adolescent mental health's language and literary nuances.

Despite this recent and growing proliferation of literature, many adolescents, particularly boys, still find it challenging to talk openly about their mental health and their experiences with mental distress. In North America, specifically, one obstacle preventing adolescent boys from discussing their mental health stems from the social conditioning of masculinity. Rather than embracing emotional vulnerability and transparency, young boys are encouraged to treat their mental distress by internalizing it and displaying warrior-like stoicism. They must dispel any semblance of weakness or fragility to demonstrate their masculinity through dominance and control, particularly in the United

States, where the concept of masculinity has been entangled with military imperialism since the turn of the twentieth century.[2] As a result of this conditioning, adolescent boys' experiences with mental distress are particularly isolating because they are rarely encouraged to discuss their difficulties, emotions, or traumas. Even when they are encouraged to talk about their distress, such conditioning is often so ingrained that many adolescent boys find it difficult to open up about their experiences. Thus, when considering what comprehensive mental healthcare looks like in adolescents' lives, we must face the hurdle of boys thinking they do not deserve, do not need, or cannot accept care. Offering comprehensive healthcare to boys means little unless we normalize that it is okay for boys to be cared for in the first place.

In this chapter, I examine how adolescent boys' discussion (or lack thereof) of their mental health is primarily informed by what I term "masculine silence." I define masculine silence as a feature of male conditioning that pressures boys into adopting an apathetic and stoic posture in response to pain (physical, mental, or emotional), trauma, or mental distress. While several YA novels explore such a concept, I trace this particular manifestation of masculine silence and mental health through Adib Khorram's 2018 YA novel *Darius the Great Is Not Okay*.[3] I argue that Khorram's novel offers both implicit and explicit critiques of how masculine silence informs boys' perspectives on mental health, preventing them from finding sustainable outlets for their emotional and psychological distress and leading them toward suicidal ideation. For Darius Kellner, Khorram's adolescent protagonist, masculine silence keeps him in a mindset that fosters suicidal ideation. Therefore, he must actively resist masculine silence despite his social conditioning. Helping to mobilize Darius's resistance to masculine silence is Sohrab, a teenage boy he meets when his family travels to Iran. Sohrab listens to Darius attentively, enabling a pathway for Darius to transform his cycles of negative self-talk into external dialogues with others regarding his thoughts, feelings, and emotional distress. As a result of the vulnerable and transparent friendship between Darius and Sohrab, Darius resists embodying traditional American masculine ideals by demonstrating how the capacities for both distress and expressiveness are interwoven into the fabric of his boyhood. Thus, *Darius the Great Is Not Okay* illustrates how boys struggle to handle their emotions and distress while also spotlighting how analyses of mental healthcare for adolescent boys must account for the ways masculine silence informs their experiences.

I focus on Khorram's novel for several reasons. First, it interrogates how father figures reinforce and perpetuate cultural norms of masculinity in rearing their male children. Darius must overcome his desire to stay silent in the face of distress, which he explicitly learns from his father. The second reason is that this novel also addresses how masculinity intersects with other social identities.

For example, it explores how masculine silence informs queer relationships and how competing models inform Darius's bicultural identity of masculinity. And last, Darius's distress is at least partially shaped by grief, as he spends much of the novel mourning the grandfather he hardly knows but who is about to die. As a result, Darius Kellner exemplifies an emotionally expressive adolescent boy and offers an example of how such a figure complicates, critiques, and skews the concept of silent, stoic masculinity rampant within US culture. And while contemporary literary scholarship increasingly considers how stoic manhood and masculine pain are central to several canonical US texts and authors, what largely remains absent from these discussions is how masculine silence shapes adolescent boy subjectivity.[4] I contend that by situating adolescent narratives within the expanding scholarship of masculine distress, we uncover both new forms of teenage rebellion and, perhaps more importantly, a deeper perspective of masculinity that does not start with men but with boys.

Before analyzing masculine silence and mental distress in Khorram's novel, I offer an overview of the conditions from which masculine silence and the internalization of distress emerged within the US, particularly following the Second World War. The following section examines how the concept of masculinity has evolved in the wake of several significant cultural moments, including, but not limited to, multiple wars, the women's liberation movement, the civil rights movement, the queer rights movement, and shifting local and global economies. After this examination, I interrogate how *Darius the Great Is Not Okay* considers the intersections of masculine silence, distress, and mental health through the framing of literary adolescence, paying particular attention to how silence informs the queer dynamics in the text. In the chapter's final section, I analyze how Darius breaks through the silences around him by speaking out about his mental health, distress, and emotions. The novel itself critiques the concept of masculine silence through its first-person narration, which signals Darius's inherent desire to speak out in some manner about his experiences. In so doing, *Darius the Great Is Not Okay* explicitly rebels against a dangerous construction of masculinity that conditions boys into living as if their mental distress does not exist, forcing them into seriously contemplating acts of suicide.

HISTORICIZING MASCULINE SILENCE

Gender theory scholars have long regarded masculinity and femininity as socially constructed and historically contingent.[5] The observation that what constitutes gender does not arise from our biology as much as our historically marked cultural practices comes with significant implications, two of which are worth noting here. First, social constructionism implies that what it means to be "manly" or "masculine" fluctuates between historical periods, so much so, in fact, that, as Michael S. Kimmel notes, "The search for a transcendent, timeless definition of manhood is itself a sociological phenomenon" (*Manhood* 4). Second, the lack of a single, transcendent masculine ideal opens the possibility of multiple masculinities. R. W. Connell, who is best known for discussing the various configurations of masculinity in her book *Masculinities* (1995), outlines conceptual differences between hegemonic masculinity, subordinated masculinity, complicit masculinity, and marginalized masculinity. This list is by no means exhaustive. Scholars such as J. A. Mangan have also written on additional concepts such as imperial masculinity, while Aaron Belkin considers military or soldier masculinity.[6] And, as sociologists C. J. Pascoe and Tristan Bridges note, defining what features of masculinity "[make] one a man" is not simple: "Most of us casually use a sort of 'I know it when I see it' approach or think of masculinity as a series of 'nots' (e.g., not feminine, not 'gay,' not interested in interior design, cooking, or clothing)" (3). Even within these categorical breakdowns, there are further nuances—for example, marginalized masculinity includes versions of manhood unique to different races, ethnicities, and the 2SLGBTQIA+ and disabled communities.[7]

While it is not within the scope of this chapter to engage directly with each configuration, I offer an overview of the varied masculinities in order to establish the arbitrary nature of the US masculine conditioning that encourages boys and men to respond to their distress through silent stoicism. Since the turn of the twentieth century, this form of masculinity traditionally signals a warrior-like personality and the ability to not just fight against but cope with physical and emotional distress. Demonstrating this ability is precisely where masculinity and mental health intersect. Stephen Wicks calls the warrior the "foremost of among male archetypes" and "the epitome of masculinity in many societies," such as those with a strong military presence (29).[8] Sam Keen argues that within these militarized societies, boys and men are taught to "value what is tough and to despise what is 'feminine' and tenderhearted" (37). Historian George L. Mosse concurs, adding, "A soldier in full control of himself, of strong power of will, would be able to cope with the experiences of battle and become accustomed to the terrible sights which surrounded him in the trenches, indifferent to death" (95–96). In *War and Gender: How Gender Shapes the War System and Vice Versa*, political scientist Joshua S. Goldstein documents the ways military ideals and practices shape masculine identity. He argues that "if a man is to carry out manly deeds, he cannot be slowed down by taking the time to psychologically heal himself after the terrible things he has witnessed and endured. He must strap down his armor and press on, willing debilitating emotions out of his mind" (Goldstein 267). This suppression of emotions and distress positions stoicism as an ideal masculine quality. Belkin adds that "warriors become stoic via practices which harden them through the disavowal of anything associated with femininity and softness.... Military training reinforces typical civilian socialization patterns in which boys are shamed if they cry or exhibit any signs of tenderness" (28).

These militaristic ideas are particularly relevant to Darius's socialization in a few important ways. First, he observes them through the television show *Star Trek*, which he and his father regularly watch together. While *Star Trek* typically depicts the human and alien members of Starfleet on diplomatic missions, they are still on a military spaceship. Moreover, some of the show's Vulcan characters, such as Spock, are also known for their combat techniques (e.g., Vulcan Nerve Pinch) and exhibiting control over their emotions. Second, airports consistently remind Darius of the military tension between Iran and the United States. While they are driving to the airport for their flight to Iran, Darius's sister Laleh asks their parents a series of inconsequential questions, which causes Darius to note, "A knot started forming, right in the middle of my solar plexus. All those questions were making me nervous, because Laleh wasn't asking the really important questions. What if they didn't let us in? What if there was trouble at Customs?" (Khorram 55–56). And last, the stoic warrior's "disavowal of anything associated with femininity" that Belkin refers to certainly informs Darius's understanding of his queerness. For instance, he plays with dolls and has tea parties with Laleh, but he hides these activities from others because he understands them as "unmanly" (16). Such efforts to conceal his "unmanly" side also directly affect how comfortable he is with his growing romantic feelings toward other boys. Near the end of the novel, his father asks him if he loves Sohrab, to which Darius responds with silence; he notes, "Dad looked at me for a moment. Like he knew there was more. But he didn't ask.... Maybe he knew, without me saying it out loud, that I wasn't ready to talk about more" (287). The subtext here matches much of the novel's engagement with Darius's queerness as something just under the surface of his silences. However, he never explicitly embraces it as part of his identity in the novel. Instead, he struggles throughout the narrative with reconciling his "masculine self" with his "queer self," as if they are somehow mutually exclusive (when they are most certainly not). Collectively, though, these experiences illustrate the ways Darius's socialization is informed, at least in part, by militaristic notions of masculinity that prohibit anything feminine and encourage silence in the face of distress.

However, the paradox of this silent and stoic form of masculinity is that the tougher one appears, the more emotions they are likely to suppress. If a boy is only mildly distressed, he need only be mildly tough to cover those emotions in a stoic exterior. If he is highly distressed, it becomes more challenging to present himself as resilient. In response to such distress, Kimmel notes, "Men try to *control themselves* . . . and when feeling too pressured, they attempt an *escape*" (*Manhood* 6). This escape can be literal, through physical relocation or attempted suicide, or symbolic, such as withdrawing emotionally from others. These efforts are primarily defined by emotional isolation and an "I don't need anyone else" attitude.

The development of this iteration of masculinity occurs particularly in the US through the twentieth century for several complex reasons. The first, of course, is due to the US's extensive military engagements throughout the twentieth century. From two world wars to the Cold War, the Korean War, the Vietnam War, the Gulf War, the war in Afghanistan, and the Iraq War, among several other wars and military interventions and occupations, the US's military industrial complex has become an economic fixture, as well as a reflection of its national image and global reputation.[9] With such a steadily expansive military presence, even civilian men are susceptible to military masculinity's sociopolitical influence, ideals, and culture. John Ibson, for example, argues that men's relationships with one another in the US changed considerably in the aftermath of the Second World War, where "a marked increase in the space between men—literal and figurative, physical and emotional—occurred during the 1950s" (xvii). It is in this new space that Ibson locates the ways "male relationships of many sorts, not just homosexual unions, were dealt a painful, damaging blow in 1950s America, a blow from which they have not recovered even yet" (xvi). Men found it increasingly difficult to develop a desire for emotionally intimate relationships and a vocabulary necessary to sustain those connections. The loss of so many men, Ibson adds, "made some returning veterans even more isolated, hesitant to risk yet additional loss, hence avoiding intimate attachments to other males with a renewed resolve" (143). In other words, men were so traumatized from WWII that it became difficult to foster relationships and emotional connections with one another once the war had ended.

Those relationships were additionally difficult to foster, Jonathan Rutherford argues, due to a changing cultural landscape wherein men in the US struggled to construct "a language of affective relations," which is not to justify such silences (9). Instead, Rutherford describes how men turned their lack of interpersonal relationships into interpersonal attacks upon others: "Men and masculinity always seemed to be exempt from the process of change. . . . It was always with someone else or somewhere else that the problem or issues was located" (8). This disconnection between men's personal and public selves—particularly for white men—would be further intensified with the rise of the civil rights, 2SLGBTQIA+, and women's liberation movements, which focused the public spotlight on personal injustices and experiences.

The rise of second-wave feminism through the 1960s and 1970s, for example, altered relationships between men and women, as men were collaborating with women more frequently in "their working, academic, political or personal lives" (Edwards 22). Additionally, the shifting US and global economies through the neoliberal policies of the 1970s and 1980s aided in transforming masculinity into something territorial, guarded, and competitive.[10] With the rise of neoliberalism and its hyper-competitive labor markets designed for individuals to prosper came decreases in the one-job-for-life employment model and depreciating wages.[11] As Barbara Ehrenreich asserts, "Patriarchal power based on breadwinning is now only an option for very wealthy men, and this is a striking change" (288). These significant cultural changes help make sense of a masculine identity in the US based on guarding oneself against other men and women. In this identity, any semblance of emotional or mental fragility jeopardizes one's masculinity and hinders an already increasingly difficult progression to economic success. And while much of *Darius the Great Is Not Okay* takes place in Iran, where concepts of masculinity may be different, I focus on the socialization of US masculinity primarily because Darius is the lens through which we receive this story, and he was socialized in the US. His sense of self as a boy and how he interprets his relationships with other boys and men are therefore primarily influenced by his upbringing in the United States.

Also shaping Darius's experiences are the ways one's immigrant identity can affect perceptions of masculinity in the US. To be clear, Darius was born in Portland, Oregon. Still, he frequently refers to himself as a "Fractional Persian" since his mom is from Iran and his dad is from the US. And since Darius looks more like his Persian mother than his white father—who Darius notes is sometimes described as "*Aryan*"—he is no stranger to explicit racism (Khorram 13). For instance, at one point in the novel, a classmate and bully named Trent Bolger calls Darius a "terrorist" during gym class, to which Darius explains, "This was not the first time I had been called a terrorist. It didn't happen often—no teacher let it slide when they heard it—but school was school, and I was a kid with Middle Eastern heritage, even though I was born and raised in Portland" (39).

This kind of racist othering has always been a part of the socialization of masculinity in the US. "Throughout American history," Kimmel argues, "various groups have represented the sissy, the non-men against whom American men played out their definitions of manhood, often with vicious results" ("Masculinity as Homophobia" 236). Today, especially in a post-9/11 context, many white men—which Trent Bolger partially stands in for—remain committed to racist and exclusionary practices. As Kimmel contends,

> [Some men] still rehearse the politics of exclusion, as if by clearing away the playing field of secure gender identity of any that we deem less than

manly—women, gay men, nonnative-born men, men of color—middle-class, straight, white men can reground their sense of themselves without those haunting fears and that deep shame that they are unmanly and will be exposed by other men. This is the manhood of racism, of sexism, of homophobia. ("Masculinity as Homophobia" 240)

Darius's socialization as a boy emerges from these practices and their history. He is subject to masculine conditioning that asks him to interrogate his identity while simultaneously framing several aspects of that identity—his queerness, Middle Eastern heritage, emotions, and mental health—as directly contributing to his "unmanliness."

Such self-reflexive politics have forced most boys and men to account for their own masculine identities. However, as bell hooks contends, despite men's overall prominence in the public sphere, the direct interrogation of their private identity was confusing: "Women demanded of men that they give more emotionally, but most men really could not understand what was being asked of them.... They simply could not give more emotionally or even grasp the problem without reconnecting, reuniting the severed parts" (66). In the face of such confusion, interrogation, and emotional uncertainty, the first line of masculine defense is to retreat from one's emotions—either externally, internally, or both. Such responses to mental distress form the conditions in which the adolescent boys in many YA novels find themselves, and Darius's boyhood is primarily shaped by the adult masculine norms reinforced by people like Trent Bolger and his father. Thus, by depicting such social conditioning, *Darius the Great Is Not Okay* highlights the importance of exploring how masculine silence inhibits adolescent boys from receiving an essential piece of comprehensive mental healthcare while simultaneously endangering their lives.

MASCULINE DISTRESS MEETS MASCULINE SILENCE

The tension between masculine silence and mental health is prevalent fairly early in *Darius the Great Is Not Okay*. The novel follows fifteen-year-old Darius and his family as they travel from Portland to Iran to spend time with his maternal grandfather before he dies. Darius struggles to connect with his Iranian cultural heritage, particularly since he does not speak Farsi. He also feels disconnected from the people around him in Portland, as he refers to his peers at school, for instance, as the "Soulless Minions of Orthodoxy" (Khorram 4). Complicating his efforts to connect with others is his depression, a diagnosis he shares with his father, Stephen Kellner, for which they both take regular medication. That Darius and his father take regular medication offers a few crucial insights regarding mental healthcare in the novel. First, it illustrates that the family has access to pharmaceutical support, likely through a health insurance provider. Darius's mother and father have stable jobs—his mother is a UX designer, and his father is a partner in an architecture firm—and this suggests they are at least comfortable financially and therefore capable of taking advantage of insurance coverage. Essentially, Darius never worries about running out of medication or about his ability to pay for it. Second, the novel's plot is not heavily informed by Darius's or his father's journey to find the "right medication." Their respective attempts to find the proper medication and dosage do arise a couple of times in the text, which shows Khorram's desire to acknowledge what can be a long and challenging aspect of mental healthcare. Still, the novel's core narrative follows Darius regularly taking an amount of medication that seemingly works for him. And third, Darius's medicinal treatments also highlight his access to doctors and mental healthcare professionals. He talks about how although he has not been diagnosed with an anxiety disorder, "Dr. Howell said that anxiety and depression often went hand in hand," indicating that he has had conversations with someone about his mental health (114). In the novel, these aspects of mental healthcare signal that while Darius and his father are diagnosed with depression, they are receiving consistent support from the medical community, both pharmaceutically and from their shared physician.

This significant similarity between them should reflect a meaningful understanding of one another's mental health; however, Darius could not feel more disconnected from his father. To Darius, Stephen Kellner is an "Ubermensch" with angular and powerful hands (Khorram 13, 61), who never struggles with gaining "medication weight" (127), never asks for directions (161), and is ashamed of needing to take medication (28), while simultaneously being "categorically opposed to self-pity" (135). Ultimately, in Darius's eyes, "Stephen Kellner [is] the Paragon of Teutonic Masculinity" (42). Implicit in these descriptions of Stephen Kellner is the Nietzschean concept of the Superman or someone who is beyond human definition, with the physical features of toughness, bodily control, supreme-level competence, and disgust for that which renders him "weak." There is also the fact that Stephen Kellner is both straight and white, reinforcing his status as a symbol of hegemonic masculinity in the novel.

These descriptions illustrate how Darius is conditioned to use masculine silence when he experiences distress. Since Darius does not observe his father as someone who talks openly about his troubles, he never learns to do the same. Just as Darius never learned Farsi, making him feel isolated from his Iranian culture, he never learns to talk openly about his mental health lest he risks his masculinity, a mode of being he adopts from his father. This parallel is explicit when Darius notes how not speaking Farsi is one of the few things that connect them: "That was the only time Dad and I were on the same team: when we were stuck with Farsi-speakers and left with each other for company. But even when that happened, we just ended up standing around in Level Seven Awkward Silence. Stephen Kellner and I were experts at High Level Awkward Silences" (Khorram 21). The fact that Darius does not speak Farsi and is aligned with his dad in this matter subtly signals how disconnected he is from both sides of his dual heritage, as well as from the normative masculine ideals that his dad symbolizes (straight, white, tough). It is also telling that Darius, who rarely has a positive opinion of himself, describes himself (and his father) as an expert when it comes to silences. They both experience depression and take medication, yet they both refuse to speak openly about these matters. Darius often refers to the moments where he internalizes his distress as "tactical withdrawals," echoing a militaristic effort to appear strong and in control (223). Such withdrawals make sense because his model of masculinity—his father—is imagined and described in purely idealized and hegemonic terms.

Unfortunately, while his father appears to be managing his depression well enough, Darius struggles mightily with his mental health. The image of swirling emotions is how he imagines his distress. He describes his depression and despair in the scientific language of black holes: "The quantum singularity in my chest churned, drawing more interstellar dust into its event horizon, sucking up all the light that drew close" (Khorram 223). Wrestling with this singularity, Darius constantly worries about mood swings; his weight; his anxiety over not being manly enough, Persian enough, or Übermensch enough; crying often; and his lingering wish to slip into a void. When the singularity swirls quickest, he observes his family and notes, "They looked happy and content without me" (223). This sentiment typifies Darius's struggle to resist his ongoing distress. He defines his subjectivity through a lens of alienation and despair, and while in isolation, he perceives his family as happy. He imagines himself as a metaphorical black hole stealing the light and positivity from those around him, making it easier to justify his musings regarding whether anyone would miss him if he died.

With Darius's emotions and distress consuming him, his adherence to masculine silence offers him no outlet through which to express his struggle. Even his positive emotions are subject to silent cover-ups. For example, although Darius deeply loves his sister, Laleh, he is acutely aware that openly expressing affection toward her is off-limits: "It wasn't the kind of thing I could ever say to anyone. Not out loud, at least. I mean, guys aren't supposed to love their little sisters. We can look out for them. . . . But we can't say we love them. We can't admit to having tea parties or playing dolls with them, because that's unmanly" (Khorram 16). But as I previously noted, Darius *does* play dolls with her *and* joins her tea parties. He just does not tell anyone he does these things. Like his male role models, he buries his emotions in the name of silent, stoic, manly toughness.

Such silent toughness likewise informs Darius's budding attraction to Sohrab, the boy he meets while his family is in Iran. Noticing Sohrab playing soccer one day, Darius's feelings overtake him:

> He was kicking his soccer ball/non-American football around, barefoot and shirtless. Sweat plastered his short hair and temples and the nape of his neck. He waved when I came out and put his hands behind his head in Surrender Cobra. His flat chest rose and fell, rose and fell, and his stomach muscles rolled with each breath. I knew if I got close enough to him, the intense thermal radiation he was emitting would scorch me. (Khorram 258)

Darius's attention to Sohrab's physical body is intense and overwhelming. His eyes notice every detail, including the repetitions of chest inhalations and stomach muscles moving. He uses a euphemism to conclude that Sohrab is so attractive that he could very well mark Darius's physical body. This intense attraction culminates for Darius in a moment of peace with Sohrab, where they are both enjoying an innocent physical connection with one another. However, it remains embedded in silence, as Darius explains, "I turned and watched Sohrab. The way his eyes lost their focus. The way his jaw finally unclenched. I put my arm over his shoulder, and he linked his over mine. And we sat like that, together. And the silence was okay" (296). Such descriptions illuminate the powerful connection between them. Sohrab sits, relaxed and at ease, in Darius's arms. Darius is attentive and at peace with their companionship. Although their relationship does not turn into anything sexual, it provides Darius with a growing sense of his queerness. What is unfortunate for Darius is no matter what he feels—intimate affection or severe mental distress—he only knows how to act like a man by suppressing it under silence and believing that silence is okay.

Such suppression is perhaps best observed, though, while Darius is with his grandfather, Ardeshir Bahrami, when they visit an ancient burial site in Iran known as the "Towers of Silence," where many of their family ancestors are buried. Once they arrive, Ardeshir—or Babou, as Darius calls him—mourns that soon there will be no more Bahramis living in Yazd and a once-great family lineage within the city will end. It is in this brief moment of sentimentality, a crack in Babou's fortified exterior, that Darius finds connection:

> My grandfather seemed so small and defeated then, bowed under the weight of history and the burdens of the future. I didn't know what to say. The singularity in my stomach was back, pulsing and writhing in sympathetic harmony with the one I knew lived deep inside Babou. In that moment I understood my grandfather perfectly. Ardeshir Bahrami

was as sad as I was. He rested his hand on my neck and gave me a soft squeeze. That was as close to a hug as he had ever given me. I relaxed against him as we studied the landscape below us. That was as close to a hug as I had ever given him. (Khorram 230–31)

I contend that what occurs at the "Towers of Silence" between Darius and his grandfather demonstrates Darius's understanding of masculine intimacy as something premised upon silence. Not only does the burial site's name connect silence with overtly phallic imagery, but Darius and Babou, who hardly know each other and struggle to relate to one another, manage to find common ground in their buried pain. Babou, mourning the loss of his family's legacy in the city, cannot talk through his grief with his grandson. And although Darius often feels distant from his grandfather, he understands this moment and its meaningfulness. Notably, however, the details of their connection are kept within Darius's internal narrative voice. They do not exchange words, nor do they exchange looks, as Babou only puts his hands on Darius's neck and squeezes. Darius leans into him in return, illustrating that their exchange of intimacy will occur physically, not verbally, which Darius interprets as enough for Babou. When Darius says he understands Babou "perfectly," he recognizes that sharing this intimate moment is meaningful to his grandfather.

This moment is also meaningful to Darius, as it signals that he is unsatisfied with his intimacy with other men, including his father. He understands that this moment is the most profound connection he will get with Babou, particularly since his time with his grandfather is limited to this visit. However, he yearns for something more from the other men in his life with whom he can connect more deeply. Knowing that this exchange is the most he will get from Babou, Darius brings the moment to an end. This particular passage closes the chapter in which it appears, which is a fitting reflection of Darius's efforts to pursue the kind of emotional connection he craves. If he can feel this connected to his grandfather without speaking, then his father and he should be capable of connecting more deeply than they do. The narrative chases this feeling by ending on this pivot point in Darius's life and shifting immediately to a new page, a new chapter, and a clearer sense for Darius that he must overcome the silences that prevent him from opening up emotionally to other men.

Still, despite Darius's yearning for deeper connections with men, his conditioning continues to keep discussions of his mental health, feelings of alienation, and queerness behind a veil of silence. With his father standing in as his primary model of ideal masculinity—straight, white, wealthy, stoic, and silent in the face of distress—Darius struggles to connect with him, his grandfather, and Sohrab, who causes Darius to feel new kinds of emotions. But with no viable outlet, no vision of masculinity that allows for a healthy dialogue between men about mental health, Darius is left alone to sit with his thoughts. Notably, he grows a dangerous fondness for this mindset, stating, "I loved the quiet. Even if it sometimes made me think of sad things. Like whether anyone would miss me if I was dead" (Khorram 223). This flirtation with suicidal ideation occurs throughout the novel, but it is directly linked to silence in this passage. The implication is that it is in the space of masculine silence where Darius is left alone to hold his distress, pain, and sadness. This connection between masculine silence and suicide appears again toward the novel's end after Darius argues with Sohrab. Running back to his grandfather's house in tears, Darius describes himself as a "coward" who "really hated [him]self"; he wishes he had "the One Ring" so he could vanish: "I wished I had a cloaking device so no one would ever find me. I wish I could just disappear forever" (280–81). Through these references to Tolkien and *Star Trek*, Darius voices a desire to remove himself from everyone around him. More importantly, he does not wish to be found. He wants to be alone, forever, by choice. It is not a stretch to suggest that these desires are euphemisms for suicide. As a result, masculine silence becomes both a space wherein suicidal ideation develops and an obstacle to overcome such thoughts. It is a mental trap that young boys are encouraged to embrace to uphold their masculinity at the cost of, at least, their mental health and, at worst, their life. Darius struggles to hold this connection between masculine silence and mental health, and Khorram's novel implores readers to examine why.

BEYOND MASCULINE SILENCE

Part of what makes *Darius the Great Is Not Okay* and other novels like it important is that they critique masculine silence through the active emotional engagements of their protagonists.[12] That is to say, their protagonists not only experience complex emotions, but they are also deeply expressive of their emotions, at least to themselves and to the extradiegetic readers. Although they are taught and encouraged by other male characters to suppress their distress and be silent in the name of manly toughness, boy protagonists such as Darius actively rebel against such expectations by eventually reaching out to others. In so doing, they ultimately find a genuine connection with other boys and men based on emotional intimacy. This rebellion does not imply that boys should not also be tough. Darius's personal development, for example, does not suggest that being emotionally vulnerable is the most critical lesson for adolescent boys to learn. Still, a conversation regarding boys' emotional and mental well-being involves reconfiguring our cultural perceptions of masculinity. As hooks contends, "We cannot teach boys that 'real men' either do not feel or do not express feelings, then expect boys to feel comfortable getting in touch with their feelings" (36).

It is precisely this struggle to get in touch with their emotions that Khorram captures in this novel. Darius's eventual effort to reach out to others about his distress is rewarded with genuine companionship, particularly with other men.

Darius finds his initial genuine companionship in Sohrab. Different from the "Soulless Minions of Orthodoxy" back in Portland, Sohrab's behavior creates space for Darius to talk openly, as Darius explains: "Sohrab nodded and waited for me. I liked that about Sohrab. That he would wait for me to figure out what I wanted to say" (Khorram 236). Sohrab provides this outlet to Darius almost immediately after they meet, and it takes time for Darius to become accustomed to this form of intimacy. As noted previously, there is a unique attraction between Sohrab and Darius. Darius routinely comments on how often they hold each other and how Sohrab smells "soapy and fresh, like rosemary" (264). Coupled with these descriptions are other intimate moments, often physically centered, as Darius finds himself learning to be more comfortable with his body and his attraction to Sohrab. In one scene, they shower following a game of soccer, and Darius experiences waves of new emotions:

> Once again, Sohrab stripped himself completely, like it was totally normal for guys to be naked around each other. His skin was a volcano, with sweat running down every valley. My face was experiencing some extreme thermal flux of its own.... I was even more amazed I managed to talk back to him while I scrubbed my belly button and my stomach jiggled like some sort of gelatinous non-humanoid life-form. Maybe I was learning to have less walls inside me too. (250–51)

Crucial here is the inversion of expectations from multiple positions. Khorram challenges readers' expectations of the conservatism in Iranian culture, while Sohrab's level of comfort in the shower challenges Darius's expectations regarding masculine intimacy.[13] Darius is initially uncomfortable in the shower for several reasons: his discomfort with his body, his attraction to Sohrab, and his unfamiliarity with this kind of vulnerability. Sohrab, however, does not care about any of those things. He expects that it is entirely normal for boys to shower together after team sports, and his attitude reinforces that this experience is typical, encouraging Darius to shower in company with others and become more comfortable with himself. Before meeting Sohrab, Darius believes it is unimaginable that other boys or men would be vulnerable around him or with him, whether physically or emotionally. When he is around Sohrab, particularly when they are alone, the two forms of intimacy are connected. Darius also alludes to the metaphorical walls within him. Those walls exist due to the social conditioning of his father and his peers in Portland specifically and masculine culture in the US generally. Around Sohrab, though, those walls begin to fall.

When Darius returns home distressed from a minor falling out with Sohrab (they eventually reconcile), the level of intimacy he has shared with his new friend leads to an unusually vulnerable moment with his father. Careful at first, Darius warns himself that he "couldn't let Stephen Kellner see [him] cry" (Khorram 282). Still, after recognizing that he has "so much anger turned inward," Darius expresses his frustrations to his father; he opens up to him about his distress: "You don't want me to feel anything at all. You just want me to be normal. Like you" (283). His father, reeling from these accusations, tells him that he only worries because he is scared that one day Darius's depression may cause him to self-harm like he almost did once. He tells Darius that several years prior, when Darius was around seven, his depression got so bad that he almost took his life. His doctor—the same physician Darius sees—prescribed him a higher dosage of medication, which took a while to work, making him distant and beginning the rift in their relationship that grew over the years. As his father explains, "Suicide isn't the only way you can lose someone to depression" (286). Taken aback by such an intimate admission, Darius describes a shift between father and son:

> Dad looked up at me again. There were no walls between us....
> There were tears in his eyes.
> Actual human tears.
> I had never seen my father cry before.
> And due to some harmonic resonance, I started crying again too. (286)

Much like Darius's moment with his grandfather, this passage reflects an instance of a male companionship rooted in an empathetic exchange. Unlike the moment Darius shared with his grandfather at the "Towers of Silence," however, Darius and his father are verbally expressive and openly crying. They talk about their feelings and the histories that contributed to their affective states. Together, they find a way to understand one another more deeply.

Moreover, their exchange notably carries two additional implications. First, it signifies the potential for an emotional connection between father and son. Darius experiences a fully developed moment with his dad, demonstrating how being open about one's emotions and mental health does not have to compromise one's masculinity. I contend that it is significant for a novel published in 2018 to exemplify this possibility, particularly considering current anxieties about masculinity. As academic and cultural discussions around masculinity continue to evolve, such literary depictions of the potential for older generations to change their behavior could go a long way in encouraging more men to express their emotional depth and talk about their mental health. Second, novels such as *Darius the Great Is Not Okay* illustrate how boys can healthily channel their expressions in discussion with others rather than bury them inward, though it is important to recognize that a range of cultural and systemic barriers may prevent boys and men from practicing such forms of communication. Darius, for example, talks to readers directly because, for much of his story, that is his only viable outlet. He frequently seeks validation from readers throughout the novel by repeating the phrase, "That's normal. Right?" (Khorram 17). Asking such a question, especially several times, begs for a response—if only the reader could provide one. But the lesson Darius must learn is how to channel his expressions toward those who can offer him emotional support, which, in this novel, begins with Sohrab and ends with his father. In perhaps the most fitting conclusion to a narrative centered on the complexities of masculine mental health and silence, Khorram's novel ends with Darius's father checking in on his son and asking him how he is feeling:

> Dad looked at me.
>   "You okay, son?"
>   "Yeah, Dad," I said....
>   "I'm great." (312)

Just as Darius always asks the reader for reassurance, his father now asks Darius to express himself and reassure *him*. Thus, Stephen Kellner joins his son in rebelling against his former embodiment of stoic, silent, Teutonic masculinity. They both realize that the silence between them, especially around their experiences with depression, is harmful to their relationship and detrimental to their mental health. As a result, *Darius the Great Is Not Okay* explicitly critiques masculine silence as a viable solution to adolescent boys' experiences with mental distress.

Additionally, Khorram's novel critiques masculine silence not only in its content but in its form. The fact that it is written through first-person narration matters. Darius does not write solely to narrate a story. He writes to be heard, speaking to his readers through a range of rhetorical questions. Thus, the framing of *Darius the Great Is Not Okay* reinforces its critique of masculine silence: by its very nature, as a cultural artifact, it illustrates a masculine yearning to open an emotional dialogue with those willing to engage. Notably, readers can offer Darius nothing in return. His rhetorical questions will always go unanswered. Still, part of working through mental distress and emotional pain means finding ways of expression that allow for honesty. Even the toughest men can be deeply emotional, and Darius actively rebels against a process of social conditioning that encourages him to define his manhood by his stoic silences. From the novel's opening lines to its final period, every thought, sentence, and word is an act of rebellion against such masculine silence. Even if Darius is not always open with other characters, his first-person perspective demonstrates how he is always describing, thinking, and speaking into reality what masculinity means to him. He learns to define his own form of masculinity with the firm acknowledgment that it is okay for boys to have feelings of sadness, grief, and despair, as well as positive feelings, such as romantic ones for other boys, and that it is okay to talk about those emotions openly and honestly. In short, while Khorram's novel does not extend its critique too far against the social structures that value masculine silence, it does critique silence as a suitable form of treatment for boys and men struggling with their mental health. It does so through its advocacy for the acceptance of expressive adolescent boys and for the spaces necessary for those boys to talk about their emotions, pain, and distress.

I contend that the encouragement of young boys to talk about their mental health remains paramount in progressive discussions about mental healthcare. As Khorram's novel suggests, even if an adolescent boy is fortunate enough to live with a family who can provide pharmaceutical treatment and medical support, which describes Darius's position, comprehensive mental healthcare must account for how young boys are taught to develop their masculinity through masculine silence. Suppose they are not provided with the spaces necessary to overcome such conditioning, or they are kept from seeing other men and boys talking openly about their mental health. In those cases, they risk internalizing their pain so intensely that their only escape is through suicidal ideation. Darius ponders his death several times throughout Khorram's novel, and it is not until Sohrab shows him how to be vulnerable that he finds the mental and emotional space to open up to his father. In turn, Adib Khorram's *Darius the Great Is Not Okay* illustrates how comprehensive mental healthcare for adolescents requires more than a pharmaceutical or medical response; it requires a thorough understanding of how masculine silence informs the way young boys are encouraged to behave as men and how to overcome this conditioning, lest they leave in search of their own life-threatening escape.

NOTES

1. While I retain the term "mental illness" when quoting critics and authors referenced here, I prefer to use the term "mental distress" when possible. Because mental health issues are complex, involving biological, social, and political components, I find the term "mental illness" reductive in its centering of the biomedical model and its viewing of experiences such as anxiety or depression as originating primarily in the brain. Thus, I find the term "mental distress" more suitable for accounting for the range of mental health issues, their severities, and the interaction between the biological and sociopolitical experience.

2. As Aaron Belkin argues in *Bring Me Men: Military Masculinity and the Benign Façade of American Empire 1898–2001*,

> While reverence for American warriors is a longstanding tradition, military masculinity did not emerge as a dominant paradigm until the end of the nineteenth century, when imperialists advocated American involvement in the 1898 war against Spain as an opportunity to remedy the nation's feminization. That war marked a turning point in how soldiers and soldiering were represented in popular culture such as literature for juvenile audiences. Before the turn of the twentieth century, magazines and books written for juvenile audiences did not epitomize soldiering as the most privileged demonstration of masculinity. After the Spanish-American War, however, the literature changed, as authors began representing soldiering as paradigmatic of what it meant to be a real man. (7)

The relationship between American masculinity and control over the self and of Others is also racialized. Michael S. Kimmel notes in *Manhood in America: A Cultural History* that "American manhood has often been built on the exclusion of others from equal opportunity to work, to go to school, to vote—to do things that allow people to compete equally" (33).

3. Khorram has since released a sequel to this novel titled *Darius the Great Deserves Better* (2020). However, for the purposes of this chapter I will only be examining Darius's story as explored through the first novel.

4. Literary scholar Jennifer Travis notes that contemporary scholarship is finally beginning to "[reframe] the 'repressive hypothesis' of masculine emotion to propose that affect is not banished from the male experience but constitutive of some of its most characteristic manifestations: flight, competition, and bonding among them" (7–8). Ryan Schneider picks up these threads in W. E. B. Du Bois's *The Souls of Black Folk*, followed by Thomas Strychacz in Ernest Hemingway, and Stephen Davenport in Jack Kerouac. See also Susan Brook, Jon Robert Adams, and the collections *Sentimental Men: Masculinity and the Politics of Affect in American Culture*, edited by Mary Chapman and Glenn Hendler, and *Boys Don't Cry? Rethinking Narratives of Masculinity and Emotion in the U.S.*, edited by Milette Shamir and Jennifer Travis.

5. See Bronner, Edwards, and Pascoe and Bridges for in-depth explorations of the historically contingent features of masculinity, and Bartky, Bordo, and Butler for discussions of cultural femininity.

6. See J. A. Mangan's *"Manufactured" Masculinity: Making Imperial Manliness, Morality and Militarism* and Belkin's *Bring Me Men* for more on military masculinity in the US context.

7. 2SLGBTQIA+ is an acronym that stands for two-spirit, lesbian, gay, bisexual, transgender, queer or questioning, intersex, asexual, and additional sexual orientations or gender identities.

8. Wicks qualifies his statement by unpacking the differences between the "warrior" and the "hunter," noting that the warrior archetype has been "the epitome of masculinity in many societies not dependent on hunting" (29). Essentially, the development of agricultural-based societies no longer necessitated the hunter role as prominently, so the warrior role—a military-like position—developed out of a need to protect societies as they developed. Some

remnants of this masculine role remain today, however, particularly in heavily militarized societies such as the United States.

9. See James Ledbetter's *Unwarranted Influence: Dwight D. Eisenhower and the Military Industrial Complex*, which examines how the US did not abandon its wartime economy after World War II; rather, military spending continued to escalate to a level that continues to shape the US's national politics and the global political landscape.

10. See David Harvey's *A Brief History of Neoliberalism*, which argues that, under neoliberalism, "Competition—between individuals, between firms, between territorial entities (cities, regions, nations, regional groupings)—is held to be a primary virtue" (65).

11. See Harvey for more on neoliberalism. See Louis Hyman's *Temp: The Real Story of What Happened to Your Salary, Benefits, and Job Security* for more on changes to employment wages in the US through the twentieth and twenty-first centuries.

12. Other YA novels that critique masculine silence include but are not limited to Stephen Chbosky's *The Perks of Being a Wallflower* (1999), Ned Vizzini's *It's Kind of a Funny Story* (2006), and Michael Thomas Ford's *Suicide Notes* (2008).

13. Khorram is writing for a primarily Western audience, so he is challenging readers' expectations, but he may also be challenging readers' stereotypes. Persian, Middle Eastern, and Mediterranean cultures have a long history of public baths, particularly in Iran. For more, see "Vakil Bath: National Heritage Site."

WORKS CITED

Adams, Jon Robert. *Male Armor: The Soldier-Hero in Contemporary American Culture*. U of Virginia P, 2008.

Bartky, Sandra Lee. "Foucault, Femininity, and Patriarchal Power." *Writing on the Body: Female Embodiment and Feminist Theory*, edited by Katie Conboy et al., Columbia UP, 1997, pp. 129–54.

Belkin, Aaron. *Bring Me Men: Military Masculinity and the Benign Façade of American Empire 1898–2001*. Hurst, 2012.

Bordo, Susan. *Unbearable Weight: Feminism, Western Culture, and the Body*. U of California P, 1993.

Bronner, Simon J. "Introduction." *Manly Traditions: The Folk Roots of American Masculinities*, edited by Simon J. Bronner, Indiana UP, 2005, pp. xi–xxv.

Brook, Susan. *Literature and Cultural Criticism of the 1950s: The Feeling Male Body*. Palgrave Macmillan, 2007.

Butler, Judith, *Gender Trouble: Feminism and the Subversion of Identity*. Routledge, 2014.

Chapman, Mary, and Glenn Hendler, editors. *Sentimental Men: Masculinity and the Politics of Affect in American Culture*. U of California P, 1999.

Chbosky, Stephen. *The Perks of Being a Wallflower*. Gallery Books, 1999.

Connell, R. W. *Masculinities*. U of California P, 1995.

Davenport, Stephen. "'Road Work': Reading Kerouac's Midcentury Melodrama of Best Sonhood." *Boys Don't Cry? Rethinking Narratives of Masculinity and Emotion in the U.S.*, edited by Milette Shamir and Jennifer Travis, Columbia UP, 2002, pp. 167–84.

Edwards, Tim. *Cultures of Masculinity*. Routledge, 2006.

Ehrenreich, Barbara. "The Decline of Patriarchy." *Constructing Masculinity*, edited by Maurice Berger et al., Routledge, 1995, pp. 284–90.

Ford, Michael Thomas. *Suicide Notes*. HarperTeen, 2008.

Goldstein, Joshua S. *War and Gender: How Gender Shapes the War System and Vice Versa*. Cambridge UP, 2005.

Harvey, David. *A Brief History of Neoliberalism*. Oxford UP, 2005.

hooks, bell. *The Will to Change: Men, Masculinity, and Love*. Washington Square Press, 2004.

Hyman, Louis. *Temp: The Real Story of What Happened to Your Salary, Benefits, and Job Security*. Penguin Books, 2019.

Ibson, John. *The Mourning After: Loss and Longing Among Midcentury American Men*. U of Chicago P, 2018.

Jensen, Kelly. "50 Must-Read YA Books about Mental Illness (Plus a Few More)." *Book Riot*, 2 Oct. 2018, https://bookriot.com/ya-books-about-mental-illness/.

Keen, Sam. *Fire in the Belly: On Being a Man*. Bantam Books, 1991.

Khorram, Adib. *Darius the Great Is Not Okay*. Dial Books, 2018.

Kimmel, Michael S. *Manhood in America: A Cultural History*. 3rd ed., Oxford UP, 2012.

Kimmel, Michael. "Masculinity as Homophobia: Fear, Shame, and Silence in the Construction of Gender Identity." *Toward a New Psychology of Gender: A Reader*, edited by Mary G. Gergen and Sara N. Davis, Routledge, 1997, pp. 223–42.

Ledbetter, James. *Unwarranted Influence: Dwight D. Eisenhower and the Military Industrial Complex*. Yale UP, 2011.

Mangan, J. A. *"Manufactured" Masculinity: Making Imperial Manliness, Morality and Militarism*. Routledge, 2012.

Mosse, George L. "Shell-Shock as a Social Disease." *Exploring Masculinities: Identity, Inequality, Continuity, and Change*, edited by C. J. Pascoe and Tristan Bridges, Oxford UP, 2016, pp. 94–9.

Pascoe, C. J., and Tristan Bridges. "Introduction." *Exploring Masculinities: Identity, Inequality, Continuity, and Change*, edited by C. J. Pascoe and Tristan Bridges, Oxford UP, 2016, pp. 1–34.

Richmond, Kia Jane. "Using Literature to Confront the Stigma of Mental Illness, Teach Empathy, and Break Stereotypes." *Language Arts Journal of Michigan*, vol. 30, no. 1, 2014, pp. 19–25. *LAJM*, https://doi.org/10.9707/2168-149X.2038.

Rutherford, Jonathan. *Men's Silences: Predicaments in Masculinity*. Routledge, 1992.

Schneider, Ryan. "'How to Be a (Sentimental) Race Man': Mourning and Passing in W. E. B. Du Bois's *The Souls of Black Folk*." *Boys Don't Cry? Rethinking Narratives of Masculinity and Emotion in the U.S.*, edited by Milette Shamir and Jennifer Travis, Columbia UP, 2002, pp. 106–23.

Shamir, Milette, and Jennifer Travis, editors. *Boys Don't Cry? Rethinking Narratives of Masculinity and Emotion in the U.S.* Columbia UP, 2002.

Strychacz, Thomas. "'The Sort of Thing You Should Not Admit': Hemingway's Aesthetics of Emotional Restraint." *Boys Don't Cry? Rethinking Narratives of Masculinity and Emotion in the U.S.*, edited by Milette Shamir and Jennifer Travis, Columbia UP, 2002, pp. 141–66.

Travis, Jennifer. *Wounded Hearts: Masculinity, Law, and Literature in American Culture.* U of North Carolina P, 2005.
"Vakil Bath: National Heritage Site." *Apochi*, https://apochi.com/attractions/shiraz/vakil-bath/.
Vizzini, Ned. *It's Kind of a Funny Story.* Hyperion, 2006.
Wicks, Stephen. *Warriors and Wildmen: Men, Masculinity, and Gender.* Bergin and Garvey, 1996.

Part 2

Bibliotherapy and Health Literacy Books

AN INTERVIEW WITH ANNA MACDONALD, GRAPHIC MEDICINE PROJECT MANAGER FOR COMICS YOUTH

SARAH LAYZELL, INTERVIEWER, AND ANNA MACDONALD, INTERVIEWEE

ABOUT COMICS YOUTH

Sarah Layzell (SL): Tell us about Comics Youth and the work you do, especially supporting children's health both inside and outside of medical settings.

Anna Macdonald (AM): Comics Youth CIC (CY) are a small creative community organization from Liverpool in the UK, founded in 2015. We are led by young people, for young people. Our aim is to empower marginalized youth across the Liverpool City Region to flourish, harnessing their own narratives, finding confidence within an inclusive community, and developing the resilience to succeed on their own path.

Comics Youth's mission is to provide creative opportunities for marginalized young people to speak truth to power and have their voices heard by creating a variety of publications about salient community and lived experience issues, as well as providing sessions and events for collaborative learning and friendship building.

Comics are a powerful tool, offering views of worlds that may be real or imagined, familiar or strange. Readers have only to imagine in order to become a part of whatever world has been created by the author. Reading can become a means of self-affirmation, and readers often seek their mirrors in books. Creating our own comics can give us the power to transform our lived experiences and be part of a larger experience.

All our varied projects seek to facilitate the creation of artwork and writing in the form of comic books, zines, blogs, poetry jams, and more, with an aim to elevate underrepresented youth voices on a national scale.

SL: Could you tell us about Marginal Publishing House and how this came about?

AM: Marginal is a revolution in publishing, the first youth-led publisher of its kind in the UK. With it, we want to change the landscape of young people's reading in the UK. We strive to use Marginal as a platform with which to nurture marginalized talent and express a diverse set of voices and experiences which are currently going unheard. Working closely with young creators to help them realize and develop their vision, Marginal aims to publish a diverse collection of books which reflect the full diaspora of identities, backgrounds, experiences, and perspectives of marginalized young people.

We piloted the Marginal Leadership Programme in 2018 as a mentorship initiative which provides underrepresented young people the opportunity to express themselves through the medium of comics, artwork, and writing, with the aim of providing a career pathway within the publishing industry. Young people aged eight to twenty-five are provided with one-to-one coaching, training, mentoring, and guidance in all aspects of publishing, including illustration, character design, writing, business development, and editorial management, so they can harness and build on their own talents and skill sets whilst also corunning the publishing house together.

Marginal seeks to give agency to young people developing narratives that reflect their identities and experiences. In doing so, we want to raise the self-esteem of young creators whilst inspiring them to become a positive point of influence for other marginalized creators to do the same.

SL: How has your work expanded to cover a wide spectrum of social marginalization, and how do you see the organization's work expanding further in future?

AM: As the first organization of its kind in the UK to deliver holistic comics-based literacy and well-being projects for youth, we provide vital, unifying services via a blended model of face-to-face and online youth work. At our core, CY provides support to marginalized youth aged eight to twenty-five, including LGBTQIA+ young people; those experiencing complex trauma and mental ill health; hospitalized youth experiencing acute, chronic, or terminal illness; and young people with neurodivergence, special educational needs, and/or disabilities.

Due to our being such a small team, we know there are areas that we could do more work to expand further into, and we are hoping that we will be able to reach out to more varied communities in the future. As an organization, we are currently going through a restructure period to reimagine the organization and how we can sustain our work into the future in light of the current cost of living crisis.

SL: What are the organization's current projects?

AM: At Comics Youth, we have many different projects on the go, including our Safe Spaces project for LGBTQIA+ young people and our Marginal Publishing House and leadership program. Our current largest project is Graphic Medicine.

There are lots of facets within each project for supporting the people we work with in various ways, but raising the voices and lifting up marginalized youth is at the forefront of everything we do. CY has won multiple national awards for our work.

SL: How have young people responded to and shaped the work you do at Alder Hey Children's Hospital?

AM: The young people that we work with, whether it's on the ward or via digital or face-to-face, one-to-one sessions, always shape the work that we do. We are a very responsive organization, and we cater to the needs of young people first.

When we visit Alder Hey, we never know before we get there which wards we'll be working on, how many young people will be there, how old they are, what conditions they might have, or what even kind of day they have had, so it really keeps us on our toes with how to work with and respond to them. We always come prepared with lots of fun, creative activities that will get them thinking about stories in a unique way, and our aim is always for them to enjoy the session and create something that they are proud of and for them to feel happy.

The Pencil Pals program that we are currently running has been shaped entirely by the sessions themselves and with feedback from the young people. We start each Pencil Pal with an intro chat where we get to know them and find out what their interests are, and then we plan our session plans around catering towards what they are more interested in doing.

Here is some of the wonderful feedback we've had from some of the young people we worked with for *Hospi-Tales* [an anthology of Pencil Pals work]:

"I had a stroke 3 years ago and I went to Alder Hey Hospital. Since it was my right hand that was affected by my stroke I couldn't really draw because it was my dominant hand before, so, Comics Youth taught me how to draw and made comics with me. It made me feel dead happy because I could draw again and bring out my creative side."

"Back in 2019 I met a few members of the comics youth [*sic*] team, and we did drawing and comics which was really fun! I thought I couldn't draw at all but thanks to Comics Youth I've become a lot more confident with my drawing and writing."

Some feedback form responses to "How did you feel after Pencil Pals?" include:

"Happy, relaxed, accepted and heard."
"I loved pencil pals."
"I really enjoyed it, it made me feel happy on the inside."
"I have loved the sessions and wish I could do more."
"I feel so happy, because it was just so fun"

ABOUT *HOSPI-TALES*

SL: Could you explain what Graphic Medicine is and how it supports and gives agency to young people?

AM: Graphic Medicine is a term coined by Dr. Ian Williams to describe "the intersection between the medium of comics and the discourse of healthcare." You can find more information on the Graphic Medicine website (https://www.graphicmedicine.org/).

The Graphic Medicine movement within comics is amazing, but whilst researching for our project, we couldn't find many published stories from the point of view of young people who are currently undergoing treatment or have done recently. Our Graphic Medicine project was founded in 2017, created from our partnership with Alder Hey Children's Hospital and their Arts for Health program, with funding from the National Lottery Community Fund. Alder Hey holds a special place in our hearts, as Comics Youth's Managing Director Rhiannon [Griffiths] spent the first eighteen years of her life traveling to and from Aberystwyth for treatment there. We created the project with Rhiannon's own lived experiences in mind as she had this unique perspective.

Over the past few years, our Graphic Medicine team have had the distinct pleasure to work with young people in a whole host of different departments in the hospital, including oncology, renal, surgical, and many more. We visited these wards with our aim of raising the confidence and voices of young people with lived experiences of acute, chronic, or terminal physical illnesses and also mental ill health. We help them to tell their stories through the medium of comics.

The young people created comics about their experiences of hospital, their illnesses, their day-to-day lives, and sometimes otherworldly and fantastical stories, as a means of fun distraction, education, building literacy and visual storytelling techniques. And we can't not mention the relaxing, self-care benefits of art and writing and the joy being creative brings that is the basis of

INTERVIEW WITH ANNA MACDONALD

Figure 1.1. The cover artwork was created by Maxine Lee Mackie, an artist who worked with Comics Youth during the creation of *Hospi-Tales*. Cover design by Anna Macdonald.

Figure 1.2. A page from *Hospi-Tales*, "Princess Home Alone," created by Riley and illustrated by Maxine Lee Mackie.

the Arts for Health program. Seeing their stories brought to life in *Hospi-Tales* has been a huge confidence boost to the young people involved.

SL: Why was it important to have children as the primary contributors to the *Hospi-Tales* collection?

AM: All the books we create through Marginal are made by young people in some capacity, whether that's contributing their stories to an anthology or being the sole author/illustrator of their own book.

The unique workshops that we did with Alder Hey meant that we were already creating fantastic content, so we decided to collate them into this anthology comic book. Our team of illustrators lovingly crafted each young person's stories into the variety of exciting styles and stunning full color comics that appear within *Hospi-Tales*.

SL: What can child and adult readers (such as healthcare professionals) find in this collection that they would not learn from adults writing on the subject?

AM: Most current Graphic Medicine books of personal experiences are of an adult experiencing them or looking back on their childhood experiences. The Graphic Medicine movement within comics is amazing and all the stories being told are important and moving, but we knew that there was a gap for these important and unique stories.

Reading can promote empathy, and seeing young people in this book have these experiences has potential to have more of an impact on another young reader. Readers of this book, and all the books released by Marginal, will gain a vital insight into the lives of young marginalized people.

SL: Could you tell us a bit about the working relationship between the young people and the illustrators? How were artistic and narrative decisions made?

AM: Our Graphic Medicine team at Comics Youth are youth workers and comic illustrators—we're a talented bunch! We work directly with the young people at the hospital, helping guide them to create their comics and hearing their stories and experiences firsthand. Then we bring all that inspiration back to our office to illustrate the final comics using the young people's drawings, direction, and wishes to create the final comics that appear in the book.

SL: What was behind the decision to structure the anthology by seasons?

AM: We visited the hospital every week over the course of two years, and when we visited during certain seasons, that would be the main topic of conversation. That led us to having some spooky stories for the run up to Halloween and young people dreaming of going away somewhere warm on holiday during the summer.

When we came to curating the order of the stories for the book, they naturally fit into the year format, and we were imagining the book akin to a comic annual such as the *Beano*, that are popular at Christmas time.

SL: What has been the response to the anthology so far? From young people, healthcare providers, other readers?

AM: All the people who have picked up copies of *Hospi-Tales* have a brilliant response to it. The comments we get most often from adults are "how important the work that we are doing is." We have had a lot of interest from the Graphic Medicine academic community, with copies being sent out to the library at Harvard Medical School, where they have a specific section for Graphic Medicine.

The best response though is seeing a young person read it and see themselves in it. I am currently working with a young girl who has a lot of complex issues that has meant she's been in Alder Hey since she was two months old. On hearing about Comics Youth, her mum picked up a copy of *Hospi-Tales*, and she has been bringing it along to all her sessions to show me her favorite comics. She is very excited for her stories to appear in the next book.

As we are only a very small team at Comics Youth, we don't have a dedicated person promoting the books as it's a full-time job in itself. We are slowly but surely getting the books out there and into the hands of the people who will love and appreciate them.

SL: How has your work been affected by the COVID-19 pandemic over the past few years?

AM: When the pandemic first hit in 2020, we had to rapidly change the way that we work to be able to provide remote support to the young people we work with. We created varied and interesting online alternatives for all our regular sessions and many more including multiplayer game servers, our own Discord channels, and a voice-only "stitch and dish" chat.

We obviously had to stop all our visits to Alder Hey Children's Hospital too, and this meant the young people on the wards were even more isolated than ever before. As a quick direct action to this, we created our Pencil Pals program. This provides young people referred to us from the hospital or via self-referral with creative online one-to-one video sessions, one hour per week for eight weeks. This really gave us the opportunity to get to know each young person we worked with better and provide them with more support and further learning opportunities that can be catered to their individual interests—including illustration, sketchbook techniques, comics 101 and in-depth comic making knowledge, creative writing, poetry, storytelling, and more. This program has been such a success that we have kept it even though the lockdown has eased.

As well as providing such varied online support, we also sent out hundreds of creative care packages for young people across the region. Each of our Stay Safe Club packages were free and packed full of thoughtful, mood-lifting treats including art supplies, stickers, and a well-being journal. It also contained a Stay Safe Club T-shirt so that every young person who received it was reminded that they are not alone, but part of a community of like-minded youths experiencing the same thing they are. Stay Safe Club packs contained products created or curated by Comics Youth, intended to help young people de-stress, find calm, get creative, or simply have a little bit of fun in a time when it was in short supply.

Knowing that young people were often struggling to connect online due to school being moved online too, a lot were experiencing video chat burnout, so we created a podcast named "Lockdown at the Disco" so there was a passive way to stay connected with the community even if they were struggling to interact.

The pandemic changed our work in many ways; we are now back to face-to-face session work, but we have kept the online portions as the variable blended model approach has proved to work well with the young people we connect with.

ABOUT LGBTQIA+ YOUTH AND MENTAL HEALTH SUPPORT

SL: What kinds of work do you do with young LGBTQIA+ people?

AM: As a service, we are in a strong position to help tackle the mental health escalation of LGBTQIA+ youth head-on within our region, providing a variety of group work and one-to-one support. We are extremely proactive in ensuring strong working relationships with other targeted services, such as LGBTQIA+ youth groups, universities, social care settings, GP practices, and inpatient settings.

We have many specific projects for LGBTQIA+ young people, but one amazing example was our Safe Spaces social action campaign. We worked with over one hundred LGBTQIA+ young people aged fifteen to twenty-five in the Liverpool City Region to reclaim spaces across the city to create development events/spaces. These cohorts of young people collaborated to create fantastic events such as the launch event for Marginal, a queer arts market, young LGBTQIA+ focused reading groups, sprawling citywide art exhibitions, and open mic events and poetry jams. All along the way learning new important life skills that aren't often taught in a fun way, such as teamwork, planning, budgeting, marketing, events management, and being given the confidence boost of knowing they have the support of our staff to help them achieve their goals.

Comics Youth are not an organization exclusively for LGBTQIA+ youth, like some other specialized youth services within the city, but by having a staff team with relevant lived experiences to the sessions provided, it stands as a testament to how welcomed and how safe we make our space and the variety of the opportunities we provide, that we get so many young people who identify as LGBTQIA+ come to access our services.

SL: Healthcare for trans and gender-diverse youth has been an especially contested issue. What reverberations do you see in your work with young people?

AM: It's becoming increasingly difficult for trans and gender-diverse young people to navigate this world fairly. Just during the time of me writing this up

[May 2024] there's news each week of more and more care and rights being stripped back, which can take an ever-increasing toll.

There are a lot of young people passionate about raising awareness of these issues in the face of all the current hatred, using their lived experiences to encourage and uplift others to find the help they need.

Here are examples of amazing projects and publications that we have helped various cohorts of LGBTQIA+ young people put together over the past two years. First is *Where We Are and Where We Should Be—Shaping a Future for Trans Young People*. We put out a call out for creative young trans, nonbinary, and gender-diverse people across the UK to come together online to create a guidebook to help others navigate through a binary world and the systems around them. They gathered research from many sources, including healthcare experts, academics, and their own lived experiences, which they were able to discuss during the sessions in a safe supportive environment. The resulting book makes a beautiful, creative, thought-provoking, and essential read for young trans and nonbinary people, but is also great for allies to learn how to better support this community.

Speaking of allies, we also have an amazing resource created by another group of LGBTQIA+ young people: *Let's Get This ~~Straight~~: A Guide to Good Allyship*. This project started off as a cohort group for activism named the Queer Agenda. Guided by the young people who felt under pressure to constantly explain themselves and their community, the project became a guidebook to help create better allies by guiding them step by step through the process. Designed with workplaces, clinics, charities, teachers, funders, and more in mind, we held a launch event where the young people who created this project got to talk directly to organizations about their reasons for the book and express how being a good ally can save people's lives. This is a free resource as we wanted it to be available to all: there's no excuse to not be a better ally.

SL: What is the importance of offering creative opportunities for LGBTQIA+ youth? How does this work contribute to the health and well-being of young people?

AM: The act of making art is known to be beneficial to the physical and mental health of individuals, but it doesn't just stop there. Art also raises the voice of young people so that others can hear, see, and feel less alone and be inspired. We started Marginal so we could focus on publishing and promoting a diverse catalog of titles created and developed through various projects within Comics Youth, whether through one of the cohorts mentioned earlier or through our Marginal Leadership Programme where we mentored young people through the creation of their own story, giving them the confidence to succeed and see themselves in an industry that hasn't been made for them.

One success story from our Marginal Leadership Programme was Ray, who was left with no choice but to leave school at age fifteen due to severe bullying. They were already a member of Comics Youth but joined our leadership program to have something to do while being out of school. Ray created a wonderful children's book called *Archie's Grand Plan*, about an anteater who decides he no longer wants to eat ants and wants to start a restaurant so everyone can try some new food, a story about acceptance when someone goes against societal norms and making the world a happier, more accepting place.

Ray's trans identity and also finally receiving an autism diagnosis helped them along this journey; with the mentoring available from Marginal, they found more and more confidence with each step. This led to them getting back into education studying art full time, leading workshops both in person and online, and attending author panels and talks.

We have recently started our Marginal Changemakers project, which has recruited a group of young people who are passionate about making change within the current publishing industry and are trying to break down the walls of mystery and make these career pathways more accessible for marginalized youth.

SL: What are the most hopeful developments you see happening for LGBTQIA+ youth?

AM: There are so many young people passionate about raising awareness of theirs and others' lived experiences in this current climate where standing up and standing out can be a dangerous and brave thing to do. We are here to guide and support them in the best way we know how, with creativity.

This interview has been edited for clarity and length.

WORKS CITED

Hospi-Tales: A Year of Stories from Alder Hey. Marginal, 2022.
Lowthian, Ray. *Archie's Grand Plan*. Marginal, 2023.
The Queer Agenda. *Let's Get This ~~Straight~~: A Guide to Good Allyship*. Marginal, 2023.
Where We Are and Where We Should Be: Shaping A Future for Trans Young People. Marginal, 2023.
Williams, Ian. "What Is 'Graphic Medicine'?" *Graphic Medicine*, https://www.graphicmedicine.org/why-graphic-medicine/.

DEALING WITH DEMENTIA

Patients and Their Caregivers in German Picturebooks

FARRIBA SCHULZ AND ANTJE TANNEN

Since about 2004, picturebooks published in German have been meeting a need for stories portraying dementia and offering insights to a young readership on the challenges of living with this condition. These developments coincide with and aim to promote its social relevance, in the same way that government alliance projects such as the National Dementia Strategy were designed to call attention to and raise awareness about the disease. In this context, the German Federal Ministry for Family Affairs, Senior Citizens, Women and Youth published a special multilingual edition of Rika Papp's Pixi-book *Lilli und ihre vergessliche Oma* (*Lilli and Her Forgetful Granny*) in 2015 in cooperation with the publishing house Carlsen. This small picturebook informs readers about the daily challenges of an elderly woman affected by dementia and the family members taking care of her. At the same time, the picturebook provides individual coping strategies. This literary example both seems to visualize objectives that are in line with the National Dementia Strategy regarding measures taken to improve the living situation of people with dementia and their relatives and also seems to foster understanding and sensitivity to the issue in our society.

By now a wide range of picturebooks approach this issue from a highly literary perspective to mediate narratively and metaphorically what life is like for people affected by dementia. A number of them depict the quality improvements suggested by the National Dementia Strategy to support the living conditions of people with dementia. Some other narratives—known as "burden narratives"—might reflect a persistent stigmatized idea of dementia as a burden (Hartung 175), but still others might even have the potential to take a stand against the "Othering" of elderly people with dementia by building counternarratives, often through the perspective of a child. In this chapter we examine how characters with dementia are represented in picturebooks and how relationships with informal and formal caregivers are constructed. We ask the following questions: What is told about the person with dementia? What is told about their relationships to formal and informal caregivers?

Based on these guiding questions, we will discuss the potential of the selected picturebooks for use in health education (of affected families as well as medical professionals) and an appreciation of elderly people with dementia within the general reading public. We specifically seek to analyze the books with attention to whether these books support master narratives of dementia or instead introduce counternarratives. The analysis is based on Vanessa Joosen's theoretical framework for understanding the construction of childhood and adulthood, as well as Hanne Laceulle's statement that counternarratives can take a stand against social silencing. Furthermore, we draw from theories about the person-centered care approach to meeting the needs of people with dementia, along with concepts of narrative pedagogy (using literature in medical education) and bibliotherapy (using literature to support patients and their families coping with the disease). Research on fictional narratives exploring dementia clarifies the social and cultural relevance of counternarratives.

Despite the existing work relating to age studies and literary studies, research such as that carried out by Elizabeth F. Caldwell et al. has only just begun to address dementia in children's literature. In the following, we will address this gap by exploring the impact of picturebooks on public discourse, healthcare education about dementia, and bibliotherapy to foster sympathetic care.

REPRESENTATION OF AGE AND ILLNESS IN CHILDREN'S LITERATURE

According to Susan Sontag, diseases—especially those which have not been fully researched—have the potential to be mystified. Just as Sontag describes the metaphorical uses of tuberculosis and cancer to show the cultural construction of the disease, so dementia seems to be comparable in its discourse: not fully understood, highly present, not yet curable, likely relevant for the elderly and those close to death. As Heike Hartung traces the discourse on dementia back to the nineteenth century, where the disease was linked to silence and its diagnosis often led to being admitted to a mental asylum, she explains the cultural fears associated with the disease in its historical dimensions as well as in its current social significance and perception (Hartung 172). "Dementia discourse as a crisis narrative, which affects the meanings and social constructions of old age, is related to the concept of 'risk,'" Hartung states (175). This concept envisages a substantial likelihood that any older person might develop dementia and reinforces stigmas and fears. Accordingly, the construction of dementia follows a social marginalization. It seems to represent what Hanne Laceulle phrases in her cultural-philosophical critique on *Aging and Self-Realization* as "everything late modern people fear about aging: loss of independence, autonomy, self-determination, control, and ultimately one's self" (80). Rebecca A. Bitenc documents the marginalization of the disease and those affected by it in *Reconsidering Dementia Narratives: Empathy, Identity and Care*, noting common descriptions of dementia and people with dementia, such as "losing one's self," "death before death," a "funeral without end," "ghosts of their former selves," "long gone," or even a "monsterizing of senility." Bitenc is not the only researcher who has raised concerns about the use of metaphors that label dementia as a threat and influence on personal identity. Martina Zimmermann argues in *The Diseased Brain and the Failing Mind: Dementia in Science, Medicine and Literature of the Long Twentieth Century* that "[l]iving with the disease and its label for an extended period can be acceptable for patients and their caregivers only when the label Alzheimer's no longer spoils the individual's social identity" (143). Amanda Grenier points out that "older people in this category become socially and culturally 'othered'—both from society and within groups of older people" (174). Against this form of social silencing, counternarratives should offer other social recognition by providing insights into the last phase of life, the Fourth Age, where illness such as dementia is highly possible.

Characteristics of a counternarrative, according to Laceulle, are as follows:

- it has to replace as well as to resist an oppressive master narrative
- it should set out to rehabilitate damaged identities
- it should deliberately cause a shift in the cultural understanding of a certain group, rather than just reflecting a shift. (73)

While fictional narratives exploring dementia have already received considerable critical attention (see Bitenc; Folkmarson et al.; Hartung; Jerónimo; Zimmermann), little research has been conducted on dementia in children's literature. Owing to the fact that children's literature, especially picturebooks, is read to children by adults, counternarratives can contribute to an intergenerational dialogue, foster understanding and sensitivity to the issue in our society, and (re)form opinions.

We follow the important preparatory work of Joosen's and Marah Gubar's research, which constructs a logical relation between age studies and childhood studies and applies the results of the analysis to children's literature. Whereas Gubar focuses on the construction of childhood through adulthood in *Artful Dodgers: Recovering the Golden Age of Children's Literature,* Joosen analyzes the construction of adulthood as a stage of life to investigate the construction of adult characters in children's literature. Their perspectives on the construction of adulthood in relation and opposition to childhood are especially important for our analysis. Characterizing childhood and adulthood "on the basis of affinity and complementarity" (Joosen 79), where the young are empowered through the old, is a common trope in children's literature. In this connection, elderly characters can be seen as wise counterparts to child characters; then again, children's literature knows "the puer senex trope," which links youth and senescence, aged and young characters, based on innocence and juvenileness, as Joosen shows. In this context the grandparent bonding with the grandchild is presented in children's literature as a form of "second childhood" and connects Romantic images of the child and the elderly figure, both associated with attributes such as creativity, spontaneity and freedom and denial of an adult status (Joosen 183). This sort of relationship creates also a "special bond" between the child and the elderly character, which makes the parents' generation look incompetent. Based on this, Zimmermann argues that the grandchildren's perspective provides an extremely important source of information, which "emphasizes the patient's continued abilities rather than losses; its [the perspective emphasizing the patient's continued abilities] limited availability then reflects the origin of (and reason for) the popular beliefs about dementia in the early 1980s" (Zimmermann 74).

To allow us to distinguish between a master and counternarrative, we will especially focus on the construction of intergenerational relationships and the mediation of the disease. As the relationship of the patient and his/her caregiver in picturebooks is narrated metaphorically between concepts of youth and age as well as between illness and sanity, metaphors can be read as cultural markers. Children's literature familiarizes children with the world, mediates general knowledge, and introduces and enforces values and ideas of society (see Reynolds). Looking at picturebooks, the cultural framework in which the story is situated is embodied in the constellation of characters, which reveals relations of the literary figure to their (social) environment in a visual and linguistic layer. To examine the representations of characters affected by dementia in picturebooks from a literary point of view, we combine different approaches to perceive the "certain functions they fulfill and meanings they convey" (Eder et al. 6). The hermeneutic approach will allow us to define the different characters as humanlike beings, and the cultural or sociological approach will allow us to understand characters as signs. The aesthetic strategies used in the selected picturebooks inform the reader explicitly and implicitly about the characters' corporality, psyche, and social relations. Between words and pictures, the characters' depiction is expanded through colors, design, and placement and symbolizes its relations to their (social) environment. Beyond that, the analysis of social relationships, values, hierarchies, and functions "is closely connected to questions of ideology, politics, and understanding texts as indicators of collective dispositions, problems, wishes and fears in a certain time and culture," as Jens Eder et al. state (27). This perspective will allow us to link extra-literary and scientific discourses, knowledge of dementia, and changed perceptions of the disease. With these modified and different narrative constructions, we gain literary figures and motifs in the picturebooks in order to understand the construction of the relationships between characters with dementia and their informal and formal caregivers.

DEMENTIA AND THE ROLE OF PICTUREBOOKS IN HEALTHCARE

As of now, there is no effective therapy for healing dementia, but there is a lot of evidence about the emotional needs of the patients, useful support, and coping strategies, as well as person-centered approaches in the care of people with dementia (see Deutsches Netzwerk). To have a better understanding of the subject, we briefly outline in the following section what is known about the epidemiology and symptoms of the disease and what treatment strategies are recommended.

Among the elderly population, dementia is the most diagnosed neuropsychiatric disease, and due to the demographic transition of western societies, the prevalence of dementia has been rising in recent decades. Among the population above sixty-five years of age, a prevalence of between 5–8 percent is estimated, and among the elderly above ninety years, the prevalence is about 30 percent (Robert Koch Institut). The generic term "dementia" includes different forms according to different causes. The most common form is Alzheimer's dementia (50–75 percent of all dementias) due to degenerative processes. The rest are vascular or other forms of dementia (Robert Koch Institut).

Usually, the development of dementia is classified in mild, average severe, and severe stages, independently of the form (Robert Koch Institut). The beginning of dementia is characterized by memory loss, difficulties in concentrating, and mistakes in judging situations. Patients often try to compensate and to hide their cognitive impairments. Because the beginning of the disease is not easy to define, it can be difficult to accept the diagnosis, for the relatives as well as for the patients. While a person may live alone without caring services in the early stages of dementia, this changes as the disease advances. The symptoms someone experiences (which may manifest more as cognitive impairment or as changes in social behavior) depend upon the damaged brain area. In an average severe stage, the patients recognize their disability in the course of everyday activities and depend on the assistance of formal or informal caregivers (e.g., nursing services or family members). They often show depressive symptoms as a reaction to their cognitive impairments. In later severe stages the patients' capability for verbal communication declines very fast (Robert Koch Institut), so they may experience problems communicating their pain, feelings, or needs. Additionally, they are likely to develop increasing difficulties with cognitive and physical abilities. Permanent nursing services are then required to ensure that the needs of the person living with dementia are being met.

Considering the progress as well as the highly individual course of the patient's disease, we now briefly describe required healthcare structures for people with dementia and their families. As healthcare systems differ internationally, we focus on the German situation.

Like the majority (76 percent) of care-dependent persons in Germany, most patients with dementia are cared for at home, receiving money from their health and long-term care insurance ("Gesundheit: Pflege"). The familiar environment and the opportunity to manage daily tasks can help people with dementia maintain functional and cognitive skills. In later stages, admission to nursing homes can become necessary; occasionally, alternative care structures, like shared houses for people with dementia, can be found. Even though family members are the most important persons for people with dementia, the healthcare system offers hardly any effective psychosocial support services and information for families. Coping with the disease and the related challenges is mainly left to the affected families, most often to women. As there is no effective drug therapy, the affected patients and their families have to deal with the symptoms of the disease—such as losing the ability to orient, understand, and judge—along with changed emotional and social behavior. Especially when the "challenging behavior" of the person with dementia increases, relationships can be disturbed, and the psychological and physical burden for the informal caregivers grows (Robert Koch Institut). The healthcare system and its health professionals therefore need to offer professional support to and maintain necessary resources for informal caregivers. Some of this gap in available support material might be filled by picturebooks.

However, caring for people with dementia is not only a question of where (at home or in long-term care institutions) but also of how. An established approach in dementia care is the humanistic concept of *person-centered care*, first developed by Tom Kitwood in the 1980s (Welling). All caring activities should be focused on the person and their needs, not on the disease or their therapy. The main features of this concept can be summarized by talking to and about the person to construct a picture of how the individuals see themselves, of how others see them, of their routines, and of their hopes for the future (see Peate et al.). The current German nursing guidelines for dementia emphasize the importance of a person-centered and relationship-based care

(Deutsches Netzwerk). According to these guidelines, it is more important *how* something is done than *what* is done, specifically for the person with dementia. In this approach, nurses need to focus on the reconstruction of biographical events and observe behavioral patterns to create a living environment, which is tailored to the patients' needs. The patient should be considered as an individual rather than as a medical problem. Implementing a person-centered and therefore an accepting attitude toward the patient's behavior requires new approaches.

Traditionally the healthcare system has been characterized by a rational and scientifically oriented culture. Healthcare professionals usually do not use picturebooks in their daily practice, but there are some approaches that show a positive effect of bibliotherapy on medical care for children (Babarro Vélez and Lacalle Prieto).[1] *Bibliotherapy* is a term broadly used for interventions using literature to support people finding solutions for their problems (see Forgan). The use of literature in a healthcare context varies broadly from its use in psychotherapy up to "reading therapy" or "story-telling" as part of (pediatric) nursing (see Robinson). The use of literature can foster understanding and problem-solving processes concerning issues relevant to the patient. Stories about characters dealing with chronic conditions illustrate new approaches to handling the situation, especially when the stories are presented by healthcare professionals (see Tielsch-Goddard). Reading stories about chronic diseases to children may create communicative situations in which children can express their feelings and speak their minds about their or others' health (see Kurkjian and Livingston).

Using children's literature—written in their particular language, told from a child's (or another nonprofessional's) perspective, and using the power of illustration—in medical education to train healthcare professionals can help them to understand the patient's perspective and therefore develop empathy and ultimately foster an accepting attitude toward the patient's behavior. This kind of *narrative pedagogy*, which is also realized by using art, film, music, storytelling, or journaling, is a humanistic educational approach pursued as an alternative to the traditional teacher-centered learning approaches in medical education. Additionally, using narratives in scientific lectures and clinical experiences brings in "society's perception of illness and the cultural construction of disease" (Brown et al. 284). In addition to showing the societal perception of illness, learning about individual perspectives and experiences can complement the expert-centered focus found in medical education. Patient stories told in picturebooks are "presented from the patient's frame of references, focusing on the personal meaning of illness or change, its significance within the context of individual patient's life" (Crawley 36). Considering the individual perspective plays an important role in the concept of person-centered care, which is also often recommended and implemented in the gerontological context of healthcare for persons with dementia, as mentioned above.

After outlining the current discourses about representation of age and illness in children's literature, findings about dementia, and possible healthcare applications of children's literature, three questions can be asked for evaluating picturebooks dealing with dementia:

1. Which counternarratives can be found in the picturebooks?
2. Which picturebooks would be suitable for supporting patients and their families?
3. Which picturebooks would be useful in nursing education?

METHODS

The picturebooks included in our research are currently in active circulation in public library systems in Germany. To get a general idea of the range of available picturebooks depicting elderly people with dementia, three leading German literature databases—those of the AJUM, the Staatsbibliothek zu Berlin, and the association of public libraries in Berlin—were browsed using the keywords "dementia" and "Alzheimer*." The two authors of this chapter read and reviewed these picturebooks closely and independently, representing two different scientific perspectives: literary studies (FS) and nursing and health science (AT). Afterward, we discussed our findings, pointing out common representations of dementia-related phenomena or strategies that were used to illustrate the content. Finally, all reviewed picturebooks were arranged into a framework with inductively built concepts drawn from the included books, such as symptoms of dementia portrayed in the book or information for health educators (see table 2.1).

Table 2.1: Overview of Analyzed Picturebooks

Concept	Content	Books mentioning	Total
Gender of the main characters	male patient	Baltscheit, Unterholzner, Barth, Welsh, Elschner, John	6
	female patient	Huppertz, Steinkeller, Papp, Nilsson, Müller, Van den Vendel, Baumbach, Van den Abeele, Shepherd, Plieth, Robben, Kratzke, Langston	13

(Continued)

Table 2.1: Overview of Analyzed Picturebooks. (*Continued*)

Concept	Content	Books mentioning	Total
Setting	patient living at home	Baltscheit, Huppertz, Steinkeller, Unterholzner, Barth, Papp, Nilsson, Müller, Van den Vendel, Baumbach, Van den Abeele, Welsh, John, Robben, Langston	15
	patient living in a nursing home	Shepherd, Elschner, Plieth, Kratzke	4
Symptoms of dementia portrayed in the book	changes in communicating and language	Baltscheit, Huppertz, Van den Vendel, Robben, Langston	5
	memory loss	Baltscheit, Steinkeller, Unterholzner, Barth, Papp, Nilsson, Müller, Van den Vendel, Baumbach, Van den Abeele, Shepherd, Welsh, Plieth, John, Robben, Kratzke, Langston	17
	changes in behavior	Baltscheit, Steinkeller, Unterholzner, Barth, Nilsson, Müller, Baumbach, Van den Abeele, Welsh, Plieth, John	11
	aggression	Unterholzner, Papp, Nilsson, Shepherd	4
	wandering	Baumbach	1
	apathy, depression and anxiety	Barth, Nilsson, Müller, Elschner, Plieth, Kratzke	6
Type of care and caring relationship	formal care	Steinkeller, Papp, Shepherd, Elschner, Plieth	5
	informal care	Baltscheit, Huppertz, Steinkeller, Unterholzner, Barth, Papp, Van den Vendel, Baumbach, Van den Abeele, Shepherd, Welsh, Elschner, Plieth, John, Kratzke, Langston	16
Information for health educators	patient-centered approach: helping them to make active choices	Baltscheit, Steinkeller, Unterholzner, Papp, Nilsson, Van den Vendel, Baumbach, Shepherd, Elschner, Langston	10
	patient-centered approach: tailoring the care to the needs of the person	Baltscheit, Steinkeller, Unterholzner, Barth, Papp, Nilsson, Müller, Van den Vendel, Baumbach, Van den Abeele, Shepherd, Welsh, Elschner, Plieth, John, Robben, Langston	17

(*Continued*)

Table 2.1: Overview of Analyzed Picturebooks. (*Continued*)

Concept	Content	Books mentioning	Total
	patient-centered approach: ensuring carers have proper training in communication and coping skills	Papp, Shepherd, Plieth, Robben	4

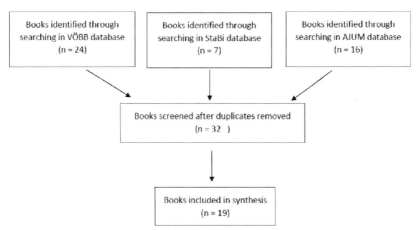

Figure 2.1. Numbers of available and included picturebooks, status as of February 2020. Image by Farriba Schulz and Antje Tannen.

After removing duplicates, a total of thirty-two books remained from the three databases. We excluded thirteen books because they had no focus on dementia, they were not written or translated in German, or because they were not picturebooks. Nineteen picturebooks were included in the final analysis (see figure 2.1).

DEMENTIA IN PICTUREBOOKS: IS THERE A POTENTIAL FOR COUNTERNARRATIVES?

Browsing through the picturebook selection, it stands out that thirteen of the nineteen main characters affected by dementia are female, which coincides with the figures given by the Federal Ministry for Family Affairs, Senior Citizens, Women and Youth (7). Conforming with the figures for patients cared for at home, the majority of characters (fifteen out of nineteen) are portrayed as living in a home care setting. Furthermore, the presence and the development of a broad variation of dementia symptoms are described in the books, as are different approaches that contribute to a person-centered care and accepting attitude (see table 2.1). As memory loss is often one of the first signs of dementia, one of the most commonly described symptoms in the picturebooks is the difficulties characters are experiencing in relation to the loss of memory (seventeen out of nineteen), such as struggling to find the right word or getting lost. Almost as commonly described are changes in behavior (eleven out of nineteen). The diversity of approaches envisaged in the books reflects not only the diversity of persons affected with dementia but also the importance of considering their individual needs (see table 2.1).

The selection of picturebooks provides different perspectives on the disease, involving a number of different psychosocial and care-related components like stress management, access to healthcare, and people's challenging behavior. As long as there is no drug therapy available to heal the dementia, relatives and caregivers have to accept the situation and increase pleasurable activities to improve people's living situations and quality of life. This is what a lot of the selected picturebooks demonstrate. For this reason, these picturebooks could effectively serve caregivers in finding ways to help patients make active choices, tailor care addressing the needs of the person, and improve communication and coping skills.

As a common symptom of dementia, memory loss plays a prominent role in recognition of the disease in the early stages and is often negotiated in the picturebooks, though from different angles. But instead of only focusing on cognitive deficits, the stories tell about the older person's selfhood, their lives and legacies. As the characters are not being reduced to their medical history, the picturebooks align with the German nursing guidelines for dementia and could serve as counternarratives to the dominant narrative in society in which the construction of dementia primarily follows a social marginalization and tells a story of loss and decline. Author Birgit Unterholzner and illustrator Leonora Leitl's picturebook *Auf meinem Rücken wächst ein Garten* (*There Is a Garden Growing on My Back*) (2016) and author Nikola Huppertz and illustrator Elsa Klever's *Meine Omi, die Wörter und ich* (*My Granny, the Words and Me*) (2017) are excellent examples of such counternarratives that could shift the cultural understanding of people living with dementia.

Unterholzner and Leitl's *Auf meinem Rücken wächst ein Garten* does not narrate a coherent story with a linear plot but offers story fragments. These illustrate different facets of Grandpa Friedel, the way he experiences dementia, and how his surrounding society responds to it. Consistent with the narrative structure, the visual technique of collage refers to the complexity of the grandfather's selfhood, which seems to peel away, piece by piece. His grandson

Fido acts out the role of the narrator while characterizing and at the same time assisting his grandpa. Sentences in bold lettering—such as "Grandpa collects treasures," "Grandpa goes for a walk at night," "Grandpa is a chicken" or "Grandpa misses a bit his cues"[2]—can be regarded as headlines (Unterholzner), which structure the picturebook in different chapters of Grandpa Friedel's experiences seen through his grandson Fido's eyes.

Introduced as a collector of treasures in the form of books about insects and birds, old newspapers, a comb, bicycle tubes, light bulbs, coffee filters and so on, Grandpa Friedel is illustrated with a crown on his head, enthroned as a king among the treasures on his bed. Gradually, another truth emerges: "His bed is filled to the brim," the text informs us (Unterholzner), while the illustration presents him sitting huddled up among his collection. In other words, there is no room left for him because of his great collection. One might interpret the scene as a mess, whereas Fido might see Grandpa Friedel's collection as rich and a treasure trove to play with. The perspective makes the difference. Fido and his grandfather's relationship is presented as what a patient-centered approach could look like: accompanying him on all his endeavors; finding out in which situations he feels comfortable; learning what he needs and helping him realize it; all while responding to his challenging behavior calmly.

In both text and images, the picturebook characterizes Fido as a well-informed caregiver. He knows about his grandfather's disease, mostly by observing his behavior, just as he knows about things that make him smile. With an unbiased approach, Fido bonds with his grandfather through acts such as inventing lists of mood-lifters in writing, which meets the needs of both. Fido can improve his writing skills, while making a list helps Grandpa Friedel to remember. The illustration portrays Grandpa Friedel's fragments of selfhood within his handwriting, silhouetted against a cloudy and foggy background. On the level of content, Fido and Friedel are presented as equal. While Fido's list contains "a collection of marbles," "words beginning with R like rainbow" and "hanging headfirst on a branch," Grandpa Friedel's list includes "walking on clouds," "singing and shafts of sunlight" and "cows, which look as if they would be called Mizzi" (Unterholzner). Accordingly, the illustration gives a clear idea of their mutual understanding on the basis of creativity, spontaneity, and freedom: both are portrayed hanging headfirst off a branch, wearing white-and-blue-striped shirts. The image is also inscribed with the words "snotty-nosed brat" in block letters (Unterholzner), emphasizing that Fido and Friedel are both pictured in their childhood—the grandfather clearly in his second.

Reading this picturebook, one could gain a good impression of some aids and strategies that might help caregivers who are confronting the difficulties people with dementia experience. Among other strategies, for example, Fido inscribes the grandfather's door with his name: "Here lives Friedel, the vagrant minstrel" (Unterholzner). By labeling his environment, Fido helps his grandfather with his memory problems. Assisting his grandfather to hold on to his selfhood might also signify a wish to hold on to a person, in order to record and shape his life story and slow the disappearance of Friedel's selfhood through "cognitive declines (e.g., memory, judgment, thinking, learning, orientation, language, comprehension or calculation)" (Reilly and Hung 268). At the same time, the reader learns about how Grandpa Friedel experiences the changes in his own behavior and how others perceive them. Being well aware that his neighbor is afraid of him, Grandpa Friedel describes his state of mind as follows: "Everything spins around me. People, things, memories. I've lost orientation, I am not really good for anything. My brain is as small as a pea" (Unterholzner). Accordingly, the illustration shows Friedel without any outlines, translucent in a forest of beanstalks, appearing lost. The only thing that marks him is a small pea sitting in his head instead of his brain. Throughout the book, Fido stays with his grandfather, accompanies him, lends him a hand, but most importantly, spends time with him. By doing so, Fido gets to know his grandfather, while his grandfather is passing on his legacy. "There is a garden growing on my back. Pick the most beautiful flowers, Fido," the grandfather offers (Unterholzner). The grandfather's legacy is built upon the sum of his life's accomplishments and the treasures he collected. Fido is provided with the opportunity to grow and allowed to choose freely. The picturebook conveys a complex and multi-perspective image with facets of different experiences; it even creates a sense of what it feels like to relate to someone affected by dementia. It outlines the challenges but also highlights the many positive and happy moments. Presenting the "special bond" between Fido and Friedel, the story emphasizes the grandfather's "continued abilities" and the legacy Fido is cherishing and serves in this way as a good example of counternarratives (Zimmermann 74).

Huppertz and Klever's *Meine Omi, die Wörter und ich* also picks up the idea of a legacy. In this picturebook, the main character's accomplishment is already introduced at the beginning. The narrator, Mio, thinks his grandmother is responsible for teaching him his first word and further playing a main role in his natural language acquisition. He describes her as someone who is hosting words and elaborates, "The words were everywhere. My granny called out for them, dug them out for me, and soon they took over so much space that it seemed as if the small room transformed into a great big palace" (Huppertz). The linguistic universe the grandmother creates for Mio spreads on a double page illustration in a panoramic representation of terms. Portraying the grandmother and her grandchild among pictures of a robot, car, bird, fish, pencil, watermelon, key, and sun creates what Jerome Bruner describes as a "predictable format of interaction that can serve as a microcosm for communicating and constituting a shared reality" (Bruner 31). The grandmother shares words in different contexts from various word categories—loud and wild, quiet and shy, cheerful and even fearful words such as "shipwreck," "thunder night" and "chattering of teeth" (Huppertz). Therefore, Mio's grandmother not only communicates her understanding of the world but also shares with him how to cope with the complexity of language. Growing up, Mio acquires the meaning of words in their functional role as mediated through conversations with and stories from his grandmother.

Referring to this communication- and usage-based perspective, Mio tries to help his grandmother as soon as he realizes that she doesn't use her vocabulary anymore. Again, the narration uses the analogy of the room visually and textually, only this time presenting an emptied room that becomes wordless and finally silent. In contrast to her previous role as a wordsmith, the grandmother is shown sitting on a table accompanied by a few last remnants. Surrounding autumn leaves signify an upcoming end. Now it is Mio's turn to fill his grandmother's empty room by sharing his words with her. Unfortunately, the words Mio wants to share concern topics that the grandmother is unfamiliar with, such as "videogames," "marshmallow blasters," "chicken nuggets" and the denotative term "memory cards." Due to Alzheimer's disease symptoms, the grandmother isn't able to encode these new memories her grandson shares with her (Reilly and Hung 270). Mio informs the reader, "My granny glanced at [the words] without any comprehension" (Huppertz), while the illustration shows disappointed and sad faces on the left and outlined objects that the grandmother could not attach to anything familiar at the right. In this transition, silence also becomes a sign of the transformation from youth to age and from health to illness. Even though the picturebook does not provide strategies for how to cope with the grandmother's problems with verbal communication, the narrator Mio reminds the reader of the grandmother's significant role in her grandchild's life. When, right before she dies, the grandmother remembers her grandson's name, she conceptualizes it physically as the result of her advanced dementia. The text informs the reader about this strategy as it follows: "Slowly she took the word in her bony fingers. She turned it back and forth, examined it tenderly and put it in my hand. Mio." This word summarizes the grandmother's legacy, which is pictured as a realm of words in which Mio grew up. This picturebook has the potential to take a stand against "othering" of persons with dementia by focusing on the person's importance for society through the perspective of the grandchild. The character of Mio's grandmother is not reduced to the status of bystander but socially recognized.

As most of the picturebook stories are told from a grandchild's perspective, the central role of the intergenerational relationship between the person living with dementia and their family members becomes more than clear. As mentioned before, a familiar environment can not only be beneficial for people with dementia but also represents the most important support, along with family members in their role of caregivers. The majority of the books represent female informal caregivers, corresponding to the reality in informal care of dependent patients (Robert Koch Institut). In author Elisabeth Steinkeller and illustrator Michael Roher's picturebook *Die neue Omi (The New Grandmother)* (2011), granddaughter Fini has a close relationship with her grandmother and is involved in care when the grandmother moves into the family's home. Fini's mother expects Fini to take on responsibilities and gets angry when Fini leaves her grandmother out of sight. Fini's capability might be her unbiased manner toward her grandmother's changed living situation (from an independent and mobile woman into a person who needs help from others), but the responsibility for the well-being of a person with dementia exceeds the ability of a small girl. Therefore, Agatha, a formal caregiver, enters the family to assist the grandmother professionally and reduce the family's pressure and burden. With different insights into everyday life situations, *Die neue Omi* introduces the reader to the daily tasks a caregiver undertakes and presents moments in which Fini observes, assists, and follows Agatha's example for home care. The illustration depicts, for instance, Agatha washing, bathing, and dressing the grandmother in a sensitive and tactful way. Everybody is smiling, and the grandmother is clearly enjoying the help. Through Fini's eyes, the picturebook introduces the reader with several big questions regarding the home care situation of a person affected by dementia, especially what person-centered care in daily living and getting professional support could look like. Supporting a family member affected with dementia at home entails a number of challenges. Alongside familiar surroundings and relationships, the organization and management of daily care such as dressing, washing, and eating have a great impact on the well-being of persons with dementia—a key issue highlighted in the picturebook. Beyond this, the grandmother's needs for privacy might be considered by choosing caregivers of the same gender (her daughter, her granddaughter, and Agatha), since washing and bathing can be very private activities ("Dementia Symptoms"). The picturebook *Die neue Omi* mediates different approaches of creating positive experiences for the person with dementia and gives an example on how to adapt to the situation as a family.

Since the person with dementia is experiencing profoundly unsettling changes, improving their living situation by preserving the person's abilities and considering all of their feelings is essential. In one of the selected picturebooks, the diagnosis is specified as Alzheimer's dementia, while in the other books the dementia diagnoses aren't specified. In Papp's multilingual[3] Pixi-book *Lilli und ihre vergessliche Oma*, the grandchild Lilli reports on her experiences with her grandmother, who lives with dementia, and how she and her family have found ways to cope with the challenges:

> When my grandmother can't remember or can't manage, she's becoming sometimes angry or sad. I know that doesn't have anything to do with me. Nevertheless, I do not understand the way she's behaving. I then speak with my mum about it. I've recognized that my granny calms down when I sing for her. Mum believes that granny makes us real singers. After all mum and dad are now singing more often for her. (Papp)

While the changes in behavior can be challenging and hard to cope with for the person living with dementia and their caregivers alike, a better understanding of the person with dementia can lead to the support they need.

This aspect is also addressed by author Géraldine Elschner and illustrator Jonas Lauströer's picturebook *Der alte Schäfer* (*The Old Shepherd*) (2011), especially when depicting a successful implementation of animal-assisted intervention. Herr Grimm (Mr. Fierceness), a former shepherd struggling with anxiety, aggression, and apathy due to dementia, experiences relief from his aggression when his nursing home integrates sheep on-site and in their program. Lauströer's illustrations highlight the therapeutic effect of animal therapy using visual and linguistic layers. Residents pictured as sheep, sheep comforting the protagonist while he is falling asleep, clouds shaped as sheep, and actively bouncing sheep demonstrate Herr Grimms's emotional state of mind and transformation to an active and even-tempered resident. When Anton encounters Herr Grimm while visiting his grandfather in the nursing home, his grandfather's explanation convinces him to take action: "In the past Herr Grimm has been always outdoors, in the nature, with his sheep. . . . Herr Grimm was a shepherd. Now it's hard for him to live here, locked up in this institution" (Elschner). As soon as Herr Grimm has the opportunity to contribute his knowledge and abilities to tending sheep, his mood lightens, and he opens up by telling stories from his past. Supporting Herr Grimm in this way shows an immediate calming effect on him and creates an environment that increases the quality of life for every home resident. "The home residents would often come together, bring a piece of dry bread and sit by," the picturebook informs the reader (Elschner). Alongside the person-centered approach, the depiction of the influence of human-animal relationship proves to be very valuable. Interacting and bonding with an animal can contribute to the well-being of the person affected by dementia, emotionally and socially. This coincides with research results of animal-assisted intervention, which document rising levels of oxytocin in both humans and animals and an increase in activity (see Hediger et al.; Kårefjärd and Nordgren). This literary example of including sheep on the nursing site clearly represents an individual response to the needs of a person living with dementia and shows an effective way of managing behavioral symptoms of dementia. In the framework of counternarratives, Elschner and Lauströer's *Der alte Schäfer* resists the narrative of loss and decline by considering Herr Grimm's individual biography and his personal needs and preferences. Illustrating person-centered care, the picturebook sets an example by raising understanding and encouraging change in help provision. This picturebook, with its appreciation of elderly people with dementia, demonstrates how quality of life is related to the richness of interactions and relationships and is therefore not only suitable for supporting families but also useful in nursing education.

Although the elderly characters affected by dementia in the selected picturebooks form a heterogeneous group that receive different coping strategies to meet their individual needs, the picturebooks reflect a general expectation of a white middle-class readership. This points to a gap in diverse and inclusive representation of characters and their families affected by dementia. Furthermore, a lack of access to healthcare is not mentioned. Such coping strategies consider the dementia-affected person's expertise, competences, former interests, and actual needs. Simplifying routines, providing reassurance, and involving the person in activities are just a few pieces of advice on coping with changes in behavior ("Dementia Symptoms"). Within the selected picturebooks, these compensatory interests and activities range from singing, playing the piano, and baking apple pies to tending sheep.

THE VALUE OF PICTUREBOOKS ABOUT DEMENTIA IN HEALTHCARE

With this interdisciplinary approach, we intended to address the overlapping concepts of age studies, literary studies, and health sciences represented in picturebooks dealing with dementia. The encounter with the disease and the depicted symptoms, the character's selfhood and its transformation, and the formal and informal caregiving relationships were of special interest to us, not least to evaluate which picturebooks would be suitable and helpful for the use in healthcare contexts—especially in patient or nursing education. Following the concept of counternarratives, we were focused on those picturebooks that have the potential to "resist an oppressive master narrative," "rehabilitate damaged identities" and "cause a shift in the cultural understanding" of people living with dementia (Laceulle 73). Those objectives coincide with those of the nursing guidelines for dementia, which emphasize the importance of a person-centered and relationship-based approach (Deutsches Netzwerk).

Even though the picturebook examples discussed here represent only a small sample of the fascinating variety possible, the selection impressively demonstrates different angles of people's lives affected by dementia. However, all these picturebooks have one thing in common: they emphasize key points of person-centered care, such as treating the person affected by dementia with dignity and respect and tailoring the care to their individual needs and preferences. Conveying an idea of the actual impact of the disease on the individual person might help family and even formal caregivers to adapt to the situation and facilitate the reduction and management of challenging behavior. Therefore, the picturebooks resonate with an affirmation of personhood by acknowledging the unique subjectivity of the person with dementia and thus validating the reality of their experience and their feelings. What does the person affected by dementia need, feel, and experience? Presenting the character with dementia integrated in a familiar environment, with family members and narratives that partly revolve around family, may serve family members as a helpful model.

Addressing patients with dementia and their (young) relatives or healthcare professionals working with patients with dementia, the abovementioned effects can become very impactful in several aspects. To begin with, the picturebooks can offer understandable information not only about the disease symptoms and the emotional responses of the patient but also of their close family. Second, these picturebooks might be useful for formal caregivers in addition to professional information. The stories provide subjective experiences of the transformation processes, which can foster empathy and the ability to adopt the perspective of the person with dementia. Counternarratives, especially told through the perspective of a child, often provide a less normative view and therefore foster an accepting attitude or even stimulate an interest in supporting a person to meet their needs. Third, offering counternarratives in which characters in their Fourth Age, affected by dementia, are respected, valued, and loved can make an important contribution in nursing education by emphasizing the value of sympathetic care. Although a diverse and inclusive cast of characters is missing in these selected picturebooks, at least recognizing and supporting selfhood during interactions mirrors a treatment which is based on dignity, compassion, and respect and above all aims at an approach by integrating the person affected by dementia in therapeutic decisions.

NOTES

1. For example, Elisabeth Nilsson et al. show some positive effects of picturebook support for children undergoing surgery.
2. All text from the German picturebooks has been translated into English by the authors of this chapter.
3. The picturebook was published in German, English, Turkish, Russian and Arabic.

WORKS CITED

Babarro Vélez, Izaro, and Jaione Lacalle Prieto. "Literature as a Therapeutic Instrument in the Health-Disease Process in Childhood." *Enfermería Global*, vol. 17, 2018, pp. 601–16.

Bitenc, Rebecca. *Reconsidering Dementia Narratives: Empathy, Identity and Care*. Routledge, 2020.

Brown, Sylvia, et al. "A Review of Narrative Pedagogy Strategies to Transform Traditional Nursing Education." *Journal of Nursing Education*, vol. 47, no. 6, 2008, pp. 283–86.

Bruner, Jerome. "The Role of Interaction Formats in Language Acquisition." *Language and Social Situations*, edited by Joseph P. Forgas, Springer, 1985, pp. 31–46.

Caldwell, Elizabeth F., et al. "Depicting Dementia: Representations of Cognitive Health and Illness in Ten Picturebooks for Children." *Children's Literature in Education*, vol. 52, no. 1, 2021, pp. 106–31.

Crawley, Josephine. "'Once Upon a Time': A Discussion of Children´s Picture Books as a Narrative Educational Tool for Nursing Students." *Journal of Nursing Education*, vol. 48, no. 1, 2009, pp. 36–9.

"Dementia Symptoms." *Alzheimer's Society*, https://www.alzheimers.org.uk/about-dementia/symptoms-and-diagnosis/dementia-symptoms.

Deutsches Netzwerk für Qualitätsentwicklung in der Pflege. *Expertenstandard Beziehungsgestaltung in der Pflege von Menschen mit Demenz*. 2019, https://www.dnqp.de/fileadmin/HSOS/Homepages/DNQP/Dateien/Expertenstandards/Demenz/Demenz_AV_Auszug.pdf.

Eder, Jens, et al. "Character in Fictional Worlds. An Introduction." *Characters in Fictional Worlds: Understanding Imaginary Beings in Literature, Film, and Other Media*, edited by Jens Eder, et al., De Gruyter, 2010, pp. 3–64.

Federal Ministry for Family Affairs, Senior Citizens, Women and Youth. *The Alliance for People with Dementia. Results of the 2014–2018 Common Efforts—Short Report*. 2019, https://www.allianz-fuer-demenz.de/report-agenda.

Folkmarson Käll, Lisa, and Kristin Zeiler. "Still Alice? Ethical Aspects of Conceptualising Selfhood in Dementia." *Routledge Handbook of the Medical Humanities*, edited by Alan Bleakley, Routledge, 2020, pp. 290–99.

Forgan, James. "Using Bibliotherapy to Teach Problem Solving." *Intervention in School and Clinic*, vol. 38, no. 2, 2002, pp. 75–82.

"Gesundheit: Pflege." *Statistisches Bundesamt*, 2018, https://www.destatis.de/DE/Themen/Gesellschaft-Umwelt/Gesundheit/Pflege/_inhalt.html.

Grenier, Amanda. *Transitions and the Lifecourse: Contested Models of "Growing Old."* Policy Press, 2012.

Gubar, Marah. *Artful Dodgers: Recovering the Golden Age of Children's Literature.* Oxford UP, 2009.

Hartung, Heike. *Ageing, Gender, and Illness in Anglophone Literature: Narrating Age Game in the* Bildungsroman. Routledge, 2015.

Hediger, Karin, et al. "A One Health Research Framework for Animal-Assisted Interventions." *International Journal of Environmental Research and Public Health*, vol. 16, no. 4, 2019, p. 640.

Jerónimo, Heather. "Family Bonds that Ensnare and Empower: Dementia as Identity Formation in Elvira Lindos's *Una palabra tuya*." *Hispania*, vol. 101, no. 1, 2018, pp. 114–24.

Joosen, Vanessa. *Adulthood in Children's Literature.* Bloomsbury, 2018.

Kårefjärd, Ann, and Lena Nordgren. "Effects of Dog-Assisted Intervention on Quality of Life in Nursing Home Residents with Dementia." *Scandinavian Journal of Occupational Therapy*, vol. 26, no. 6, 2018, pp. 433–40.

Kurkjian, Catherine, and Nancy Livingston. "The Right Book for the Right Child for the Right Situation." *Reading Teacher*, vol. 58, no. 8, 2005, pp. 786–95.

Laceulle, Hanne. *Aging and Self-Realization: Cultural Narratives about Later Life.* Transcript Verlag, 2018.

Nilsson, Elisabeth, et al. "Picture Book Support for Preparing Children ahead of and during Day Surgery." *Nursing Children and Young People*, vol. 28, no. 8, 2016, pp. 30–35.

Peate, Ian, et al., editors. *Nursing Practice: Knowledge and Care.* Wiley Blackwell, 2014.

Reilley, Jamie, and Jinyi Hung. "Dementia and Communication." *The Cambridge Handbook of Communication Disorders*, edited by Louise Cummings, Cambridge UP, 2015, pp. 266–83.

Reynolds, Kimberley. *Children's Literature: A Very Short Introduction.* Oxford UP, 2011.

Robert Koch Institut. *Gesundheitsberichterstattung des Bundes.* Heft 28 Altersdemenz. RKI, 2005.

Robinson, Sally. "Children's Books: A Resource for Children's Nursing Care." *Paediatric Nursing*, vol. 14, no. 5, 2002, pp. 26–31.

Sontag, Susan. *Illness as Metaphor.* Farrar, Straus and Giroux, 1977.

Tielsch-Goddard, Anna. "Children's Books for Use in Bibliotherapy." *Journal of Pediatric Health Care.* vol. 25, 2011, pp. 57–61.

Welling, Karin. "Der person-zentrierte Ansatz von Tom Kitwood—ein bedeutender Bezugsrahmen für die Pflege von Menschen mit Demenz." *Unterricht Pflege*, vol. 9, no. 5, 2004, pp. 2–12.

Zimmermann, Martina. *The Diseased Brain and the Failing Mind: Dementia in Science, Medicine and Literature of the Long Twentieth Century*, Bloomsbury, 2020.

APPENDIX: SELECTED PICTUREBOOKS

Baltscheit, Martin. *Geschichte vom Fuchs, der den Verstand verlor.* Illustrated by Baltscheit, Beltz and Gerstenberg, 2010.

Barth, Rolf. *Mein Andersopa.* Illustrated by Daniela Bunge, Hanser, 2018.

Baumbach, Martina. *Kuddelmuddel in Omas Kopf.* Illustrated by Michaela Heitmann, Gabriel, 2014.

Elschner, Géraldine. *Der alte Schäfer.* Illustrated by Jonas Lauströer, Minedition, 2011.

Huppertz, Nikola. *Meine Omi, die Wörter und ich.* Illustrated by Elsa Klever, Tulipan, 2017.

John, Kirsten. *Opa Rainer weiß nicht mehr.* Illustrated by Katja Gehrmann, Knesebeck, 2018.

Kratzke, Daniel. *Oma isst Zement!* Illustrated by Kratzke, arsEdition, 2014.

Langston, Laura. *Omas Apfelkuchen.* Illustrated by Lindsay Gardimer, Friedrich Wittig Verlag, 2004.

Müller, Dagmar. *Herbst im Kopf. Meine Oma Anni hat Alzheimer.* Illustrated by Verena Ballhaus, Annette Betz, 2006.

Nilsson, Ulf. *Als Oma seltsam wurde.* Illustrated by Eva Eriksson, Beltz and Gerstenberg, 2008.

Papp, Rika. *Lilli und ihre vergessliche Oma.* Illustrated by Miriam Cordes, Carlsen, 2015.

Plieth, Martina. *Mia besucht Frau Turboschnecke.* Illustrated by Lena Miller, Neukirchener, 2018.

Robben, Jaap. *Josefina. Ein Name wie ein Klavier.* Illustrated by Merel Eyckerman, Carl-Auer, 2015.

Shepherd, Jessica. *Oma, vergiss mich nicht!* Illustrated by Shepherd, Brunnen, 2015.

Steinkeller, Elisabeth. *Die neue Omi.* Illustrated by Michael Roher, Jungbrunnen, 2011.

Unterholzner, Birgit. *Auf meinem Rücken wächst ein Garten.* Illustrated by Leonora Leitl, Picus, 2016.

Van den Abeele, Véronique. *Meine Oma hat Alzheimer.* Illustrated by Claude K. Dubois, Brunnen, 2006.

Van de Vendel, Edward. *Anna Maria Sofia und der kleine Wim.* Illustrated by Ingrid Godon, Carlsen, 2006.

Welsh, Clare Helen. *Mit Opa ist alles anders.* Illustrated by Ashling Lindsay, 360 Grad, 2019.

CAREGIVING CHILDREN AND ABSENT MEDICAL PROFESSIONALS

Hyperemesis Gravidarum in Picturebooks

B.J. WOODSTEIN

In this chapter, I analyze the two existing children's picturebooks[1] on hyperemesis gravidarum in order to understand how they explain illness to children while also placing an expectation on those children that they are to become "heroes" who must care for and help their sick mothers. The mothers in these books lose their caregiver roles and become patients, while the children are placed in a dual role where they want and need the usual attention and care from their parents and yet are pressured to help support, protect, and care for their ill mothers. In other words, there is some conflict between what we usually expect from and offer to children and what seems to be expected from and offered to them in this particular situation. Meanwhile, medical professionals are not shown to be particularly involved in caregiving.

Hyperemesis gravidarum (HG) is a serious complication that affects around 1 percent of pregnancies and can be best described as extreme pregnancy sickness, with nausea and vomiting all day and night, along with other symptoms, such as excess saliva, fatigue, depression, and more. It often leads to the pregnant person[2] being hospitalized, being put on bed rest, and/or needing medication. The two picturebooks that I have found in English both depict children whose mother is ill with HG, and while they give factual information about HG and can thus be called issue books, they also show the child characters helping out at home and caring for their mothers, with one book even explicitly calling the child a "hero" for their caring efforts. This in turn sends a message that children may need to become carers or helpers when their mother is ill. While it is certainly natural for children to contribute to the family—throughout history, they have worked both in and outside the home—and some children do end up in caregiver roles in their families, encouraging children to become caregivers, even temporarily, could be problematic, especially when other people are not sharing the burden with the children. It is important to acknowledge the reality of caregiving children without encouraging it, which is what I argue that these books do.

The two works, which are both limited in terms of diversity and inclusivity, take slightly different approaches, with one depicting the child as a protector for the mother and the other focusing on the child as the helper. In both cases, the father does very little and, similarly, the healthcare system is depicted as something distant, which is a surprise, as one might think it would be beneficial and comforting to child readers to see doctors and midwives actively taking care of the ill mother. In addition, mental health is referred to, but the child protagonist is not given much support with it. Caregiving is in many ways placed onto the child protagonist's shoulders in these two picturebooks. Young caregivers can face significant problems in their lives, so my question is whether this is an appropriate approach to take in these works. As a brief comparison, I will look at one other work that also features an ill parent but takes a different approach. In this book, the child is not expected to be a carer or a hero, but rather is given the space to explore their own feelings around the illness and to be the focus of attention; this is in contrast to the pressure I perceive the children to be under in the two picturebooks that comprise the main case study.

BACKGROUND TO THIS PROJECT

My interest in this subject developed because I myself suffered from hyperemesis gravidarum twice. I was very ill in both my pregnancies and received almost no support from healthcare professionals, colleagues, relatives, or friends. Indeed, my first time around, my doctor did not even deign to tell me that I had HG; I only found out because I saw a form where he wrote it down, and that was when I learned that what I was suffering from had a name and that there were treatments available. I never would have made it through either pregnancy without the care of my wife; this is interesting to me in part because of how little involvement the partner seems to have in caregiving in the two picturebooks discussed in this chapter.

My second HG pregnancy was much harder in many ways. In part, this was because I was even more ill than I had been the first time, although I was also more prepared and was able to give the doctors information on the medications I required.[3] But another reason why this second pregnancy was harder was because we had our older child to look after. I was still breastfeeding her[4] but was otherwise unable to interact with her in the ways I usually did, and it was confusing for her that I was lying in bed much of the time. I could not play, I could not drive her to nursery, I could not take her to her other activities, and in general I was not the mother she was used to. She was three years old and found my sickness terrifying and traumatizing. She grew used to calling out to my wife, "Mummy, Mama is throwing up again!" We naturally explained to her what was wrong, but she was worried that I would die, and this has had a long-standing impact on her. As a children's literature scholar, one of the resources I turned to was literature. I found two picturebooks about HG, and I read them regularly to her; she requested them most days and seemed to find them useful starting points for discussions. Still, I often wished there were more books or different books available. I was uncomfortable with the depiction of HG and of families in these works.

After I gave birth for the second time and we as a family recovered as best as we could from this difficult experience, I decided I wanted to analyze the books from a more academic perspective and try to understand what role they played not only in our life but also in the lives of children and families more generally. Since I have explored "issue books" in the context of LGBTQ+ literature (Epstein, *Are the Kids All Right?*), I felt I could use that lens to analyze these two books.

BACKGROUND RESEARCH

I was interested to learn more about children as caregivers, and while I found a lot of research on children who need special care, such as fostering or educational support, as well as some research on children and grief after a bereavement and some generally on the children of ill parents, it was harder to find studies of children who provide care, perhaps because it has been a more hidden subject. I did find some sociological studies of children as caregivers and also popular websites that discuss issues around children being caregivers.[5]

Such research notes that, as Ruth Evans puts it, childhood is considered to be a protected time that should be free of tasks and duties, and yet many children have what we might view as adult responsibilities (1894). This could include housework, although this is less common in the Global North (where my corpus of texts take place), and may also involve care of adults or siblings, running errands, earning money to financially support the family, and more.[6] For example, "[a]s many as 1.4 million U.S. children age 8 to 18 are caring for a parent, grandparent or sibling with a disability or illness" (Chamberlin). The two HG books represent slightly different circumstances, as the child protagonists appear to be much younger than eight and also are not either long-term caregivers or the sole caregivers, but some of the research around child caregivers is nonetheless relevant.

Caregiving is a political issue, but an often invisible one, despite the existence of the UN Convention on the Rights of the Child (Bibby and Becker 29). Andrew Bibby and Saul Becker write that in the UK, few people are aware of the UN Convention, even though several of the articles in the Convention would seem to suggest that children should not be caregivers (25).

Evans writes that "the work that 'young carers' do is distinct from the usual household work that young people engage in because of the wider range of household and caring tasks undertaken by 'young carers,' particularly children's involvement in the personal or 'intimate' care of their parent/relative, as well as the frequency, time spent, and outcomes of these tasks" (1895). She points out that there is a continuum of how much work children put in, distinguishing between low levels, or "caring about," and high levels, or "caring for" (1896). The familial situation, location, and relevant health issues in part determine which term is applicable; as discussed below, it is low levels, or "caring about," that I see in the HG texts.

Another important factor for discussion here is the impact caregiving has on young people. As Evans points out, being a child caregiver comes with adult responsibilities. Making children feel they need to take care of the parent or protect the parent places expectations on the child and decreases their freedom to just be children. Evans differentiates between "*well-being*, in terms of their lives in the present, [and] *well-becoming*, in terms of their personal development, future lives, and transitions to adulthood" (1893, emphasis in original). Evans refers to a variety of other potential issues, such as "anxiety about a parent/relative's illness, anticipatory and unresolved grief" (1903), undernourishment, getting infected with illnesses (from parents or other relatives), difficult relationships with relatives or friends, missing school, an inability to take part in hobbies or other community activities, uncertainty about their future, and more (Evans 1903–6; see also Austin). It is not a surprise that given how much time and energy caregiving can take, child caregivers will not necessarily have the ability to form healthy bonds with other people or be able to devote time to schoolwork or extracurricular or extrafamilial activities.

I could not find any research specifically on the depiction of children as caregivers in fiction, even though some authors, such as Jacqueline Wilson, are known to have tackled the subject in their writing due to their aim of portraying the realities of children's lives. In general, when looking at both scholarly research and literary texts, I found material on children with their own health conditions or children grieving the death of a parent, grandparent, or pet, but very little on children doing the caregiving themselves for an adult with an illness. This is an important gap, which is why my intervention, in the form of this chapter, is needed; I aim to understand what it means when children are depicted in picturebooks as the caregivers and what messages that might send to children.

THE CORPUS OF TEXTS

My corpus of texts is admittedly very small, in that I am only aware of two picturebooks about hyperemesis gravidarum. Indeed, when I have searched for depictions of HG in literature more generally and asked other people for recommendations, I have found almost nothing. As noted before, around 1 percent of pregnant people get HG. According to UK statistics, around 605,479 babies were born in 2022 in England and Wales (Scotland and Northern Ireland were not included in this figure) (Office of National Statistics); this was a lower rate than in previous years, but if I take it as an average number and also assume that some of those births may have been twins or multiples, I can use the number of 500,000 as a low average. This implies that around 5000 people are ill with HG each year. Similar figures for the US show 3.66 million live births (not including the pregnancies that did not result in live births) in 2021 (Statista), so if I try to account for multiple births, perhaps a conservative figure is at least three million, or 30,000 people with HG. In other words, I would suggest that HG affects a significant number of people every year in the UK and US alone: at least 35,000 pregnant people are impacted by HG, and in fact the actual figure is much higher than that, if one also takes into consideration the older children, spouses, and relatives of the pregnant person, since having someone ill in the family has a wide-ranging effect on other people too. Given how many issue books exist for children on a range of subjects, such as divorce or diabetes, and also how common pregnancy is, I had anticipated finding more picturebooks on HG or other challenging aspects of pregnancy, such as miscarriage, bed rest, stillbirth, birth defects, and more. It strikes me that there is a lack of knowledge around HG, combined perhaps with a lack of interest in or comfort with writing about it for children.

The two texts I found are *Mama Has Hyperemesis Gravidarum (But Only for a While)* (2009) by Ashli McCall, illustrated by Anna-Maria Crum, and *How to Be an HG Hero!* (2015) by Caitlin Dean, with illustrations by Paul Colledge. The former text is from the US and the latter from the UK. Jamie Chamberlin claims that the United Kingdom, Australia, and New Zealand are more advanced in terms of recognizing and supporting child caregivers than the United States is, but I found no difference along these lines based on where these two books were written and published.

Both books were self-published, which suggests that mainstream publishers perhaps did not consider the topic of HG to be of interest.[7] While I do not have the space here to explore this in great detail, it could be argued that a book that is self-published or only published by a specialized publisher indicates that its subject matter is not considered to be of general interest.[8] Both authors are women who experienced HG themselves and also have produced nonfiction works for adults about HG.

The two works depict the low level of caregiving, which Evans calls "caring about" (1896). Neither child protagonist has to earn money to support the family, carry out the intimate care of the parent, manage the household, or educate a younger sibling, among other higher-level tasks. Nonetheless, the books do still feature children caregiving, and what they show seems typical of child caregiving in the world. Evans notes that "the majority of children are involved in low levels of caring, while a small proportion are involved in much higher levels of caring" (1897).

The books in my HG corpus also both take place in the West and appear to depict comfortable, middle-class families; although, as Evans writes, it is generally "difficult to distinguish the negative impacts of caring from wider processes of poverty, social exclusion, and marginalization that many children living in households where family members have impairments, chronic illness, or other care needs are likely to experience" (1906), this does not seem relevant here.

McCall's and Dean's picturebooks take slightly different approaches to explaining and discussing HG, as I explore below. They are otherwise similar in that they do not have plots per se; rather, they focus on the issue of HG, showing child characters whose mothers are pregnant with hyperemesis, and they explain the illness to the child.[9] Both books feature a child character who is non-gender-specific, presumably so any child could see themselves in that character. The main difference in terms of the characters is that McCall's work uses rabbits while Dean's depicts humans.

In what follows, I will describe the stories and discuss the tensions in them between the ill mothers' and their children's varying roles. These books matter not just because they are a space to explain HG to children but also because they can help child caregivers know they are not alone (Chamberlin).

CHILDREN AS PROTECTORS

Mama Has Hyperemesis Gravidarum (But Only for a While) (2009) is the older of the two books and, as noted, uses rabbit protagonists. The book begins by emphasizing all the things that Mama does: "[s]he cooks and cleans and plays with me every day." The mother, in other words, is stereotyped from the start, in that she plays the typical woman's role of being caregiver and homemaker. She wears a variety of different aprons throughout the book, without any other clothes under the apron; the only other outfit she wears is a hospital gown in the scene in which she is an inpatient. That is to say, the mama character is only ever shown in homemaker clothes or patient clothes. The father, on the other hand, wears no clothes at all, so he is not stereotyped into roles based on his garments. However, he does wear reading glasses and is depicted as being out of the house at times; Daddy, as he is called, thus works outside the house and is portrayed as a reader through his glasses. It is also implied that he cannot or will not cook, because on the first day that Mama is ill, he gives the child character cereal, unlike the pancakes that the mother usually makes.

In the book, the child rabbit is told that the mother is pregnant. "Mama says she might get sick. Very sick. Daddy says that things might change a lot. But only for a while" (McCall). My assumption from this description is that Mama had HG with her first pregnancy, so they suspect she will have HG with this second one, too. The family enjoys thinking about the baby and what its sex might be, but then the mother gets ill and makes "scary noises"—that is, she has begun vomiting (McCall). Mama "stays in bed . . . [and] does not cook or clean or play. . . . [She] throws up. A lot" (McCall). To emphasize the gendered stereotypes in this book, the grandmother comes to help, and she cooks and plays, as if the father is unable to do those things. The father does not step into the mother's caregiving role for the child.

Mama goes to stay in the hospital, and this scares the protagonist. When Mama comes home and is visited by a nurse,[10] the protagonist turns into a protector. The nurse tries to take blood from the mother, who has her eyes squeezed shut and her head turned away in the illustration, as if she is in pain or frightened. The text reads, "She pokes my mama, and I see blood. Daddy says she is helping. I pop the balloon. GO AWAY, Nurse Bunn!" (McCall). The child rabbit is trying to scare the nurse away by making a loud noise, as if the nurse is doing something bad to the mother, even though the father explains that the nurse is "helping." A short time later, the child sees a bin, and this brings up memories of how her mother gags and possibly throws up into a bin; the story then reads, "Trash cans are bad! I kick this one" (McCall). In other words, the young rabbit tries to show concern for and protection of her mother first by attempting to make the nurse go away, out of an assumption that the nurse is hurting her mother, and then by kicking the "bad" bin, as if blaming it for her mother's illness. Although the father does "take[s] Mama to the doctor" and is also seen with an arm around her in one illustration (McCall), he does not seem to protect her or to offer caregiving in the way the child does.

Soon the mother gets better—some people with hyperemesis gravidarum do find their symptoms ease as their pregnancy progresses, while others only return to wellness after their baby's birth—and she comes out of her bedroom. The story says, "Mama spends more time with me each day. Very slowly she begins to cook and clean and play" (McCall). This again has the impact of depicting her role as extremely limited: Mama is either an ill patient, who is in bed or the hospital, or else she is the caregiver and homemaker for the family. Mama makes pancakes again, which signals to the child, "I've got my mama back!" (McCall). This may be accurate to some children's home lives; indeed the back cover describes the author as a "stay-at-home, homeschooling mother," but perhaps it is not particularly common in a society and era in which many people suffering from HG would need to negotiate their work roles as well as their responsibilities at home.

The book finishes with the family being "very happy" as they once again consider the forthcoming baby's sex and name. The final, wordless page shows Daddy, Mama, and child standing around a cot, arms around each other, a small paw only just visible as it pokes out of the blanket (McCall). In other words, the baby has arrived and all is well with the family once again; the HG only lasted "a while" and all is back to normal. No long-term consequences on the family or the child's mental health are mentioned. In regard to this, the back cover points out that "[t]he debilitating effects of hyperemesis gravidarum (HG) can be bewildering for adults, so it's no surprise that children's lives are greatly affected . . . but only for a while," which suggests that once the HG has passed, or the pregnancy is over, all is well again and there are no more effects. As discussed above, there can be long-term impacts on both the patient and the caregiver; Austin notes that child caregivers may change their behavior to become more adult-like in inappropriate ways—they may regress, become disruptive in school, express mood swings or fatigue or anger, look for ways to escape, and so on—but none of this is seen in this book, nor is there any depiction of an adult helping the child rabbit through what is an emotionally challenging time.

To sum up, *Mama Has Hyperemesis Gravidarum (But Only for a While)* shows a very traditional nuclear family, albeit in rabbit form and not human, with the mother only allowed two roles. She either takes care of the family or she is ill; she does not have a job outside the home, nor does she ever combine her roles, such as by playing with her child even though she feels ill. On the other hand, the child is used to being taken care of and when they no longer receive this attention from the mother, the child worries about whether the mother "still love[s] me" (McCall). Although the father does take the child out to the cinema and the grandmother also comes to help, much of the standard caregiving has been withdrawn; the father is not depicted as doing much caregiving for the mother or for the child. In response to the lack of caregiving, the child turns into a would-be protector, wanting to take care of the mother.

It is implied that the child can relinquish this caregiving role once the mother feels better. The roles are thus depicted as very distinct, in that both mother and child can apparently not both take care of one another simultaneously; it is one thing or the other at any given time.

CHILDREN AS HEROES

The approach is slightly different in *How to Be an HG Hero!* (2015). Dean's book has even less of a plot than McCall's, in that McCall's book starts with the mother and child's relationship and shows how it changes over the course of the HG pregnancy, while Dean's mostly gives information about what it means to have HG. Dean's work begins with the lines, "Mummy has a teeny tiny baby growing in her tummy. Some mummies get very sick when they have a baby in their tummy." The latter of these two sentences is accompanied by an illustration of a mother with a greenish tinge to her face. The story goes on to explain how "some mummies" take medicine or go to the hospital to have a drip, as well as that this experience might make the child of such a mummy feel "sad . . . [or] scared or worried" (Dean). While the book suggests that the child speak to someone if they feel this way, most of the text consists of suggestions for how the child can be an "HG hero" (Dean). That is, the book briefly shows that a child can suffer when their parent is ill, but then implies that the child needs to pick themselves up and make an effort for their mother and for the family.

Some of the things an "HG hero" can do, according to the book, include getting dressed by themselves, tidying, getting water for the ill mother, helping with laundry, being quiet so as not to disturb the mother, and generally being a "super helper for mummy" (Dean). The child is told that some days the mother might feel better and "might be able to play with you again or go for a walk with you" (Dean), which, as with McCall's work, implies that the mother can once again take on her caregiving role. However, where the two works differ is through the ending. McCall shows a clear end point to the child having this protectionist role; when the mother gets better, the child can once again become only the cared-for and not the caregiver. In Dean's work, the reader is told that "Mummy won't be sick any more," and yet the child is said to have learned so much through "all that practice helping mummy" that they will then go on to "be the best brother or sister around" (Dean). This suggests that the child will continue to be a helper and to play a caregiving role, this time to the new baby. In fact, in the very last image, the mother is depicted holding the new baby, while the older child, wearing a superhero outfit, is larger than their parents. This emphasizes the child's heroic role, supporting and taking care of the mother, and also separates the hero child from their parents and sibling, because they are bigger and standing apart.

The last page in the book has an "HG Hero" certificate that the adult can fill in that notes that "[y]our support, compassion and care has made a massive difference" (Dean). . Both the adults and the children who read or who have this book read to them are thereby encouraged to expect care and help from the child when the mother is ill with HG. While it is certainly important to help develop empathy and compassion in children, the question is whether expecting too much may add pressure and stress to what is already likely to be a difficult situation for the child. Again, as with McCall's book, there is little suggestion that the child might have big feelings to process.

Neither of the last two images in the book show the now-well mother engaging with her older child; in the first, she is holding and looking at the baby only, and in the second, as stated, she is staring down at the baby and the father is looking at the reader, while the extra-large HG hero looms over them both. A possible message is that the young reader or read-to can no longer expect caregiving and needs to be more independent now, with additional pressures or expectations placed on them. As in McCall's work, there is no reference at all to the potential trauma that a child in this situation might have experienced.

How to Be an HG Hero!, like *Mama Has Hyperemesis Gravidarum (But Only for a While)*, portrays a nuclear family with distinctly delineated roles. In *How to Be an HG Hero!*, the father is even less present, in that he is only referred to in words or thought bubbles until the very end, when he is standing next to the mother, who is holding the baby, and he is shown doing absolutely no caregiving at all. It is as if he is not involved in the family, except to take pride in the children he helped create. The mother is said to be so ill that she is not able to "play" or "cuddle," so she does seem to be the primary caregiver, although her cooking and cleaning tasks are not highlighted in Dean's book as they are in McCall's. The child does not comment as much on the lack of caregiving in Dean's book, but focuses instead on worries such as "When will mummy be home?" (Dean). Then the child becomes the HG hero. The child provides some care for the mother, as in bringing her a drink, but primarily supports her through carrying out household tasks and trying to be unobtrusive. This new role is shown as positive in that the child learns from it and can carry on with it even after the HG is over and the new baby has arrived, perhaps because there is no indication in the book that the mother will resume her caregiving role for this child. This relates back to Evans's concept of "well-becoming" (1893), as there is an implication that the child has become a caregiver and has transitioned to an adult role, but I would not suggest that this is healthy, since the child's own "well-being" has not been dealt with (Evans 1893).

MENTAL HEALTH

While both these picturebooks clearly depict children responding to their mothers' illness by stepping into new roles, they do also, to their credit, briefly explore the impact of a mother's illness on the child's mental health and acknowledge the challenges that the child might face, although only during the time of the illness itself.

Both picturebooks acknowledge that the child might feel sad, worried, or frightened, and they show a range of other feelings. McCall's book also depicts confusion when the mother sends the child out of her room, as well as the child experiencing nausea (it is implied that this gagging has been copied from the mother's behavior). There is anger, too, when the child tries to protect the mother from the nurse. The child in McCall's book is thrilled when they can cuddle and play together again; Dean's book, of course, does not show the mother and child together again in this way, possibly leaving the reader to consider whether the HG has effected a permanent break in their relations. A missing feeling here is resentment, whether toward the mother for being ill and not providing her usual caregiving, or toward the baby for taking the attention away from the older child, and this seems a surprising absence.

Another thing the two works have in common in relation to mental health is that they show the child wondering if the mother is going to die. In McCall's book, the answer to this question is, "Daddy says no. He says she will just be sick. Very sick. But only for a while" (McCall). Strangely, this fear is never answered in Dean's book. The child ponders this and other questions, such as "Why is daddy upset?" and "Does the drip hurt?" but is not shown discussing them with anyone or getting any answers (Dean). Instead, the reader or read-to is told that it is "okay to ask questions and talk about how you feel" and then is encouraged to discuss them with "Daddy," "Granny or Grandad," "my teacher," "my friends" or "my teddy bear" (Dean), although whether a stuffed toy or other children could appropriately answer such questions is debatable.

As already made clear, neither book refers to any long-lasting impact of HG. My own experience of having an older child while I was ill from HG suggests that it can be traumatic and upsetting even once the period of illness has finished. Likewise, research on young caregivers discusses how being forced into a caregiving role can have effects on the child (Evans; Austin). Although HG is arguably different from some other situations, such as alcoholism or disability, in part because it is for a defined period of time (i.e., at most the length of a pregnancy), it is certainly possible that young people would need some support in getting past what happened to them during the pregnancy. Picturebooks are short and perhaps there was no scope in the two discussed here for depicting, for instance, a visit to a therapist or a discussion between the child and the mother about how things felt while the mother was ill, but it may nonetheless have been important and true to life to nod to this in some way. My reading of these picturebooks suggests that the child protagonists also have to become caregivers to themselves; while they are encouraged to ask questions, they are not always given answers within the book, nor are they shown receiving the kind of support from others that they might actually require in this situation.

Given the explanations of the mothers' illness and the references to feelings, I would potentially suggest that these two books could be called bibliotherapeutic. Eileen H. Jones defines bibliotherapy as "the practice of using books and stories as part of the treatment of emotionally and mentally disturbed people" (15). I would define it more broadly, however. Books of any type can support people and help them feel less alone, while also educating them.[11] McCall's and Dean's works are, like many picturebooks about illness, issue books, which focus on the topic—here, the illness—rather than weaving it into a larger plot. Indeed, lists of other such picturebooks reveal that no matter what the particular illness—fibromyalgia, say, or multiple sclerosis, depression, or cancer—the books tend to explain it, often with an aim of educating children and inducing empathy and caregiving in them.[12] Interestingly, however, in their guide to HG for adults, Dean and her coauthor Amanda Shortman make many recommendations for preparing for a second HG birth, such as getting a nanny or other childcare, but they do not recommend reading children picturebooks as a way of helping them learn about and understand HG. It seems that despite the emphasis on hyperemesis, including feelings around it, in these works, the bibliotherapeutic benefits of picturebooks are not yet recognized in general research on HG.

THE LACK OF MEDICAL PROFESSIONALS

Rather oddly, perhaps, for picturebooks about illness, medical professionals are notable here for their absence. I had expected to see them throughout the books, maybe portrayed as saviors who were going to make the women slightly better, although not well, since medicine cannot bring about wellness in cases of HG.

Mama Has Hyperemesis Gravidarum (But Only for a While) shows the mother in the hospital with a tube in her arm; the reader is told that the hospital "smells funny" and that the young rabbit wants "to go home" (McCall). However, no doctor, midwife, or nurse is in evidence, as if the mother is by herself, having to manage alone. A nurse does appear later in the story, as mentioned above, when the mother has come home and Nurse Bunn arrives to take blood, much to the annoyance of the child.

The only reference to a medical professional in *How to Be an HG Hero!* is early on: "Some mummies have to see the doctor and take lots of medicine so they aren't so sick" (Dean). That page shows the doctor alone, not interacting with the mother. The doctor is a balding man with reading glasses. The very next page states that "[s]ome mummies have to go to hospital to have more medicine through a special needle in their hand or arm. Sometimes this is called a drip" (Dean). But, as in McCall's work, the mother is in her hospital bed without any doctor or nurse helping her.

The health establishment could have been featured after the birth of the new baby as well. In part, one could have imagined a visit from a midwife, doula, or lactation consultant to check on and support the mother-and-baby dyad specifically and the family as a whole more generally. Likewise, a therapist, counselor, or psychologist could also have been shown, helping the family move past the confusing and distressing experience they have gone through. However, as already noted, this does not happen in either text.

The authors may not have wanted to scare readers by focusing too much on the need for medical help and intervention or giving too many details about hospital stays, although given how much they discuss worries and refer to the idea of death, this seems unlikely. Rather, I would suggest that the books instead focus on the role the children can play. Children are not experienced or educated medical professionals, of course, and cannot prescribe medication or attach tubes or take blood—even if Austin notes that some children do carry out these age-inappropriate tasks—but they are depicted as being there to help and take care of their mothers. Instead of the "mother bear" protecting them, they become the powerful "baby bears." This may help some child readers or read-to feel empowered; in what is a frightening situation, they can gain and retain power by taking the place of medical professionals and of fathers, who likewise do very little in these works. The focus of the books is thus squarely on the children, their experiences, and their contributions.

DIVERSITY, OR THE LACK THEREOF

Although this article is primarily about caregivers in HG picturebooks, I do feel it is essential to briefly discuss diversity. Given the extremely small corpus here, it is perhaps not surprising to say that there is no real diversity in these books. Both books feature apparently heterosexual families, in that there is a mother and a father. It is the mother (called "mummy" in one book and "mama" in the other) who is ill; in other words, it is not a trans man carrying the child. The assumption is that the reader or read-to also has a mother and a father;

Dean's book says "[t]here are lots of things you can do to help mummy and daddy," as if that is the family setup for anyone who might be reading this book.

The gender roles are quite defined, too, as already mentioned above. The "mummy" in *How to Be an HG Hero!* wears a dress when she is out of bed and has long hair (Dean). The "mama" in *Mama Has Hyperemesis Gravidarum (But Only for a While)* is depicted in an apron and as being the one to cook meals for the family; indeed, part of what the child protagonist misses about her when she is ill is that she cannot make pancakes (McCall). Neither mother is said to work outside the home, and there is no discussion of the mother having to take sick leave from her job. In addition, the nurse in *Mama Has Hyperemesis Gravidarum (But Only for a While)* is female, and the doctor in *How to Be an HG Hero!* is male, and this too emphasizes traditional gender roles, as do the relatively unengaged fathers. There is, I hasten to say, nothing wrong with a stay-at-home parent, of whatever gender, but many women do in fact work today. Indeed, around half the world's women are in the paid workforce (World Bank). Surely these two books could have challenged gender stereotypes and depicted the tensions caused by a working and caregiving woman becoming a patient and needing care from her family, including her partner.

The illustrations in *How to Be an HG Hero!* depict a white family and those in *Mama Has Hyperemesis Gravidarum (But Only for a While)* depict a gray rabbit family. Nurse Bunn is a brown rabbit, which may simply be to differentiate her from the family, or it may be to signal that she is a darker color, as are many nurses; between 20 and 40 percent of the UK nursing workforce is from an ethnic minority background (NHS England), and US figures seem to be between 25 and 30 percent (Minority Nurse). Using animals in the illustrations as the protagonists in picturebooks is a relatively common approach, and one that other scholars have noted, especially in regard to stories about minorities or nonnormative situations; there is no space here to discuss the issues with this in great depth, but it is worth pointing out that some people feel that animals are not racialized and thus anyone can relate to them, while others worry that the approach of employing animals instead of humans reproduces a challenging dynamic (e.g., Chetty and Sands-O'Connor).[13] Despite HG being relatively common, disease and illness may still be seen as a non-norm or tricky subject to feature in picturebooks. It may also be easier for readers, whether adults or children, to relate to the animals. Interestingly and unsurprisingly, there are more animal characters in children's literature than there are people of color (Flood), which says something about how readers relate to animals in picturebooks as well as about what authors, illustrators, and publishers consider to be valuable to depict in literature.

THE POSITIVE

Finally, although I have been generally negative about the two works, it is important to note that they may also be read from a more positive perspective.

As Becker et al. note, there is much ongoing discussion about whether children should be providing caregiving work, in part because of the detrimental impacts mentioned above and how caregiving can restrict their lives (54). And yet, "children often want to care in some way . . . so it is important to identify ways of reconciling their wishes with their rights as carers, as well as their rights as children to protection, participation and the promotion of their physical and mental well-being (under the UN Convention and the Children Act)" (Becker et al. 55).

Besides their genuinely wanting to be involved, there may be other positive benefits to child caregiving. Evans writes that some research reveals that

> caring developed children's knowledge, understanding, sense of responsibility, maturity, and a range of life-, social-, and care-related skills . . . [and] helped to bring many children closer to their parents in terms of a loving, caring relationship. . . . [C]hildren's caregiving [for a parent with severe mental illness] helped to allay some of the fears, concerns, and anxieties that they had about their parent's condition because it gave children control and direct involvement in the provision and management of care work. . . . In some instances caring helped to enhance parent–child relationships and helped children to feel included when often, outside the domain of the family, they were ignored and not recognized by health, social care, and other professionals. (1906)

Perhaps depicting or encouraging these positive impacts are part of the aim of these works, even if not stated or always shown explicitly. As I noted before, becoming a protector can feel empowering. It may be positive to feel strong and hero-like in a scary, uncertain situation. And the children in these books are encouraged to ask questions relating to their concerns and anxieties, even if they do not always get answers. Nevertheless, I do not see evidence in these two picturebooks of caregiving bringing parents and children closer; indeed, I would suggest the opposite, given the way the older children do not seem fully integrated into the newly expanded family, as well as the absence of open discussion about the effects of the period of illness on the children or the families as a whole.

Despite my overarching concern for the emphasis on children as caregivers in these two HG books, I do recognize that there are some positive aspects to child caregiving and that some of these aspects can be read into these works.[14]

A COMPARISON

This analysis suggests a limited depiction of illness in children's literature, but I felt it was important to explore other books to see if there were different models available in regard to diversity, caregiving, room for feelings and so on. Intriguingly, many of the picturebooks about other illnesses are also self-published[15]—presumably by people for whom these illnesses are personally relevant—and they seem to be issue books that have the aim of explaining the illness to the child. This means that there appears to me to be a tension between pedagogy and pleasure; in other words, the authors seem to intend to inform children about the illnesses and how to handle them, and sometimes this happens to the detriment of having a plot or a book being more inclusive.

One of my favorite counterexamples is the Swedish-language book *Dyksommar*, written by Sara Stridsberg and illustrated by Sara Lundberg (2019). I admit a connection to it that perhaps makes me biased: I translated it to English as *The Summer of Diving*, published in June 2022, which is the version I will discuss here.

In *The Summer of Diving*, the protagonist, Zoe, has a father who is suffering from mental health problems and has to go to a mental hospital. As Zoe puts it, "One day, the man who was my dad is gone" (Stridsberg).[16] While Zoe does consider how she can help him, such as by thinking, "He likes parties. Maybe we should plan a party now so he'll come back?" (Stridsberg), there is no suggestion that Zoe needs to care for him or to be a hero for him. In fact, much of the book focuses on Zoe's experiences of visiting him and dealing with her own feelings.

There is undeniable empathy in this book for the pain Zoe's father is going through, and there is space for explaining to a child reader or read-to what it means to suffer from poor mental health, but the book prioritizes Zoe's needs. Unlike the child protagonists of the HG books discussed above, Zoe is not expected to be a caregiver. She does not need to do the protecting, healing, or physical work of caring, whether for herself or her father. Instead, the medical staff are present. Zoe says, "There are angels everywhere in the building, checking on him. But they haven't come to take him. They're just watching over him on earth now so he doesn't fly away" (Stridsberg). These "angels" are two female nurses and a male nurse, and it is these professionals and not Zoe who are the heroes, playing the role children are sometimes seen as playing in other picturebooks where parents are ill. Zoe certainly cares about her father but, in Evans's terms, neither has to provide "caring about," as in the two HG books, nor "caring for."

In Stridsberg's text, Zoe questions why her father is depressed and why he does not want to live, and she is allowed to express these thoughts. Zoe also goes to visit her father on her own, and she makes friends with another patient on his ward. By the end, Zoe's father is able to return home, but although he is well in some ways, Stridsberg makes it clear that his illness is not over: "My dad never really got happy but things turned out okay for him anyway. Some people are never happy. It doesn't matter what you do, they're still sad. Sometimes they get so sad they have to stay at the hospital until it passes. It isn't dangerous." This, too, is in contrast to the other books discussed here, where illness is shown as having a finite end point. Zoe and her father manage to reforge some sort of relationship, whereas in the HG books, the caregiving children seem outside of the new family dynamic.

I recognize that hyperemesis gravidarum and depression are not comparable in scope, and also that I must acknowledge that an ill father could be depicted differently from an ill mother, for some of the gender-based reasons already discussed in this chapter. Furthermore, the books were written in different languages and published in different ways (self-published versus by a mainstream publisher). However, I would suggest that Stridsberg and Lundberg's picturebook shows that it is possible to depict parental illness in another way. A parent can be unwell without the child taking on the role of being a protector or a hero. An illness can impact patients and children, but people can have "okay" lives nonetheless. Illness can be part of life without placing an undue burden on a child.

CONCLUSION

While this chapter is undeniably a limited case study of two books on a very specific subject, I think it does have something interesting to say about depictions of caregiving and healthcare in children's literature. It seems clear from sociological research that caregiving can have both positive and negative effects on young people, but this small research project has primarily found the negative in literary depictions. The two books show illness as something to be explained; they depict children who are put in caregiving roles that may not be appropriate while also having to accept a lack of the expected caregiving in return; they are not particularly inclusive or challenging of stereotypes; they do not offer in-depth explorations of mental health and especially not long-term effects of illness and caregiving; they largely omit medical professionals despite illness being the key feature; and they do not portray fathers contributing much care to their spouses or children. Children may feel empowered to a certain extent, because they see that they can make a significant contribution to their families, but this may also be too much power or too heavy an expectation for some children in certain situations and at specific ages.

McCall's and Dean's books are both issue books, without plots. Issue books are problematic, I claim, because they focus on the issue to the detriment of having a plot. In other words, they might as well be nonfiction works giving information, because they generally simply explain depression, diabetes, divorce, or whatever else it might be. They do not show someone living with that issue and having a life beyond it. That gives the impression that if you have a medical or mental health condition or if you are going through something difficult, you are no more than that. And these books do not show much in the children's lives beyond their mothers' illness. This is in contrast to Stridsberg and Lundberg's picturebook, which is likewise about parental illness but focuses on the child's needs and shows the child continuing to live life beyond the difficult situation.

Future research needs to compare these two HG texts with other picturebooks in English that depict children of ill parents in order to explore how common it is to show young carers in children's literature and to analyze how they are portrayed. But this study suggests that the children of ill parents are pressured to protect and care for their parents and to resign themselves to not receiving the care they would usually expect and that the UN Convention on the Rights of the Child suggests children ought to receive (United Nations).

NOTES

1. I write "picturebook" as one word to show the close connection between words and images.

2. I use "pregnant person" to show awareness that some people who are pregnant do not identify as mothers or women, although the two picturebooks I discuss in this book both focus on women who are pregnant.

3. By this time, I had also learned about the charity Pregnancy Sickness Support (PSS), which has a website and a forum (see https://www.pregnancysicknesssupport.org.uk/). I spoke to a staff member there, who provided me with information to give to the doctor, and I was also given a peer supporter, who texted me once in a while to check in with me and to help me feel less alone. I later trained as a peer supporter for PSS and have worked with many pregnant people who are ill with HG since then.

4. I wrote an article about breastfeeding while ill with hyperemesis (Epstein, "Breastfeeding").

5. See, for example, Jones on bereavement; Rutter on children with ill parents; Becker et al., Evans, and Bibby and Becker on children as caregivers; and Chamberlin on children as caregivers.

6. Some of the research on child caregivers explores major differences between the Global North and the Global South, but here I focus on the North, given that the books are from the US and the UK. Similarly, some scholarly work analyzes differences between gender roles when it comes to caring responsibilities, but since both of my texts feature gender-neutral child protagonists, I will not discuss this in any depth.

7. In addition, self-publishing often has some implications for editing, including some inconsistencies of style or phrases that could be more carefully written or illustrations that are not as professional as what one might find in books published by publishing companies.

8. See Sarles.

9. I have discussed the lack of plot in issue books elsewhere (Epstein, *Are the Kids All Right?* 26–62).

10. The nurse is called "Nurse Bunn," where "bunn" presumably refers to "bunny." But perhaps there is also a link to "bun in the oven," referencing pregnancy.

11. See Elderkin and Berthoud.

12. See, for example, Joy; Clevinger; Wonders and Worries; What Do We All Day?; and Little Parachutes.

13. See, for example, DePalma and Naidoo and Zabawa, which both discuss animals in LGBTQ+ picturebooks.

14. Evans points out that more research needs to be done on the positive aspects of child caregiving for a variety of reasons, because even if caregiving can help children develop resilience, there is a suggestion "that younger siblings of children with caring responsibilities could be 'highly vulnerable,' since they witness the 'chronic and debilitating illness' of parents/relatives but do not benefit from developing closer emotional ties through a caring role or gain from a sense of responsibility, pride, and emotional maturity" (1908). It would be interesting to explore picturebooks that show families with multiple children, where only the oldest has a caregiving role, to see if this is the case.

15. Indeed, my local library system generally refuses to order the self-published ones, making them difficult for me to access and analyze unless I buy them myself.

16. All quotes are from my own English translation.

WORKS CITED

Austin, LeAne. "Children as Caregivers." *Today's Caregiver*, https://caregiver.com/articles/children-as-caregivers/.

Becker, Saul, et al. *Young Carers and Their Families: Working Together for Children, Young People and Their Families*. Blackwell Science, 1998.

Bibby, Andrew, and Saul Becker. *Young Carers in Their Own Words*. Calouse Gulbenkian Foundation, 2000.

Chamberlin, Jamie. "Little-Known Caregivers." *APA Monitor*, vol. 41, no. 9, 2010. *American Psychological Association*, https://www.apa.org/monitor/2010/10/children.

Chetty, Darren, and Karen Sands-O'Connor. "Beyond the Secret Garden: Animal Fables and Dehumanization in Children's Books?" *Books for Keeps*, no. 238, Sep. 2019, https://booksforkeeps.co.uk/article/beyond-the-secret-garden-animal-fables-and-dehumanization-in-childrens-books/.

Clevinger, Brandi. "9 Children's Books Kids of Chronically Ill Parents Should Read." *Mamas Facing Forward*, 19 June 2023, https://www.mamasfacingforward.com/2020/04/14/9-childrens-books-kids-of-chronically-ill-parents-should-read/.

Dean, Caitlin, and Amanda Shortman. *Hyperemesis Gravidarum—The Definitive Guide*. SpewingMummy, 2014.

Dean, Caitlin. *How to Be an HG Hero! Helping Children Understand Hyperemesis Gravidarum*. Illustrated by Paul Colledge, SpewingMummy, 2015.

DePalma, Renée. "Gay Penguins, Sissy Ducklings . . . and Beyond? Exploring Gender and Sexuality Diversity through Children's Literature." *Discourse: Studies in the Cultural Politics of Education*, vol. 37, no. 6, 2016, pp. 828–45.

Elderkin, Susan, and Ella Berthoud. *The Story Cure: An A–Z of Books to Keep Kids Happy, Healthy and Wise*. Canongate, 2016.

Epstein, B.J. *Are the Kids All Right? Representations of LGBTQ Characters in Children's and Young Adult Literature*. HammerOn Press, 2013.

Epstein, B.J. "Breastfeeding and Hyperemesis Gravidarum." *ABM Magazine*, 2019, https://abm.me.uk/wp-content/uploads/mag11-featured.pdf.

Evans, Ruth. "Children as Caregivers." *Handbook of Child Well-Being: Theories, Methods and Policies in Global Perspective*, edited by Asher Ben-Arieh et al., Springer, 2014, pp. 1893–1916.

Flood, Alison. "Children's Books Eight Times as Likely to Feature Animal Main Characters as BAME People." *The Guardian*, 11 Nov. 2020, https://www.theguardian.com/books/2020/nov/11/childrens-books-eight-times-as-likely-to-feature-animal-main-characters-than-bame-people.

Jones, Eileen H. *Bibliotherapy for Bereaved Children: Healing Reading*. Jessica Kingsley Publishers, 2001.

Joy, Kevin. "10 Great Children's Books for Talking About Surgery, Sickness and Feelings." *University of Michigan Health* blog, 25 Jan. 2018, https://healthblog.uofmhealth.org/childrens-health/10-great-childrens-books-for-talking-about-surgery-sickness-and-feelings.

Little Parachutes. "Picture Books about . . . Serious Illness in the Family." https://www.littleparachutes.com/category/issues/serious-illness/.

McCall, Ashli. *Mama Has Hyperemesis Gravidarum (But Only for a While)*. Illustrated by Anna-Maria Crum. Self-published, 2009.

Minority Nurse. "Race and Ethnicity Statistics." *Minority Nurse*. 2021. https://minoritynurse.com/nursing-statistics.

Naidoo, Jamie Campbell, and Mercedes Zabawa. "Sameness and Difference in Visual Representations of Same-Sex Couples in International Children's Picture Books." *International LGBTQ+ Literature for Children and Young Adults*, Edited by B.J. Epstein and Elizabeth L. Chapman, Anthem, 2021, pp. 183–98

NHS England. "Ethnic Minority Nurses and Midwives." 2020, https://www.england.nhs.uk/nursingmidwifery/delivering-the-nhs-ltp/cno-black-and-minority-ethnic-bme-leadership/.

Office of National Statistics. "Births in England and Wales: 2022 (Refreshed Populations)." 2024, https://www.ons.gov.uk/peoplepopulationandcommunity/birthsdeathsandmarriages/livebirths/bulletins/birthsummarytablesenglandandwales/2022refreshedpopulations.

Pregnancy Sickness Support. 2021, https://www.pregnancysicknesssupport.org.uk/.

Rutter, Michael. *Children of Sick Parents: An Environmental and Psychiatric Study*. Oxford UP, 1966.

Sarles, Patricia. "Heather Has a Donor: 30 Years of International Lesbian-Themed Children's Picture Books About Donor Insemination, 1989–2019." *International LGBTQ+ Literature for Children and Young Adults*, edited by B.J. Epstein and Elizabeth L. Chapman, Anthem, 2021, pp. 147–80.

Statista. "Pregnancy—Statistics & Facts." 2024, https://www.statista.com/topics/1850/pregnancy/.

Stridsberg, Sara. *Dyksommar*. Illustrated by Sara Lundberg, Mirando, 2019.

Stridsberg, Sara. *The Summer of Diving*. Illustrated by Sara Lundberg, translated by B.J. Woodstein, Triangle Square, 2022.

United Nations General Assembly. "Convention on the Rights of the Child." *Office of the High Commissioner*, 20 Nov. 1989, https://www.ohchr.org/en/instruments-mechanisms/instruments/convention-rights-child.

What Do We Do All Day? "Middle Grade Books with Characters Who Have Medical Challenges." https://www.whatdowedoallday.com/childrens-books-characters-medical-challenges/.

Wonders and Worries. "Recommended Reading." https://www.wondersandworries.org/for-parents/recommended-reading/.

World Bank. "Labor force participation rate, female (% of female population ages 15+) (modeled ILO estimate)." https://data.worldbank.org/indicator/SL.TLF.CACT.FE.ZS.

MOVING TOWARD LITERATURE-BASED DENTISTRY TO BOOST ORAL HEALTH LITERACY OF CHILDREN

Interprofessional Partnerships between Dentists, Doctors, and Librarians

VALERIE A. UBBES, MADISON MINER, AND MANJUSHRI KARTHIKEYAN

This chapter focuses on the oral health literacy of children and their ability to read and understand print and electronic books about teeth, dentistry, and oral health behaviors. In this chapter, we provide a narrative review of selected picturebooks that promote oral health hygiene and dental checkups for children. We also describe a new genre of electronic texts that were designed into an *eBook for Oral Health Literacy©* curriculum with integrative themes of oral health hygiene, nutrition and beverages for healthy teeth, and dental checkups. The curriculum gives children access to visual, textual, and gestural (nonverbal) messages to persuade them to act on their oral health in one-minute chapters that can be read and listened to via a digital device or from an academic library website.

We have three goals with this chapter with an overall aim of boosting the oral health literacy of children using a new approach called literature-based dentistry. Our first goal is to review the role of oral health as a key component of overall health. A contemporary shift is occurring to include oral health content into health professions education and to include more person-centered approaches with increased referrals between pediatric dentists and doctors. A renewed strategy for interprofessional partnerships is predicated on the fact that more than fifty systemic diseases start in the mouth. Therefore, children and their families will need to experience more "oral health education to increase oral health literacy and oral health knowledge" (Jang and Yoon 93). School-age children and their families will also need to experience more patient referrals between dentists and doctors in order to boost the expectancy of integrative healthcare across the lifespan.[1]

Our second goal is to promote children's oral health literacy by highlighting the need to depict interprofessional partnerships between dentists and doctors in children's literature. Oral health literacy has been defined as "the ability to understand and act on oral health information" (California Department of Public Health 4). If children can gain access to more integrative storylines about dental and medical checkups, these narratives will increase children's functional health knowledge, language, and lexicon about integrative healthcare and the importance of health-promoting behaviors and preventive checkups. There is a need to increase access to print and electronic books about oral health showing dentists and doctors working together, leading to improved social norms and cultural expectations to enhance oral health behaviors and health literacy.

Our third goal is to advocate for public librarians as health literacy professionals to increase children's access to oral health literature in a variety of settings such as public libraries, school libraries, school-based health clinics, and school health education classrooms using our annotated bibliography (provided in the Appendix). We conclude with a reminder for dentists and doctors to reach out to public librarians to seek high-quality children's literature for families to access and read in clinic waiting rooms. In short, we advance a school-community-clinical approach for oral health literacy that seeks to improve and increase the general health and oral health of children and their families through literature-based dentistry.

BACKGROUND

Oral health is an integral component of overall health for children and their families. Some expository texts have begun to focus on relationships that children can form with their dentists while in the setting of the dental clinic. When realistic books do surface for younger children,[2] dentistry and medicine have been written about as separate and disconnected narratives in children's literature, often mirroring the ways in which these pediatric fields have operated as distinct and separate clinical practices for more than one hundred years. In general, children's books do not typically show children and their families going to visit a dentist and a doctor within the same storyline. This practice certainly mirrors the lack of referrals between dentists and doctors in pediatric healthcare, resulting in gaps in routine care instead of interprofessional collaborations that build social, cultural, and behavioral norms for children and their families.

Although most oral healthcare in the United States occurs in private dental clinics, children and their families receive "care where they live, work, and learn—including in community health centers, government-run clinics, dental schools, or in schools" (National Institute of Health, *Oral Health in America*). As such, children and their families could benefit from more school-community-clinical approaches. Children still do not receive planned, sequential, and consistent time to learn health education in schools where they also may experience inadequate exposure to oral health education in the curriculum (U.S. Centers for Disease Control, "School Health Policies"). Providing children from all social, economic, and geographic backgrounds access to valid and reliable health information, products, and services is an important aim of health literacy, which is one of eight National Health Education Standards in a skill-based school health curriculum (National Consensus for School Health Education).

Access to more print and electronic books about oral health content will help children to boost the oral health literacy skills that lead them to practice self-care behaviors. Dentists and doctors in training also need access to age-appropriate and developmentally appropriate information literacy as part of their education about how to promote health literacy for children. National literacy programs like Reach Out and Read have been vital in building book-sharing, reading aloud programs for children and families in medical contexts (Jackson and Mell; Needleman et al.; Diener et al.), but access to literature-based interventions still needs to grow in dental contexts.

GOAL 1: ORAL HEALTH AS A KEY COMPONENT OF GENERAL HEALTH

Our first goal highlights the importance of oral health as a key component of general health for Americans within the context of dental and medical history. Historically, dentistry and medicine have been studied and practiced as separate disciplines. However, more recent agendas call for better communication and referrals between the two disciplines in order to deliver more effective integrative care so that children and their families are more aware of the important connections between dentistry and medicine. This historical context is necessary for readers of this volume with interests in the role of children's literature in healthcare because dental caries, the disease that causes tooth decay, affects more than 50 percent of children in the United States (Dye et al.). Tooth decay especially affects children in poverty and in rural areas where access to dental clinics is limited and affordability of dental care remains challenging (National Institute of Dental and Craniofacial Research, "The Invisible Barrier").

Moreover, children lack access to literature about teeth, dentistry, and oral health behaviors, with no children's books showing how dentists and doctors work together to make referrals between their clinics to improve child health.

Oral healthcare is often viewed as a personal health habit rather than a major determinant of health and disease. However, oral health is much more than a hygiene habit. Oral health has a significant impact on overall health and is a major indicator of an individual's health status and quality of life. Oral health infections are associated with diabetes, heart disease, cancer, and stroke. According to the American Medical Association, dental care is the most prevalent unmet health need in US children (Mouradian et al.). Many children are at risk of missing school, with dental cavities being the most common childhood disease in the United States. Children with poor oral health status are three times more likely to miss school due to dental pain, resulting in poorer school performance (Guarnizo-Herreño and Wehby; Jackson et al.). In the US, 42 percent of children aged two to eleven years have experienced tooth decay (Edelstein and Chinn; Wehby). Oral health literacy (OHL) is a determinant of oral health, and low OHL reduces self-care skills and the ability to understand instructions from dentists.

In the 1800s, Horace H. Hayden and Chapin A. Harris were credited for founding the Baltimore College of Dental Surgery, the first dental school in the United States, which had intentions to "educate and train dentists with the understanding that it was important to create interdisciplinary connections between medicine and dentistry" (Mays 1). To date, the Health Sciences and Human Services Library (HSHSL)[3] at the University of Maryland, Baltimore, has a collection and list of dental health books for children that were chosen by an interprofessional review team of academic and public librarians, a pediatric dentist, registered dental hygienists, pediatric nurses, health education specialists, a professor of public health, a classroom teacher, a school nurse coordinator, and students of dentistry and dental hygiene. (For some of these titles, refer to the Appendix.)

After the first nonmedical college to promote the study and practice of dentistry was established with the first Doctor of Dental Surgery (DDS) degree, the overlap between these two professions declined, despite significant "linkages between systemic health and oral health" (Tiwari). In order to combat this disciplinary separation, current thinking promotes a more interdisciplinary approach between dentistry and medicine to increase knowledge about the signs and symptoms associated with the fifty-seven systemic illnesses that begin in the mouth.[4] This contemporary research reveals an even greater need to increase dental services and oral health education in our nation's schools and to increase the number of educational materials available for children and their families through interdisciplinary teams of librarians, writers, and researchers.[5]

As recent history has demonstrated, in order to advance a specialized discipline like pediatric dentistry, dentists need a formal professional education about children, a membership in a professional organization that promotes children, and access to a professional scientific literature that publishes research about children within dentistry.[6]

Before turning to our second goal of highlighting interprofessional partnerships between dentists and doctors in children's literature, we'd like to assess whether interprofessional partnerships between dentists and doctors are actually occurring. This idea for pediatricians and not just dentists to promote oral health and caries prevention among children was recently summarized by Melinda B. Clark and Patricia A. Braun, who state that "primary care clinicians could ensure the delivery of more effective whole-person care; help ameliorate oral health inequities that may be related to socioeconomic status, race and ethnicity, and insurance status; and potentially assist the dental profession in meeting the overwhelming demand for preventive dental care and improving oral health for children" (2140).

Research shows that primary care clinicians (pediatricians) who also deliver preventive oral health services for young children can reduce caries and tooth decay (Kranz et al.). A 2021 editorial associated with the scientific journal *Nature* suggests that "breaking down the division between mouth and body should lead to better healthcare" since more than one hundred million people visit their physician annually but do not go to their dentist (Molayem). These ideas are supported by several initiatives, including a framework to foster oral health literacy and oral and general health integration (Kleinman et al.); a model for integrated medical–dental delivery systems (Jones et al.); and a medical–dental integration program where children at a rural community health center are seen by medical and dental providers during the same visit (Pawloski et al.).

In short, the academic literature supports the need for interdisciplinary cooperation between dentists and doctors based on the relationship between oral disease and systemic disease (Nikolić et al.) and the fact that the mouth is an integral part of the digestive and respiratory tract (Lobbezoo and Aarab). Joint recommendations by the American Academy of Pediatrics, the American Academy of Pediatric Dentistry, and the American Dental Association urge a dental visit by age one, owing to the fact that 87 percent of children have had at least one visit to a doctor but only 2 percent will have seen a dentist by their first birthday (Clark and Braun). Based on the success of these integrative models, we now transition to our second goal, which advocates for a fresh approach to children's literature that reflects the increasing need to model an interprofessional team of dentists and doctors in print and electronic books for children and their families.

GOAL 2: INTERPROFESSIONAL PARTNERSHIPS BETWEEN DENTISTS AND DOCTORS IN CHILDREN'S LITERATURE

Our second goal is to promote children's oral health literacy through integrative storylines about dental and medical checkups. Language-based approaches are essential between parents and their children in order to boost and amplify children's understanding about health, including their ability to make inferences for how to think about and then actually do oral health behaviors every day as a self-care routine. Moreover, oral language, written language, and body language should be integrated together in multimodal health literacy activities (Ubbes and Njoku). The shared reading of books provides parents and their children, and teachers and their students, opportunities for talking and thinking about health-related storylines. Through shared reading of books and especially the conversations indicative of interactive health literacy, children learn the "what, when, where, why, and how" of different health behaviors. The effective use of inquiry-based question prompts between children and their parents help to stimulate reciprocal verbal and nonverbal interactions that increase the learning of healthy behaviors.

Books like those provided in the Appendix at the end of this chapter can play an important role in fostering interactive health literacy, which includes "interpersonal communication between people and their use of print and electronic materials for health enhancement" (Ubbes and Ausherman). Print books with dental themes, like those in table 3.1, may build familiarity with what to expect in a dental clinic so that children can feel more comfortable with the people that they will talk to and with the dental equipment, tools, and procedures that they will experience when going to their checkups every six months.

Formal and informal conversations among children and caregivers in a dental clinic can help to foster interactive health literacy in three ways within a dental context: when using and building upon an oral health vocabulary, when asking and talking about what children understand about their dental checkup, and when explaining the health benefits of practicing oral hygiene behaviors every day. Children who are exposed to literature-based dentistry in school-community-clinical settings have the potential to benefit from narratives that provide social role models, environmental cues, situational prompts, and language and literacy development about oral health. Figure 3.1 shows upstream, midstream, and downstream factors that influence public health initiatives for oral health. In the upstream position, dentists who practice in community and school-based health clinics can play a critical role in providing children and their families access to high-quality print books in their waiting rooms and access to electronic e-books on their websites or

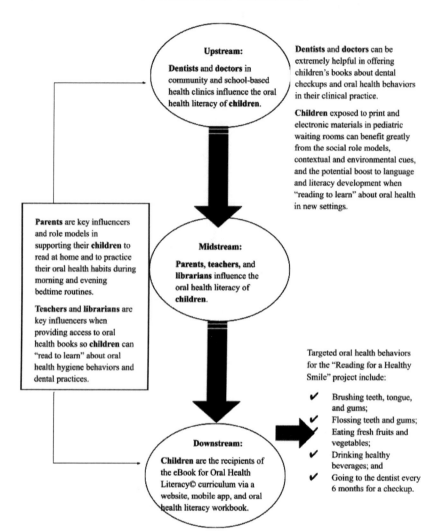

Figure 3.1. Upstream, midstream, and downstream flow chart for oral health literacy. Created by Valerie Ubbes, Madison Miner, and Manjushri Karthikeyan

clinic monitors. In the midstream position, parents, teachers, and librarians can influence children to read books about oral health hygiene and dental practices in the school community. As Rima E. Rudd and Alice M. Horowitz outlined more than two decades ago, the linkages between literacy and health need to be advanced into an oral health research agenda with a "broad-based collaborative effort . . . for reducing literacy barriers to oral health" (National Institute of Dental and Craniofacial Research, "The Invisible Barrier" 174). Thus, there is an ongoing need for building functional knowledge about oral

Table 3.1. Thematic Analysis of Dental Content in Recommended Children's Books

Dental Content	Books
Dental Clothing	Adamson, Clark, Schuh
Dental Equipment	Adamson, Ready, Schuh
Dental Processes and Procedures	Adamson, Ready, Smith, Murphy
Dental Tools	Adamson, Clark, Smith, Schuh, Murphy
Friendly Clinic Environment	Clark, Smith, Murphy
Gender and Ethnic Diversity	Adamson, Clark, Murphy
Inquiry-Based Approaches	Clark, Ready
Interprofessional Collaboration	Adamson, Smith, Murphy
Numeracy	Smith, Schuh, Murphy

health hygiene through more child-centered educational resources (e.g., print and electronic books, websites) while simultaneously advancing literacy and reading comprehension about oral health that leads to improved oral health behaviors—a downstream intervention. Further upstream, these educational resources need to exist before dentists, doctors, and librarians can recommend them.

We turn now to a selection of three expository texts that indicate the separate approaches that authors have taken to date when writing about the clinical practices of pediatric dentists and doctors. One approach is Dee Ready's book, *Dentists Help*; children learn about different types of dentists and their specialties, including how they work to provide care for their patients. The colorful book gives an authentic photo depiction of a dental practice environment and uses question prompts—"What is a dentist?" and "What do dentists do?"—to explain what to expect. *Dentists Help* is from the Our Community Helpers book series, so separate books are available for doctors, librarians, and nurses, to name a few. *Dentists Help* also uses teeth models with word cues and labels of dental equipment to help children gain a vocabulary reading at grade level 1.

In a text written by Heather Adamson, children learn about *A Day in the Life of a Dentist*, which is from a First Fact book series comprised of a narrative storyline and a photographic glossary (e.g., instruments, uniform, appointment, cavity, clinic, decay, disease, germs, hygienist, prevent). Research has shown that photographic visuals are particularly helpful in building neurological links to word learning (López-Barroso et al.), and pictorial representations are superior in capturing attention (Pieters and Wedel). The reader learns different picturebook facts about having twenty baby teeth and twenty-eight to thirty-two adult teeth, including how sugary foods can harm the teeth and gums.

Through different question prompts, the reader is shown the dental clothing (e.g., goggles, mask, gloves) and equipment (e.g., X-ray machines) that the dentist uses when examining a patient. The office manager and hygienists are assistants to the dentist who represent different gendered and ethnic diversities—and they all demonstrate the interprofessional collaboration needed between the dentist and dental hygienist in the same clinic. The procedural actions of a dental checkup from the dentist's perspective (e.g., takes X-ray; counts patients teeth; looks for tooth decay; checks gums for disease; writes report about each; sometimes puts fluoride on teeth) will give young readers and their families an insider's view of visiting the dentist for a checkup. The photo narrative of this book also describes the importance of visiting the dentist regularly.

In Penny Smith's book called *A Trip to the Dentist*, the reader can improve their familiarity with and knowledge of dental care services, including how to brush teeth in the back of the mouth to prevent the buildup of plaque. Set in a friendly clinical environment with toys, stuffed animals, and reading books, the narrative shows interprofessional collaboration between the dentist and a dental assistant who model several "how to" processes (e.g., brushing teeth, putting in a filling, cleaning out a cavity, and drying a cavity). This photographic book is part of "A Trip To" book series (e.g., A Trip to the Doctor; A Trip to the Dentist), but these storylines remain separate without modeling interprofessional collaborations between dentists and doctors. Like the books described above, this book shows a visualization of dental procedures, such as filling a cavity, and also highlights visuals of dental tools on each page (e.g., drill, suction tip, cup, mirror). Visualization of the dental procedures and tools help to break down and demystify the clinical environment for children and parents, providing a helpful way to activate prior knowledge when they enter a dental clinic in the future. In a picture glossary, the reader learns about plaque, molars, incisors, fillings, saliva, and spit, with additional practice in numeracy when the reader counts the number of baby teeth and adult teeth in the mouth. As part of the Level 1 Reader book series called Learning to Read, this book provides behavioral cues for health-related skills by explaining and demonstrating teeth brushing and eating habits for oral health hygiene.

The previous three books, although exemplary in scope and authenticity for pediatric dentistry, indicate the need for newer titles that show partnerships and referrals between dentists and doctors for children. We advocate for new books that can be written as photographic narratives showing a pediatric referral process after children visit either a dentist or doctor practicing in the same clinic (e.g., school-based health clinic, children's hospital) or in the same neighborhood (e.g., community clinic). As indicated, the publishers and the writers of our reviewed titles have chosen to write separate books for dentists and doctors in their book series, even though they do provide a realistic view of what children and their families will experience when visiting a dentist and a dental hygienist in the same clinic. Since social and behavioral modeling of dental and medical partnerships are not currently happening in these books (or in any other books currently available for children), we explain below how interprofessional collaborations can improve the knowledge, attitudes, and beliefs of children toward health-related checkups while also increasing their health literacy. Regardless, we highly recommend the placement of these three books, as well as all other vetted titles in this chapter, in the waiting rooms of dental and pediatric clinics in hospitals, community practice settings, and schools, so children and their families gain access to a health-related lexicon and realistic visual images from which to build their background knowledge of health professionals in different health services environments when reading the books—before, during, and after their health checkups.

The need for a model curriculum for improving oral health literacy for children and their families was the impetus for the development of the *eBook for Oral Health Literacy©* led by our team at Miami University. The project drew upon two of the 355 measurable objectives of the federal initiative called Healthy People 2030. Healthy People 2030 indicates that evidence-based public health improvements are needed in literacy *and* oral health. Over the next decade, the US needs to "increase the proportion of 4th grade students whose reading skills are at or above the proficient achievement level for their grade," since current data indicates that only 36.6 percent of fourth grade students attending public and private schools had reading skills at or above their grade level in 2017 (Office of Disease Prevention). The US also needs to "increase the proportion of children, adolescents, and adults who use the oral healthcare system," since current data indicates that only 43 percent of children, adolescents, and adults used the oral healthcare system in 2016. By advancing both national objectives at the same time, the *eBook for Oral Health Literacy©* helps to boost literacy and dental checkups in tandem with the potential to prevent disease and reduce school absenteeism. If children are not in school due to tooth pain and unmet dental needs, they cannot learn. Current research suggests that children's oral health before they reach kindergarten is associated with academic achievement during their later school years and that children who had a comprehensive oral health exam or a dental treatment had higher reading and math scores (Wehby). Other evidence shows that children who achieve proficiency in knowledge and skills across the prekindergarten to twelfth grade developmental years and make it to high school graduation will have the potential to live six to nine years longer in their lifetime (Wong et al.).

As shown in figure 3.2, the *eBook for Oral Health Literacy©* consists of seventeen chapters organized by five themes, e.g., oral health hygiene, oral

Figure 3.2. This landing page for the *eBook for Oral Health Literacy*© shows its organization into five themes: oral health hygiene, oral health and nutrition, oral health and beverage consumption, oral health and medicine safety, and dental checkups for children.

health and nutrition, oral health and beverage consumption, oral health and medicine safety, and dental checkups for children. The *eBook for Oral Health Literacy*© curriculum consists of an oral health literacy workbook, educational bookmarks, teacher-parent newsletters, published research papers, and accommodations for the blind. Dental education materials are typically rated at or above a ninth-grade reading level (Garrett et al.), but the *eBook for Oral Health Literacy*© is written at the upper-sixth-grade level and has been evaluated for readability, suitability, understandability, actionability, and gist-based message design (Ubbes et al., "Evaluation of an eBook for Oral Health").

The *eBook for Oral Health Literacy*© is a free, academic curriculum for use by children in schools, libraries, health clinics, and at home with their families. The eBook was designed to be a collection of electronic texts that are multisensory, multigenre, and multidisciplinary in order to build functional health literacy, which is the "ability to read, write, and speak about health" (Ubbes and Ausherman). The accompanying *eBook for Oral Health Literacy*© *Curriculum Workbook* by Valerie A. Ubbes and Lindsay M. Wallace promotes literacy skill development through spelling, vocabulary, and comprehension activities—all of which are available online or via a digital app. Chapter materials can be accessed from each page of the workbook via a QR code that takes users right to the website with free access to all of the electronic materials. Our *eBook for Oral Health Literacy© Curriculum Workbook* endeavors to extend the reading of the chapters into explicit literacy instruction within health education. The design of the workbook is based on Orton Gillingham, a popular reading assessment program for children that teaches spelling, writing, and reading skills while using "a multisensory approach through auditory, visual, and kinesthetic modals" (Myers 5). Teachers instruct reading skills using explicit guidelines of Orton Gillingham through the use of sounds, syllables, words, sentences, and written language for building literacy skills (Magpuri-Lavell et al.). Title I teachers in schools could use the eBook with children who are "learning to read," whereas classroom teachers could use the eBook with children who are "reading to learn" about health.

The *eBook for Oral Health Literacy©* curriculum as a whole was designed from an American child's perspective, with visual representations of inclusive ages, genders, and racial identities. We acknowledge that unless elementary children read all seventeen chapters of the curriculum, there could be gaps in their contextual understanding of oral health from a critical health literacy perspective, which focuses on access and equity for people of different backgrounds, health needs, and interests (Ubbes and Ausherman). The curriculum has been transcribed into Braille for the visually impaired, and audio narration provides support for all learners who benefit from multimodal access. There is an ongoing need for more culturally relevant oral health materials that can help to reduce oral health disparities, especially when considering the underlying social and cultural determinants of health (Neves; Patrick et al.). In the *eBook for Oral Health Literacy©* curriculum, low-literacy needs are addressed, but not low-income needs. However, we have recently piloted our Reading for a Healthy Smile© campaign for low-income children and their families to benefit from the distribution of dental kits, a home checklist, and access to the eBook curriculum via social media channels such as Facebook and Instagram in order to boost their oral health literacy and oral health behaviors at home.[7]

The Appendix at the end of this chapter shows a booklist of children's literature that represents children and health professionals from a variety of backgrounds (e.g., race, gender, and age) who can read about oral health hygiene behaviors at home, at school, and in the community. The annotated bibliography addresses some of the National Culturally and Linguistically Appropriate Services (CLAS) Standards from the U.S. Office of Minority Health, which aims "to advance health equity, improve quality, and help eliminate healthcare disparities" when health professionals use easy-to-understand print and multimedia materials with target populations (U.S. Department of Health, "HHS Action Plan"). CLAS in oral healthcare has not yet been fully implemented in children's literature, but our call to action with health professionals, authors, and publishers is to advance the design of more clinic-friendly, child-centric oral health literacy materials for young people and their families. Hence, our new approach is called "literature-based dentistry."

The Cultural Variance Framework may also be useful for authors, publishers, and educators in designing more books and websites for oral health literacy because the framework differentiates three ways to represent cultural influences: identity affiliations, cultural attributes, and cultural specificity (Davis and Resnicow). In the case of children looking at photographs of their peers in a print or electronic book, each child will identify and draw upon beliefs, behaviors, norms, and assumptions toward identify affiliations depending on who is demonstrating the oral health actions of teeth brushing and flossing. The second route of cultural variance is cultural attributes, which are those specific beliefs, norms, values, and behaviors that combine to form an individual's subjective culture. For example, languages other than English or culturally appropriate foods and drinks could be implemented more in children's books about oral health. Contextual cues, the third route of the framework, can influence the degree to which a particular identity affiliation or cultural attribute may be salient to an individual in a specific situation. For example, contextual cues inside a bathroom when brushing one's teeth should look somewhat similar to a children's environment at home in order for it to appear realistic and salient to them.

According to a dental study conducted by Marija Nikolić and her colleagues, "the majority of subjects go to the dentist only after the toothache starts" (135). These results indicated that not only do younger and older populations fail to visit the dentist regularly, but they also often rely first on primary care physicians for their dental care until a more severe problem arises. Insufficient awareness of how the oral cavity and the rest of the body's health are interrelated places patients at risk and leads to insufficient healthcare. Nikolić et al. summarize it this way: "Interdisciplinary cooperation of doctors and dentists should be a prerequisite for good health of all patients" (140). Tamanna Tiwari et al. have argued for "the next generation of dental health specialists [who] are well prepared to function in a whole person-focused practice" and who do not just focus on the mouth, teeth, and gums.[8] Conversely, Shalinie King et al. provide specific guidelines on how doctors can support good oral health by asking their patients: "Do your gums bleed when you brush? Do you have bad breath? Do you have loose teeth? Do you have pain or difficulty chewing? How many teeth do you have?" (King et al 203). Authors of new books for children may benefit from these physician-to-dentist referral questions to help develop child-centric content for storylines using an inquiry-based approach.

As early as 2004, the need for interprofessional collaborations in health literacy was promoted in the seminal book from the Institute of Medicine,

Health Literacy: A Prescription to End Confusion. A key recommendation was for all health professionals to work on health literacy initiatives in a systematic way to ensure that health systems integrate with education systems and sociocultural systems. As such, we designed our work from a health literacy framework by Donald Nutbeam, who differentiated three types of health literacy (e.g., functional, interactive, and critical) that are used in health promotion research. As one example applicable for this chapter with an aim to boost oral health literacy, we believe a collaboration of librarians, clinicians, educators, and parents will need to help children get access to literature-based dentistry to increase their oral health knowledge and beliefs while using an interactive process of conversations, print materials, and electronic materials known as interactive health literacy.

GOAL 3: LIBRARIANS AS PARTNERS IN LITERATURE-BASED DENTISTRY TO PROMOTE ORAL HEALTH LITERACY

Our third goal is to advocate for public librarians as partners in literature-based dentistry. Research supports the value of public libraries, school libraries, and school-based health clinics for public health initiatives.[9] As was discussed in goal one, increasing pediatric referrals between physicians and dentists can boost dental checkups and overall health for children and youth. Similarly, the involvement of librarians, children's book publishers, and authors in partnership with health professionals will foster the interprofessional collaboration needed to advance health literacy in general and oral health literacy specifically.

What prerequisites should literacy professionals think about in their search for high-quality oral health books for children? First, literature-based dentistry for children should contain persuasive messages that promote oral health hygiene behaviors, which are essential for building children's knowledge, attitudes, beliefs, and intentions to do self-care routines that lead to daily habits. Literature-based dentistry is characterized as persuasive messages for brushing, flossing, rinsing, eating nutritious foods, and dental checkups. Oral health messages for children should also rely on visual persuasion. Patients will have increased message understanding and recall of information when visuals are combined with text (Houts et al.). Health professionals who use multimodal communication (e.g., verbal, gestural, kinesthetic, and aural) enhance information processing for individuals by increasing attention to the behavioral tasks to help children to make inferences from the information (Houts et al.). Individuals with lower literacy levels can benefit from multimodal reading approaches so they can access the information in more than one way to understand it.

Hence, youth in middle school who reported that they did not like to read or had trouble reading had significantly fewer dental checkups even after controlling for socioeconomic status (Zullig et al.). Youth with reduced reading abilities got fewer dental checkups. Constructivist theoretical approaches in the teaching and learning of health education have acknowledged the importance of social role models, social interactions, and collaborative meaning making (Ubbes et al., "Teaching for Understanding"). As such, students who saw a parent or caregiver reading in the previous two days had significantly more dental checkups. Conversely, youth who did not see their parent or caregiver reading in the past two days had significantly fewer dental checkups. Similar results occurred if the youth had visited a public library or bookstore during the past year versus not visiting a public library or bookstore. In conclusion, youth reported significantly fewer dental checkups if they did not go to the public library or bookstore in the last year where they could access books of any topic (Zullig et al.).

Picturebooks can be cultural tools for language development and for demonstrating a wide variety of health-related skills and behaviors (Ubbes). The books in our annotated bibliography were selected because they represent culturally diverse healthcare providers working with culturally diverse children and their families within a dental clinic environment. If children read books with visual-textual narratives showing other children demonstrating oral health behaviors, they may be more willing to seek the healthcare that they need throughout their life and even be more likely to envision a future where they become dentists and physicians themselves.

A third prerequisite for high-quality oral health books for children involves nudging. Nudging is "any small action or arrangement that prompt[s] people to do things which will have [a] positive impact on their life" (Cherukodan 255). Nudging is also a practice of making healthy options more "apparent, appealing, and available" to a population (du Pré 315). Nudges, or environmental cues, have been used to encourage parents to attend oral health promotion programs for their children (Marciano et al.), as well as to help librarians to be "nudge architects" by "organizing the context in which people make decisions" (Cherukodan 258; Thaler and Sunstein). Librarians practice nudging when they place documents in locations where library patrons will select a particular book but also pick up other books that may be useful to them at the same time. Thus, we hope that nudging can be incorporated in literature-based dentistry programs led by librarians so that more oral health books can be read by children and their families who frequent libraries, including any dental or medical clinic where there is a waiting room for a checkup.

Print books, including electronic books with authentic photographs, should represent a wide variety of children from different backgrounds because children are the next generation of new dentists and pediatricians. If children from underrepresented racial backgrounds get a late start in seeing themselves as professionals in public health campaigns and published books, they may remain limited and disadvantaged in their career trajectories and aspirations. Current data reflects a lack of diversity in the healthcare workforce. According to the 2020 U.S. Census, African Americans and Latinos together comprised approximately 30 percent of the US population, but they currently represent only 6 percent of all physicians (U.S. Department of Commerce). For example, of physicians in the US, only 5.16 percent are Black or African American physicians and 0.628 percent are Hispanic physicians (Data USA, "Physicians"). Similarly, within the field of dentistry, of the dentists in the US, only 4.94 percent are Black or African American dentists and 0.976 percent are Hispanic (Data USA, "Dentists"). Among registered nurses, only 11.6 percent are Black or African American and 1.51 percent are Hispanic (Data USA, "Registered Nurses"). Therefore, in order to achieve more inclusive and accessible oral health books, librarians, publishers, and authors will need to focus on ways to boost critical health literacy that empowers all children and their families.

In the three children's books reviewed below, we selected the titles for their authentic and inclusive use of photographs to depict positive dental clinic interactions. Readers are also provided language-specific jargon that is common when visiting a dental clinic. For example, language-related cues are often depicted in visible office signage and within the written narratives exchanged by people in the dental clinic. A few books from our list stand out as examples of what to look for in authentic storylines for oral health literacy. The books also model diversity of race and gender in both providers and patients, and Rosalyn Clark's book utilizes an inquiry-based approach conducive to critical health literacy.

In Patricia Murphy's book, *A Visit to the Dentist's Office*, children visit the dentist for a checkup to ensure a healthy smile. From the moment the reader enters the Oz Family Dentistry practice, we meet friendly people like the front desk receptionist and the dental hygienist wearing a name tag. Interprofessional collaboration between the dentist and dental hygienist is shown with child-friendly patient experiences for a boy and a girl who are sitting in dental chairs in the exam room. Several dentists and hygienists from multicultural backgrounds conduct dental procedures such as cleaning, polishing, and viewing a photo of teeth on an X-ray film. Three main sections of this book take us from the Dentist Office to the Exam Room, and then Healthy Smiles where children express a variety of teeth conditions. *A Visit to the Dentist's Office* is written for early intervention students, prekindergarten through second grade, and is one title from the "Visit to Community Helpers" book series, which includes a second title called *The Doctor's Office*. At the end of the book, the dentist instructs three children about healthy teeth and gums while using a teeth model and a poster with directions for brushing, flossing, and rinsing teeth. As the children leave, they are reminded to visit the dentist twice a year.

We turn next to a children's book that uses an inquiry-based approach called *Why We Go to the Dentist* by Rosalyn Clark. This book focuses on how to clean teeth using a toothbrush, why teeth should be flossed each day, and why it is important to go for dental checkups on a regular basis. This title is in the "Caring For Our Bodies" book series and provides a picture glossary of scientific vocabulary words such as bacteria, cavities, gums, and X-rays. Additionally, we've selected one of the six titles in the Pebble Plus Healthy Teeth book series called *At the Dentist* by Mari Schuh. Written for early intervention students in first grade, a young girl, a dentist, and a dental hygienist are fully introduced, along with dental tools and dental clothing. Indeed, both texts represent diverse ethnicities receiving care at the dental office surrounded by dental tools (e.g., picks, small mirror, X-ray machine); oral hygiene products (e.g., toothbrush, floss); and dental clothing (e.g., scrubs, mask, lab coat). Furthermore, both books integrate and define dental terminology (e.g., sealants, cavity, plaque) for children.

Dental content from these three books and others found in our Appendix provide direction to dentists and doctors when choosing books for their pediatric waiting rooms and to librarians when selecting children's books for library collections and displays. As such, librarians fill multiple roles, and in each role, they can contribute to health literacy (Vassilakaki and Moniarou-Papaconstaninou), and oral health literacy specifically, when guiding dentists and doctors in book selections. In this next section, we will address public librarians who promote oral health literacy in the community, in school libraries, and in school-based health centers.

Public Librarians Who Promote Oral Health Literacy in the Community

Public librarians can help to foster an improvement in oral health literacy among children and their families by partnering with dentists and physicians in the community. Both sectors can work together to promote increased access to print and electronic books for children in community dental clinics and private dental practices. Public librarians could also join with health education specialists to make dentists and doctors aware of high-quality children's books to place in their waiting rooms for use by children and their families. Our annotated bibliography of children's books can help to build a lexicon and narrative around going to the dentist as an integral component of pediatric primary care. To date, we have found no printed books showing children going to the dentist and the pediatrician in the same storyline. As we have suggested, children and their families need early and continuous exposure to interprofessional partnerships between dentists and doctors who need to make patient referrals between them.

There are three electronic book chapters of the *eBook for Oral Health Literacy©* that show doctors and dentists in the same narrative and we wish to use these titles as a prototype for distribution. In theme 4 of the curriculum, "Oral Health and Medicine Safety," children improve their oral health literacy in three electronic chapters: "Coping with the Stress of Dental Pain," "Communicating How to Take Medicine Safely with a Trusted Adult," and "Deciding to Follow Rules for Taking Medicine." By reading declarative sentences and child-centric photographs in one-minute stories, children learn the value of who to trust when improving their oral healthcare or what rules to follow when taking medicine from dentists, doctors, or parents.

Librarians who are interested in advancing public health can be guided by a summative review by Morgan M. Philbin et al., who argue that health disparities for ten different determinants of health can be addressed and narrowed by librarians who work in the 17,000 public libraries in the United States. The authors state, "Because libraries are distributed across myriad jurisdictions (e.g., rural, urban, rich, and poor), they offer an existing structure through which targeted investments in high-disparity areas could be part of a multisectoral strategy to promote health and mitigate disparities" (Philbin et al. 193). Two examples include the National Library of Medicine, which trains public librarians to help patrons gain access to "social services, welfare and public assistance, health, education, and employment resources" (Cabello and Butler), and summer reading programs, which are offered in 95 percent of US libraries to prevent the "summer slide" in reading achievement among school-aged children and youth (American Library Association).

Active and retired librarians have been known to participate as volunteer readers in the waiting rooms of the 6,000 Reach Out and Read pediatric clinics around the country. Reach Out and Read, funded by the American Academy of Pediatrics, has a focus on all children who receive their well-child checkups between ages six months and five years, but the program has a special emphasis on low-income families. Furthermore, early literacy supports in the form of Reach Out and Read programs among Latino children have fostered emergent literacy skills for preparing them to enter kindergarten (Diener et al.). This is important because Mexican American children living below the poverty level have the highest incidence of untreated, decayed teeth (Garrett et al.). New data indicate that literacy-enriched Reach Out and Read programs significantly boost an increase in child attendance for well-child checkups. Specifically, there was a twofold increase in the odds of parents reporting that they took their children to the recommended number of preventive pediatric visits as a result of participating in a Reach Out and Read program (Needlman et al.).

Librarians Who Promote Oral Health Literacy in the School Library and Elementary Classroom

School librarians can play an important role as "health information gatekeepers" (Lukenbill and Immroth 3), and they have "a unique opportunity to improve the health literacy of children and teachers" (Barr-Walker 200). School librarians can help teachers to know about the annotated bibliography in this chapter and be advocates for buying those same books for their school library or classroom libraries. School librarians can help the school know about certain health observance months that match themes in the academic curriculum by providing a book display during National Children's Dental Health Month in February or National Health Literacy Month in October. When ordering books for the school library from publishers, librarians can be advocates for requesting books that depict children and their families going to dentists and doctors in the same storyline.

Research indicates that students who attend schools with enriched libraries scored an average one-half a standard deviation higher on standardized tests for reading comprehension than students from control schools (Nielen and Bus). Similarly, schools with libraries have a stronger reading culture and a higher student engagement with books, leading to higher levels of reading achievement. Similar findings have been found in childcare centers where high-quality children's books and a ten-hour staff training were provided as an intervention. Children with the literature-based intervention "outperformed children in comparable day care centers without the intervention on four out of six measures of early literacy development" (Neuman; Nielen and Bus 2).

Librarians Who Promote Oral Health Literacy in School-Based Health Centers

School-based health centers began in the US in 1995 and have grown to more than 2,500 programs to serve children and youth with dental, medical, and vision care within public school districts. The School-Based Health Alliance is a nonprofit organization that coordinates a network of twenty state affiliates and forms partnerships with community organizations and hospitals. In 2021, school-based health centers received an increase in federal funding so that children and their families can obtain the healthcare they need. School-based health centers "place critically needed services like medical, mental, dental, and vision care directly in schools where young people spend the majority of their time" (Arenson et al.). School-based health centers operate within two sectors—education and health—and can contribute to child health by providing preventive healthcare services and primary healthcare to underserved populations. Sometimes the school-based health centers may provide a medical or dental home for students who would not have access to healthcare services (Arenson et al.).

When children leave their academic classrooms and head down the hall toward the school-based health centers for their clinical appointments during the school day, they have an increased potential to lose instructional time on various curriculum topics, concepts, and skills. To prevent this from happening, interprofessional partnerships can be formed between the clinic staff and school librarians, who can help to acquire a collection of health-related print books for the children to read in the school-based health centers while waiting for their dental, medical, or vision checkups. Chapters from the *eBook for Oral Health Literacy*© can also be accessed from digital devices using the Internet or mobile applications. Librarians can help to place books on tabletops and in bookshelves in the clinic waiting rooms and help to load electronic materials on waiting room monitors and computers. Weblinks and QR codes can be promoted on wall posters in the clinic and accessed by mobile devices so children can gain a working vocabulary and background knowledge about going into a dental and medical checkup. Print and electronic books can help children boost their oral health literacy and functional health literacy skills in tandem. Librarians who promote the annotated booklist in the Appendix will help children learn how to talk with their dentists and doctors and know what to expect and do during their appointments. Additionally, school-based health centers can be excellent settings for librarians, dentists, doctors, and nurses to work together in interprofessional partnerships.

Pediatric Dentists and Doctors Who Link with Librarians

We conclude with the need to empower pediatric dentists and doctors to build interprofessional bridges for health literacy and oral health literacy by reaching out to librarians when possible to seek high-quality children's literature for families to access and read when visiting their clinical practice. In short, we advance a school-community-clinical approach for oral health literacy that improves and increases the general health of children and their families through literature-based dentistry. At minimum, we encourage dentists and pediatricians to put children's literature in their clinic waiting rooms to boost critical health literacy and to support children with access to print and electronic books that increase their functional and interactive health literacy skills.

CONCLUSION

We have advanced a new call to action called literature-based dentistry. Literature-based dentistry can contribute to the development and improvement of health literacy and oral health literacy—both are integral ways to boost the quality of life and longevity of children and their families. In order to improve and advance two of the leading health indicators of the federal initiative called Healthy People 2030, interprofessional pediatric partnerships need to move quickly toward literature-based dentistry to boost the oral health literacy of children and their families and ultimately, their improved oral health knowledge and behaviors. More interprofessional collaboration between dentistry and medicine is needed in clinical practice settings, flanked by librarians and health education specialists who can help to bridge the literacy gap with print and electronic books so children and their families can learn about oral health in the context of their overall health status as determined by preventive checkups. We return to the premise that future storylines in print and electronic books for children will need to depict interprofessional partnerships of dentists and physicians in both the words and images so as to provide social norms and role models for oral health and general health integration. Publishers and authors will need to write print and electronic books about doctors referring children to dentists and pediatric dentists referring children to pediatricians. Recent collaborations have begun to take place in school-based health centers where children experience seamless coordination between medical, dental, and vision checkups in one on-site location while attending school. Librarians and health education specialists can advocate for literature-based dentistry in many different waiting rooms where children and their families go for their dental and medical checkups. Intentional steps in fostering interprofessional partnerships between dentists, doctors, librarians, health educators, publishers, and authors will make it possible to improve health literacy and oral health literacy for current American children and future generations.

NOTES

1. For more background on shifts in curricula and integrative approaches, see Gill et al.; Jones et al.; National Institute of Dental and Craniofacial Research, "Invisible Barrier"; Gauger et al.; and Harnagea et al.

2. Historically, children's literature has not portrayed dentists and doctors as human helpers who form reciprocal relationships with patients in their communities. Instead, dentists and doctors have often been portrayed as animal protagonists in picturebooks, with some storylines written about fantastical adventures of teeth or toothbrushes, which are not realistic contexts for children to make connections to their own health.

3. The HSHSL is distinguished as the first library established in 1813 by a medical school in the United States. The library also serves as the Regional Medical Library (RML) for the National Network of Libraries of Medicine, Region 1.

4. For more on this need, see Vieira and Caramelli and the National Institute of Dental and Craniofacial Disease, *Oral Health in America*.

5. For more on promoting oral health in schools, see Arenson et al.; Patrick et al.; and Tzoc and Ubbes.

6. In 1969, pediatric dentistry was founded by the International Association of Pediatric Dentistry (IAPD) with its mission "to promote good oral health for children worldwide" (Gelbier et al. 391). In 1927, the American Society for the Promotion of Children's Dentistry (ASDC) was established, followed by the publication of the *Journal of Dentistry for Children* in 1934. In 1947, the American Academy of Pedodontics, later known as the American Academy of Pediatric Dentistry (AAPD), was founded. In 2002, the ASDC and AAPD successfully merged. In 2018, there were 8,033 pediatric dentists practicing in the US, with this number expected to increase to 10,560 pediatric dentists by the year 2030 (Casamassimo 31).

7. Explaining how we considered issues of accessibility for low literacy and multiple home languages is outside the scope of this chapter. For more information about these considerations, see a variety of prototypes at https://dlp.lib.miamioh.edu/healthliteracy/, which served as a pilot project for the final multimodal design of the *eBook for Oral Health Literacy©* curriculum. All curriculum materials and our digital app are available at no cost at https://dlp.lib.miamioh.edu/ebook/

8. Dentists frequently refer patients to physicians when poor oral health is associated with diabetes, heart disease, and stroke (U.S. Centers for Disease Control, "Oral Health Conditions"), even though the start of inflammation usually had its origin in the oral cavity (Iwata and Sessle). F. Lobbezoo and G. Aarab advocate for medicine and dentistry working side by side to improve global health equity with the need for physicians to reach out to dentists and dentists to reach out to physicians. Provider collaboration is essential for reducing the economic burden of untreated dental care, which is estimated at 545 billion US dollars—comparable to the economic burden of the two most expensive illnesses of cardiovascular disease and diabetes (World Health Organization). Thus, the most vulnerable populations (e.g., low income, older people, people with disabilities and chronic diseases, uninsured, limited access to oral healthcare) could benefit the most from dental and general health collaborations (Lobbezoo and Aarab).

9. See, for example, Cahill and Ingram; Abidin and ShaifuddinI.; Philbin, et al.; Merga; Barr-Walker; Nielen and Bus; and Arenson et al.

WORKS CITED

Abidin, Nur Syazwanie Zainal, and Norshila Shaifuddin. "Systematic Literature Review of the Bibliotherapy Practices in Public Libraries in Supporting Communities' Mental Health and Wellbeing." *Public Library Quarterly*, vol. 42, no. 2, 2021, https://doi.org/10.1080/01616846.2021.2009291.

Adamson, Heather. *A Day in the Life of a Dentist*. Capstone Press, 2008.

American Library Association. "Summer Reading Programs: Research." *ALA*, 2015, http://libguides.ala.org/summer-reading/research.

Arenson, Michael, et al. "The Evidence on School-Based Health Centers: A Review." *Global Pediatric Health*, vol. 6, 2019, https://doi.org/10.1177/2333794X19828745.

Barr-Walker, Jill. "Health Literacy and Libraries: A Literature Review." *Reference Services Review*, vol. 44, no. 2, 2016, pp. 191–205, https://doi.org/10.1108/RSR-02-2016-0005.

Cabello, Marcela, and Stuart M. Butler. "How Public Libraries Help Build Healthy Communities." *Brookings*, 30 Mar. 2017, https://www.brookings.edu/blog/up-front/2017/03/30/how-public-libraries-help-build-healthy-communities/.

Cahill, Maria, and Erin Ingram. "Extratextual Talk in Public Library Storytime Programs: A Focus on Questions." *Journal of Early Childhood Research*, vol. 20, no. 4, 2022, https://doi.org/10.1177/1476718X221098662.

California Department of Public Health. "Oral Health Literacy in Practice" *California Oral Health Technical Assistance Center*, https://oralhealthsupport.ucsf.edu/sites/g/files/tkssra861/f/wysiwyg/CDPH_Toolkit_HL%20Guidebook_210617_Final_single_OOH%20logo%20updated.pdf.

Casamassimo, Paul. "Pediatric Dental Workforce Study: What Does It Mean for The Future of Your Practice?" *The Magazine of the American Academy of Pediatric Dentistry*, March 2020, pp. 30–33, https://www.aapd.org/globalassets/media/pdt/march2020pdt.web.pdf.

Cherukodan, Surendran. "Adopting Nudge Theory in Academic Libraries." INFLIBNET Centre, 2019, https:// https://ir.inflibnet.ac.in/handle/1944/2307.

Clark, Melinda B., and Patricia A. Braun. "Promotion of Oral Health and Prevention of Dental Caries among Children in Primary Care." *JAMA*, vol. 326, no. 21, 2021, pp. 2139–2140.

Clark, Rosalyn. *Why We Go to the Dentist*. Learner Publishing Group, 2018.

Data USA. "Dentists." *Data USA*, 2021, https://datausa.io/profile/soc/dentists.

Data USA. "Physicians." *Data USA*, 2021, https://datausa.io/profile/soc/physicians.

Data USA. "Registered Nurses." *Data USA*, 2021, https://datausa.io/profile/soc/registered-nurses.

Davis, Rachel E., and Ken Resnicow. "The Cultural Variance Framework for Tailoring Health Messages." *Health Communication Message Design: Theory and Practice*, edited by Hyuni Cho, SAGE Publications, 2012, pp. 115–35.

Diener, Marissa L., et al. "Kindergarten Readiness and Performance of Latino Children Participating in Reach Out and Read." *Journal of Community Medicine and Health Education*, vol. 2, no. 133, 2012, https://doi.org/10.4172/jcmhe.1000133.

du Pré, Athena. *Communicating About Health: Current Issues and Perspectives*. 5th ed., Oxford UP, 2016.

Dye, Bruce A., et al. "Trends in Dental Caries in Children and Adolescents According to Poverty Status in the United States from 1999 through 2004 and from 2011 through 2014." *Journal of American Dental Association*, vol. 148, no. 8, 2017, pp. 550–65, https://doi.org/10.1016/j.adaj.2017.04.013.

Edelstein, Burton L., and Courtney H. Chinn. "Update on Disparities in Oral Health and Access to Dental Care for America's Children." *Academic Pediatrics*, vol. 9, no. 6, 2009, pp. 415–19, https://doi.org/10.1016/j.acap.2009.09.010.

Garrett, Gail M., et al. "Parental Functional Health Literacy Relates to Skip Pattern Questionnaire Error and to Child Oral Health." *Journal of the California Dental Association*, vol. 40, no. 5, 2012, pp. 423–30, https://www.ncbi.nlm.nih.gov/pmc/articles/PMC3488587/.

Gauger, Tylor L., et al. "Integrative and Collaborative Care Models between Pediatric Oral Health and Primary Care Providers: A Scoping Review of the Literature." *Journal of Public Health Dentistry*, vol. 78, no. 3, 2018, pp. 246–56, https://doi.org/10.1111/JPHD.12267.

Gelbier, Stanley, et al. "History of the International Association of Paediatric Dentistry: A 50-year Perspective." *International Journal of Paediatric Dentistry*, vol. 29, no. 3, 2019, pp. 387–402, https://doi.org/10.1111/ipd.12492.

Gill, Stephanie A., et al. "Integrating Oral Health into Health Professions School Curricula." *Medical Education Online*, vol. 27, no. 1, 2022, https://doi.org/10.1080/10872981.2022.2090308.

Guarnizo-Herreño, Carol Cristina, and George L. Wehby. "Children's Dental Health, School Performance, and Psychosocial Well-being." *The Journal of Pediatrics*, vol. 161, no. 6, 2012, pp. 1153–59, https://doi.org/10.1016/j.jpeds.2012.05.025.

Harnagea, Hermina, et al. "Barriers and Facilitators in the Integration of Oral Health into Primary Care: A Scoping Review." *BMJ Open*, vol. 7, no. 9, 2017, https://doi.org/10.1136/bmjopen-2017-016078.

Houts, Peter S., et al. "The Role of Pictures in Improving Health Communication: A Review of Research on Attention, Comprehension, Recall and Adherence." *Patient Education and Counseling*, vol. 61, no. 2, 2006, pp. 173–90, https://doi.org/10.1016/J.PEC.2005.05.004.

Institute of Medicine, et al. *Health Literacy: A Prescription to End Confusion*. The National Academies Press, 2004, https://doi.org/10.17226/10883.

Iwata, K., and B. J. Sessle. "The Evolution of Neuroscience as a Research Field Relevant to Dentistry." *Journal of Dental Research*, vol 98, no. 13, 2019, pp. 1407–17, https://doi.org/10.1177/0022034519875724.

Jackson, Jasmyne, and Anthony Mell. "Beyond the Cover—Children's Books as Tools for Positive Social Identity Formation." *JAMA Pediatrics*, vol. 176, no. 7, 2022, pp. 637–38, https://doi.org/10.1001/jamapediatrics.2022.1060.

Jackson, Stephanie L., et al. "Impact of Poor Oral Health on Children's School Attendance and Performance." *American Journal of Public Health*, vol. 101, no. 10, 2011, pp. 1900–6, https://doi.org/10.2105/AJPH.2010.200915.

Jang, Sun-Ju, and Sung-Uk Yoon. "The Relationship of Oral Health Behavior with Oral Health Literacy and Oral Health Knowledge Among Elementary School Students." *Journal of Korean Society of Dental Hygiene*, vol. 19, no. 1, 2019, pp. 93–103, https://doi.org/10.13065/jksdh.20190011.

Jones, Judith A., et al. "Integrated Medical-Dental Delivery Systems: Models in a Changing Environment and Their Implications for Dental Education." *Journal of Dental Education*, vol. 81, no. 9, 2017, pp. eS21–eS29, https://doi.org/10.21815/JDE.017.029.

King, Shalinie, et al. "Oral Health and Cardiometabolic Disease: Understanding the Relationship." *Internal Medicine Journal*, vol. 52, no. 2, 2022, pp. 198–205, https://doi.org/10.1111/imj.15685.

Kleinman, Dushanka V., et al. "A Framework to Foster Oral Health Literacy and Oral/General Health Integration." *Frontiers in Dental Medicine*, vol. 2, 2021, https://doi.org/10.3389/fdmed.2021.723021.

Kranz, Ashley M., John S. Preisser, and R. Gary Rozier. "Effects of Physician-Based Preventive Oral Health Services on Dental Caries." *Pediatrics*, vol 136, no. 1, 2015, pp. 107–14, https://doi.org/10.1542/peds.2014-2775.

Lobbezoo, F., and G. Aarab (2022). "Medicine and Dentistry Working Side by Side to Improve Global Health Equity." *Journal of Dental Research*, vol. 101, no. 10, 2022, https://doi.org/10.1177/00220345221088237.

López-Barroso, Diana, et al. "Impact of Literacy on the Functional Connectivity of Vision and Language Related Networks." *NeuroImage*, vol. 213, 2020, https://doi.org/10.1016/j.neuroimage.2020.116722.

Lukenbill, Bill, and Barbara Immroth. "School and Public Youth Librarians as Health Information Gatekeepers: Research from the Lower Rio Grande Valley of Texas." *School Library Media Research*, vol. 12, 2009, pp. 1–35.

Magpuri-Lavell, Theresa, et al. "The Effects of a Summer Reading Program Using Simultaneous Multisensory Instruction of Language Arts on Reading Proficiency." *Reading Improvement*, vol. 51, no. 4, 2014, pp. 361–72.

Marciano, Deborah, et al. *Nudging Parents to Improve Children's Oral Health: A Field Study*. Social Policy Institute at Washington University in St. Louis, 2021.

Mays, Keith A. "Designing an Oral Health Curriculum that Facilitates Greater Integration of Oral Health into Overall Health." *Frontiers in Dental Medicine*, vol. 2, 2021, https://doi.org/10.3389/fdmed.2021.680520.

Merga, Margaret. "How Can School Libraries Support Student Wellbeing? Evidence and Implications for Further Research." *Journal of Library Administration*, vol. 60, no. 6, 2020, 660–73, https://doi.org/10.1080/01930826.2020.1773718.

Molayem, Shervin. "Dentists and Doctors Need to Play on the Same Team." *Nature*, 27 Oct. 2021, https://www.nature.com/articles/d41586-021-02919-3.

Mouradian, Wendy E., et al. "Disparities in Children's Oral Health and Access to Dental Care." *JAMA*, vol. 284, no. 20, 2000, pp. 2625–31, https://doi.org/10.1001/jama.284.20.2625.

Murphy, Patricia. *A Visit to the Dentist's Office*. Capstone Press, 2005.

Myers, Lisa. *The Effects of a Multi-Sensory Reading Program on Students with Disabilities*. 2017. Georgia College, EdS Thesis. *Georgia College Knowledge Box*, https://kb.gcsu.edu/eds/12.

National Consensus for School Health Education. *National Health Education Standards: Model Guidance for Curriculum and Instruction*. 3rd ed., 2022, www.schoolhealtheducation.org.

National Institute of Dental and Craniofacial Research. "The Invisible Barrier: Literacy and its Relationship with Oral Health." *Journal of Public Health Dentistry*, vol. 65, no. 6, 2005, pp. 174–82.

National Institute of Health. *Oral Health in America: Advances and Challenges*. National Institute of Dental and Craniofacial Research,, 2021, https://www.nidcr.nih.gov/research/oralhealthinamerica.

Needlman, Robert D., et al. "Attendance at Well-Child Visits after Reach Out and Read." *Clinical Pediatrics*, vol. 58, no. 3, 2019, pp. 282–87, https://doi.org/10.1177/0009922818822975.

Neuman, Susan B. "Books Make a Difference: A Study of Access to Literacy." *Reading Research Quarterly*, vol. 34, no. 3, 1999, pp. 286–311. https://doi.org/10.1598/RRQ.34.3.3.

Neves, Érick Tássio Barbosa, et al. "Oral Health Literacy, Sociodemographic, Family, and Clinical Predictors of Dental Visits Among Brazilian Early Adolescents." *International Journal of Paediatric Dentistry*, vol. 31, no. 2, 2021, pp. 204–11.

Nielen, Thijs M. J., and Adriana G. Bus. "Enriched School Libraries: A Boost to Academic Achievement." *AERA Open*, vol. 1, no. 4, 2015, https://doi.org/10.1177/2332858415619417.

Nikolić, Marija, et al. "Dentistry in the Eyes of Medical Students." *Serbian Dental Journal (Stomatološki Glasnik Srbije)*, vol. 67, no. 3, 2020, pp. 135–43, https://doi.org/10.2298/SGS2003135N.

Nutbeam, Donald. "Health Literacy as a Public Health Goal: A Challenge for Contemporary Health Education and Communication Strategies into the 21st Century." *Health Promotion International*, vol. 15, no. 3, 2000, pp. 259–67.

Office of Disease Prevention and Health Promotion. *Healthy People 2030*. U.S. Department of Health and Human Services, https://health.gov/healthypeople.

Patrick, Donald L., et al. "Reducing Oral Health Disparities: A Focus on Social and Cultural Determinants." *BMC Oral Health*, vol. 6, no. 1, 2006, https://doi.org/10.1186/1472-6831-6-S1-S4.

Pawloski, Catherine, et al. "Medical–Dental Integration in a Rural Community Health Center: A Qualitative Program Evaluation." *Health Promotion Practice*, vol. 23, no. 3, 2022, pp. 416–24, https://doi.org/10.1177/15248399211002832.

Philbin, Morgan M., et al. "Public Libraries: A Community-Level Resource to Advance Population Health." *Journal of Community Health*, vol. 44, no. 1, 2019, pp. 192–99, https://doi.org/10.1007/s10900-018-0547-4.

Pieters, Rik, and Michel Wedel. "Attention Capture and Transfer in Advertising: Brand, Pictorial, and Text-Size Effects." *Journal of Marketing*, vol. 68, no. 2, 2004, pp. 36–50, https://doi.org/10.1509/jmkg.68.2.36.27794.

Ready, Dee. *Dentists Help*. Capstone Press, 2013.

Rudd, Rima E., and Alice M. Horowitz. "Health and Literacy: Supporting the Oral Health Research Agenda." *Journal of Public Health Dentistry*, vol. 65, no. 3, 2005, pp. 131–32, https://https://onlinelibrary.wiley.com/doi/10.1111/j.1752-7325.2005.tb02801.x.

Schuh, Mari. *At the Dentist*. Capstone Press, 2010.

Smith, Penny. *A Trip to the Dentist*. Penguin Random House, 2006.

Thaler, Richard H., and Cass R. Sunstein. *Nudge: Improving Decisions about Health, Wealth, and Happiness*. Penguin Books, 2009.

Tiwari, Tamanna, et al. "What Is the Value of Social Determinants of Health in Dental Education?" *NAM Perspectives*, 6 Apr. 2020, https://doi.org/10.31478/202004a.

Tzoc, Elias, and Valerie A. Ubbes. "The Digital Literacy Partnership Website: Promoting Interdisciplinary Scholarship between Faculty, Students, and Librarians." *New Review of Academic Librarianship*, vol. 23, no. 2–3, 2017, pp. 195–208, https://doi.org/10.1080/13614533.2017.1333013.

Ubbes, Valerie A. "Picture Book Database Strengthens Children's Vision of Literacy and Health." *ASCD Curriculum Technology Quarterly*, vol. 11, no. 3, 2002, p. 3.

Ubbes, Valerie A., and Judith A. Ausherman. "A Historical Comparison of Reading Materials Originating in the 19th and 20th Centuries that Contributed a Language and Vocabulary for Functional Health Literacy." *The Health Educator*, vol. 50, no. 2, 2018, pp. 26–40.

Ubbes, Valerie A., and Benedict Njoku. "A Curriculum, Instruction, and Assessment (CIA) Framework for Health Literacy Education (HLE) in Medical and Health Professions Schools." *World Journal of Social Science Research*, vol. 9, no. 1, 2022, pp. 15–55, https://doi.org/10.22158/wjssr.v9n1p15.

Ubbes, Valerie A., and Lindsay M. Wallace. "Curriculum Workbook: Let's Practice Your Oral Health Literacy!" *eBook for Oral Health Literacy©*, 2021, https://dlp.lib.miamioh.edu/ebook/more-resources.php

Ubbes, Valerie A., and Abby M. Witter. "Parental Influences on Children's Oral Health Behaviors, Reading Behaviors, and Reading Attitudes Associated with the Sharing of a Digital Story from the eBook for Oral Health Literacy© Curriculum." *Children and Teenagers*, vol. 4, no. 3, 2021, pp. 26–55, https://doi.org/10.22158/ct.v4n3p26.

Ubbes, Valerie A., et al. "Evaluation of an eBook For Oral Health Literacy© to Promote Child Health: Readability, Suitability, Understandability, Actionability, and Gist-Based Message Design." *Children and Teenagers*, vol. 3, no. 1, 2020, pp. 54–80, https://doi.org/10.22158/ct.v3n1p54.

Ubbes, Valerie A., et al. "Evaluation of an Oral Health Curriculum: Design Feedback from Three Audiences." *The International Journal of Health, Wellness, and Society*, vol. 8, no. 4, 2018, pp. 1–10.

Ubbes, Valerie A., et al. "Teaching for Understanding in Health Education: The Role of Critical and Creative Thinking Skills Within Constructivism Theory." *Philosophical Foundations of Health Education*, edited by Jill M. Black, et al., Jossey-Bass, 2009, pp. 95–107.

U.S. Centers for Disease Control and Prevention. "Children's Oral Health." *CDC*, 2014, https://www.cdc.gov/oralhealth/children_adults/child.htm.

U.S. Centers for Disease Control and Prevention. "Oral Health Conditions." *CDC*, 2022, https://www.cdc.gov/oralhealth/conditions/index.html.

U.S. Centers for Disease Control and Prevention. "School Health Policies and Practices Study (SHPPS)." *CDC*, 2016.

U.S. Department of Commerce. "U.S. Census—Quick Facts." *United States Census Bureau*, 2021, https://www.census.gov/quickfacts/fact/table/US/PST045219.

U.S. Department of Health and Human Services. "Healthy People 2010: Understanding and Improving Health." *U.S. Department of Health and Human Services*, 2000, https://www.healthypeople.gov/2010/Document/pdf/uih/2010uih.pdf/.

U.S. Department of Health and Human Services. "HHS Action Plan to Reduce Racial and Ethnic Health Disparities: A Nation Free of Disparities in Health and Health Care." *U.S. Department of Health and Human Services*, 2011, http://minorityhealth.hhs.gov/npa/files/Plans/HHS/HHS_Plan_complete.pdf.

Vassilakaki, Evgenia, and Valentini Moniarou-Papaconstaninou. "Librarians' Support in Improving Health Literacy: A Systematic Literature Review." *Journal of Librarianship and Information Science*, vol. 55, no. 2, 2022, https://doi.org/10.1177/09610006221093794.

Vieira, C. L. Z., and B. Caramelli. "The History of Dentistry and Medicine Relationship: Could the Mouth Finally Return to the Body?" *Oral Diseases*, vol. 15, no. 8, 2009, pp. 538–46, https://doi.org/10.1111/j.1601-0825.2009.01589.

Wehby, G. L. "Oral Health and Academic Achievement of Children in Low-Income Families." *Journal of Dental Research*, vol. 101, no. 1, 2022, pp. 1314–20, https://pubmed.ncbi.nlm.nih.gov/35426350/.

Wong, Mitchell D., et al. "Contribution of Major Diseases to Disparities in Mortality." *New England Journal of Medicine*, vol. 347, no. 20, 2002, pp. 1585–15.

World Health Organization. "Oral Health." Seventy-Fourth World Health Assembly, Agenda item 13.2, 31 May 2021, https://apps.who.int/gb/ebwha/pdf_files/WHA74/A74_R5-en.pdf.

Zullig, Keith.J., et al. "Early Adolescent Literacy Influences, Reading Ability, and Preventative Health Behaviors." *American Journal of Health Studies*, vol. 28, no. 3, 2013, pp. 134–41.

APPENDIX: ANNOTATED BIBLIOGRAPHY OF ORAL HEALTH AND DENTAL BOOKS FOR CHILDREN

The authors have compiled this bibliography as an example of the potential of a book-centric approach to teaching children about going to the dentist. We want people to use books to teach oral health—and health in general. It is our hope that this annotated bibliography will be disseminated to dentists and doctors to make the process of identifying useful books for their waiting rooms easier. More information and additional titles can be found by visiting the Children's Picture Book Database at Miami University (http://dlp.lib.miamioh.edu/picturebook) and entering the search term "dentist."

Adamson, Heather. *A Day in the Life of a Dentist.* Capstone Press, 2008.
Dr. Fong provides readers with an outline of what she does in her job as a dentist. Starting at the beginning of her day, Dr. Fong describes the various articles of clothing that she as well as the office staff and hygienists wear. After eating her lunch, Dr. Fong demonstrates various technologies that she uses to visualize a patient's mouth. Finally, Dr. Fong shows the tools she uses when examining a patient and describes the importance of visiting dentists, like her, regularly.

Adler, Sigal. *Bacteria Joe.* CreateSpace, 2017.
One night, a boy does not brush his teeth and eats chocolate before going to bed. Bacteria Joe comes along and begins eating away at any remaining sugars and sweets in the boy's mouth. After causing cracks to form in the boy's teeth, Bacteria Joe is finally washed away, and the boy promises his mom that he will always brush his teeth twice a day in order to prevent tooth decay!

Brush, Brush, Brush! Children's Press, 2010.
Following a series of questions, the narrator provides details of proper oral hygiene. These recommended dental health behaviors include brushing your teeth thoroughly twice a day. If done properly, patients will maintain a healthy smile.

Clark, Rosalyn. *Why We Go to the Dentist.* Learner Publishing Group, 2018.
Let's take a trip to the dentist to learn more about what dentists do. First, the dentist takes X-ray images of the patient's teeth and performs a routine checkup on the teeth and gums. Next, the dentist explains how to properly clean your teeth using a toothbrush and floss each day. Now you know more about the dentist, and why it is so important to go for checkups on a regular basis.

Courtad, Jeanette. *Toothful Tales.* Mentors International Publications, 2009.
Incisa tells the story of how she and her friends, Cuspi, Mola, and Tongo, are attacked by a "sticky sweet" given to them by Grandma. After the friends are covered in sugar, germs begin to attack them and dissolve holes in Incisa and her tooth friends. Then, Incisa, Cuspi, Mola, and Tongo get a pleasant surprise when Grandma brings other things to make the teeth happy: an electric toothbrush and floss! Finally, after a good cleaning, Incisa and her friends Cuspi, Mola, and Tongo are once again all shiny and bright, just in time for lunch.

Dentist. Child's Play, 2011.
Children go in and out of this dentist's office for checkups! First, a little boy gets his teeth examined by the dentist, and he finds out that they are a little dirty. Then, the dentist teaches the boy about how teeth develop over time and what he should do to take care of his teeth properly. Next, a little girl visits the dentist, and they find out that she has a hole in her tooth or a cavity. Finally, the little girl gets a filling, and her mouth is good as new.

Geisel, Theodor. *The Tooth Book.* Random House Children's Books, 2000.
Using clever rhymes, Dr. Seuss describes why teeth are important and what they help people and animals do. The structure of the mouth and the different stages of tooth development are described. Finally, Dr. Seuss explains what his readers should and should not eat in order to maintain a healthy smile.

Hallinan, P.K. *My Dentist, My Friend.* Ideals Children's Books, 1996.
Take a tour through the sights, sounds, and care of the friendly dentist's office! After spending time in the waiting room and visiting with the oral hygienist,

the children are seen by the dentist. Some of their teeth may need to get some X-ray scans during the dental checkup. After a successful appointment, the children are given the knowledge and tools to practice oral health behaviors at home.

Hallinan, P.K. *My Doctor, My Friend*. Ideals Children's Books, 1996.
Explore the sights, sounds, and care that kids experience at the doctor's office. After explaining why they go to the doctor for a medical checkup, the children describe the different tests that are performed at every appointment to diagnose their illness. Afterward, the children are much less afraid about going to the doctor.

How to . . . Brush Your Teeth. Cottage Door Press, 2016.
Learn from the tiger how your teeth develop over time, how teeth are classified, and why it is so important to take care of them regularly. The tiger gives you a step-by-step explanation of how to brush your teeth, and he reminds you how to brush for two minutes twice a day. Finally, the tiger explains other ways to care for your teeth that include proper nutrition and visits twice a year to the dentist.

Jones, Jill. *The Teeth That Looked for a New Mouth*. Spirala Publishing, 2014.
Luke refuses to brush his teeth despite his mom's warnings about sugar bugs coming to eat his teeth. That night, Luke has a dream that his teeth try to find another mouth to live in because they are tired of being dirty with food stuck between them. In a startling end, Luke wakes from his dream and quickly goes to brush his teeth, promising that he will brush at least twice a day.

Klingel, Cynthia, and Robert Noyed. *Mouth*. Weekly Reader Early Learning Library, 2002.
A group of children demonstrate all of the different things they can do with their mouths so that other kids can do the same. However, in order to be able to do all of these things, the children make sure to explain why it is so important to go to the dentist to take care of their mouths and keep their teeth clean and healthy.

Maccarone, Grace. *My Tooth Is About to Fall Out*. Scholastic, 2003.
A little girl describes her wiggly tooth and all the places where she doesn't want it to fall out. Then, while she is eating spaghetti, the tooth falls into her bowl and a giant hole is left in her mouth. That night, she places the tooth that fell out under her pillow, and the Tooth Fairy leaves a nice little surprise for her in the morning.

Miller, Edward. *The Tooth Book.* Holiday House, 2008.
Let's learn how oral health and the mouth develops over a lifetime. The mouth grows a set of primary teeth and then a set of secondary teeth. Readers can learn proper dental hygiene and interesting historical facts about tooth decay and different techniques to treat oral health issues when and if they occur.

Murphy, Patricia. *A Visit to the Dentist's Office.* Capstone Press, 2005, Patients visit Oz Family Dentistry for a checkup to ensure that they have a healthy smile and know how to care for their teeth. After meeting the dental hygienist in the exam room, patients get their teeth cleaned and polished before getting X-rays of their mouth. Then, the dentist meets with patients to teach them more about oral hygiene.

Ready, Dee. *Dentists Help.* Capstone Press, 2013.
Learn who a dentist is, what their job entails, and how they work to provide care for their patients. Children also learn about different types of dentists and what specialists they should see if they have crooked teeth. Details are shared about the clothing and tools a dentist may use when caring for their patients' teeth. The goal is for children to know these details, so they can relax and enjoy going to the dentist.

Schaefer, Lola. *Loose Tooth.* HarperCollins Publishers, 2004.
A young boy wakes up and realizes he has a loose tooth. He wiggles the tooth and shows his mom, dad, sister, brother, and dog, but it won't fall out. He tries to eat hard food or have his brother yank it out with a wrench, but the tooth finally comes out all on its own!

Schuh, Mari. *All About Teeth.* Capstone Press, 2008.
Lee acts as a role model for others and describes what he does in order to maintain a healthy smile by brushing and flossing his teeth every day and visiting the dentist regularly. To explain why taking care of your teeth is so important, Lee also demonstrates the structure of a tooth and the unique functions of canines, incisors, premolars, and molars in the mouth that allow him to eat and digest food.

Schuh, Mari. *At the Dentist.* Capstone Press, 2010.
Lena goes to see Dentist Doug and Deb, the hygienist, because her teeth need a checkup. During her appointment, Deb explains good dental hygiene to Lena and, soon after, Deb takes X-rays of her teeth and cleans them. After Dentist

Doug checks for cavities, Lena goes home and continues to brush and floss every day in order to maintain her healthy smile.

Schuh, Mari. *Brushing Teeth*. Capstone Press, 2008.
Lee sets an example for other children like him by describing how to properly brush his teeth in order to get rid of food and plaque that could build up and cause cavities. Every morning and night, Lee uses his own toothbrush and a small amount of toothpaste to clean his teeth, gums, and tongue. After brushing, Lee makes sure to rinse with water. Lee also uses a new toothbrush every few months so his teeth get brushed well.

Schuh, Mari. *Flossing Teeth*. Capstone Press, 2010.
Anna acts as an example for how to floss her teeth properly. Anna demonstrates flossing her teeth with traditional floss and a flossing tool in order to remove any plaque from surfaces of her teeth that cannot be reached by a toothbrush. By flossing daily, Anna is able to prevent cavities from forming in between her teeth.

Schuh, Mari. *Loose Tooth*. Capstone Press, 2008.
Andy shows other kids just like him what to do when they have a loose tooth. Andy got his first loose tooth when he was five and every time since, when the permanent tooth inside his gum pushes on his baby tooth, he wiggles it with his tongue and tries his best not to eat hard foods. When he is older, Andy will have a total of thirty-six permanent teeth, all of which will be healthy because he brushes and flosses them every day.

Schuh, Mari. *Ready, Set, Brush!* Printers Row Publishing Group, 2017.
Elmo and his gang teach the reader how to brush teeth. First, Elmo teaches how much toothpaste to use, and Marvin Monster explains where to brush. Then Zoe describes how to brush the tongue while Cookie Monster shows how to rinse the mouth. Next, Martha Monster visits the dentist for a checkup, and he tells her that she, and all of her friends, do a great job of taking care of their mouth by brushing and rinsing twice a day!

Schuh, Mari. *Snacks for Healthy Teeth*. Capstone Press, 2008.
Tessa sets an example for other children by describing all of the healthy snacks that she eats in order to keep her teeth and gums healthy. Instead of eating sugary sweets, Tessa enjoys eating fruits, vegetables, dairy products, and popcorn as snacks to protect her teeth and keep them strong. Tessa also explains how she brushes her teeth every day to make sure the enamel protecting her teeth does not wear down and form a cavity.

Smith, Penny. *A Trip to the Dentist*. Penguin Random House, 2006.
Sarah and Josh go to see Dr. Richards, their local dentist, for routine checkups. Josh is examined first and, after the dentist checks his mouth for evidence of cavities, Dr. Richards shows Josh how he can do a better job of brushing teeth in the back of his mouth in order to prevent the buildup of plaque. Next, Dr. Richards examines Sarah's mouth and finds a cavity, which he fixes by adding a filling. After explaining how to maintain a healthy smile by avoiding sugary foods and beverages, Sarah and Josh are done with their appointments and ready to keep taking good care of their teeth.

Smith, Stacy. *A Toothbrush Tale*. Outskirts Press, 2020.
A little boy goes to sleep one night without brushing his teeth, and then he hears a song coming from his bathroom. When he goes to investigate the noise, he finds his toothbrush singing and dancing about why it is so important to brush his teeth every morning and night. Scared that he will develop cavities (or even worse, that his teeth might fall out), the little boy brushes his teeth well every day.

Tourville, Amanda. *Brush, Floss, and Rinse*. Picture Window Books, 2008.
Kyle and Alen demonstrate their habits of proper dental hygiene to other children by brushing and flossing their teeth every day. Just as the dentist would like, the two brothers replace their toothbrushes regularly and rinse with fluoride after brushing to remove any food or plaque that may get stuck between their teeth. Finally, in order to protect their teeth from breaking or decaying, Kyle and Alen also make sure to avoid eating hard foods, choose healthy snacks with little to no sugar, and always wear their mouth guards while playing contact sports.

Weisz, Sam, and Erica Weisz. *Sugar Bugs*. Trism Books, 2014.
The Mutans family moved into Robbie's mouth after searching for a sugary new home. Robbie ate candies and sweets every day, so the Mutans loved living there. Over time, the Mutans began to rot his teeth, causing Robbie to have horrible pain when chewing. Then Robbie goes to visit Dr. Sam, his dentist, who removes the Mutans family from their home. Dr. Sam shares some habits that will help Robbie improve his oral health in the future and keep the Mutans family out forever!

Woodruff, Amira. *My Wiggly Smile*. AMW Solutions, 2018.
Olive wakes up one day and finds that she has a loose tooth! She runs downstairs to tell her parents and keeps wiggling it all day, but it won't come out! At

school, Olive talks to a girl named Jordan who tells her about the "My Wiggly Smile" book, which says to keep track of the teeth she's lost. When Olive gets home, her dad surprises her with a "My Wiggly Smile" book of her own, and they leave for the dentist, where Olive's tooth is finally pulled by the dentist. That night, while she is fast asleep, the Tooth Fairy comes to visit Olive, and she wakes up with a gift under her pillow!

Part 3

Storytelling Ethics and Speculative Care

AN INTERVIEW WITH SUDESHNA SHOME GHOSH, PUBLISHER FOR TALKING CUB, ABOUT *A BEND IN TIME: WRITINGS BY CHILDREN ON THE COVID-19 PANDEMIC*

SARAH LAYZELL, INTERVIEWER,
AND SUDESHNA SHOME GHOSH, INTERVIEWEE

Sarah Layzell (SL): In 2020, we saw publishers, writers, and other creators respond to the COVID-19 pandemic in different ways. Could you tell us a bit about how *A Bend in Time* came about?

Sudeshna Shome Ghosh (SSG): In March 2020, India went into one of the severest lockdowns in the world, at a mere four hours' notice. This resulted in great hardship for millions of daily wage earners and migrant workers stuck in cities without work, with no way to reach their villages thousands of miles away. Our TV and other media were awash with images of whole families trekking across the country with a few belongings, children lying exhausted by their parents, and more. We also read reports about how with the closure of government schools, children were going without their free midday meals, sometimes their one source of nutrition. Even in affluent society, children were suddenly caught at home, all over the world, severed from their daily routines. This got us thinking about how children were coping and the difficulties they are facing. All around us we saw kids dealing with a sudden upturning of their usual patterns of life. I was so impressed by how they adapted, and yet wondered what was going on really in their minds. At this time, a lot of online activities were being planned to keep children engaged, but most of it was one-way, with adults telling children their thoughts. How many children were being asked to express their fears and insecurities in this situation? And what of the many many children in this country with no access to the Internet? Was there a way to reach out to at least some of them and create a book on their thoughts on these unprecedented times?

It was also a time when a lot of our publishing work was at a bit of a standstill, because the printing presses were not working, and bookstores were closed, including online delivery of books. Our entire publishing schedule got disrupted, so we thought of doing this book as a sort of small experiment, perhaps just as an ebook. But as the idea grew and the pieces came in, we wanted it to be a printed book that would go out there and be available for anyone to pick up and read.

SL: Why was it important to have children as the primary contributors? What can readers find in this collection that they would not learn from adults writing on the subject?

SSG: I felt there was a lot of talking to children happening in these months. As adults we were constantly in their faces, telling them what to do, how to do, what to think, what to watch, what to read. This collection was a way of giving autonomy to children to articulate their thoughts. Our brief to the writers was broad—they could write anything they wanted: fiction, nonfiction, pieces that are happy, sad, adventure, mystery, anything. We waited to see what would emerge, and happily we got a good mix of ideas and thoughts. Since adults usually get the stage to pontificate enough, here children could say exactly what was going on in their minds. We saw raw sadness and anxiety, but we also saw incredible flashes of humor. We saw how even in the space of twelve pieces, minds worked in different directions. The writing was much more immediate, more unpolished than what an adult writer would do, but I felt therein lay their charm.

SL: Many of the writers reflected explicitly on healthcare, illness, and death. For some, writing seems to have served a therapeutic purpose: for example, Lavanya talks of finding a "cure" or "remedy" for writer's block. How far do you think the writing in this book acts as self-care?

SSG: I think, surprisingly, it did become a form of self-care, though that was not one of our explicit objectives when we started on the book. As the pieces started coming in, and I got to know the writers better, interacted with them as their editor, I learnt how much of their daily lives and what they were imbibing from the world around them was coming into their stories and essays. For example, Shivani's story, "A Prayer," originally written in Hindi, is about a poor Muslim man, a daily wage earner, and the story is told by the daughter. Shivani herself lives in a not very affluent neighborhood, and though she herself is not Muslim, she chose to write about such a family. A little context here is that in the initial months of the pandemic, an Islamic event in Delhi was portrayed in the media as a super-spreader event, and there was a vilification of Muslims across the country, for no reason at all. It was a manifestation of the religious divide that has been growing in India for the last few years. What Shivani was showing through her story was the pain she felt at what she saw around her, at the nonsensical communalization that was happening, and through her story showed that sickness and grief is universal.

SL: Writing can also be an act of care for others. I felt buoyed by what the writers in this collection had to say about taking responsibility for each other, for our planet, for the future. Did you feel you were creating something that could provide comfort and care to readers?

SSG: Yes, definitely, because in all the gloom and doom it was easy to lose perspective and get sucked into the sorrow all around. Teenagers being such masters at looking on the dark side, I felt that we also needed to inject some facts, some perspective, and to look at the planet as a whole in the pieces as well. Ishaan's piece "A Pale Blue Dot" was born out of this, as well as Shiv's, which looked at epidemics and lockdowns from a historical perspective. Both of these tried to say that humanity has gone through worse, and there will always be challenges, and that we need to keep learning and innovating.

SL: One of the most powerful pieces I read in 2020 was Neil Singh's essay on coronavirus and cholera, which asked, "Who will die of coronavirus in 200 years' time?" I was reflecting on Shiv's piece, which highlights past pandemics, and Sharvari's piece, which considers future inequalities relating to COVID-19. Do you think that this collection will become part of our "history of COVID," that it can speak to the future and help inform what happens next in terms of the stories we tell and the care we provide?

SSG: I certainly hope so. We had an online event to release the book (available to watch on YouTube) where all the writers spoke about their pieces, and Bijal, a children's author and editor who wrote the introduction, said something that stuck in my head. She said, this book will be a time capsule. If we bury objects from 2020 to be found in the future, this book should be one of them, so that future generations get an idea of the events, ideas, and thoughts that were buzzing in our children's heads here and now. It is important to keep a record of these precisely because they are a snapshot of what we as a country and society lived through. Sharvari's piece with its sad outlook that COVID will stalk our society even decades from now was an eye-opener to me on how bleak the world was looking to a thirteen- to fourteen-year-old. It serves as a wake-up call to actually not let that happen.

SL: The title recalls Madeleine L'Engle's *A Wrinkle in Time*. How does the theme of time inform the collection? Was this a focus provided for the writers, or did it emerge from their writing?

SSG: The title was the last thing we decided on in the book! It came about thanks to Bijal's introduction, where she talks about finding a new superpower during the lockdown—the ability to bend time. At that point we read the pieces from that perspective and realized that this thought or feeling echoed through the book, whether it was Shiv's piece on history, Tishya's story on losing her dreams, Sharvari's story set a decade later, Lavanya's almost stream-of-consciousness essay on longing for ordinary activities from the past, Shreya's essay on finding solace in reading through the nights, Ishaan's essay, which looked at time at a cosmic level, Sofia's essay filled with allegory. That's when we knew we had the title—*A Bend in Time.*

SL: How did the book's cover art come about, and what is your response to it?

SSG: The cover art by Kavita Singh Kale was initially created as part of a series she was doing on the lockdown and pandemic. She was posting them on her Instagram page, and our art director had seen this one in that series. She decided to use this as it serendipitously gave such a good idea of the feelings in the book. But we also wanted it to be bright and attractive, since this was after all a book written by children. We wanted it to show the hope as well as the note of mischief and cheekiness that runs through some of the pieces. I feel between Maithili, our art director, and Kavita, the artist, they managed to capture this very well.

UPDATE MAY 2024

SL: Four years on from the start of the COVID-19 pandemic, what are your reflections looking back on the publication of *A Bend in Time*? Have you received feedback from readers?

SSG: *A Bend in Time* now seems like a book that lives up to its name—that it had to occur at a time of unprecedented change at a global level, and that it had to reflect the thoughts of the youngest and most vulnerable at the time. It seems both distantly in the past, and yet as if it was published recently. I hear from people now and then about it still, and how some stories will always stay with them or bring back feelings from that phase in their lives. The contributors themselves have grown up; many are now college students or young working professionals. Most were young readers and writers, and they have continued to hold on to that part of themselves. While the sales of the book have dropped off, which is understandable given its topical nature, it is a book that we at Talking Cub (Speaking Tiger) treasure closely as a unique experiment and one we will always be proud that we were courageous enough to do at the time.

SL: How do you think the children's book market and publishing industry in your context has changed as a result of the pandemic?

SSG: There has been a change in the role of bookshops and the way people buy books. The role of independent bookstores was highlighted during the pandemic, and many of them have continued to thrive since. Smaller lending libraries too flourished at the time, and many have survived. Reading itself became an important activity for children and adults, and many parents still seem to recognize this and encourage their children to read more. But on the whole, for children, life is back to what it was—school and activities and sports—as it should be. If the pandemic created lifelong readers or not is yet to be seen. Publishing too has slowly found its feet after all the disruptions, and book sales are up, as well as author events and school visits. In the case of school visits, we are seeing more of that occurring than pre-pandemic times. The popularity of easy reading books remains high—books that are fun, visual, and quickly finished are ideal for attention spans that had to deal with online school and screen time.

This interview has been edited for clarity and length.

WORKS CITED

Cosy Nook Library. "Book Launch of A Bend in Time: Writings by Children on the COVID-19 Pandemic." *YouTube*, 24 Oct. 2020, https://www.youtube.com/watch?v=Bmh41wsoHns.

L'Engle, Madeleine. *A Wrinkle in Time*. 1962. Square Fish, 2007.

Singh, Neil. "Cholera and Coronavirus: Why We Must Not Repeat the Same Mistakes." *The Guardian*, 1 May 2020, https://www.theguardian.com/society/2020/may/01/cholera-and-coronavirus-why-we-must-not-repeat-the-same-mistakes.

Vachharajani, Bijal, et al. *A Bend in Time: Writings by Children on the COVID-19 Pandemic*. Talking Cub, 2020.

"UNVILING" ALIFE

Ethical Choices of Healthcare Practitioners about Future Children

ANNA BUGAJSKA

Progress in medicine and biotechnology is contingent upon uncertainty—scientists must verify whether discoveries will ultimately ameliorate the lives of humans. Experimental therapies, including those that allow for the control of reproduction and lifespan, require a series of stringent tests and rigid trials, reviews and verification studies. However, before all of these can be performed on human subjects, the undeveloped and unsafe versions of drugs and treatments are first tested on so-called vile bodies[1]: the bodies of those beings that dominant social actors have designated as eligible for experimentation for various reasons. Such vile bodies have traditionally been corpses, but have also been (and still are) live animals and humans deprived of their humanity by a master status trait like being a prisoner, a person of color, a slave, or a disabled or mentally ill person. It is now becoming possible to create artificial life (ALife), which lacks person status and thus is not protected by law from harm that they might suffer in the course of medical experimentation.

In the formation of attitudes and ethical stances that subsequently impact the fate of future posthuman children, contemporary children's literature has an important role to play. It has been shown that the texts that impact readers in their formative years continue to influence their later life choices and the goals they pursue, including their relation to science and technology.[2] Children's science fiction, in addition, when compared to its equivalent for adult audiences, demonstrates bolder visions and is less constrained with the formal demands of the genre (like verisimilitude and scientific exactness), and it constitutes a perfect environment for creating empathy narratives, putting the modified beings in the center rather than pushing them away and casting them as villains or existential tormented heroes.

The above role of children's literature for the posthuman world and the interrelationship between the rapid biotechnological progress and children and young adult novels has been subject to multiple readings. Researchers like Noga Applebaum, Zoe Jaques, Anita Tarr, Donna White, Jennifer Harrison, and others, have discussed at length various facets of posthumanities in books written for young audiences. For the most part, the common denominator in the existent scholarship is the understanding of posthumanities as the expression of the contemporary crisis of Enlightenment humanism in its many shapes, from patriarchalism to anthropocentrism. The aim of the present chapter is not, however, to provide a bird's-eye view of the conceptualizations of what it means to be human and nonhuman within a bigger body of texts. I aim here at posing more concrete questions directed toward medical professional ethics—namely, what kind of professional ethical model is apparent from those literary texts that attempt to show positive doctor–patient interactions? In the subsequent sections I analyze the representations offered by Nancy Farmer in her Matteo Alacrán series (2002; 2013), and by James Patterson in the Maximum Ride series (2005–2015). Both suggest it is necessary to rethink medical ethics relating to the numerous challenges that traditional models face from the abovementioned criticism of Enlightenment humanism, and both juxtapose veterinary ethics with medical ethics to answer the challenges of the extended concept of care needed for relations with the posthuman beings.

OVERVIEW OF POSTHUMANISM AND THE ETHICS OF CARE

The term ALife here is employed after the essay of John Johnston in *The Routledge Companion to Literature and Science* as a counterpart for and a pun on AI. However, one should be aware that in the majority of contemporary commentary, the term "ALife" is used scantily and the general term "posthuman" is mostly applied. And despite the fact that ALife would probably be understood more narrowly in posthumanist discourse and situated solely within the scope of synthetic biology, with regard to literary studies I am going to follow the definition outlined in the abovementioned chapter by Johnston.[3] This definition encompasses all forms of lab-created life, including augmentations of natural life, hybrid machine-organic life, and entirely artificial life. Such ALife forms encompass human-animal hybrids, cybrids (so-called three-parent babies), synthetic organisms, organoids, and cloned animals. Artificial life is an experiment in itself and is often created with the sole purpose of being submitted to tests, providing parts for transplants, or fulfilling societal and personal needs regulated by political powers, market forces, or individual desires.

Not only lawyers and government officials, but also ethicists find themselves at a loss when it comes to determining the status of ALife. It is at the convergence point of various well-established fields of philosophy, such as technoethics, bioethics, scientific ethics and medical ethics, and the challenges that the creation of ALife poses for contemporary ethics are manifold. Many potential approaches are being proposed: Rosi Braidotti's posthuman ethics,[4] Maria Puig de la Bellacasa's speculative ethics,[5] the ethics of uncertainty,[6] or the ethics of complexity,[7] to name but a few. However, relatively little is done to provide ethical direction for practicing professionals, such as nurses.

First, and more generally, the notion of care is fundamental for medical practitioners, as they deal with those who by definition are in need of special care and attention. In the wake of George Church's and Daniel Gibson's 2013 attempts to print life, He Jiankui's 2018 experiment with editing the human genome, and the increasingly broad leeway given to embryo experimentation (e.g., human-animal hybrids), it becomes imperative to discuss the care medical personnel should display toward all patients. Puig de la Bellacasa in her book on speculative ethics asks: "But what is care? Is it an affection? A moral obligation? Work? A burden? A joy? Something we can learn or practice? Something we just do?" (1). The instinctual care we extend toward the members of our own species or people related to us by blood collapses in the face of artificially created beings (Dawkins), and the existence of such beings calls for a new basis for the extension of care toward nonhumans.

Second, nursing ethics is a complex[8] phenomenon in itself, quite distinct in its very origins from medical ethics. The profession is strictly connected with a particular organization of care within a certain political and operational context. This is why, besides the notion of care understood as a humanitarian approach to the patient, nursing care depends on institutional values like economy and objectivity: the availability of resources, understaffing, "routinization of care." Nurses are also involved in the multiple loyalties dilemma (e.g., loyalty to the patient, their family, the employer, the leading physician). Since its origins are to be sought on the battlefield, nursing is underpinned by many of the assumptions of military ethics, embracing efficiency and crisis management principles (Storch). In a critical situation, it is imperative to act fast, and usually consequentialist ethics is applied, guided by the "greatest good for the greatest number" principle and heavily influenced by the dichotomy between ally and enemy.[9] Thus, it is prone to fall into the pitfalls of speciesism or other forms of bias, which may potentially be harmful for newly created ALife. On the battlefield, there is no time to ponder on the complexity of the novel being, the harm caused to a synthetic creature, or the actual status of the printed organism. The novelty of the contemporary challenge is also caused by the fact that there are few or no existing legal guidelines that would regulate working with ALife, and healthcare practitioners are not provided courses on these emerging forms of life. They are left with the patterns supplied—for the most part—by bioalarmist rhetoric, framing posthumans and postbeings as monsters or inhumans, potential enemies. This rhetoric seriously prevents them from exercising proper care.[10]

Contemporary bioethics provides a set of rules to be used by healthcare practitioners; nevertheless, they are already being violated in the creation of ALife, who usually have no say as far as the type and purpose of the medical procedures they are subjected to. Harm that they suffer is not taken into account, as the good of the creator, the "owner," or simply the natural (rather than artificial) human beings is valued higher. Some examples include experiments on such organoids as minibrains or the destruction of hybrid embryos after they are used in tests. These violations mark the special character of the technologically devised creations and beg the question about the justice of these practices.

If we accept human subject rights as basic in dealing with the creation of new artificial life, we have to consider such issues as informed consent, respect for persons, autonomous agency, protection from any type of harm, the right to end the procedure at any moment, and protection of privacy. Clearly, these conditions for an ethical human experiment are not and cannot be met in the case of tampering with a person's genome at its embryonic stage, encoding a life code in the computer and printing it out, or growing a minibrain from a tissue culture in a lab. The various forms of ALife are from the beginning conceived as not participating in the legal framework protecting human beings. What is more, they are burdened with imaginative bias fueled by fictional productions and sensationalist discourse, operating with horror and thriller images from adult media, which—often misapplied—provoke strong anthropocentric bias in handling new life forms. The creation of ALife forces us to weaken this anthropocentric position or else to devise an anthropological model that accounts for the facts we are dealing with now. Are the posthuman bioethics of Braidotti or some other models proposed by critical posthumanism applicable to the problems? Certainly, it would take time before these posthuman models were developed and enriched by the complexity and uncertainty models, which, nevertheless, do not give clear guidance.

Contemporary bioethics does not offer rules or support to healthcare practitioners who would need to reconcile themselves to working with a new type of life. This lack may lead to degeneration into a military ethics of crisis or simply utilitarian business ethics, both threatening ALife with objectification. It is to be understood, though, that these issues emerge at the current cutting edge of research, and although some headway has been made, no normative solutions are in sight. Thus, in the following paragraphs I investigate how contemporary fiction for young readers imagines situations that may well soon be faced by healthcare practitioners who would be forced to proceed without determining the ontological and legal status of ALife and perform ethical evaluations on the spot without relevant training.

ALIFE HEALTHCARE: INSIGHTS FROM JUVENILE LITERATURE

The motif of ALife in juvenile fiction is increasingly popular, especially in recent years. Characters like Matt Alacrán and the robot-like eejits from Nancy Farmer's narcotopia (*The House of the Scorpion*, *The Lord of Opium*), Heron and Samm from Dan Wells's *Partials*, Total and the Flock from James Patterson's *Maximum Ride*, or Camus Comprix from Neal Shusterman's *Unwind* dystology, are only some of the most prominent examples. Out of a considerably big corpus, I have chosen for analysis two texts, Farmer's Matt Alacrán duology and Patterson's Maximum Ride series,[11] as the instances that most foreground both the creation and care of artificial life. In Farmer's books, Matt Alacrán[12] is both the name of the clone-protagonist and a cartel boss (known as El Patrón) who donated his tissue to have an infinite supply of organs for transplantation harvested from his clones. The boy is brought up in a small house by a carer, Celia, and subsequently moves to live in the house with his original; he is educated and socializes with others. When he learns, however, that at fourteen he is going to become the donor, sacrificing his life, he escapes, only to return in the second novel and discover that all his enemies from the Alacrán estate are dead. He takes the place of El Patrón, trying to right the wrongs of his predecessor. In *Maximum Ride*, the titular heroine-narrator has been genetically modified to develop avian features—most importantly, the ability to fly thanks to wings and pneumatic bones. Maximum lives with her Flock—other modified avian kids—first in the School (the laboratory where they were created) and then on the run. The Flock is being hunted by scientists who want to destroy them, use them for further experiments, or—eventually, in the case of Maximum—to make them reproduce in an effort to create a better human race. In both series, the authors are interested in the socialization of ALife, the difficulties posthumans face in everyday life, and the types of prejudice and abuse they are prone to suffer.

The phenomenon of ALife in children's and young adult literature has been well described by, among others, Applebaum, Clare Bradford et al., and Harrison, who devote considerable space to the discussion of varieties of posthumanity, especially clones and artificial people. Applebaum's argument concentrates on showing the liminality of clones, as they both reinforce and challenge traditional patterns and are embodiments of both technology and organic humanity.

Her posthuman is recognized simply as an "identical twin"—that is, sharing all features of the original and, in consequence, the status of the original. Thus, it is bound to be included in the original's humanity, rather than excluded from it. Harrison, importantly, engages in the discussion of the transformations—and possible rejection—of Enlightened humanism as an anthropocentric obstacle to proper relations between human and nonhuman entities. Her stance thus invites the rise of medical posthumanities,[13] a direction into which I would like to extend the existing research.

ALife in literature, like in real life, originates in medical facilities and is created for military or medical/scientific purposes, and experiences treatment combining the ethical stances of these contexts. All three contexts are clearly shown in these texts as dystopian. The objectification of clones, Biosynths, Avians, and uplifted animals stems from the mental framework adopted by the practitioners of human experimentation, quite clearly presented as looking at contemporary "vile bodies" with the disinterested "medical gaze" of which Foucault has extensively written in relation to the practices of the past. It turns out, though, that the "medical gaze" has not disappeared with the development of more humane approaches in doctor–patient relations; it has simply shifted its focus.

In the Matteo Alacrán series by Nancy Farmer, the cartel boss and the ruler of the fictional state of Opium has his clones created to provide him with spare parts for transplants. The readers are shown both the production and the care process for the clones. First of all, the embryos are implanted into cows' uteruses and, if they survive the fetal stage, they are born and transferred into the hands of healthcare practitioners. The level of care depends on the level of the clone's initial damage and its final destination. If their organs are to be used soon, or if they have multiple developmental deficiencies, they are treated no better than things. One such case is witnessed by Matt when he sees a screaming, thrashing creature strapped to a bed:

"It's a boy," whispered María.

It was. Only at first Matt thought it was some kind of beast, so alien and terrible was its face. It had doughy, unhealthy skin and red hair that stuck up in bristles. It seemed never to have been in the sun, and its hands were twisted like claws above the straps that held it down. It was dressed in green hospital pajamas, but these had been befouled by its terror. Worst of all was the terrible energy that rolled through the trapped body. The creature never stopped moving. It was as though invisible snakes were rippling beneath the skin and forcing its arms and legs to move in a ceaseless bid for freedom.

"It's not a boy," Tom said scornfully. "It's a clone."

> Matt felt as though he'd been punched in the stomach. He'd never seen another clone. He'd only felt the weight of hatred humans had for such things. He hadn't understood it because, after all, clones were like dogs and cats, and humans loved them. If he'd thought about it at all, he had assumed he was a pet, only a very intelligent one. (Farmer, House 119–20)

The clone on the bed has been created as deficient because only some organs needed to be healthy. It is also partly because of his intentional disability that he is treated as a "creature" rather than a patient. In this passage Farmer seems to reach to the intuitions arrived at in disability studies and mental illness studies (such as Johnson's or Foucault's), which critique the objectification of disabled bodies and their treatment as objects of horror or pity or hopeless "cases" upon whom care would be wasted. The passage borrows images from books and movies on mental institutions or from the debates of the proponents of the right to life for the severely disabled. Farmer seems to suggest that ALife is getting no professional care at all, but even more so if it is created as disabled from the start: here, according to the "normal" children in the novel, the thing on the bed does not even deserve animal status. Thus, a subtle link is introduced between the care extended toward animals, the disabled, and the posthuman, suggesting the possibilities for further inspirations for building relevant ethical models that would benefit marginalized humans as well as posthumans.

In addition to the above biases of the characters, replicating the ableist and anthropocentric leanings of today, people filling in the posts of nurses are unqualified and full of prejudice. Such is the case of Rose and Fiona, two servant-women who fulfill the roles of nurses or caretakers and cooperate with doctors. By association, they usurp for themselves posts requiring special sensitivity and training. It is especially telling to recall the scene in which Matt, who is closed in the house, observes children playing outside and breaks a window in an attempt to join them. When Matt is brought to the house of El Patrón, bloodied from trying to break the "glass wall" between himself and other children, Rose takes over the role of the doctor. The figurative boundary between human and ALife gets shattered, but it appears that it leaves him in a liminal sphere where there is nobody to take care of him. Instead, Rose closes him in a room turned into a chicken pen and treats him like a nonverbal animal, with the tacit agreement of the residents of the mansion and the doctor supposedly in charge of this case. In the second volume, we see the dispassionate behavior of Dr. Rivas and Dr. Kim, resulting in lack of care, and the open malevolence of "nurse" Fiona, who has also usurped a place in the medical hierarchy; she used to be a dishwasher, but her ambitions were much higher. She enjoys telling morbid tales of harvesting organs from live, not anesthetized clones, and of replacing the "eejits" instead of curing them. In *The Lord of Opium*, she abuses

Waitress Mirasol, a girl who is supposed to serve Matt and who is injected with nano-chips that make her an "eejit," little more than a highly functioning robot. For instance, when the girl suffers burns as a result of torture, Fiona refuses to treat her:

> "Oh, but I don't work on eejits," faltered Fiona. "There's the vet hospital for that, over by the horse barn. Only, I don't think they fix eejits either. They replace them."
> "You will take care of Waitress's hands and do it immediately," said Matt. "She's as human as you are, and despite your stupid prejudice, she can feel pain. Isn't that so, Cienfuegos?"
> The jefe had the grace to look ashamed. "Eejits can feel pain, mi patrón, otherwise I couldn't train them. I don't think they suffer in the same way we do. They scream, but it's an automatic function, like your heart beating or your stomach digesting food. You don't think, 'Today I'm going to digest that omelet I had for breakfast.' The omelet arrives in your stomach and the reaction happens. To suffer implies emotion, and eejits don't have that."
> "I don't believe you," said Matt, and left the room. (Farmer, *Lord* 76)

Here we witness multiple points of view and doubts stemming from the lack of understanding of the status of posthumans within the medical system. Fiona, presented as uneducated and prejudiced, thinks that people modified with nanotechnology ("chips") are either animals—so they should be treated by vets—or machines. The use of the words "fix" and "replace" suggests objectification of clones in popular understanding, while at the same time implying that the animal status might be a better one for a posthuman, because this at least affords them some type of care. Matt, himself a clone, underlines that from his perspective there is no difference between a modified human and a nonmodified human in terms of rights and ethical obligations. However, he seeks assurance in Cienfuegos, his right hand. El Jefe, himself modified with nanotechnology, tries to be objective: on the one hand, he protects his status as equal to humans; on the other, he justifies his cruel, pain-based methods of behavioral training. To teach "eejits" that are modified to be fully obedient, he electrocutes them. He attempts to prove that people like Mirasol feel pain, but they cannot suffer because they do not have emotions. And although Matt violently opposes this idea—he has developed a complex emotional relationship with Mirasol—it turns out that the "medical gaze" objectifying posthumans is not simply a matter of lack of education or self-interest. A medical professional, Dr. Kim, confirms Fiona's words, not even trying to save Mirasol when she ultimately breaks down and refusing to sedate her.

The behavior of Dr. Kim and "nurse" Fiona stands in contrast to that of Tam Lin, Celia, and María, all sensitive to Matt's plight. None of them is a skilled medical professional: Tam Lin is a bodyguard and former terrorist, Celia is a caregiver of Matt and a cook in El Patrón's household, and María is the daughter of the powerful Mendoza family, linked to the United Nations. They befriend Matt and treat him like any other child, helping to get him out of Rose's imprisonment and to socialize. In fact, Celia does have medical training, albeit not officially recognized,[14] and she ultimately uses her knowledge to save Matt from being dismembered for transplants. The healthcare system is thus shown unequivocally as abusive and corrupted, and the only care that can be expected comes from outside of it. Tam Lin, Celia, and María are deeply connected to nature, which perhaps helps them to extend the feelings they have toward plants and animals to a clone. However, although Celia and María form a well-functioning relationship with Matt, which conditions the extension of care to a representative of ALife, both have difficulty breaking out of their deeply ingrained anthropocentrism, and they rely on personal patterns of attachment, much like we can observe in the cases of emotional involvement with cloned pets or even limited artificial intelligence. The moment such a bond cannot be formed, their ethics wanes and sometimes collapses—for example in Celia's discrimination against Mirasol. While she raised Matt and treats him like her son, she treats Mirasol like a thing, not worth any care; only Matt tries to reach out to the "chipped" slaves and wake them up from their stupor.

The Patterson series offers a more reliable form of ethics through the introduction of human-avian and human-lupine characters extending professional veterinary care toward posthuman subjects.[15] The hybrid characters are created via genetic engineering and experimentation on both embryos and grown children. The resulting characters have superhuman powers but also have numerous developmental issues and special needs. Many experiments fail, and the resulting so-called patients are kept in cages or dog crates at the medical facility called School. The medical staff clearly objectify the patients, not caring for their consent or accounting for the pain they feel. What is more, the same attitude is displayed in the hospitals the characters have to attend when they manage to break out from under the inadequate care of their creators. When doctors, who usually deal with humans, realize they have admitted Avians for some simple treatment, they persist in trying to keep them in hospitals to study them, rather than cure them. Max and her chosen family are treated, and perceive themselves, as "freaks."

Real help is provided by a veterinarian, Dr. Martinez, whom Max meets in the first volume and who continues to support the flying girl. In *Angel Experiment* she attends to Max's injuries and treats her like a so-called normal kid. Later on, she confronts the representatives of those who consider themselves the owners of Avians, speaking up for mutants, which she clearly links to her veterinary practice. The scene takes place at her workplace, during her practice. She insists on being called a doctor by the intruders and does not draw a distinction between human and animal "patients": "'I'm a veterinary surgeon,' said Dr. Martinez in a chilling voice. 'To tell you the truth, I usually don't look at my patients' owners much. And I haven't seen any strangers around. As for unusual *animals*, last week I treated a cow that had a bicornuate uterus. She had a healthy calf in each side. Does that help?'" (Patterson, *The Angel Experiment* 145–46). Her words imply that she is concentrated on the patient, whose good is of primary importance for her, and that she would be unlikely to switch to an institutional ethic or a military one and put government purposes over the care for the patient, however nonhuman or otherwise unusual. (Mutants would not be strange or unusual either: they would still receive her help.) It is telling that yet again a cow appears in a meaningful way, this time giving birth to twins. The words of Dr. Martinez suggest that animals should be included in the same kind of care humans receive. The cow is not an "it" but a "she," and the doctor clearly utilizes the language that could well be used with a human mother giving birth to healthy children. It is worth noting that in *Saving the World and Other Extreme Sports*, Dr. Martinez removes Max's tracking chip, in this manner removing her from the "livestock" or "pet" category. This is the extension of her humane treatment of animals, and—on the part of the author—a tacit statement that just like we classify and chip people, we classify and control animals and other live organisms and decide their fate on the basis of predetermined categories.

Dr. Martinez provides a balancing weight in the narrative for such characters as Jeb Batchhelder, an abusive father-scientist, or Dr. Gunther-Hagen, who injects his enhancement serum into unwilling subjects to forcefully create a superior breed of humans and who in the end makes "Horsemen" to kill the rest of those "unfit for the future" (Persson and Savulescu). In *Fang*, the sixth volume, he justifies his inhumane experiments on people and ALife, saying, "in an apocalypse, there are no doctors. There are no hospitals and certainly no insurance companies. You are on your own. It is you against the forces of nature, which at this point in Earth's history surely see it as in their best interest to eradicate the human race" (Patterson, *Fang* 52). Healthcare in the face of crisis succumbs to crisis ethics reduced ad absurdum: the very subjects that are supposed to be saved are targeted for eradication. Such reductionism obviously leads to the instrumentalization of research subjects. Here fiction and reality permeate each other in the exploration of an even more dire perspective—in an attempt to save humanity, we might bring about its destruction.

It is apparent that characters like Dr. Martinez or Celia establish relational ethics with ALife, thus breaking anthropocentric bias and going against species solidarity that should prompt them to objectify the biological artifacts. It then seems valid to ask about the grounds on which this relation is built: is it a question of individual virtue, moral training, religion, or profession? Celia, as a *curandera*, is taught a more holistic perception of nature, which might result in more humane treatment of ALife forms. Her practice outside the system, within the realm of alternative medicine, has perhaps prepared her for dealing with alternative life forms. The case of hybrids and chimeras is more complex when it comes to species solidarity. In fact, Dr. Martinez has her own genetic interest in helping and protecting Max, to whom she is biologically related. According to the theory of Richard Dawkins, her care for Max could be read in terms of parental investment: she subconsciously wants her genes to be perpetuated, even in a modified form. Thus, biological continuity merges here with discontinuity, provoking tensions between being a healthcare professional and a mother. The relationship between the two, although it cannot be taken for a case of altruistic coexistence between species, allows Dr. Martinez to form similar relations with other Avians. This could indicate that forming a bond with at least one posthuman can help to extend care to others who are not related in any way.

Judging by the sensibilities and system of values presented by characters that display bonds with animals, most prominently Dr. Martinez, one is led to ask further questions about the ethical system that they form in relation to nonhuman people. Whereas individual bonds and relationships are not sufficient, they can still act as a stepping-stone to a broader and more reliable ethics. Furthermore, from the existing models in young adult literature, it seems that successful caretakers combine the two vast systems of veterinary ethics and animal ethics: the first being more often understood in institutional terms and the second providing ontological grounds for medical procedures and limits of care. In the case of dealing with ALife, both systems are helpful to conceptualize our relationship to the artificially created children of the future.

VETERINARY ETHICS FOR BEINGS OF UNCERTAIN STATUS

The professional ethics of vets rests on similar principles as medical ethics; however, it has to account for the specific case of a subject whose voice is not understood and whose rights are not secured. Most often, the decision of the owner (or the client) is binding, and the doctors should not speak up trying to protect animal life—only do what they are paid to do. As Elein Hernandez et al. write in their article, the issue of business and species loyalty is one of the most fundamental in veterinary ethics: "In reality, many ethical dilemmas are 'solved' by prioritising the interests of the client over the interests of the animal. This is facilitated by legislation that reinforces the status of animals as property, without equivalent legal (and by extension, moral) standing to humans. If animals had equal legal and moral standing, it would be difficult to justify their use, for example, as sources of food or fibre." The authors also survey various ethical standpoints relating them to animal care within a specific veterinary context. They describe two models that are of particular interest for the analysis in the present chapter since the very name relates directly to the juvenile patients in the above texts:

> The veterinarian's actions can fall into what Rollin refers to as either the garage mechanic or the paediatrician model, based on the moral value of the animal. In the garage mechanic or human-centred (anthropocentric) model, the animal's needs are not directly taken into consideration. Conversely, a veterinarian in the paediatrician model would primarily look after the well-being of the animal and discuss potential ethical concerns with the owner. (Hernandez et al.)

These issues can be observed in the case of Rose from Farmer's *The House of the Scorpion*; although she is not a trained nurse or a veterinarian, she has experience with raising animals. Unfortunately for Matt, she was taught to breed chickens for food, and she sees them in terms of the problems they cause and the benefits they bring. The same attitude is displayed by Willum the doctor, who cares for Matt only as much as his client El Patrón does. The garage mechanic model is here transferred from other spheres of life to dealing with ALife, which leads to developmental delay and physical emaciation of the clone.

A perhaps more overarching approach to applying veterinary ethics to future children is animal ethics, especially regarding the ontological status of animals in relation to humans and the questions of personhood, sentience, and consciousness. The liminal status of Patterson's Maximum is phrased as human, animal, "or a combination thereof" (Patterson, *Saving the World* 231); that of Farmer's Mirasol is phrased as "neither human nor animal" (Farmer, *Lord* 77). Matt witnesses the worst version of ethics: "a thing on the bed" (Farmer, *House* 134).

The best ALife can hope for, in fact, turns out to be some kind of animal ethics: Matt quite rightly observes that livestock is not the only potential category while considering conduct toward nonhuman people. He notices that "people keep all kinds of things" and treat them well without hope for the return on their emotional investment (Farmer, *Lord* 77). The same idea appears in the Maximum Ride series: the Avians are called "really expensive pets" and "unusual animals" (Patterson, *The Angel Experiment* 142). The biggest obstacle for Farmer to surmount, it seems, is justifying the ontological status of animals as equal to humans—and this she does by instituting an interpretation of Franciscanism. Sor Artemisia believes that "animals are just as good as people," (Farmer, *Lord* 87), which reflects on the attitude to clones; by extension, they are just as good. María calls Matt "Brother Wolf," trying to imitate St. Francis, and eventually cries out that Matt is "not an animal" (Farmer, *House* 226). However, by law he is considered "livestock" because he was gestated inside a cow and "[c]ows can't give birth to humans" (*House* 226). María apparently displays care ethics, which are still anthropocentric. She draws Matt under the protective umbrella of human-centric theology she does not fully understand. She does not address the question of what would happen if the ontological difference between herself, an ALife, and her dog Furball were obliterated.

But what constitutes possible common ground shared by ALife, animals, and people? The difficulty in choosing the right conduct with ALife is usually predicated on the carer's perspective on artificially created life and their stance in the realm of reproductive ethics. If a medical carer believes in the naturalistic paradigm, which as a rule favors sentience as a criterion for personhood, then the genetic manipulation of nonpersons will not violate bioethical principles of conduct. Thus, naturalism would allow for the creation of ALife and its use as an object in experimentation as long as its rights as a person are not recognized. Ethicist Julian Savulescu claims,

> However, the embryo is not the future person. Genes are not persons. To manipulate a gene or embryo is not to manipulate a person. One can still have a communicative relation with a future child if an embryo's genes were modified, or a genetic disorder cured. One can treat a future child as an end while still having selecting [*sic*] it as stem-cell donor (savior sibling), or improving its genetic hand. At the heart of all these concerns is a reductionism that reduces persons (and their treatment) to genes or embryos. How we choose to treat persons is entirely separable from how we choose to treat the genes of an embryo. (3)

Still, it can be seen that in this paradigm, the notion of personhood decides the ethics applied to ALife, which can be treated on par with an embryo. And if for Savulescu the difference between an embryo and a "rightful" person seems clear, there are some who propose an extended notion of a person, whether by including other beings into the personhood of humans (by stating we all partake in the same nature) or by pointing out that our integrity as humans is already compromised.[16]

Nevertheless, it does point to one of the difficulties and limitations in applying veterinary ethics to humans and posthumans, which is also present in the Matteo Alacrán and Maximum Ride series. Farmer in particular seems to be acutely aware of the personhood problem, although she phrases it as a human-animal dichotomy. Matt is treated like an animal only from the moment when a tattoo saying "The Property of the Alacrán Estate" is discovered on his foot. The children that bring an injured boy to the white mansion of El Patrón look for a doctor, but one of the drug lord's employees claims he needs a vet. This is later repeated by María, who is more sympathetic but still claims that Matt "doesn't have a soul" and that "all animals are like that" (Farmer, *House* 159). In the end, Matt accepts his status as an animal; however, he embraces this in defiance and rejection of narrowly understood humanity. María, in fact, attempts to find a conceptual framework that would breach the divide between humans who go to heaven and clones that slip out of the boundaries of traditionally understood humanity.

In contrast, Matt, thanks to his experience, realizes that this oppressive understanding of veterinary ethics is not the only possibility. In fact, when Celia points out to him that it is a waste of time to extend care toward Mirasol because she cannot love him back, he says, "That would be true if Mirasol were a Real Person . . . but I've decided that she's a pet. People keep all kinds of things, dogs, horses, cats, even fish" (Farmer, *Lord* 77). Matt ironically uses the category of "Real Person" to signify a being that is able to formulate an emotional response to humans, which in the book can be understood as roughly corresponding to sentience. It is clear, though, that he is seeking some kind of ethical leverage to validate the existence of beings such as himself, who also have been denied both the status of a Real Person and care. As he notices in *The House of the Scorpion*, people create children and buy pets and form with them an emotional relation that is the basis for their inclusion into the ethical system of humans (120). He and other clones, as he learns, are only "property"—part of a bioeconomy. Farmer's novels suggest the limitations of using veterinary ethics; however, the character of Matt suggests a way forward by using the modified pediatrician approach. Such a concept can be used by care providers to establish a viable ethical response to and a relation with the artificially created beings.

CONCLUSIONS

Even before his successful creation of "humanzee" (human-monkey) embryos (Barash), Juan Carlos Izpisúa Belmonte, a Spanish scientist, stated, "History teaches us time and again that, with time, our ethical and moral boundaries change and mutate, like our DNA, and what yesterday has been ethically unacceptable, if it constitutes real advancement in the progress of humanity, today is already an essential part of our lives" (qtd. in Carretero).[17] This statement shows that the model of retrospective adaptation of ethics is common in the field of medicine and biomedical engineering. While it is understandable that principles are formed in reaction to actual cases that occur, for posthuman subjects it is too late—as even juvenile fiction warns us, the problem is not so much that ALife is created, but that we fail to "love our monsters" (Latour). In the books of Farmer and Patterson, it is too late for "the thing on the bed," for Marisol, and for many other unnamed posthumans created without any specific medical ethics model in mind or, rather, created by employing the utilitarian one and treating ALife as resources. Their texts, though, come right on time to pose important ethical questions and suggest solutions that should be at least investigated for the possibilities of their application. Among others, one value of the texts to young readers lies in their function to more boldly explore the available models and present them for further consideration.

Veterinary ethics does bring new insights into the ethics of healthcare of new life forms insomuch as it alerts the practitioners to the dilemmas that are often not present in their daily practice with humans. It shows the way out of the false dilemma of full recognition of an entity's personhood and its full denial, covering the gray zone between a human and an object. Philosopher Isaiah Berlin perceives positive freedom and agency as proper to subjects, to the exclusion of animals and slaves:

> I wish my life and decisions to depend on myself, not on external forces of whatever kind. I wish to be the instrument of my own, not of other men's, acts of will. I wish to be a subject, not an object; to be moved by reasons, by conscious purposes, which are my own, not by causes which affect me, as it were, from outside. I wish to be somebody, not nobody; a doer—deciding, not being decided for, self-directed and not acted upon by external nature or by other men as if I were a thing, or an animal, or a slave. (Berlin 178)

It is, then, a complicated notion of freedom that accords special dignity to one group over others—and yet, animals can hardly be called objects. As could be seen from the above discussion, the contemporary conundrums of ontology and ethics are far from resolved, and focusing on various criteria (e.g., sentience) for the emancipation of different groups of ALife remains contestable. What, then, inspires Celia, María, and Dr. Martinez to act toward biotechnological artifacts as they would toward people? A belief in their intrinsic "soul" or the will of the "owners"? Hardly: they act against scientific practice, contractual ethics and religious teachings. Rather, a broad understanding of their own dignity as conscious agents allows them to recognize the dignity in another being, and it is from this foundation that their care results. Veterinary and animal ethics go beyond the notion of a person or a human and demonstrate the possibility of extending care toward nonhuman beings. These systems of ethics show that what brings the desired communication and coexistence is not according dignity from a privileged position, but recognizing it as pertinent to all beings—not humanizing ALife but accepting its Otherness.

However, before these texts serve as inspiration for the young and the old in their relations with ALife—and, more broadly, with marginalized groups escaping normative regulations—they have to be thoroughly analyzed. The above discussion of the novels signaled numerous problems, which might transfer harmful stereotypes about some groups while inculcating positive mindsets about others. What is especially disturbing in the contemporary juvenile texts is the presentation of healthcare providers, especially the nurses, as a nameless mass at best. At worst, they are incompetent and malicious women, envying male doctors and scientists and taking out this anger on the children. This reflects the biases Geoffrey Hunt and Barbara Ehrenreich and Deirdre English write about and implies that healthcare practitioners cannot be trusted, that they are malevolent or uneducated or both. In fact, what is tacitly promoted is ceding the care for ALife to others—specifically, to children, which has been shown by Derek Thiess to be a questionable practice. We can easily see how Maximum and María feel pressed to "othermother" their posthuman charges (Thiess 74). This replaces the care the Avians and Matt should receive from professionals, but—especially in the case of Max—it comes with an associated burden and psychological damage. Two exceptions to the generalized negativity, especially hurtful toward female healthcare providers, are Dr. Martinez, who breaks the stereotype of an uneducated, malicious, and insensitive care worker, and Celia, who challenges the stereotypes of the type of education future healthcare workers need. It turns out that scientific training is not always enough; conversely, it may result in prioritizing institutional and utilitarian approaches, whereas sensitivity training would allow medical professionals to build relations and extend care over the hardwired biases and the "yuck factor."

As can be seen, the analyzed novels fulfill one of the basic functions of utopian literature: they challenge the existing social system and offer an alternative for its improvement. In this case, it is especially the medical system with its professional ethics that is contested and shown as lacking in many respects. Especially, though, it is the question of care that calls for reconsideration. It seems that Farmer and Patterson try to go beyond anthropocentrism in medical ethics; however, what they arrive at is mostly a grim picture of institutional regulations that impede attempts to make a change. It is also evident from the texts that medicine now is seen as shackled by economic and political relations and that healing seems to be slowly replaced by science, with alternative ways of practice discarded as not productive or "unscientific." Finally, the authors remind the readers that ethics begins in relations, and unless these relations are acknowledged and the status of beings entering the relation is determined, it is extremely hard to bring about real change in the world of actual, not fictional, healthcare. Importantly, they help to "unvile" yet another group of "vile bodies," at least in the minds of the audience, providing hope and sensitizing future medical practitioners to the complexities of their profession.

NOTES

1. It is worth recalling that vile bodies in medical practice are always situated within a concrete historical context, connected with the necessity to perform human trials in medical research. Grégoire Chamayou provides a historical overview of how vile bodies were used in medical practice before the twentieth century, while William A. Lafleur et al. relate famous cases of the twentieth century, including Nazi and Unit 731 experimentation. This practice is frequent during military conflicts, but not limited to them (as in the cases of race or ability bias). Judith L. Newman et al. also note unethical experimentation on children.

2. See, for example, Bugajska; Mills; Jaques; Kaku; and Sullivan.

3. "Here, 'ALife' will simply refer to new and non-natural forms of life brought into existence through external and technical means at least initially under human control" (Johnston 4).

4. Braidotti describes the category of assemblage in which the constituent elements enter in nonnecessary relations between one another (i.e., they are nonessential and can be changed at any given moment), and each part can be replaced or sacrificed if the well-being of the whole system is at stake. The assemblage is made out of human and nonhuman elements; thus, the ethics to be applied is nonanthropocentric.

5. According to her own definition, "it speaks in one breath of nonhumans and other than humans such as things, objects, other animals, living beings, organisms, physical forces, spiritual entities, and humans" (Puig de la Bellacasa 1).

6. This form of ethics takes into account various instances in which the calculation of risk, probability, or good faces serious difficulties due to the lack of measurable data that would enable a strong normative rule (i.e., one that would allow for the creation of possibly universal legal solutions).

7. As argued by Carlos E. Maldonado and James Wilson, for example, bioethics needs to acknowledge nonanthropocentric perspective as it takes into account multiple new variables, such as life in space, new life forms, and biosocial, economic, and political systems.

8. This complexity is underlined by Geoffrey Hunt's discussion of the "perennial question" about nursing. He states that "nurses often express unease about a lack of freedom to care for patients and clients as they feel is decent, as they feel they themselves would like to be cared for or have their loved ones cared for" (Hunt 2). It is important to notice that nurses sometimes can be pressured to commit crimes or comply with the existent conditions, just like doctors. See Hunt's illuminating discussion of the biomedical model and the military model in nursing, as well as the relationships between doctors and nurses and the dependence on various sources of power.

9. Some regulations instituted to ensure correct conduct on the battlefield are the Nightingale Pledge and the Code of Ethics for Nurses. The latter is a set of soft standards that can be dynamically applied to the situation at hand (see Lachman).

10. The experiments leading to the creation of ALife that I enumerate above show that the problem of extending proper care toward different kinds of beings is not only fictional, but emergent, and there are not enough studies into the matter, as the research into 3D bioprinting led by Church or human-animal hybrids by Hiromitsu Nakauchi and Juan Carlos Izpisúa Belmonte are within a gray zone.

11. The choice of texts has been motivated by various factors. First of all, neither are frequently studied, and it is worth bringing them to critical attention. Second, the authors are clearly interested in the patterns of care, and the hypothetical situations they construct are less entangled with the limitations of the chosen conventions than, for example, Dan Wells's texts. Third, the ALife is foregrounded: Matt Alacrán and Maximum Ride are the main heroes, and the readers have insight into their emotions.

12. "Alacrán" in Spanish means "scorpion," hence the title of the first novel. It is worth noticing the entanglement of symbols surrounding the clones in the novel. They are seen as animals and embodiments of evil. Importantly, originally El Patrón comes from the lower class; it is only in adulthood that he lives in a mansion referred to as the white house, which clearly symbolizes the White House. Therefore, the political and economic contexts, as well as ethnic and cultural biases surrounding the Mexican border, come into play.

13. Although the term "medical posthumanities" is recent, it has already gained some currency, especially in the reflection on the status of the emerging forms of life and their possible socialization, and determining their legal status (see Cohn and Lynch; Bryson et al.). This is the perspective I am working from, and my assumptions underpinning the use of this term, are first, that medical posthumanities are inviting the insights of posthumanities into medical practice, or at least philosophical-ethical formation and second, medical posthumanities are determining what posthuman is and developing reflection and legislation over what it means to be posthuman. This is how I use the term in this chapter with regard to literary texts: my inquiry is about how texts help us to manage reality, and not so much how we can understand texts better thanks to new frameworks.

14. As Barbara Ehrenreich and Deirdre English write, whereas it is true that male medical experts were better educated than female healers,

> too often the experts' theories were grossly unscientific, while the traditional lore of the women contained wisdom based on centuries of observation and experience. The rise of the experts was not the inevitable triumph of right over wrong, fact over myth; it began with a bitter conflict which set women against men, class against class. Women did not learn to look to an external 'science' for guidance until after their old skills had been ripped away, and the 'wise women' who preserved them had been silenced, or killed. (37)

15. Clémentine Beauvais and Evelyn Tsitas discuss interpretations of hybrid characters. Beauvais focuses on the trans-and the resultant hybrid offspring as an expression of political power and social role of children, whereas Tsitas constructs her analysis around the notion

of Haraway's cyborg (here a term used for ALife) and the Frankensteinesque mad scientist. Many of the points made, especially by Tsitas, are relevant to this chapter, for example the anthropocentric treatment of nonhumans, presented in fiction as chimeras. However, I take the debate further toward practical applications: I concentrate on the ethical response to emergent biotechnological issues.

16. To understand the robust debate about personhood, it is helpful to read the ideas of Peter Singer, Ingmar Persson, and Georg Dvorsky, who call for extending personhood, and the ideas of H. Tristram Engelhardt and Grzegorz Hołub, who insist that medical ethics should be applied only toward "persons," as differentiated from "impostors," and that for now there is no certainty about the personhood of artificially created life.

17. This is my translation.

WORKS CITED

Applebaum, Noga. *Representations of Technology in Science Fiction for Young People.* Routledge, 2009.

Barash, David P. "It's Time to Make Human-Chimp Hybrids." *Nautilus*, 8 Mar. 2018, http://nautil.us/issue/58/self/its-time-to-make-human_chimp-hybrids.

Beauvais, Clémentine. "Romance, Dystopia, and the Hybrid Child." *Contemporary Adolescent Literature and Culture*, edited by Mary Hilton and Maria Nikolajeva, Routledge, 2016, pp. 71–86.

Berlin, Isaiah. *Liberty: Incorporating Four Essays on Liberty.* Edited by Henry Hardy, Oxford UP, 2002.

Bradford, Clare, et al. *New World Orders in Contemporary Children's Literature: Utopian Transformations.* Palgrave Macmillan, 2011.

Braidotti, Rosi. Utrecht Summer School 2018: Posthuman Ethics, Pain and Endurance, 20–24 Aug. 2018.

Bryson, Joanna J., et al. "Of, for, and by the People: The Legal Lacuna of Synthetic Persons." *Artificial Intelligence and Law*, vol. 25, 2017, pp. 273–91.

Bugajska, Anna. *Engineering Youth: The Evantropian Project in Young Adult Dystopias.* Ignatianum UP, 2019.

Carretero, Nacho. "Juan Carlos Izpisúa: 'Avances así permiten la vida.'" *El País*, 22 Aug. 2017, https://elpais.com/elpais/2017/08/22/ciencia/1503411254_955787.html.

Chamayou, Grégoire. *Les corps vils: expérimenter sur les êtres humains aux XVIIe et XIXe siècles.* Kindle ed., Éditions La Découverte, 2011.

Clarke, Bruce, and Manuela Rossini, eds. *The Routledge Companion to Science and Literature.* Routledge, 2012.

Cohn, Simon, and Rebecca Lynch, eds. *Posthumanism and Public Health.* Routledge, 2017.

Dawkins, Richard. *The Selfish Gene.* Oxford UP, 1989.

Dvorsky, Georg. "All Together Now: Developmental and Ethical Considerations for Biologically Uplifting Nonhuman Animals." *Journal of Evolution and Technology*, vol. 18, no. 1, 2008, pp. 129–42, https://jetpress.org/v18/dvorsky.htm.

Ehrenreich, Barbara, and Deirdre English. *For Her Own Good: Two Centuries of Expert Advice to Women.* Anchor, 2005.

Engelhardt, H. Tristram. *The Foundations of Bioethics.* 2nd ed., Oxford UP, 1996.
Farmer, Nancy. *The House of the Scorpion.* Simon and Shuster, 2013.
Farmer, Nancy. *The Lord of Opium.* Atheneum Books for Young Readers, 2014.
Foucault, Michel. *The Birth of Biopolitics: Lectures at the Collège de France, 1978–79.* Palgrave Macmillan, 2008.
Foucault, Michel. *Madness and Civilization: A History of Insanity in the Age of Reason.* Routledge, 2001.
Gibson, Dan. "How to Build Synthetic DNA and Send It across the Internet." *TED*, 11 July 2018, https://www.ted.com/talks/dan_gibson_how_to_build_synthetic_dna_and_send_it_across_the_internet.
Harrison, Jennifer. *Posthumanist Readings in Dystopian Young Adult Fiction: Negotiating the Nature/Culture Divide.* Lexington Books, 2019.
Hernandez, Elein et al. "Speaking Up: Veterinary Ethical Responsibilities and Animal Welfare Issues in Everyday Practice." *Animals*, vol. 8, no. 1, 2018, https://doi.org/10.3390/ani8010015.
Hołub, Grzegorz. "Is a Post-Human Personalism Possible?" *Studia Sandomierskie*, vol. 25, no. 1, 2018, pp. 261–70.
Hunt, Geoffrey, "Ethics, Nursing and the Metaphysics of Procedure." *Ethical Issues in Nursing*, edited by Geoffrey Hunt, Routledge, 1994, pp. 1–20.
Jaques, Zoe. *Children's Literature and the Posthuman: Animal, Environment, Cyborg.* Routledge, 2015.
Johnson, Harriet McBryde. *Too Late to Die Young: Nearly True Tales from a Life.* Picador, 2006.
Johnston, John. "AI and ALife." *The Routledge Companion to Literature and Science*, edited by Bruce Clarke and Manuela Rossini, Routledge, 2011, pp. 4–16.
Kaku, Michio. *Physics of the Impossible: A Scientific Exploration into the World of Phasers, Force Fields, Teleportation, and Time Travel.* Doubleday, 2008.
LaFleur, William R., et al. *Dark Medicine: Rationalizing Unethical Medical Research.* Indiana UP, 2007.
Lachman, Vicki. *Applied Ethics in Nursing.* Springer, 2005.
Latour, Bruno. "Love Your Monsters: Why We Must Care for Our Tehnologies as We Do Our Children." *Breakthrough Journal*, vol. 2, Feb. 2012, https://thebreakthrough.org/journal/issue-2/love-your-monsters.
Lee, Keekok. "Biology and Technology." *The Companion to the Philosophy of Technology*, edited by Jan Kyrre Berg Olsen et al., Blackwell Publishing. 2009, pp. 99–103.
Maldonado Castañeda, Carlos E. "Complejidad de la Bioética." *Rev Thelos*, 2015, https://www.academia.edu/20089390/Complejidad_de_la_bio%C3%A9tica.
Maldonado Castañeda, Carlos E., ed. *Complejidad: Revolución Científica y Teoría.* U del Rosario, 2009.
Mills, Claudia, ed. *Ethics and Children's Literature.* Ashgate Publishing, 2014.
Newman, Judith L., et al. *Against Their Will: The Secret History of Medical Experimentation on Children in Cold War America.* Palgrave Macmillan, 2014.
Patterson, James. *Angel.* Arrow, 2012.
Patterson, James. *The Angel Experiment.* Headline, 2006.
Patterson, James. *Fang.* Arrow, 2011.

Patterson, James. *The Final Warning*. Arrow, 2009.

Patterson, James. *Max*. Arrow, 2010.

Patterson, James. *Maximum Ride Forever*. Arrow, 2015.

Patterson, James. *Nevermore*. Arrow, 2013.

Patterson, James. *Saving the World and Other Extreme Sports*. Headline, 2008.

Patterson, James. *School's Out—Forever*. Headline, 2007.

Persson, Ingmar, and Julian Savulescu. *Unfit for the Future: The Need for Moral Enhancement*. Oxford UP, 2012.

Puig de la Bellacasa, María. *Matters of Care: Speculative Ethics in More Than Human Worlds*. U of Minnesota P, 2017.

Savulescu, Julian. "Rational Freedom and Six Mistakes of a Bioconservative." *The American Journal of Bioethics*, vol. 19, no. 7, 2019, pp. 1–5.

Storch, Janet L. "Ethics in Nursing Practice." *A Companion to Bioethics*, 2nd ed., edited by Helga Kuhse and Peter Singer, Blackwell Publishing, 2009, pp. 551–62.

Sullivan, C. W., III., ed. *Young Adult Science Fiction*. Greenwood Press, 1999.

Tarr, Anita, and Donna R. White, eds. *Posthumanism in Young Adult Fiction: Humanity in a Posthuman World*. UP of Mississippi, 2018.

Thiess, Derek J. *Embodying Gender and Age in Speculative Fiction: A Biopsychosocial Approach*. Routledge, 2016.

Tsitas, Evelyn. "Boundary Transgressions: The Human-Animal Chimera in Science Fiction." *Relations. Beyond Anthropocentrism*, vol. 2, no. 2, 2014, pp. 97–112.

Wilson, James. "Embracing Complexity: Theory, Cases and the Future of Bioethics." *Monash Bioethics Review*, vol. 32, no. 1–2, 2014, pp. 3–21.

White, Donna R. "Posthumanism in *The House of the Scorpion* and *The Lord of Opium*." *Posthumanism in Young Adult Fiction. Humanity in a Posthuman World*, edited by Donna R. White and Anita Tarr, UP of Mississippi, 2018, pp. 135–55.

SHIFTING STORIES

Care Ethics and Masculinities in the Television Series *Teen Wolf*

CARRIE SPENCER

INTRODUCTION: MASCULINITY, MONSTERS, AND MORALITY

Ethical questions raised by scientific and medical practices have provided a rich source of material for literature from Mary Shelley's *Frankenstein* (1818) to popular television series such as *House* (2004–2012). Conflicts and dramatic tension in healthcare settings often arise through power imbalances between scientist or physician characters and patients and through contrasting perspectives on illness, patient experience, and physician goals. Physician characters are usually depicted as approaching moral decision-making as the result of objective, detached deliberations, whereas patients' views on the medications, treatments, and interventions they want are more often informed by subjective experience and contextualized in their lives and relationships with friends and family. In formal healthcare institutions, decisions about the organization, distribution, and practices of care are developed within a "larger political context that reflects a given society's values, laws, customs, and institutions" (Tronto, *Who Cares?* 10). These wider contexts include dominant social ontologies and ideologies, such as individualism in the twenty-first century US. However, narrative explorations of healthcare needs and practices may variously assert a moral rationale for recognizable healthcare policies and practices or encourage readers and audiences to question those practices and to consider alternatives. Care ethics (or ethics of care) theory offers an alternative to detached deliberations that are abstracted away from the emotional, experiential, and contextual. Instead, care ethics theories propose moral practices and principles that begin in the inevitable interdependencies of life, taking relationality as "the most basic nature of human existence" (Robinson 4). Care ethics is not only concerned with the morality or practice of a single care act, but also takes relationality as a basis for offering fundamentally different approaches to the organization and distribution of healthcare.

Care ethics has developed from the work of second-wave feminists, particularly Sara Ruddick, Carol Gilligan, and Nel Noddings, who considered gendered differences in women's moral decision-making and care practices. Although there is not one singular care ethics theory, the ontological starting point of relationality, the importance of attention and response to others, and the need for understanding particularities and contexts are themes shared by care ethicists (Engster and Hamington 4). Over the last forty years, care ethics theory has critiqued the distribution and structuring of care through political, economic, and sociocultural forces that sustain the privilege of those who already have power, as well as the idealization of independent, autonomous, self-interested moral individuals as fundamental to systems that continue to devalue care and those who are expected to practice care. Care ethics, as an approach based in relationality, has rejected models that essentialize care as so-called women's work or suggest that men are somehow feminized by caring. Globally, the distribution and organization of care, including but not limited to looking after households, children, sick, injured, disabled, or elderly relatives, remains devalued, gendered, raced, and classed (Robinson 63–64; Tronto, *Who Cares?* 19). Power and inequality are fundamental to theorizing care ethics and, therefore, so are considerations of race, class, gender, and other forms of disadvantage and marginalization. Care ethics not only critiques existing systems and practices, but also offers an alternative that recognizes good care as essential for flourishing and well-being.

This chapter takes a care ethics lens to consider how the devaluation and unequal distribution of care reinforces gender stereotypes that disassociate men from caring. The concept of hegemonic masculinity theorizes how unequal gender-based relations are sustained through changing historical and social contexts. In positing hegemonic masculinity as socially, culturally, and historically produced, this concept describes a social "practice (i.e., things done, not just a set of role expectations or an identity) that allowed men's dominance over women to continue" (Connell and Messerschmidt 832). Hegemonic masculinity does not propose an essentialized or trans-historical way of "being a man" that is more advantageous in every society or situation, although the contemporary traits of hegemonic masculinity are recognizable as those which are typically advantageous for boys and men in particular contexts. In young adult (YA) literature, werewolves are often portrayed to affirm hegemonic masculinity as heterosexual, aggressive, and seemingly natural for adolescent boys and alpha males at the top of the social hierarchy, such that these aspects of a teen werewolf's "animality can be read as affirmative" (Waller 47). The original film *Teen Wolf* (1985) depicts the teenage protagonist Scotty (played by Michael J.

Fox) struggling to control his werewolf side when he kisses a girl or plays basketball. By directly associating this adolescent boy character's animality with heterosexuality, aggression, and physical strength, "becoming a werewolf is the path to popularity and athletic prowess for the film's hero" (Schell 112). In the final scene, Scotty gains control of his "inner animal" to win the basketball game and female love interest in his human shape. The film's portrayal of Scotty's werewolf embodiment within the constraints of mainstream male adolescence and hegemonic masculinity means that "Scotty . . . couldn't be more conventional, even in his wildest form" (Kidd 161).

However, in remaking the 1985 film of the same name, the more recent television series *Teen Wolf* (2011–2017) responded to its twenty-first century adolescent audience by shifting away from concern with socialization and idealized male adolescence toward a greater engagement with moral questions regarding interpersonal relationships and appropriate uses of power. As such, *Teen Wolf* (*TW*) can be considered within the wider trend of popular US teen television programming since the 1990s that has made "significant changes in the portrayal of masculinities and a man's role on the small screen" (Feasey 4). A number of popular US television series with adolescent boy protagonists explore concepts of masculinity and social power through regular scenes of formal and informal healthcare practices. In *TW* the eponymous teenage werewolf, Scott McCall (played by Tyler Posey), has a job at the animal clinic, which provides a setting for many werewolf-human interactions, as well as human-animal ones. Although it is commonplace for teenage protagonists to have part-time jobs, it is unusual for teenage male protagonists, particularly superpowered ones, to find satisfaction in low-status healthcare work, in contrast to the higher-status ambition of becoming a doctor or surgeon. As such, Scott's work at the animal clinic and his ambition to become a vet emphasize his concern with the thoughtful and skilled practice of meeting the needs of others over his own social status.

The depiction of Scott learning and practicing healthcare at the animal clinic contrasts with other superpowered adolescent protagonists of popular US teen television, who can only practice healing in secret. Typically, superpowered or alien characters can heal much faster than humans, reducing their own need for healthcare, as seen in shows such as *Buffy the Vampire Slayer* (1997–2003), *Roswell* (1999–2002), and *Smallville* (2001–2011). Like Scott, the adolescent boy protagonists of *Smallville* and *Roswell* use their powers to heal or save others, seeming to counter the traditional disassociation of men from caregiving. However, it is a convention that the supernatural or alien protagonist must hide their nonhuman identities and abilities from society at large, with the result that only a small group of trusted individuals knows their secret (Levy and Mendlesohn; Banks). In contrast to Scott's work at the clinic, in *Smallville* and *Roswell*, the protagonists' acts of care or healing are constructed as the alternative masculinities of nonhuman boys who must remain hidden from mainstream society. The construction of caring masculinities as outside of the dominant culture sustains hierarchical social relations, as hegemonic masculinity "requires all other men to position themselves in relation to it" (Connell and Messerschmidt 832). The depiction of teenage boy characters who must enact healing and care in secret limits their potential to disrupt hegemonic processes or offer viable alternatives to the current organization and distribution of care practices.

In contrast to the depiction of a lone superpowered protagonist and the more typical association of werewolves with an aggressive hierarchical social order, *TW* centers the mutually supportive friendship between Scott (werewolf) and Stiles (human). By taking relationality as ontologically basic, care ethics theorizes a "morality of responsibility in which the emphasis is on connection, and the relationship itself, rather than the individuals in it" (Robinson 30). Through six seasons, Scott and Stiles's shared interdependence is the foundation from which they approach the moral dilemmas posed by the supernatural events that they encounter. *TW* alludes to the more common relationship of hero and sidekick that is structured on terms of unequal power relations between two male characters: soon after Scott is bitten and becomes a werewolf, Stiles complains that it is "starting to feel like you're Batman and I'm Robin" ("Pack Mentality" 17:39–17:41). However, Scott assures Stiles that "nobody's Batman or Robin any of the time" ("Pack Mentality" 17:44–17:45). Scott's response highlights that, even though he is physically stronger and faster than Stiles, these traits do not require a reordering of their friendship with Scott as dominant or superior to Stiles. This mutually supportive friendship between a werewolf and human demonstrates that differences in strength or abilities do not inevitably result in nor require hierarchical social relations. The relational values of *TW*'s protagonists demonstrate a care ethics founded in moral attention and response to others and the importance of the quality of interpersonal encounters for well-being.

Through its depiction of thoughtful and responsible adolescent relationships, *TW* has attracted some critical attention for its depictions of gender relations, consent in sexual activity, masculinities, and sexualities that "makes significant progress over other recent young adult paranormal romance series" (Kendal and Kendal 38). Rather than the depiction of gender relations or sexualities, my focus is on the moral decision-making processes that inform healthcare practices and shape patient experiences for both human and supernatural characters. I similarly aim to focus my application of care ethics theory in a slightly different direction than existing scholarship. Although there has been growing interest in care ethics in children's and YA scholarship since Mary

Jeanette Moran's article "'Use Your Head, Judy Girl': Relationships, Writing, and an Ethic of Care in the Judy Bolton Mysteries," work to date has generally concentrated on familial relationships and female protagonists. Lisa Sainsbury's monograph *Ethics in British Children's Literature: Unexamined Life* considers a range of moral frameworks portrayed in British children's and YA novels, including care ethics alongside other more familiar Western philosophical approaches. Sainsbury's astute analysis includes an examination of male and female characters to analyze gender relations and the detrimental consequences of the "rules" of masculinity in children's novels mostly from the twentieth century. Similarly, Moran's chapter "Making a Difference: Ethical Recognition through Otherness in Madeleine L'Engle's Fiction" considers depictions of male and female characters' relational moral deliberations and values but does not reflect on hegemonic masculinity. In this chapter I seek to add to existing scholarship by applying care ethics to twenty-first century adolescent masculinities in one popular US teen television series and to the moral dilemmas that arise in healthcare situations and settings. As I demonstrate in this chapter, the values and ideologies that shape the everyday interactions between various human and werewolf characters also shape how each of these characters responds to healthcare needs, with dramatically different results. Through these contrasts, and by depicting ethical care values and practices through its protagonists, *TW* exemplifies for teen audiences that there is nothing inevitable about the prevailing systems that structure unequal social relations and that organize and distribute healthcare.

PETER AND THE NURSE: GENDER AND POWER IN A PATIENT-PRACTITIONER RELATIONSHIP

Despite the ability of werewolves in *TW* to heal almost immediately from severe injuries, healthcare practice is a recurring theme throughout the series that repeatedly destabilizes hierarchical social relations. While later seasons of *TW* consider social relations within networks, as I discuss in the following sections, season one depicts a hierarchical dyadic practitioner-patient relationship between adult werewolf character Peter Hale and his human nurse. Peter adheres to dominant social values, including hegemonic masculinity and autonomy, seeking power through a process of domination that requires the subordination and devaluation of others' needs and labor. Peter's willingness to use violence in pursuit of his self-interest positions him as an antagonist character to the teenage protagonists, Scott and Stiles. The distance between the target teen audience of *TW* and the undesirability of Peter's values as an adult character are emphasized, as both Peter and Derek (Peter's adult werewolf nephew) allude to the original 1985 *Teen Wolf* film (e.g., "Second Chance at First Line" 22:14; and "Co-Captain" 03:52). These references to a werewolf narrative from the adolescent years of an older generation directly associate Peter and Derek's aggression with an outdated concept of masculinity that is distanced from the experiences of a contemporary teen audience.

Peter's character is first introduced in "Magic Bullet" (season 1, episode 4) as a resident of the hospital's long-term care facility. Due to injuries that he sustained in an arson attack, Peter is initially portrayed in a healthcare relationship of paternalistic control. When Derek and Scott visit him, Peter sits in silence in a wheelchair in his darkened room ("Magic Bullet" 36:34–38:00), evoking individualistic values that construct lack of health as lack of self-determination and the patient as passive object of fear or pity. The arrival of Peter's female nurse further suggests that Peter's injuries have resulted in a loss of autonomy and social power, as she demands of Derek and Scott (off-screen), "What are you doing? How did you get in here?" ("Magic Bullet" 38:00–38:03). The shot from inside Peter's room widens to show the silhouette of the nurse standing in the doorway (38:03). The nurse acts as gatekeeper; her confrontational demand and position in the doorway, surveying the room, assert her authority over both visitors and her patient. Notably, the nurse does not pay attention or respond to Peter. There is no good care in this scene, either from the visitors or the nurse.

However, in fictional portrayals of healthcare, "medical content is always in the service of core story lines" (Shapiro 22). The introduction of Peter Hale in this episode in a passive patient role is revealed to be a ruse to sustain the mystery of the identity of the violent alpha werewolf who has been murdering people in each episode. The revelation that Peter is the alpha destabilizes his initial presentation as a subordinate patient to the controlling nurse. Peter is now understood as the dominant figure in the dyad, with the nurse as his subordinate carer and helper. By drawing attention to who carries out care work and how care is valued in society, care ethics exposes how powerful individuals are constructed as autonomous within "existing structures of power and inequality" (Robinson 3). The nurse's role in helping Peter to become the powerful alpha emphasizes that this healthcare relationship is structured by prevailing systems of gender inequality, sustaining hegemonic masculinity. The nurse's assistance directly contravenes her professional duties as a healthcare worker, as she lures Peter's werewolf niece to the town so that Peter can kill her, thus stealing her powers and becoming the alpha ("Wolf's Bane" 33:44–54). As an alpha Peter has greater supernatural abilities, including faster healing, such that Peter rationalizes killing his niece from an objective and disinterested viewpoint, explaining that "becoming an alpha . . . pushed me over a plateau in the healing process" ("Wolf's Bane" 35:16–35:21); he adds "I can't help that" (35:22–23). Peter's detachment and objectivity in these statements abdicates his moral responsibility, problematizing universalist ethics that require detachment, objectivity, independence, and autonomy for moral reasoning.

Furthermore, Peter's rationalization of murder on health grounds and the facilitating role of the nurse draw attention to care as a site of entrenched gender inequalities, sustained by the inattention of the powerful to carers. Critical attention to gender inequality draws attention to the paradox of care within an individualistic and patriarchal "system that depends on care yet also views that care as a threat to autonomy" (Moran, "Mother" 182). As the nurse aids Peter, first in his recovery, then to become the alpha and to get away with murder, her assistance simultaneously emphasizes the nurse's subordinate role and Peter's dependence on her help. However, those at the top of the social hierarchy are constructed as independent individuals. Sustaining this illusion requires Peter as alpha to eliminate any source of dependency: he kills the nurse. The murder is not depicted, but when Stiles sees the nurse's body in the boot of a car, Peter simply states, "I got better" ("Code Breaker" 07:23–07:32). For Peter's character, being "better" is synonymous with autonomy that demands a violent rejection of all interdependent relationships. From Peter's perspective, once the nurse is no longer serving his needs, there is no reason for her existence, demonstrating how structural inequality legitimizes violence and injustice against those with less social power. Yet, in killing his nurse, Peter's character denies his dependence on her care labor at the same time as he draws attention to it. Far from the nurse posing a threat to his autonomy, *TW* makes clear that Peter could not have become the alpha without her. The murders of Peter's niece and nurse demonstrate how men's violence against women can become legitimized by social contexts that position women as carers and helpers who should privilege men's goals and needs, even at the cost of their own well-being.

Peter's conflicted relationship with the nurse—in which he seeks to assert his dominance over her even as he is dependent on her help—extends to his other relationships, including those with the other male werewolves, Derek and Scott. Social values that naturalize gender roles, such as feminine caring or masculine aggression, can create compliance with practices of oppression and inequality, as the concept of hegemony expresses "an idea that embeds certain notions of consent and participation by the subaltern groups" (Connell and Messerschmidt 841). In YA monster texts in which werewolves are part of a pack, participation in sustaining hegemonic masculine practices is typical among werewolf characters who submit to the authority of the (usually male) alpha, such as in Stephenie Meyer's *Twilight* saga (2005–2008) or Cassandra Clare's *The Mortal Instruments* series (2007–2014). In line with this trope, once Peter is the alpha, he needs other werewolves to dominate and seeks to recruit Derek and Scott to his pack, attempting to coerce them with violence. However, in response to repeated threats that Peter will either make Scott kill someone or kill him ("Magic Bullet" 24:34; "The Tell" 06:47), Scott demands "Seriously? Who made up these rules?" ("The Tell" 06:49–06:50). This adolescent male protagonist exposes hegemonic masculinity as constructed, contingent, and contextual, rather than inevitable or "natural"—even for male werewolves.

The idea of an alternative to mainstream systems and values is emphasized when Peter is defeated at the end of season one, such that the caring relationship between Scott and Stiles is successful and preferable to the violence of the older male werewolves. Unusually for any adolescent supernatural protagonist in a twenty-first-century YA monster text, Scott never kills anyone, either human or supernatural. Furthermore, Scott is not alone in his refusal of masculine violence. He and Stiles demonstrate their shared values as they both repeatedly reject the aggression of the adult werewolves (e.g., "Heart Monitor") and work together to find nonviolent ways of solving human and supernatural problems alike. As Scott and Stiles's friendship is the principal relationship throughout the series, their care ethics offers an alternative to competitive hierarchies of interpersonal and social relations.

CONTRASTS IN INFORMAL CARE: FRIENDS AND WOLF PACKS

In season three of *TW*, care ethics within social groups, rather than dyadic relations, is explored through the contrast of Scott's friendship group with a violent werewolf pack led by the alpha male Deucalion. In "Frayed" (season 3, episode 5) the urgency of life-threatening injuries enables a narrative exploration of how the values underpinning social relations can influence healthcare decisions and practices. Since the latter half of the twentieth-century, developments in healthcare policy and practice have sought to move away from paternalistic models of physician authority over patients, recognizing that care networks may include communities and family members. Outside of formal institutions that typically reflect mainstream values and ideologies, individuals and social groups can deploy alternative moral frameworks in deciding whether, when, how, by whom, and on what basis care will be provided. After Scott and adult werewolf Ennis are injured in a violent conflict between werewolves, their social groups of high school friends and werewolf pack, respectively, must each determine how best to respond to their needs. The structure of the episode juxtaposes healthcare scenes involving Scott and Ennis, inviting viewers to contrast each group's responses and decision-making processes, as well as the differing results for the werewolf patients, healthcare practitioners, and other group members.

To analyze what good care looks like and if, how, and when it is happening, I apply the four stages or principles of ethical care to the healthcare scenarios

I consider here. The four interrelated stages of care proposed by Joan Tronto and Berenice Fisher are "caring about," "caring for," "care-giving," and "care-receiving" (qtd. in Tronto, *Who Cares?* 5–7). These stages begin from the principle of attentiveness, that is, paying attention to other people in order to notice that they have a need ("caring about") (Tronto, *Who Cares?* 5). However, noticing that someone has a need does not necessarily produce a response; for example, in cities people often walk by someone who has fallen without stopping or offering assistance. When care does take place, the second stage of "caring for" involves taking responsibility for doing something to address the need. Notably, this does not mean that the individual has to address the need directly themselves; in many medical emergencies, the appropriate act of "caring for" may involve taking someone to hospital. Having paid attention and taken responsibility, the third stage is the actual practice of caregiving. In healthcare this involves many different people—for example, surgeons, nurses, and anesthetists. The final stage of care is continued attention and response to assess whether and how well the needs have been met. Although a person or fictional character may notice a need, try to do something about it, and take an interest in the outcome, *ethical* care takes place as a moral encounter that centers the experiences of the person in need and the quality of the interpersonal interaction as important to well-being.

In care ethics, the recognition that any interaction may be a site for a moral encounter proposes that responsibilities are "distributed based on the assumption that all persons are bearers of responsibilities to care for others" (Robinson 83). Care is not the natural responsibility of women or people who are assumed to be more virtuous or better at care tasks but constitutes a shared responsibility produced through the inevitable interdependencies of human lives. Furthermore these distributed responsibilities occur within contexts in which people actually live, including care networks that extend beyond traditional self-contained family units. In the twenty-first century, friendships are increasingly recognized in studies of social policy as a vital source of the "intimacies and practices of care" (Roseneil and Budgeon 154). YA literature since the twentieth century has also emphasized friendship groups as an important source of meaningful relationships and moral considerations for its teenaged characters. In the late 1990s, *Buffy the Vampire Slayer* was the first teen monster television series to emphasize the importance of high school friendships over sexual relationships or the end of the world (Levy and Mendlesohn 197). It is now a convention of US teen television series that friendships are a primary source of long-term caring relationships alongside familial relationships. In "Frayed," on the way to a lacrosse match, it is Scott's best friend Stiles who first notices that Scott is not healing and immediately does something about it. Rather than assuming authority as the sole person responsible, Stiles phones their friends Lydia (a banshee) and Allison (a human) to discuss what to do ("Frayed" 21:52–22:24). The friends agree to make the school bus pull over so that they can assess how to help Scott, and the public toilet at the roadside rest stop becomes the unlikely therapeutic space of informal healthcare.

When responsibility is shared within a social friendship group—in contrast to a group of nurses and doctors who have formal roles, responsibilities, and duties—decisions cannot be made on the basis of roles and structures in which each person carries out particular care tasks. Mutually supportive friendship groups must negotiate shifting situations of varying needs and dependencies while sustaining long-term relationships, raising "questions of how care may be given and received by equals" (Roseneil 414). The depiction of the friends' responses to Scott's life-threatening injuries explores how shared responsibility and mutual support can operate in practice. Scott cannot participate in the conversation or consent to treatment as he drifts in and out of consciousness while his wound oozes black goo ("Frayed" 23:34).[1] However, *TW* rejects the construction of the injured, dependent individual as abject or subordinate, as Scott remains centered visually through repeated shots of his prone form, as well as being the subject of his friends' discussion. The composition of the scene gives equal weight to each character's perspective through the use of alternating mid-shots of Lydia, Stiles, and Allison, suggesting shared responsibility that is also portrayed through the dialogue as they each offer ideas. Visual and aural cues emphasize the urgency of the situation, as the shots cut rapidly between each character and the soundtrack sustains a continuous rapid succession of high notes, connoting both the accelerated heartbeats and anxiety of the teens as well as time ticking away as Scott's condition worsens. Stiles, Allison, and Lydia cannot conduct a medical evaluation but together apply their knowledge of the individual, context, and limited medical skills. Stiles suggests that Scott is not healing because he blames himself for failing to prevent the violent conflict and, he fears, for Derek's death ("Frayed" 24:06–24:10). Lydia suggests that they stitch Scott's wounds to make him "believe he's healing" ("Frayed" 24:23), in the hope that his supernatural abilities will then take over. Stiles and Allison agree, reaching a consensus about Scott's treatment. Although Lydia and Stiles do not have any medical training, they participate in Scott's care by fetching him clean clothes and ensuring that the bus doesn't leave while Allison uses her medical skills to stitch Scott's wounds ("Frayed" 24:46–24:58).

However, Allison is Scott's close friend and ex-lover: she cannot shift into a position of detached, objective physician with Scott as patient or body. At first, Allison's emotions overwhelm her healthcare practice. A number of close-up shots show Allison crying and her hands shaking as she repeatedly attempts and fails to thread the needle. Allison imagines her mother demanding that Allison remembers her training and work "clinically" and ("Frayed" 26:09),

Allison adds with a sob in her voice, "And unemo—unemoti—" (26:12–14). Importantly, Allison's training is to become a werewolf hunter and the family's "clinical" code of objective detachment is used to justify killing all supernatural creatures on the assumption that they are inevitably violent. However, Allison has rejected her family's code, recognizing that there are werewolves, such as Scott, whose actions and values are not shaped by their embodiment alone. Allison also rejects the construction of rational detachment as superior because her relationship with Scott is not a weakness to be eradicated but is important and meaningful. The concept of "finding a safe path through two opposing forces" is deployed through the metaphor of "threading the needle" in this episode ("Frayed" 36:35–38), a position that Allison finally manages to achieve when she rejects the opposition between clinical and emotional practice and her imagined mother disappears (26:27). Once Allison recognizes that care *sustains* her relationship with Scott, she can balance her emotions with Scott's needs, and she is able to swiftly stitch his wounds ("Frayed" 26:29–26:42). After Scott regains consciousness, the use of close-ups and extended eye contact between the characters emphasizes their ongoing intimacy and mutual attentiveness ("Frayed" 27:34–28:00), rather than distance or detachment.

The distributed responsibilities in Scott's friendship group, through which Allison, Lydia and Stiles participate in each stage of care, contrast with scenes in which Deucalion's violent werewolf pack seeks help for Ennis from the human vet character, Deaton, who has knowledge of the supernatural. Within the strictly hierarchical wolf pack, Ennis's life-threatening injuries constitute a loss of self-determination and an inability to defend his position in the competitive social order. His loss of status is evident in the objectifying distance between Ennis and the rest of the pack, connoted through the absence of the alpha, Deucalion; through the lack of dialogue about Ennis's needs; and through shot composition in which Ennis is obscured from view ("Frayed" 19:27–20:38). Within hierarchical social structures, responsibilities are unevenly distributed across the stages of care, such that within patriarchal and individualist societies "caring about, and taking care of, are the duties of the powerful. Care-giving and care-receiving are left to the less powerful" (Tronto, *Moral Boundaries* 114). These divisions are seen in formal healthcare as well as the ordering of other social relations. Although the members of the pack are subservient to their alpha, they wield their superior physical strength to gain power over Deaton. Through objectifying the injured pack member, the other members of Deucalion's pack disassociate themselves from care and must ensure that someone else bears the responsibility for direct caregiving, producing coercive interactions with Deaton. The scene evokes the risk of conflict, deploying deep, ominous music and long pauses between dialogue as well as heightening dramatic tension through static shot composition that "allows space to contemplate performance" (Bignell 98). The camera lingers on the werewolves and Deaton's reactions as the pack deploys a number of threats against the vet until Deaton finally admits them to the clinic ("Frayed" 19:37–20:37).

Having constructed Ennis's injuries as inability and lack, the wolf pack perceive their care responsibilities to have been fulfilled once they have secured Deaton's help. Inside the clinic Ennis's objectification as patient or body is emphasized through shots that do not show his face but linger on his wounds in gory detail as Deaton prepares Ennis for treatment ("Frayed" 24:26–24:30). The pack's static poses and silence connote their emotional detachment and dissociation from direct caregiving (24:32; 24:41). The scene ends with a static shot at table height so Ennis's face cannot be seen, centering the patient on-screen but as the passive object of clinical attention ("Frayed" 24:41). The distancing composition and silence in this scene provide a stark contrast with the intimacy generated through the use of frequent close-ups and urgent soundtrack while Allison stitches Scott's wounds.

The hierarchical structure of Deucalion's pack demands that the other werewolves adhere to the alpha's violent methods and work together only in the service of his goals while their own needs are devalued or ignored. At the top of the hierarchy, Deucalion is in a position of extreme privilege: he can overemphasize his own needs and is simultaneously the most distanced from the responsibilities or practices of care. This type of privilege has been termed "privileged irresponsibility," a concept that articulates how the most powerful in society have "the opportunity simply to ignore certain forms of hardships that they do not face" (Tronto, *Moral Boundaries* 121), including poverty, sexism, racism, queerphobia, and ableism. For example, as long as the social organization and distribution of care work are such that powerful people are not expected to take responsibility for meeting the needs of others, those in socially powerful positions—including white, rich, heterosexual men—can continuously prioritize their own perceived needs, such as having someone else care for their children or clean their houses, without a moral obligation to consider the needs of the people carrying out this work. This concern with the needs and interests of the most privileged, along with its detrimental consequences for those in less powerful positions, is depicted when Deucalion finally arrives at the animal clinic after Ennis's treatment. Rather than enacting the final stage of care that would require attention to how well Ennis's needs were met, Deucalion's visit is entirely self-serving. Eerie background music and Deaton's wary expression suggest that Deucalion poses a threat, calling into question Deaton's claim that Ennis "is gonna make it" ("Frayed" 32:04). In a close-up shot in which Ennis's face and neck fill the screen, the viewer can see that Ennis is alive and conscious as Deucalion puts a hand over Ennis's face before killing Ennis by crushing his skull in order to steal his power and escalate the conflict between werewolves from which Deucalion hopes to benefit ("Frayed" 32:15–32:41). This act demonstrates how parochial concern with one's own ever-expanding "needs" and the lack of moral responsibility for others can legitimize violence within hierarchical social orders.

The contrast between the provision of healthcare in response to the similar injuries sustained by Scott and Ennis demonstrates how the values of social groups produce varying responses to vulnerability and dependency with significantly differing results for patient experiences and well-being. Through the responses of Scott's friends, *TW* exemplifies for teen audiences that vulnerability and dependency need not be undesirable or result in a loss of status when experienced within social groups that share relational values. Instead, practices of good care provide a source of meaningful support and "an occasion for developing our capacities of thought, empathy, sensitivity, trust, ingenuity and creativity" (Kittay 310). Scenes of complex, emotional, practical caregiving that center on Scott are contrasted with the hierarchical social arrangements of Deucalion's wolf pack that stymie the conditions in which good care might take place. Unlike Scott, who remains an important part of his social group when injured or unconscious, Ennis's injuries result in his abjection, objectification, and ultimate elimination from the hierarchical pack. Even though the werewolf pack secures healthcare for Ennis, good care is absent from the pack's interactions with both the patient and the vet practitioner. Within the competitive social order of Deucalion's pack, each werewolf prioritizes their own position and power over the importance or meaning of their relationship with Ennis. In contrast, the relational values of the high school friendship group are expressed through the friends' shared responsibilities for Scott's care, emphasizing the value of relationships. While medical training and skills are needed to address his injuries, this example demonstrates how care ethics principles and practices support flourishing.

CONTEXTS OF URGENT CARE: HOSPITAL POLICY AND THE PRINCIPLES OF CARE ETHICS

In the informal healthcare scenarios examined above, characters responded to the werewolves' life-threatening injuries in different ways according to the values of their social groups. I now turn to the provision of healthcare for human characters within the formal healthcare setting of Beacon Hills Memorial Hospital. In formal healthcare institutions, prevailing social values and ideologies have a much greater role in determining healthcare policies and procedures. In the US context, ideals of autonomy and individualism have been evident in the increasing emphasis on patient choice in healthcare and social policy (see Derse; Orfali and DeVries). The argument for patient choice within contemporary neoliberal democracies arises from the assumption that patients are informed, objective, rational, autonomous consumers who want to shop for their preferred treatment on the market of healthcare providers. There are important principles in these policies, particularly the recognition of patient agency and knowledge that may redress traditional power imbalances between patients and practitioners. However, the policy conceptualization of patient choice in terms of autonomy and pursuit of self-interest constructs patient choice as an issue of competing rights, knowledge claims, and agency between independent individuals. Doctors, nurses, hospital managers and administrators, patients, friends, and family all make judgments about the quality and goals of healthcare, yet an individualistic approach to patient choice continues to exclude the interpersonal and contextual from these judgments with potentially negative impacts on good care (see Mol; Barnes). Care ethics offers an alternative approach that centers the needs and well-being of the patient in formulating responses to illness and vulnerability but also considers patient needs and interests through a framework of attentiveness and responsiveness, rather than assuming patient autonomy and informed consent.

The limits to the extent to which healthcare practices can be predetermined by institutional procedures are explored in the urgent care scenarios depicted in "Currents" (season 3, episode 7). The opening sequence of "Currents" is set in the hospital's emergency room and contrives a narrative situation in which there are no doctors available to conduct consultations or to treat patients. The episode begins by establishing the context of an understaffed and overwhelmed emergency department through brief dialogue and shots of a corridor crowded with injured patients ("Currents" 00:22–00:58). As a stream of patients flows into the emergency room, the lack of doctors raises questions of what constitutes appropriate medical and ethical responses in these circumstances. After Scott brings his mother, Melissa, a take-away dinner during her long night shift as an emergency room nurse, they are approached by a woman clutching her arms around her abdomen, her face contorted in pain ("Currents" 00:56–00:58). Standing in the busy corridor, the woman begs Melissa for "something for the pain" ("Currents" 00:59–01:01), but Melissa responds, in a sympathetic tone, that "giving you something could actually complicate things" and guides the woman gently to a chair to wait (01:05–01:11). The interaction between Melissa and the woman demonstrates how institutional procedures distribute care within a formal healthcare setting; although Melissa is aware of a need, she is not in a position to address it, suggesting that hospital policy creates a conflict between addressing the woman's pain and Melissa's moral obligation to ease her pain. This conflict is resolved through appeal to the higher principle that the hospital should not *worsen* the woman's suffering; that is, it is morally preferable for the woman to continue suffering as she waits, regardless of the fact that there are no doctors available, than for Melissa to unintentionally make things worse if she attempts to help during the doctors' absence. Melissa's response thus follows hospital rules that apply universal principles to patient-practitioner encounters, regardless of context.

However, Scott's relational values oppose the idealized moral individual as independent, objective, and self-interested and, after witnessing the exchange between Melissa and the woman, demonstrates his care ethics by taking responsibility to attempt to address the woman's need. According to universalism, Scott would have no personal responsibility for attempting to redress her pain himself nor to do so in a way that values interpersonal interaction. In contrast, care ethics centers relationality in moral decision-making, regardless of reward or reciprocity, including for those who are unknown, unlike, or distant to ourselves (Barnes 34). On these terms Scott hesitantly approaches the woman and sits in the empty seat next to her ("Currents" 01:14–01:15), and the shot composition changes to close-ups with the rest of the emergency area now off-screen in a visual suggestion of an interpersonal connection. The woman is gasping with pain and grimacing as Scott gently tells her that "sometimes human contact can help with pain" ("Currents" 01:20–01:23). The viewer at this point in season 3 is aware that when Scott mentions "human contact," he means his supernatural werewolf ability to temporarily take another's pain away through touch. This supernatural process is physically draining on the werewolf, so if the woman agrees, then Scott will also experience a degree of discomfort. Scott's vague wording also aims to protect his own secret that he is not human. Rather than relying on hospital rules to determine "what is right?" or "what should I do?" the dialogue and televisual strategies used for this exchange emphasize personal interaction and recognize that Scott and the woman are both vulnerable, albeit in different ways.

Relational morality emphasizes that the "quality of those encounters [with strangers] can make an important difference to well-being" (Barnes 124). Although Scott and the woman are strangers, after the woman has consented to contact with a brief nod, Scott carries out the third and fourth stages of ethical care. These are the act of caregiving and continued attention to assess whether caregiving has met the need (Tronto, *Who Cares?* 6–8). Scott gently rests his hand on the woman's hand, and there is a brief shot of something black traveling up the veins on the back of Scott's hand and arm in a visual depiction of taking pain away ("Currents" 01:32–36). The woman is shown in profile through mid-shots as if from Scott's point of view ("Currents" 01:41; 01:46–48), emphasizing Scott's attention to the effect of his care as he watches the woman: at first she is hunched over and grimacing, then she gasps and her face begins to relax ("Currents" 01:37). As the pain relief is felt, the shot changes to the woman's point of view, watching Scott watching her ("Currents" 01:45). A somber but uplifting soundtrack distinguishes this moment of caregiving from the hectic activities of the emergency area around them. Scott is able to relieve the woman's suffering without side effects because he is a werewolf, but the reason *why* he does so is founded in relational principles of ethical care. The soundtrack, point-of-view shots of both characters, and the conclusion of the caregiving with eye contact connote the significance of responding to strangers and the importance of Scott's actions to improving the well-being of a stranger ("Currents" 01:46).

While the scenario with the woman in pain, although only lasting around a minute, calls into question the care provided on the basis of following hospital policy, the next urgent care scenario also questions the job satisfaction that can be achieved by nurses who must follow institutional rules. A number of theoretical and empirical studies have challenged the contemporary Western conceptualization of healthcare as a service to be purchased as failing to provide a "basis on which to enable well-being for those cared for or satisfaction for those paid to care" (Barnes 72). The conceptualization of "care" as a list of tasks that can be prescribed in advance in policy documents and employment contracts not only eschews the centrality of relationships to good care, limiting attention and response to patients, but also stymies the value that care providers find in their work. In other words, if relational morality is fundamental to good care, then the question arises of how hospital staff can practice good care or experience personal or professional satisfaction from their practices if they are only held accountable for rule-following.

In "Currents," the second urgent care scenario involves human character, Danny, a school friend of Scott and Stiles, in a life-threatening situation that requires Melissa to transgress hospital rules to save his life. The importance of interpersonal relations to good care is modeled through the scenario that involves Melissa and Danny as well as Scott and Ethan, who is Danny's boyfriend and a werewolf in Deucalion's violent pack. Ethan brings Danny to the emergency room as he is having difficulty breathing. Scott and Ethan both enact the values of care by prioritizing Danny's needs rather than their own concerns with werewolf rivalries and follow Melissa and Danny into the ward ("Currents" 02:05–02:30; 02:49–02:53). Although Danny is struggling to breathe and cannot participate in the conversation, he is positioned at the center of the group of characters facing the camera, as well as being the subject of the dialogue. As there is a shortage of doctors, Scott immediately asks, "How can *we* help?" ("Currents" 03:00). Melissa tells him, "You can't" ("Currents" 03:01). Ethan and Scott are positioned on one side of the bed, willing to act but lacking medical skills. On the other side, literally, is Melissa, who is willing to help but, as a nurse, is bound by hospital rules and procedures. But when Danny stops breathing and Scott asks, "He's going to die, isn't he?" ("Currents" 03:06–07), Melissa decides to act anyway.

Melissa's awareness that her actions will transgress hospital policy are suggested through a close-up of Melissa in profile, looking over her shoulder, her eyes moving to see who else is in the ward ("Currents" 03:08–03:11). In considering how institutions organize, distribute, and remunerate paid healthcare workers, care ethics directs attention to the "disempowerment nurses can experience because of their subservient position within the health system" (Barnes 69). Nurses generally occupy less powerful positions within hospital staff hierarchies; Melissa's glance to check that she won't be seen indicates her awareness of her lack of power with respect to institutional authority. The power of the hospital authority, even in the absence of doctors, is suggested through a shot from above, looking down at the bed ("Currents" 03:14). This camera angle suggests that the characters are being observed and surveilled in this formal healthcare setting and, therefore, the possibility of disciplinary action against Melissa if she transgresses hospital policy. However, although fear of surveillance may typically have the disciplining effect of normalizing behaviors through self-policing and adherence to institutional rules, as suggested by Michel Foucault, paid care workers do not necessarily act in accordance with policies and procedures. The portrayal of effective transgressive healthcare practice in a context of policy failure exposes the limits of both institutional power and the care that can be determined by rule-following. Not only are transgressive practices possible but, where these are informed by relational morality, they can enhance patient experiences and well-being.

Furthermore, the potentially positive effects of Melissa's unauthorized healthcare practice entails a risk that is mitigated as Ethan and Scott enact care for her. These two adolescent boy werewolves do not simply observe Melissa's transgression or hold their knowledge of it over her. As both teenage male werewolves are clearly concerned for Danny, Melissa may feel somewhat confident of their support. They are not passive witnesses but actively help Melissa as she prepares to carry out the procedure to alleviate the pressure on Danny's lung ("Currents" 03:12–19). All these characters are participants in a temporary network of care that produces trust, even though Melissa and Ethan are strangers, and Ethan and Scott are ostensibly enemies. The acts of caregiving in this scene flow in multiple directions at once: Melissa cares for Danny by performing the unsanctioned medical procedure, while Ethan and Scott care for both Danny and Melissa, as they not only assist Melissa in the procedure but also keep her transgression a secret. After the procedure, close-up shots of Scott ("Currents" 04:14), then Ethan (04:15), then Melissa as each character peers down at Danny indicate their shared attention to the outcome of their care until Danny takes a breath (04:18; 04:21). The audience is not a voyeur to the spectacle of Danny's vulnerability, there is a point-of-view shot from the level of the bed that positions the audience as patient, looking up at Melissa's cheerful face ("Currents" 04:22–24). Her expression indicates that her transgressive practice of good care has not only saved Danny's life but has also produced professional pride and emotional reward.

The healthcare scenarios in the opening sequence of "Currents" suggest that attention and response to others, including healthcare practitioners, is fundamental to good care. In other words, effective healthcare provision cannot be limited to policy prescriptions and rule-following but must include negotiations of the needs and vulnerabilities of those who give and receive care, making use of situated knowledge to inform judgments and practices of good care. As well as exploring a context in which hospital rules and procedures cannot be followed due to the shortage of doctors, the scenes also destabilize an understanding of "patient choice" within a practitioner-patient relationship as a transactional exchange between autonomous individuals. Neither the unknown woman nor Danny are able to choose their doctors or the timing and courses of treatment. When the expected hospital system fails, the moral response to their needs, alleviation of suffering, and improvement to well-being rests on relationality. Furthermore, as Melissa is the character who takes control of the situation with Danny, using her knowledge, skills, and judgment to both involve Scott and Ethan in Danny's care and also carry out a medical procedure that saves Danny's life, ethical care also destabilizes expected power and gender relations within hospital hierarchies. Although she is not a doctor, Melissa saves a life, and even though she is human and less physically powerful than Ethan and Scott, they follow her instructions, trusting Melissa to save Danny. As both Ethan and Scott seek and respect Melissa's help, the thoughtful, emotional, and skilled care that they enact together suggests the openness of possible masculinities within frameworks that emphasize relationality rather than hierarchical gender and power relations.

Healthcare scenarios are a key way in which *TW* proposes that the values and practices of ethical care are essential to the conditions in which all characters can flourish. Through a range of informal and formal healthcare scenes and settings involving both human and supernatural characters, *TW* presents a number of contrasts between the outdated ideals of 1980s hegemonic masculinity and the mutual care of the series' teenage protagonists, as well as between aggressive social hierarchies and the protagonists' relational morality. These contrasts demonstrate to the twenty-first-century teen audience that the values and ideologies of mainstream society that structure and distribute care are not universal or inevitable but can be changed over time, perhaps with a new generation who is willing to practice ethical care and reject the injustices and inequalities entrenched in the current organization, distribution, and devaluation of care. Although *TW* could have improved some of its depictions of gender, race, and sexualities, it remains unusual among twenty-first-century US teen monster television programs in centering caring masculinities as socially successful for both human and supernatural characters, as well as in depicting relational morality as more desirable than prevailing social structures for both personal relationships and healthcare interactions. The innovation that *TW* moves toward is not a "new" masculinity portrayed by a caring yet physically powerful male adolescent protagonist, but the centrality of attentive, responsive relationships and distributed responsibilities for caring in which there is no mandate for a dominant masculinity at all.

NOTE

1. A visual convention in *TW* is that a supernatural wound is life-threatening.

WORKS CITED

Averill, Lindsey Issow. "Sometimes the World Is Hungry for People Who Care: Katniss and the Feminist Care Ethic." *The Hunger Games and Philosophy: A Critique of Pure Treason*, edited by George A. Dunn and Nicolas Michaud, Wiley, 2012, pp. 162–76.

Banks, Miranda J. "A Boy for All Planets: *Roswell*, *Smallville* and the Teen Male Melodrama." *Teen TV: Genre, Consumption, Identity*, edited by Glyn Davis and Kay Dickinson, British Film Institute, 2004, pp. 17–28.

Barnes, Marian. *Care in Everyday Life: An Ethic of Care in Practice*. Policy, 2012.

Bignell, Jonathan. *An Introduction to Television Studies*. 3rd ed., Routledge, 2013.

Buffy the Vampire Slayer. Created by Joss Whedon, Mutant Enemy, 1997–2003.

"Co-Captain." *Teen Wolf*, created by Jeff Davis, directed by Russel Mulcahy, season 1, episode 10, MGM Television and Music Television (MTV), 2011.

"Code Breaker." *Teen Wolf*, created by Jeff Davis, directed by Russel Mulcahy, season 1, episode 12, MGM Television and Music Television (MTV), 2011.

Connell, R. W., and James W. Messerschmidt. "Hegemonic Masculinity: Rethinking the Concept." *Gender and Society*, vol. 19, no. 6, 2005, pp. 829–59.

"Currents." *Teen Wolf*. Created by Jeff Davis, Directed by Russel Mulcahy, season 3, episode 7, MGM Television and Music Television (MTV), 2013.

Derse, Arthur R. "The Ethics of Self-Determination." *The Picture of Health: Medical Ethics and the Movies*, edited by Henri Colt et al., Oxford UP, 2011, pp. 49–54.

Engster, Daniel, and Maurice Hamington, editors. Introduction. *Care Ethics and Political Theory*. 1st ed., Oxford UP, 2015, pp. 1–16.

Feasey, Rebecca. *Masculinity and Popular Television*. Edinburgh UP, 2008.

Foucault, Michel. *Discipline and Punish: The Birth of the Prison*. Translated by Alan Sheridan, Vintage, 2012.

"Frayed." *Teen Wolf*, created by Jeff Davis, directed by Robert Hall, season 3, episode 5, MGM Television and Music Television (MTV), 2013.

Gilligan, Carol. *In a Different Voice: Psychological Theory and Women's Development*. Harvard UP, 1982.

"Heart Monitor." *Teen Wolf*, created by Jeff Davis, directed by Toby Wilkins, season 1, episode 6, MGM Television and Music Television (MTV), 2011.

House. Created by David Shore, Heel and Toe Films, Shore Z Productions, Bad Hat Harry Productions, Moratim Produktions, NBC Universal Television (2004-2007), Universal Media Studies (2007-2012), 2004-2012.

Jacques, Wesley S. "Reading Relational in Mildred D. Taylor: Toward a Black Feminist Care Ethics for Children's Literature." *Research on Diversity in Youth Literature*, vol. 2, no. 2, 2020, pp. 1–23. https://iopn.library.illinois.edu/journals/rdyl/article/view/1548.

Kendal, Zachary, and Evie Kendal. "Consent Is Sexy: Gender, Sexual Identity and Sex Positivism in MTV's Young Adult Television Series Teen Wolf (2011–)." *Colloquy: Text Theory Critique*, vol. 30, 2015, pp. 26–41.

Kidd, Kenneth B. *Making American Boys: Boyology and the Feral Tale*. U of Minnesota P, 2004.

Kittay, Eva Feder. "Centering Justice on Dependency and Recovering Freedom." *The Disability Studies Reader*, 5th ed., edited by Lennard J. Davis, 2017, pp. 305–10.

Levy, Michael, and Farah Mendlesohn. *Children's Fantasy Literature: An Introduction*. Cambridge UP, 2016.

"Magic Bullet." *Teen Wolf*, created by Jeff Davis, directed by Toby Wilkins, season 1, episode 4, MGM Television and Music Television (MTV), 2011.

Mol, Annemarie. *The Logic of Care: Health and the Problem of Patient Choice*. Routledge, 2008.

Moran, Mary Jeanette. "Making a Difference: Ethical Recognition through Otherness in Madeleine L'Engle's Fiction." *Ethics and Children's Literature*, edited by Claudia Mills, Ashgate, 2014, pp. 75–88.

Moran, Mary Jeanette. "The Mother Was the Mother, Even When She Wasn't: Maternal Care Ethics and Children's Fantasy." *Mothers in Children's and Young Adult Literature: From the Eighteenth Century to Postfeminism*, edited by Lisa Rowe Fraustino and Karen Coats, UP of Mississippi, 2016, pp. 182–97.

Moran, Mary Jeanette. "'Use Your Head, Judy Girl': Relationships, Writing, and an Ethic of Care in the Judy Bolton Mysteries." *Clues: A Journal of Detection*, vol. 27, no. 1, 2008, pp. 22–32.

Noddings, Nel. *Caring, a Feminine Approach to Ethics and Moral Education*. U of California P, 1984.

Orfali, Kristina, and Raymond G. DeVries. "A Sociological Gaze on Bioethics." *The New Blackwell Companion to Medical Sociology*, edited by William C. Cockerham, 1st ed., Wiley Blackwell Publishers, 2010, pp. 488–510.

"Pack Mentality." *Teen Wolf*, created by Jeff Davis, directed by Russel Mulcahy, season 1, episode 3, MGM Television and Music Television (MTV), 2011.

Robinson, Fiona. *The Ethics of Care: A Feminist Approach to Human Security*. Temple UP, 2011.

Roseneil, Sasha. "Why We Should Care about Friends: An Argument for Queering the Care Imaginary in Social Policy." *Social Policy and Society*, vol. 3, no. 4, 2004, pp. 409–19.

Roseneil, Sasha, and Shelley Budgeon. "Cultures of Intimacy and Care beyond 'the Family': Personal Life and Social Change in the Early 21st Century." *Current Sociology*, vol. 52, no. 2, 2004, pp. 135–59.

Roswell. Created by Jason Katims. Jason Katims Productions, New Regency Productions, 20th Century Fox Television, 1999–2002.

Ruddick, Sara. "Maternal Thinking." *Feminist Studies*, vol. 6, no. 2, 1980, pp. 342–67.

Sainsbury, Lisa. *Ethics in British Children's Literature: Unexamined Life*. Bloomsbury Academic, 2013.

Schell, Heather. "The Big Bad Wolf: Masculinity and Genetics in Popular Culture." *Literature and Medicine*, vol. 26, no. 1, 2007, pp. 109–25.

"Second Chance at First Line." *Teen Wolf*, created by Jeff Davis, directed by Russel Mulcahy, season 1, episode 2, MGM Television and Music Television (MTV), 2011.

Shapiro, Johanna. "Movies Help Us Explore Relational Ethics in Health Care." *The Picture of Health: Medical Ethics and the Movies*, edited by Henri Colt et al., Oxford UP, 2011, pp. 19–28.

Smallville. Created and developed for television by Alfred Gough and Miles Millar, Tollin, Robbins Productions, Millar Gough Ink, Warner Bros. Television, DC Comics, DC Entertainment, Smallville 3 Films, Smallville Films, Tollin/Robbins Productions, Warner Bros., 2001–2011.

Teen Wolf. Created by Jeff Davis, MGM Television and Music Television (MTV), 2011–2017.

Teen Wolf. Directed by Rod Daniel, Atlantic Entertainment Group, Wolfkill Productions, 1985.

"The Tell." *Teen Wolf*, created by Jeff Davis, directed by Toby Wilkins, season 1, episode 5, MGM Television and Music Television (MTV), 2011.

Trites, Roberta Seelinger. *Twenty-First-Century Feminisms in Children's and Adolescent Literature*. UP of Mississippi, 2018.

Tronto, Joan C. *Moral Boundaries: A Political Argument for an Ethic of Care*. Routledge, 1993.

Tronto, Joan C. *Who Cares? How to Reshape a Democratic Politics*. Cornell Selects, 2016.

Waller, Alison. *Constructing Adolescence in Fantastic Realism*. Routledge, 2011.

"Wolf's Bane." *Teen Wolf*, created by Jeff Davis, directed by Tim Andrew, season 1, episode 9, MGM Television and Music Television (MTV), 2011.

THE METAPHOR OF MADNESS

Metaphor and Mental Illness in Contemporary YA Fiction

MELANIE GOSS

From the legless Velveteen Rabbit who must be loved to be truly whole to the vision-impaired child whose blindness allows her to "truly see," disability has long been used as a narrative device to further plot and character development. Though there has been great progress made in depictions of physical disability and illness, representations of mental disability and illness remain largely stagnant. Partially because mental illness is perceived as a largely "invisible" disability, it remains a topic written about in heavy metaphor to convey an experience to a readership who may not have lived it and can't necessarily picture it.

However, when authors lean too far into regressive or stereotypical metaphor, lived experience can become erased in favor of harmful tropes. From linking madness to creativity to using psychiatric disorders to signify characters' inability or unwillingness to survive in society, young adult (YA) literature has long erased the reality of life with mental illness, instead using these conditions as plot devices to convey larger ideas and ideologies. This paper addresses the lingering tropes and metaphors that permeate YA texts such as Suzanne Young's *The Program* (2013) and Madeleine Roux's *Asylum* (2013), as well as those texts that are making strides in improving representation, such as Patrick Ness's *The Rest of Us Just Live Here* (2015) and Neal Shusterman's *Challenger Deep* (2015). I argue that the metaphors we use to describe mental illness can shape our understanding of what these illnesses are, as well as how they are treated and experienced; ultimately, I call for the use of novel metaphors to present a more nuanced view of life with a mental illness.[1]

In John Green's 2017 novel *Turtles All the Way Down*, protagonist Aza, who lives with obsessive-compulsive disorder, thinks, "I wanted to tell [my psychiatrist] I was getting better, because that was supposed to be the narrative of illness: It was a hurdle you jumped over, or a battle you won. Illness is a story told in past tense" (85). In many ways, this is the resounding metaphor of mental illness in the YA novel: mental illness is a hurdle to clear, not a road to travel. If we conceive of illness as a hurdle, then the expectation is that the hurdle will be crossed and left behind. If it is not, one has failed to reach a goal as expected.

We can contrast this with the image of illness as a road to travel, where the expectation is that one will stay on the road indefinitely but still make forward progress. Statistical evidence supports the metaphor of a road over that of a hurdle: Roughly 50 percent of adults with mental illness say their symptoms were present by the age of fifteen, and 75 percent say that they were present by the age of twenty-four (Kessler et al.). In short, young people with mental illnesses often become adults with mental illnesses. Thus, the ways that young people see themselves represented in their literature may have a major impact on how they conceptualize their conditions and what an "acceptable" life with a mental illness can look like. As more authors recognize and respect the varied experiences of mentally ill people, including the fact that many individuals will never achieve a tidy "recovery" arc where the goal is to become not mentally ill, recent texts work to find a balance in the power of metaphor to share experience while also respecting characters as people instead of narrative or ideological props.

In this paper, I explore a selection of YA fiction texts from the fifteen-year range of 2006 to 2021, focusing on texts from the United States and Canada with narrators whose primary (if not native) language is Standard American English. In discussing YA literature, I apply the broad definition given by Chris Crowe, who writes that YA literature includes "all genres of literature published since 1967 that are written for and marketed to young adults," whom Crowe classifies as young people from grades seven to twelve, or around ages twelve to eighteen (121). Another hotly contested term I will use is *mental illness*. Though the definition of mental illness has been and remains a controversial one,[2] for the sake of establishing common vocabulary, I use the term in accordance with the definition from the *DSM-5*: "a syndrome characterized by clinically significant disturbance in an individual's cognition, emotional regulation, or behavior that reflects a dysfunction in the psychological, biological, or developmental processes underlying mental functioning" (American Psychiatric Association 20). For this study, my focus is on those disorders, like obsessive-compulsive disorder or major depression, that cause substantial impairment to a character's cognitive or emotional functioning. Thus, I am omitting autism spectrum disorders and attention-deficit hyperactivity disorder (ADHD) from consideration for this paper, as these conditions constitute different, not necessarily impaired, ways of being in the world.

Though the majority of work about literary depictions of mental illness focuses on classical characters such as Bertha Rochester or Prince Hamlet, research on mental illness in children's and YA literature is an emerging field. In recent years, scholars such as Alyssa Chrisman and Kia Jane Richmond have focused largely on the medical accuracy of depictions of mental illness so that texts may educate young readers. Others, such as Ashley Corbett and Diane Scrofano ("Not as Crazy as It Seems"), have centered their work on using literature in the classroom as a tool to build understanding and empathy. Still others, such as Kathryn Caprino and Tara Anderson Gold and Scrofano ("Disability Narrative Theory"), have turned their attention to the narrative structures of YA texts and how texts can allow characters to demonstrate agency and show the possibility of a full life with mental illness.

A common thread throughout these research studies is the power of literature to reduce stigma and increase understanding of individuals with disabilities. In *Disabling Characters: Representations of Disability in Young Adult Literature*, Patricia Dunn argues that qualities of some narratives can be harmful to disabled people. Texts can worsen discrimination and stigma "in several ways: the stereotypical way in which disabled characters are portrayed; a tired plot structure in which they die or get cured at the end, suggesting there's no place for disability in mainstream society; and unchallenged discriminatory remarks reflecting assumptions of an ableist society, that is, a society that privileges so called 'able-bodied' people" (2). It is my contention that the metaphors authors use to describe and explain the condition of mental illness can also have a deleterious effect on young readers if those metaphors are stigmatizing, regressive, or stereotypical; conversely, novel and compelling metaphors may help readers to view mental illness with more nuance and empathy.

To begin, I want to first define how I am using the term *metaphor*. In George Lakoff and Mark Johnson's seminal work *Metaphors We Live By*, the authors define metaphor, and specifically conceptual metaphor, as a figurative comparison in which one idea is understood in terms of another. Far from being bound only to language, conceptual metaphor "is pervasive in everyday life, not just in language but in thought and action" (Lakoff and Johnson 3). The authors continue, "If we are right in suggesting that our conceptual system is largely metaphorical, then the way we think, what we experience, and what we do every day is very much a matter of metaphor" (3). According to the linguist Andrew Goatly, the metaphors embedded in any given language can have major impacts on how a speaker understands concepts (24). As a framework for this research, I align with the assumption of the linguistic relativity hypothesis,[3] a linguistic theory that posits that "the particular language we speak predisposes us to think and act in certain ways" (Goatly 24). It is important to separate this hypothesis from linguistic determinism, which holds that one's thoughts are entirely bound by one's native language; instead, linguistic relativity argues that the language one uses can shape how one thinks about the world. This is particularly relevant in the discussion of metaphors, which can vary greatly across language systems.

The physicist Evelyn Fox Keller argues that metaphor is useful "not so much as a way of guiding us toward a more precise and literal description of phenomena but rather as a way of providing explanatory satisfaction where it is not otherwise available" (120). Likewise, disability theorist Ann Jurecic writes that "language . . . orders the disordered experience of illness, which makes it possible for readers to attend to the details of an otherwise unimaginable experience" (60). Because the idea and experience of mental health or illness can be so abstract, we use more concrete analogies to make sense of it. Unfortunately, a good deal of the metaphor that English-speaking cultures use to explain mental illness works on the assumption that neurodiversity[4] represents damage or defect. For instance, some of the most prevalent metaphors in the English language system include "an unhealthy mind is a damaged object," as is evidenced by terms like *crazy* (from the Old English meaning *cracked* or *flawed*), *unsound*, or *unhinged*; or "mental states are physical spaces," represented by phrases like *fell into a depression* or *on the edge of madness*. Even the term *depression* itself represents a metaphor: "good is up; bad is down."

Disability in literature has long been steeped in metaphor, with authors often using physical or cognitive disabilities to illustrate aberrant character traits. In *Narrative Prosthesis: Disability and the Dependence of Discourse*, authors David T. Mitchell and Sharon L. Snyder use the phrase "materiality of metaphor" to refer to this use of disability as "a metaphorical signifier of social and individual collapse" (47). In *Chronic Youth: Disability, Sexuality, and U.S. Media Cultures of Rehabilitation*, Julie Passanante Elman writes, "disability studies scholars have shown how popular media rarely portrays the fullness or political realities of disabled lives and instead uses disability as corporeal otherness that signifies otherwise intangible character traits" (5). This tendency to use disability as an indicator of character traits is especially true in YA literature, which is often used as a socializing or moralizing agent for the young reader. Anastasia Wickham argues that YA authors can "influence the perception of youth culture, and arguably, with the rise of YA fiction's popularity among adults, the perception of the wider culture" (22). For this reason, it is especially crucial to examine how authors use metaphor when writing about mental illness, which is particularly prone to ideological judgments about what constitutes normal or abnormal behavior.

In her work *Illness as Metaphor*, Susan Sontag writes, "Any important disease whose causality is murky, and for which treatment is ineffectual, tends to be awash in significance. First, the subjects of deepest dread (corruption, decay, pollution, anomie, weakness) are identified with the disease. The disease itself becomes a metaphor" (58). Sontag here is writing of physical illness, specifically leprosy, but the comparison stretches. Though I disagree with Sontag's overall call to eliminate metaphor entirely from the conversation of illness, I do find the use of reductive, uncritical metaphor to describe illness to be inherently limiting. Throughout literary and social criticism, metaphorical readings of psychiatric illness abound. Hysteria is read as a pushback against a patriarchal society, anorexia is a rebellion against restrictive beauty standards, and suicide is an escape from the troubles of the modern world.

This desire to read illness as purely metaphorical is very tempting, especially when the metaphors seem to match up so neatly. What happens when we lean too far into the metaphor, though, is that the actual experience of living with a mental illness becomes distorted and misrepresented. Individuals may first understand a metaphor, then extend that metaphor outward to shape their understanding of a condition. For instance, if one is familiar with the term *bipolar* primarily as referring to unstable weather patterns or the poles of the earth, it should come as no surprise when one's understanding of bipolar disorder is limited to a stereotypical "hot and cold" or "high and low" temperament, instead of a fuller understanding of the complexities of the actual condition. Similar distortions may occur when a politician is referred to as *psychotic* or a tidy person is *so OCD*.

One specific example of this distortion occurs with eating disorders, as the over-reliance on symbolism often completely permeates narratives wherein characters live with these issues. Eating disorders in particular are often ascribed symbolic attributes that may not be entirely accurate and certainly aren't especially helpful. In her book *Abject Relations: Everyday Lives of Anorexia*, Megan Warin writes, "Theorists with a Foucauldian perspective have offered some quite convincing explanations of anorexia itself, but . . . have tended to 'read the anorexic body' as a metaphor for the social body" (10). In doing so, theorists make the anorexic body into a symbol for social ills. Though there is immense value in the critical consideration of the intersections of societal pressures, beauty ideals, and the physical body, such critiques run the risk of reducing individuals to tragic bellwethers of cultural currents. For people living with eating disorders, these interpretations can not only feel profoundly alienating and condescending, but they can also directly impact public perception of eating disorders and, in turn, the stigma that individuals face (Blodgett Salafia et al.).

In Hannah Moskowitz's *Not Otherwise Specified*, there is a conversation in which one character, Rachel, tells another character, Bianca, "You don't need to be this skinny to be beautiful," to which protagonist Etta mentally replies, "As if being beautiful is the point. There's a part of this that laypeople are just never, ever going to get" (200). Viewing eating disorders as desperate attempts to conform to patriarchal beauty standards in turn complicates how people with eating disorders are viewed: as shallow, vapid, and image-obsessed. This characterization of people with eating disorders also factors into how these people and conditions are treated. When eating disorders are understood solely as a desire to be pretty or attractive, the condition is trivialized, viewed as self-inflicted, and not taken seriously by medical professionals and the general population alike. When we rely on flimsy understandings of disorders, the metaphors that follow are sure to be treacherous.

In addition to non-mentally ill people misunderstanding disorders, people with mental illness may also struggle to make sense of their lives when their experiences don't fit the metaphors that are set up for them, such as when texts attempt to erase the social stigma of mental illness by comparing it to physical illness. In 2006, the American Psychiatric Foundation partnered with the National Alliance on Mental Illness (NAMI) and several other advocacy groups for a public education campaign called "Depression is Real." In a series of print, television, and radio public service announcements, the campaign compared mental illnesses with physical illnesses using phrases like "You never hear, 'Snap out of it, it's just diabetes'" and "You'd never say, 'It's just cancer, get over it'" (American Psychiatric Foundation). Why, then, should mental afflictions be treated any differently? The campaign aimed "to educate Americans that depression is a serious, debilitating disease that can be fatal if left untreated and to provide hope for recovery to the nearly 19 million Americans who suffer from depression each year" (National Alliance on Mental Illness). Though the stigma-reducing aim of such awareness campaigns is certainly valuable, the complex reality of the nature of mental illnesses makes such a comparison troublesome nonetheless. There is still no well-supported consensus on what actually causes many types of mental illness, with new studies casting doubt on the chemical imbalance theory of depression (Moncrieff et al.), research corroborating the influence of viral infections on the development of OCD (Della Vecchia and Marazziti), and continued questioning of the role of environmental factors in schizophrenia (Brown). Despite the numerous metrics that have been created to diagnose mental ailments, all still rely upon self-reporting of symptoms and clinicians' subjective observations of clients' behavior, nor is there dependable consistency in diagnoses across clinicians, whereas a bone fracture can be seen and insulin levels can be empirically measured (Weir 30). Nor does there exist an agreed-upon definition of what constitutes "recovery" from a mental illness (Bonney and Stickley).

Most significant to my argument, though, is that there exists a great disparity between the stigma surrounding mental illness in comparison to physical illness, and YA novels can help readers interrogate this metaphor by showing individuals' thought processes when they encounter it. Despite its intended goal of reducing stigma, the *mental illness is physical illness* metaphor rings hollow to many characters, who lament that their illnesses don't garner the same sympathy as physical illnesses. In *Challenger Deep*, protagonist Caden says, "Dead kids are put on pedestals, but mentally ill kids get hidden under the rug" (Shusterman 168). In *All the Bright Places*, protagonist Violet says, "The fact is, I was sick, but not in an easily explained flu kind of way. It's my experience that people are a lot more sympathetic if they can see you hurting, and for the millionth time in my life I wish for measles or smallpox or some other recognizable disease just to make it simple for me and also for them" (Niven 15). In *Wintergirls*, protagonist Lia says, "I wish I had cancer. I will burn in hell for that, but it's true" (Anderson 27). These characters are acutely aware that, although they have been told that mental illness is just as serious as physical illness, the public reaction is nowhere near so sympathetic.

The slippery nature of the *mental illness is physical illness* metaphor is present in Suzanne Young's *The Program* series, which plays on the well-documented phenomenon of suicide contagion[5] and repositions suicide as a literal transmissible disease—one can "catch" suicide. *The Program* sets its characters in a world where suicide is an epidemic and the treatment renders young people docile, compliant, and fragile, stripped of their memories and, in turn, of their individuality. The main character, Sloane, describes the treatment process when one of her classmates is taken away:

> To fight the outbreak, our school district implemented the pilot run of The Program—a new philosophy in prevention. Among the five schools, students are monitored for changes in mood behavior, flagged if a threat is determined. Anyone exhibiting suicidal tendencies is no longer referred to a psychologist. Instead, the handlers are called. And then they come and take you. Kendra Phillips will be gone for at least six weeks—six weeks spent in a facility where The Program will mess with her mind, take her memories. She'll be force-fed pills and therapy until she doesn't even know who she is anymore. After that they'll ship her off to a small private school until graduation. A school designated for other returners, other empty souls. (Young 10)

Sloane then embarks on the long fight to resist this depersonalizing treatment, lamenting all the while the ways that psychiatrists push drugs to brainwash youth into conformity.

To an extent, this presentation of psychiatry is a fair criticism. Since the advent of psychotropic medications in the US, there has been a persistent outcry based on the perception that doctors overprescribe medication in lieu of more involved and time-consuming therapeutic approaches (Perring 1–2).

I also find immense value in books where teens have agency and the ability to work through their own issues. However, *The Program*'s foundational metaphor of mental illness as physical illness creates problems within the narrative as characters vehemently resist any medical intervention for an ailment that, in the novels, claims the lives of one in three teenagers. One struggles to imagine calling a person undergoing chemotherapy an "empty soul," or a person using insulin as "brainwashed," and yet this is the language used in *The Program* to describe individuals who receive intervention efforts against suicide.

The implications become much more distressing when we think about the novel in terms of the lived experience of people with mental illnesses, who might include the young reader herself. If a young person has been hospitalized and has benefited from psychiatric medication, what does it say to them when these often lifesaving interventions are presented as brainwashing and erasure of the self? It is not difficult to believe that such a dehumanizing presentation of mental health treatment might dissuade readers from seeking help. In his writings about depictions of mental illness in children's media, Otto F. Wahl asserts, "Few, if any, of those concerned with the problem of mental illness stigma . . . would argue that the documented negative attitudes toward mental illness emerge full-blown in adulthood. Rather, it seems more likely that these ideas and attitudes are acquired gradually over a lifetime and that their roots are established in childhood" (250). As suicide rates rise across the United States, increasing nearly 60 percent from 2007 to 2018 among youth aged ten to twenty-four, we should not accept passively those texts that may further stigmatize mental illness and its treatment (Curtin 1).

Sometimes the metaphors that we use in an attempt to explain abstractions can actually end up causing more confusion. An excellent example of this occurs when mental illness is conceptualized as an invader or intruder. In Faith Gardner's *Girl on the Line*, protagonist Journey describes her depression as "like some stranger had taken over my head. Like an uninvited guest had invaded me" (40). This metaphor centers around the idea that there is one essential self and the illness is not part of it; instead, it is a parasite that creeps into the brain and wrests it away from its owner's will. This metaphor is also present in Lois Metzger's *A Trick of the Light*, which tells the story of Mike, a young man with anorexia nervosa. Darpana, Mike's therapist, uses a Venn diagram to explain the eating disorder by drawing Mike as one circle and the eating disorder as another. As the circles overlap, Mike becomes "eclipsed" until "the only real thing about [him] is the eating disorder" (Metzger 158). In some ways, separating out the eating disorder as an invader can be useful to help one compartmentalize disordered thoughts. However, the implicit meaning in the metaphor from the therapist, a medical authority within the text, is that one cannot have a real self and an eating disorder at the same time, which is a deeply dehumanizing manner of viewing a person with a mental illness.

Casting the illness as an invader can lead to confusion as characters then begin to question where their own self ends and the illness begins. Aza in *Turtles All the Way Down* grapples with this, and she finds herself frustrated by her inability to express what she sees as a lack of an essential self. It's not difficult to see how the metaphor of *mental illness as invader* can be disconcerting and puzzling. An invader clearly does not belong, forced its way in, and can (at least in theory) be forced back out. But this metaphor doesn't match up with the experience of living with a chronic mental illness, where the distorted thinking is so much a part of one's way of engaging with and interpreting the world that it can feel inextricable from the rest of oneself. When faced with the metaphor of "losing one's mind," Aza thinks, "Actually, the problem is that I can't lose my mind. . . . It's inescapable" (Green 240).

Aza is profoundly unsettled by this thought, but to explain it she must rely on metaphor, which confuses her further: "Felt myself slipping, but even that's a metaphor. Descending, but that is, too. Can't describe the feeling itself except to say that I'm not me" (211). By the end of the novel, she comes to the understanding that she can't escape her OCD because it is part of her, and instead she has to learn to live with it. This is Aza's ultimate realization, that "she would go on, that she would grow up, have children and love them, that despite loving them she would get too sick to care for them, be hospitalized, get better, and then get sick again" (285). The invader becomes a permanent resident. In this conceptualization, the mental illness is integrated into the overall self. Casting the disorder as part of oneself instead of as something that takes over oneself is, for many people with chronic conditions, a much more realistic (though, admittedly, less narratively satisfying) approach.

In addition to the many metaphors that surround mental illness itself, there exists a multitude of metaphors in literature around psychiatric healthcare. Though there are, of course, numerous avenues for a client to access psychiatric healthcare, for the purposes of this paper, I am keeping my focus on inpatient and residential treatment settings, which tend to be the most frequently represented in my sampling of young adult texts. The two most prevalent metaphors about psychiatric hospitalization that I have found in my research are *psychiatric hospitals are zoos* and *psychiatric hospitals are prisons*. Each of these metaphors situates clients of psychiatric services in a position of incarceration and confinement, stripping away individual freedoms and agency. To be certain, conditions in psychiatric hospitals prior to the era of deinstitutionalization could be horrific, and modern conditions can be very inconsistent across institutions, from understaffed public hospitals to cushy private clinics, but the persistence of these metaphors further stigmatizes mental health treatment and the people who utilize it.

The metaphor *psychiatric hospitals are zoos* appears frequently in literature and is particularly damaging in its implications of psychiatric healthcare as dehumanizing and clients of psychiatric services as animals. In *Get Well Soon*, protagonist Anna says, "I feel like a zoo animal. No—I feel like a circus freak, locked up in a cage!" (Halpern 10). In *Words on Bathroom Walls*, a father writes of his son's school administrators, "They won't be satisfied until he is caged off from the others like a beast in a wildlife exhibit" (Walton 272). In *Kiss of Broken Glass*, protagonist Kenna describes her anxiety as a snake, thinking that "something coils around me like a boa constrictor squeezing, tightening, crushing" (Kuderick). This type of language encourages readers to view people with mental illness as wild and in need of taming, and characters with mental illness often come to see themselves and their conditions as beastly and animalistic.

A similar metaphor is *psychiatric hospitals are prisons*, which hearkens back to the era of forced institutionalization while simultaneously overlooking the fact that, in the modern-day United States, people who would previously have been confined to psychiatric hospitals are now increasingly being placed in actual prisons (Parsons). One particularly striking example of the *psychiatric hospitals are prisons* metaphor is Madeleine Roux's 2013 horror novel, *Asylum*, about sixteen-year-old Dan Crawford, who attends a summer college preparatory program housed in Brookline, a former psychiatric facility. While there, Dan and his friends explore the building's abandoned basement and find evidence that a rogue psychiatrist was performing monstrous experiments on his patients. When students begin turning up murdered, the plot twists into a story of ghostly possession, with Dan seeing through the eyes of the psychiatrist (referred to as a "warden," furthering the *psychiatric hospitals are prisons* metaphor) and another student embodying the spirit of a serial killer patient.

Wildly sensationalistic, *Asylum* is also a particularly interesting case because it is so profoundly exploitative, using altered photos of real psychiatric doctors, patients, and institutions as illustrations to scare the reader. Later in the book, Dan claims that modern psychiatry is no better than it was in the past, his understanding of which involves patients chained to walls as they await experimental surgery. When considering his therapist, Dr. Oberst, Dan thinks, "What did she know? She was no better than the doctors who'd been at Brookline fifty years ago. At least their treatments had gotten results" (Roux 262). The book backpedals some of its more extreme statements in its concluding chapters, saying that the murderer needs "the right kind of help . . . not the kind of help this place had to offer" (305). Yet the uncommonly regressive depiction of mental illness is striking, with patients being depicted as either bloodthirsty killers or pathetic lost souls, both of which perpetuate negative and stigmatizing stereotypes of people with mental illness. The extended metaphor of *psychiatric hospitals as prisons* in *Asylum*, paired with the fact that the majority of the patients from the defunct Brookline are "criminally insane," makes it easy for an uncritical reader to think that the patients deserve the abuse that they receive at the hands of their doctors; after all, prisons are—in theory, at least—reserved for the guilty.

Some variation of the *psychiatric hospitals are prisons* appears frequently in contemporary texts, from characters in *Skin and Bones* referring to their "sentences" and "incarceration" to Lia in *Wintergirls* speaking of her time in a residential eating disorders clinic as "the prison" (Shahan 13, 3; Anderson 27). The metaphor is so prevalent that characters even expect facilities to look like prisons and are surprised when they don't; in *Kiss of Broken Glass*, Kenna says, "I thought it was gonna look like jail inside, with steel bars and silver toilets. But it doesn't" (Kuderick). In this metaphor, clients of psychiatric services are cast as prisoners, while providers of psychiatric services are jailers. Certainly, this vestige of the era of forced institutionalization speaks to the inherent power imbalance between clients and providers, between patients and doctors. But it also fosters and perpetuates an "us versus them" mentality in the doctor–patient relationship that can be counterproductive to treatment goals and that keeps alive ideas of outdated treatment models and settings.

The impact of these depictions of treatment facilities is felt in the texts, as characters in these novels often understand their experiences with psychiatric illness and healthcare via their consumption of texts and media. In *The Memory of Light*, the protagonist's stepmother says that the psychiatric hospital "reminded her of *One Flew Over the Cuckoo's Nest*" (Stork 59). In *The Art of Starving*, protagonist Matt says, "I'm pretty sure boys can't even *get* eating disorders. Lord knows there aren't any afterschool specials about it" (Miller 12). The lack of representation of males with eating disorders leads the character to doubt his own experiences and remain in denial about his condition. In *Skin*, Karen, who has anorexia nervosa, laments that being in the hospital wasn't at all like the "disease of the week" books from which she learned about the disorder (Vrettos 131). She recounts the simplistic, triumphant narrative arc of a novel called *Dying to Be Thin*, then explains her confusion when her own experience didn't mirror that represented in the book. Characters measure their own experiences in comparison to the media they encounter, and it is possible for authors to model new metaphors to create texts that give them a more nuanced picture to consider.

According to Goatly, "We may be aware of alternative ways of conceptualising reality because (1) we speak a second language or (2) are sufficiently alert to notice the choices made within the language we speak. But, if not, the texts we encounter may seem the only natural way of representing experience" (27).

Texts from nonwhite authors that feature characters who speak more than one language can offer a glimpse into alternative metaphors about mental illness, though there appears to be significant overlap in metaphors across cultures.

One trend that seems more prevalent among texts wherein the sole language is not Standard American English is the presentation of mental states as especially embodied. In *Counting Down with You*, Karina, the American daughter of Bangladeshi immigrants, experiences physical symptoms of anxiety and views her body, not her mind, as "traitorous" (Bhuiyan 140). Throughout the text, Karina describes her anxiety through physical sensations, saying that it "tugs on my heartstrings" or feels like "an unknown pressure building in my chest" (290, 20). Similarly, the unnamed Trinidadian protagonist of *Home Home* experiences depression in a strongly embodied way, "like I had this big hole in my belly between my heart and my stomach" (Allen-Agostini 19), while Melati in *The Weight of Our Sky*, set in 1960s Malaysia, says that her OCD makes her "brain hot and itchy" (Alkaf 2). While this characterization of mental illness is not unique to these narratives, it does seem to be more pronounced within them.

One common cross-cultural metaphor is that of *mental illness as invader*. In *The Weight of Our Sky*, protagonist Melati conceptualizes her OCD as a djinn, an Islamic spirit able to possess humans. Melati is familiar with djinn as fantastic creatures and as beings from the Quran, but she "didn't realize they could be sharp, cruel, insidious little things that crept and wormed their way into your thoughts" (Alkaf 2). In the author's preface, Hanna Alkaf acknowledges that a portion of her readership may not be familiar with the Islamic religious tradition, writing, "As you read, you may also want to keep in mind that for Muslims, djinn are real. They aren't just wacky blue creatures with a Robin Williams voice, or mythical beings that pour out of old lamps and ancient rings to grant you three wishes; they exist for us in ways that they may not for you" (ix). Despite being couched in a uniquely Islamic tradition, the conceptualization of mental illness as an invasive being appears to be a ubiquitous metaphor.

Similarly, the depiction of people with mental illness as wild or animalistic appears to be present across language systems. In *The Surprising Power of a Good Dumpling*, the language spoken in protagonist's Anna's home is Cantonese. When Anna's mother begins exhibiting symptoms of bipolar disorder, she is frequently referred to in language that closely aligns her with animals, so that Anna is approaching her "like I would a wounded tiger" or "like a rabid dog" (Chim 139, 180). Anna's mother describes her illness as like a large, black dog. An episode of psychosis climaxes with her mother brutally maiming a fish. Talking to her father about her mother's condition reminds Anna of a Cantonese phrase describing an impossible task: "dragging a cow up a tree. Neither party wants to be in that situation" (188). Interestingly, Anna says that "the language is missing" when she tries to discuss her mother with her father; her inability to find the words to describe her mother's condition means that she cannot convey to her father the seriousness of this condition (198). It is not until Anna is able to find the language to communicate with her father that her mother is able to get the treatment she needs.

Clearly, the use of metaphor in regard to mental illness is a challenge that exists across languages and cultures. The way metaphor is used to discuss mental illnesses is crucial to establishing an understanding about various conditions. The metaphors authors use to describe psychiatric illnesses and healthcare are especially important in breaking down stigma and misconceptions, as many young readers will have no other frame of reference for these conditions. Their knowledge may stem only from understanding the metaphor itself, resulting in a faulty and damaging perception of a condition. How, then, do we resist reductive metaphor without policing or censoring language? Authors must first recognize the limitations and implications of regressive metaphors, then understand the value of more nuanced metaphors. I am not calling for simple avoidance of metaphor, but instead for the creation of novel metaphors that more clearly convey the complexities of a life with mental illness. As disability theorist Amy Vidali writes, "Creative engagement with disability metaphors can further complicate, or 'denaturalize,' ideas of how bodies and metaphors interact" (17). This type of engagement can show the socially constructed nature of the metaphor and provide an opportunity for authors to construct something different and more profound. Doing so requires "a willing embrace of the opportunity to diversify our writing to represent a wider range of bodily and cognitive experience" (15). The same holds true for metaphors about mental illness, as authors have the opportunity to create metaphors that complicate and expand readers' understanding of mental illness.

Some authors already embrace novel metaphors of mental illness. In Francisco X. Stork's *The Memory of Light*, narrator Vicky describes the need for imagery and metaphor to convey the experience of depression, and she recognizes that there is not one single way to describe it: "I call it a sticky, thick, smelly kind of fog. Emily felt boots of lead creaking across her soul. Gabriel's was a deflated basketball" (265). Elsewhere in the novel, a psychiatrist describes depression as like seeing the world through "dirty glass goggles" (51). This diversity of metaphors allows for representation of a range of experiences and encourages readers to hold more complex and varied views of the experience of depression.

Patrick Ness's *The Rest of Us Just Live Here* is an excellent example of a text that uses more nuanced metaphors about mental illness to explain the full weight of the condition. Narrator Mikey lives with obsessive-compulsive disorder, and his sister Mel nearly died from anorexia nervosa. Mikey's OCD manifests in real, devastating ways: his hands bleed from washing, he finds himself helpless to perform basic tasks, and he often wonders if he would be better off dead. He's frustrated and made angry by his behavior, but he can't stop. Mikey describes his obsessive thought patterns as "loops" from which he cannot extract himself. This metaphor presents a very different picture from the cute and quirky depictions of OCD that we see over and over in popular media. If a reader can understand a loop—nonstop, inescapable, and repetitive—she can have a clearer understanding of the realities of OCD beyond a simple desire for tidiness or order, as OCD is commonly presented.

Mel's recovery from her eating disorder is also represented in its full complexity, as is its impact on the rest of her family. She had a heart attack at age fourteen. She regained some weight, but not much. Her mother resents her for the "missed opportunities" that resulted from the time commitments of family-based treatment (Ness 47). Mel is depicted as in a constant struggle against her eating disorder, despite the fact that she is presumed to be recovered. She compares her struggle to a physical scar, something that lingers long after the worst injury has been mended. "The thing about scars, though," Mel says, is that there is "nothing you can do except wear them with pride" (82). Mel's experience with her eating disorder destroyed her life and her health, but she recognizes it as an integral part of herself, and she is proud of what she has overcome despite not being cured.

In *Skin*, Karen describes her eating disorder in terms of a seed being plucked from the soil, leaving a void in its place: "[A]fter you dig down to find out the things that make you this way, after you flick out the seed that everything grew from, there's still a hole there where the seed was. You still have to do something about the hole" (Vrettos 133–4). Karen's novel use of metaphor here shows how deeply ingrained a disorder like anorexia nervosa can be, how central it can become to a person's sense of self. Recovery from an eating disorder involves much more than just weight stabilization, a fact that many books about the topic neglect.

Novel metaphors can also reshape how readers view psychiatric hospitalization. In *Not Otherwise Specified*, one of Bianca's friends reflects on the way that her family treats Bianca's eating disorder: "I love the girl, but it feels all the time that we're making this little dream world for Bianca. Like a house made out of candy. Shitty metaphor but whatever" (Moskowitz 93). Far from presenting the psychiatric hospital as a prison or a zoo, this metaphor acknowledges the limitations of psychiatric hospitalization without unnecessarily stigmatizing patients. Though there is certainly a need for safe spaces, it is, arguably, not ideal for clients of psychiatric services to be insulated apart from the outside world and away from the problems of everyday life. The metaphor of the hospital as a house made out of candy reflects larger questions of the efficacy of psychiatric hospitalization and points to the conflicts that family members and friends may encounter when a loved one seeks intensive treatment.

Finally, Neal Shusterman's 2015 novel *Challenger Deep* is a text that makes effective use of novel metaphor, immersing the reader in the mind of a young person with schizophrenia. Protagonist Caden Bosch, who is experiencing a first episode of psychosis, experiences his illness as a quest into Challenger Deep, the deepest known point in the oceans. Caden's voyage takes him to dark and treacherous places, both literal and metaphorical, as he sublimates events from his time in a psychiatric hospital into scenes on a ship. Switching back and forth from fantasy to reality, *Challenger Deep* crafts the sea as an extended metaphor for mental illness: unknown and formidable, but ultimately navigable with the right tools and companions.

As he comes to terms with his illness, Caden thinks, "This is the weight chained to my ankle, and it is far heavier than any anchor. That is the overwhelming never that I must face. And I still don't know if I'll disappear into it, or find a way to push beyond" (Shusterman 287). Caden's lingering uncertainty in the face of life-altering diagnosis reflects the very real probability that he will continue to face psychotic episodes in his future. His mental illness doesn't resolve at the end of the novel, but he has hope that he will be able to cope, thinking, "Maybe one day I'll dive so deep that the Abyssal Serpent will catch me, and I'll never find my way back. No sense in denying that such things happen. But it's not going to happen today—and there is a deep, abiding comfort in that. Deep enough to carry me through till tomorrow" (308). Like many young people coping with a new diagnosis, Caden faces an uncertain future, and *Challenger Deep* stands as an example of a text that doesn't have to rely on literary realism in order to present a realistic picture of a life with serious mental illness.

Language is fluid and constantly evolving, and our use of metaphors can shift as our understanding of mental illness deepens. In their discussion of how metaphors can change over time, Lakoff and Johnson write that we can create new metaphors by "consciously recognizing previously unconscious metaphors and how we live by them" (233). Texts that engage with mental illness by using creative, innovative metaphors can play a crucial part in jump-starting this evolution as young readers seek out literature that helps them make sense of their experiences. In doing so, these texts challenge harmful stereotypes and expand readers' assumptions of what life with a mental illness can look like. I'm hopeful that the thoughtful consideration of the ways that we explain our internal worlds will encourage authors to consider the implications of their metaphors; this challenge is a continuous road to travel, not a single hurdle to overcome.

NOTES

1. It is impossible to discuss our current understanding of the psychiatric healthcare system without also acknowledging the great changes that have been implemented in the latter half of the twentieth century through the tireless work of patients, advocates, and activists. It is essential not to erase the inhumane treatment of people living with mental illness, and it is crucial to remember the undeniable harm that psychiatric institutions have caused. Psychiatric healthcare has a fraught history, and it is difficult to argue that all practitioners, both individual and institutional, have always acted and will always act in good faith. Systemic racism and classism permeate the mental health landscape and severely limit access to treatment. These are imperfect institutions that we must navigate, and this paper is not meant to imply that all psychiatric treatment is inherently right or good. Instead, my goal here is to consider the ways that regressive metaphors can shape our perceptions of or openness to mental healthcare in a way that limits the options for characters and, in turn, for young readers.

2. For a concise but complex consideration of this issue, see Bolton.

3. The linguistic relativity hypothesis is sometimes referred to interchangeably as the weak Whorfian hypothesis.

4. *Neurodiversity*, a term first associated with autism spectrum disorder, has since been embraced by a range of activists representing many types of cognitive and psychiatric conditions, including dyslexia, ADHD, mood and anxiety disorders, and schizophrenia. See Armstrong.

5. Suicide contagion refers to the phenomenon of "cluster suicides" that often follow an initial report of suicide. See O'Caroll et al. and Gould and Lake. Interestingly, suicide contagion is sometimes referred to as the Werther Effect, so named because of the spate of suicides that followed the 1774 publication of Goethe's *The Sorrows of Young Werther*, showing the long association of literature with popular understandings of mental health and illness.

WORKS CITED

Alkaf, Hanna. *The Weight of Our Sky*. Salaam Reads, 2019.
Allen-Agostini, Lisa. *Home Home*. Delacorte Press, 2020.
American Psychiatric Association. *Diagnostic and Statistical Manual of Mental Disorders*. 5th ed., American Psychiatric Association, 2013.
American Psychiatric Foundation. *Depression Is Real*. 2006. Internet Archive, https://web.archive.org/web/20061205212717/http://depressionisreal.org/
Anderson, Laurie Halse. *Wintergirls*. Penguin, 2009.
Armstrong, Thomas. *The Power of Neurodiversity: Unleashing the Advantages of Your Differently Wired Brain*. Da Capo Press, 2010.
Bhuiyan, Tashie. *Counting Down with You*. Inkyard Press, 2021.
Blodgett Salafia, Elizabeth H., et al. "Perceptions of the Causes of Eating Disorders: A Comparison of Individuals with and without Eating Disorders." *Journal of Eating Disorders*, vol. 3, Apr. 2015.

Bolton, Derek. "What is Mental Illness?" *The Oxford Handbook of Philosophy and Psychiatry*, edited by K. W. M. Fulford, et al., Oxford UP, 2013, pp. 434–50.

Bonney, S. and T. Stickley. "Recovery and Mental Health: A Review of the British Literature." *Journal of Psychiatric and Mental Health Nursing*, vol. 15, no. 2, 2008, pp. 140–53.

Brown, Alan S. "The Environment and Susceptibility to Schizophrenia." *Progress in Neurobiology*, vol. 93, no. 1, Jan. 2011, pp. 23–58.

Caprino, Kathryn, and Tara Anderson Gold. "Examining Agency in Contemporary Young Adult Illness Narratives." *The ALAN Review*, vol. 46, no. 1, 2018, pp. 75–86.

Chim, Wai. *The Surprising Power of a Good Dumpling*. Scholastic, 2020.

Chrisman, Alyssa. "Living with It: Disabling Depictions of Obsessive-Compulsive Disorder in Young Adult Literature." *The ALAN Review*, vol. 46, no. 1, 2018, pp. 54–64.

Corbett, Ashley. "We're Not Crazy: Overcoming the Mental Health Stigma in YA Literature." *English Journal*, vol. 105, no. 6, 2016, pp. 92–99.

Crowe, Chris. "What Is Young Adult Literature?" *English Journal*, vol. 88, no. 1, 1998, pp. 120–22.

Curtin, Sally C. "State Suicide Rates among Adolescents and Young Adults Aged 10–24: United States, 2000–2018." *National Vital Statistics Reports*, vol. 69, no. 11, 2020.

Della Vecchia, Alessandra, and Donatella Marazziti. "Back to the Future: The Role of Infections in Psychopathology. Focus on OCD." *Clinical Neuropsychiatry*, vol. 19, no. 4, 2022, pp. 248–63.

Dunn, Patricia A. *Disabling Characters: Representations of Disability in Young Adult Literature*. Peter Lang, 2014.

Elman, Julie Passanante. *Chronic Youth: Disability, Sexuality, and U.S. Media Cultures of Rehabilitation*. New York UP, 2014.

Gardner, Faith. *Girl on the Line*. Harper Teen, 2021.

Goatly, Andrew. *Washing the Brain: Metaphor and Hidden Ideology*. John Benjamins, 2007.

Gould, Madelyn S., and Alison M. Lake. "The Contagion of Suicidal Behavior." *Contagion of Violence: Workshop Summary*, National Academy of Sciences, 2013, pp. 68–72.

Green, John. *Turtles All the Way Down*. Penguin, 2017.

Halpern, Anna. *Get Well Soon*. Fewer and Friends, 2007.

Jurecic, Ann. *Illness as Narrative*. U of Pittsburgh P, 2012.

Keller, Evelyn Fox. *Making Sense of Life: Explaining Biological Development with Models, Metaphors, and Machines*. Harvard UP, 2002.

Kessler, Ronald C., et al. "Age of Onset of Mental Disorders: A Review of Recent Literature." *Current Opinion in Psychiatry*, vol. 20, no. 4, 2007, pp. 359–64.

Kuderick, Madeleine. *Kiss of Broken Glass*. Kindle ed., Harper Collins, 2014.

Lakoff, George, and Mark Johnson. *Metaphors We Live By*. U of Chicago P, 1980.

Metzger, Lois. *A Trick of the Light*. Balzer and Bray, 2013.

Miller, Sam J. *The Art of Starving*. Harper Collins, 2017.

Mitchell, David T., and Sharon L. Snyder. *Narrative Prosthesis: Disability and the Dependencies of Discourse*. U of Michigan P, 2000.

Moncrieff, Joanna, et al. "The Serotonin Theory of Depression: A Systematic Umbrella Review of the Evidence." *Molecular Psychiatry*, vol. 28, 2023, pp. 3243–56.

Moskowitz, Hannah. *Not Otherwise Specified*. Simon Pulse, 2015.

National Alliance on Mental Illness. "Diverse New Coalition Launches Education Campaign to Counter Misconceptions about Depression." 14 Sep. 2006, https://www.nami.org/Press-Media/Press-Releases/2006/Diverse-New-Coalition-Launches-Education-Campaign.

Ness, Patrick. *The Rest of Us Just Live Here*. Harper Teen, 2015.

Niven, Jennifer. *All the Bright Places*. Alfred A. Knopf, 2015.

O'Carroll, Patrick W., et al. "Suicide Contagion and the Reporting of Suicide: Recommendations from a National Workshop." *Morbidity and Mortality Weekly Report*, vol. 43, 1994, pp. 9–18.

Parsons, Anne E. *From Asylum to Prison: Deinstitutionalization and the Rise of Mass Incarceration after 1945*. U of North Carolina P, 2018.

Perring, Christian. "Medicating Children: The Case of Ritalin." *Bioethics*, vol. 11, no. 3–4, 1997, pp. 228–40.

Richmond, Kia Jane. "Using Literature to Confront the Stigma of Mental Illness, Teach Empathy, and Break Stereotypes." *Language Arts Journal of Michigan*, vol. 30, no. 1, 2014, pp. 19–25.

Roux, Madeleine. *Asylum*. Harper Collins, 2013.

Scrofano, Diane. "Disability Narrative Theory and Young Adult Fiction of Mental Illness." *The Journal of Research on Libraries and Young Adults*, vol. 10, no. 1, 2019, pp. 1–33.

Scrofano, Diane. "Not as Crazy as It Seems: Discussing the New YA Literature of Mental Illness in Your Classroom or Library." *Young Adult Library Services*, vol. 13, no. 2, 2015, pp. 15–20.

Shahan, Sherry. *Skin and Bones*. Albert Whitman, 2014.

Shusterman, Neal. *Challenger Deep*. Harper Teen, 2015.

Sontag, Susan. *Illness as Metaphor and AIDS and Its Metaphors*. Picador, 2001.

Stork, Francisco X. *The Memory of Light*. Arthur A. Levine Books, 2016.

Vidali, Amy. "Seeing What We Know: Disability and Theories of Metaphor." *Journal of Literary & Cultural Disability Studies*, vol. 4, no. 1, 2010, pp. 33–54.

Vrettos, Adrienne Maria. *Skin*. Margaret K. McElderry Books, 2006.

Wahl, Otto F. "Depictions of Mental Illnesses in Children's Media." *Journal of Mental Health*, vol. 12, no. 3, 2003, pp. 249–58.

Warin, Megan. *Abject Relations: Everyday Worlds of Anorexia*. Rutgers UP, 2010.

Weir, Kirsten. "The Roots of Mental Illness." *Monitor on Psychology*, vol. 43, no. 6, 2012, pp. 30–4.

Wickham, Anastasia. "It Is All in Your Head: Mental Illness in Young Adult Literature." *The Journal of Popular Culture*, vol. 51, no. 1, 2018, pp. 10–25.

Young, Suzanne. *The Program*. Simon Pulse, 2013.

"NO ONE WOULD BE MOVED BY ANY FEELING SAVE PITY"

Children, Narrative, and Healthcare in Annie Fellows Johnston's *Little Colonel* Series

DAWN SARDELLA-AYRES

Those who can tell a story possess social power. As Lee Anne Bell writes in *Storytelling for Social Justice*, the stories we tell each other and ourselves about social injustice can provide "a roadmap for tracing how people make sense of social reality," as well as "helping us to see where we connect with and where we differ from others in our reading of the world" (4). Rudine Sims Bishop has discussed the importance of young readers accessing stories that reflect the "multicultural nature of the world" in which children live, especially marginalized ones, and used the phrase "windows, mirrors, and sliding glass doors" to describe how child readers can see themselves and others in the books they read (ix–xi). However, what is a sliding glass door for one reader is a window or mirror for another, and social realities are varied, contextual, and all valid. While multiple perspectives coexist, hegemonic narratives are almost always white, heteronormative, middle-class, Christian, male, and, in one element that is too often overlooked, healthy. In Annie Fellows Johnston's *Little Colonel* series (1895–1912), disenfranchised characters, usually sick children experiencing poverty and abuse, rarely give firsthand accounts of their own stories. Either they are denied the opportunity due to their lack of social power, or they are disenfranchised as a result of not being able to tell their stories in the first place; usually it is a vicious circle of both. The idea of who tells whose story to whom, under what circumstances, has been explored in a variety of critical framings and children's texts. However, Johnston's problematic *Little Colonel* novels reveal complicated systemic oppression at work, further illuminated when contextualized with the written and practical work of her sister, reformist Albion Fellows Bacon.

First, narrative displacement in the *Little Colonel* series is not always straightforward. When explored through specific critical lenses, the child-advocates in the series provide insights to now-outdated attitudes, allowing interrogation into how ideologies and misinformation about reform literature, healthcare, and responsibility have developed. Second, particularly when read alongside Johnston's sister's concurrent social reform texts, the books are examples of American reform literature that clearly link illness and lacking healthcare with poverty, dirt, insufficient light and fresh air, and unsanitary housing conditions. Housing reform in their texts *is* public healthcare, often in lieu of accessible medical care. Ultimately, the texts blame intersectional systems of oppression in America for these lacks and empower children, especially girls and young women, to confront and change those systems. Thus, scholars might consider children's literature as a kind of healthcare of its own, giving rise to advocacy.

In these texts, one can explore the storytelling techniques and the messages about healthcare issues for both child readers and their parents. At the time Johnston was authoring her *Little Colonel* books, political, social, and healthcare reforms in response to urbanization and industrialization were emerging along with the new middle class, including the popular health movement, the efficiency movement, the hygienic movement, conservation, and the American Red Cross. Furthermore, many of these reforms were women-dominated; domestic science, birth control, anti-child labor reform, temperance, and suffrage were all linked to ideology about health, resources, and poverty, discussed openly in women's homes and gatherings. A hundred years later, contemporary conversations include similar ideas of reform, but further question the ethics of storytelling. These questions have given rise to new awareness movements in the late 2010s, including #OwnVoices (coined by Corinne Duyvis) and We Need Diverse Books (established by Ellen Oh, Dhonielle Clayton, and Judy Schricker), meant to elevate marginalized voices and increase representation, with marginalized women themselves in charge. Many narrative and social awareness movements also emphasize counterstorytelling to challenge dominant representation.

However, in the *Little Colonel* texts, as in real life, who gets to tell whose story is a complicated dynamic. Sometimes contradictory ideas are held together in a state of tension; stories may need to be told by outsiders' voices in order to get those in power to listen and bring about social change, while *at the same time* they can patronize or receive precedence over a firsthand voice. There are constructive ways to interrogate this power dynamic regarding who has "the right" to tell a story and under what circumstances. I would argue that, rather than a simplistic binary of silencing versus centering, an even more diverse, polyphonic, multivoiced approach is essential in effective storytelling and counterstorytelling: multiple voices speaking up from a variety of perspectives and experiences without silencing each other, still centering marginalized voices, with narratives coexisting, balancing. The *Little Colonel* books provide possibilities for exploring more effectively multifaceted approaches to healthcare advocacy and reform. Johnston's texts eventually reveal an unintentionally transgressive feminism in the complicated role privileged girls play as social advocates, especially on behalf of other children. They also demonstrate the complications inherent in advocacy today: instead of flat, single-centered, and simplistic either/or lessons about social reform and privilege, it is crucial to acknowledge that complex, multidimensional things have multiple centers.

ANNIE FELLOWS JOHNSTON AND ALBION FELLOWS BACON

In 1895, Johnston published *The Little Colonel*, the first of what became a popular series of girls' books featuring Lloyd Sherman, a five-year-old girl nicknamed "the Little Colonel" because of the hot temper and imperious ways that link her with her grandfather, a Confederate Kentucky colonel who lost an arm in the Civil War. The series grew to thirteen books, ending in 1912 with Lloyd as a young married woman, but relatively unchanged as a character. Interestingly, two other girls emerge not only as primary characters, replacing the static Lloyd, but also as active heroines and writers: Betty Lloyd Lewis, Lloyd's foster sister, comes to live at the family home in Lloydsboro when the girls are pre-teens, and Betty's diary forms sections and book chapters. Many of the didactic stories in the books, including those highlighting social reform, are told or re-told by Betty the writer. Mary Ware, the "Little Colonel's Chum," is the youngest daughter of family friends who live out in the "Wild West" of Arizona and Texas. By the last books of the series, Mary takes over the titular role, and in the final *Little Colonel* book, *Mary Ware's Promised Land* (1912), she becomes active in social reform for tenement housing.

Johnston's model for Mary Ware's reform work was her sister Albion Fellows Bacon. Bacon was a poet, an artist, and eventually a prominent social reformer who organized the Indiana Housing Association and, after several attempts, successfully pushed through a bill of statewide housing reform in 1913. Johnston and Bacon collaborated on projects from the time they were children, and their first published works were composed, submitted, and published together (Johnston, *The Land* 80). As adults, both belonged to the Author's Club, a group in Louisville that met during summers for over twenty years to read, write, and critique each others' work (122). Many of Bacon's poems are included in *Little Colonel* books.

Most significantly, at the same time Johnston was writing *Mary Ware's Promised Land*, Bacon was writing and lobbying for statewide reform laws in Indiana and had been active in housing reform, children's rights, and improving sanitation conditions locally for many years. Two years after Johnston published her final Little Colonel book, Bacon published her 1914 memoir, *Beauty for Ashes*, documenting her three housing reform campaigns from 1909–1913. From childhood, the sisters were often inseparable as writers and companions, always in close communication. Their archived papers at the Willard Library in Evansville, Indiana, were conceived as a joint project (although, after the library flooded in 1937, little archival material remains). Thus, I would suggest that, much like Wilder scholars approach the *Little House* books as a mother-daughter collaboration, we can and should examine Johnston's and Bacon's works collectively, even synergistically.

REFORM LITERATURE AND THE ROLES OF WOMEN AND CHILDREN

Numerous critics have examined reform literature in the United States during a time of rapid technological, industrial, and social change known as the Progressive Era. In *Reading for Reform: The Social Work of Literature in the Progressive Era*, Laura R. Fisher explores American texts produced during this time, spanning the latter years of the nineteenth century through the 1920s. During the Progressive Era, literature was seen as an accessible way to repair damages across class boundaries and was an accepted venue for women to pursue social and career ambitions as well. Harriet Beecher Stowe's abolitionist novel, *Uncle Tom's Cabin* (1852), is usually referenced as a standard for this kind of practical literature and, from the Civil War on through the first decades of the twentieth century in America, "women activists developed a relatively autonomous and nonpartisan reformist culture anchored in suffrage, temperance, and settlement reform" (L. R. Fisher 5). Like the Industrial era's social problem novel in England, American reform literature "held a special power to shape the U.S. social order" in new ways during the turn of the century, as "reform institutions from the settlement house to the African American college generated their own nuanced institutional vocabularies to describe the unequal but still friendly relations" existing "between reform's benefactors and its beneficiaries" (3). However, Fisher is critical of the ways reform movements, associations, and literature served to "conceptualize the connection between the privileged benefactor and underprivileged beneficiary as friendship" (19), which often diminished the realities of class and racial hierarchies.

While she doesn't distinguish between the burgeoning genre of "youth" or children's literature and texts aimed at adult readers, Fisher recontextualizes writers such as Grace H. Dodge, Booker T. Washington, Nella Larsen, Louisa May Alcott, Lillian Wald, Edith Wharton, and Jane Addams—many who are now considered children's authors, who concerned themselves with the rights and welfare of children, and who were and continue to be read by young readers—demonstrating how their literature of reform and activism help shape US history. Emily Hamilton-Honey roots much of women's reform work in church activity, specifically, the Christian charitable societies that emerged as new spaces for women beginning around the mid-1800s, post–Civil War (55). There, Hamilton-Honey identifies "a cultural shift in the beliefs about the role of young women in U.S. society," reflected in postbellum series fiction for girls, which opens up "more space for women's social and political activism" (2). This moral reform was "no longer confined to the home" as women "took their moral authority into city slums and the political arena" and did "their best to alleviate the effects of poverty, hunger, poor sanitation, and illness" (2). Bacon's *Beauty for Ashes* fits this genre description of American women's reform literature in those same middle-class Christian contexts; Johnston, who was considered a direct literary descendant of (and even replacement for) Alcott, also fits within this model, allowing for the *Little Colonel* series to be read in the context of reform literature as well.

The role of the child in relation to reform movements became increasingly active as the nineteenth century moved into the twentieth, both within and outside of the texts themselves. Roberta Seelinger Trites "notice[s] the strain of social criticism that permeates adolescent literature in the United States" (xiv) including Twain and Alcott, as well as Dodge, Warner, and Stowe, all mentioned in Alcott's novels; in addition, Alcott is often intertextually referenced in Johnston's *Little Colonel* books. Youth literature during this era, writes Trites, "relied on adolescents as metaphors for reform" because, for authors like Alcott, "the young represented the capacity for change that is necessary for a culture itself to change" (xiv). Bacon echoes this ideology when she writes of hosting countless housing reform and sanitation meetings in her home parlor so that "the children will grow up with the idea of using the home for social services" (65). Children, especially girls, were encouraged to participate in reform activities; if their literature was a central vehicle for ideologies of social reform, the *Little Colonel* series is no exception. And if, as Fisher suggests in *Reading for Reform*, reform literature in America at this time can be gathered and explored as a distinct genre, Johnston must be included in that conversation.

Inside these *bildungsroman* texts (see Sardella-Ayres and Reese), the fictional girls grow to womanhood in specific social contexts by, in part, engaging in kind, charitable Christian acts in their local communities with those who are sick, poor, and needy. Outside the texts, the child readers of the books are encouraged to do likewise; this resulted in their (mostly middle-class) readers forming clubs and hosting events, *Little Colonel* plays, and other assorted fundraisers described in letters to Johnston in her archives. "To feel that one has a part in making such conditions, in starting these ripples which go on and on in ever widening circles, is a happiness that cannot be estimated" (*The Land* 130), Johnston writes in her memoir, describing letters from girls who have incorporated the stories into their own lives, engaging in "charitable work" inspired by Lloyd Sherman and her friends. Additionally, women writers, including Johnston, Alcott, Dodge, and Burnett, wrote this kind of youth literature to support their own "increasingly ill and needy families" (Trites xiii), adding layers to the idea of girls' literature not just as social practice, but as healthcare. This slippage between writers advocating for othersand experiencing their own financial and health-related hardships offers points of inquiry requiring longer, more detailed study.

In plot points that revolve around illness and poverty, Johnston employs the language of reform literature, including referring to the relationships between her child-activists and the sick, poor children they rescue as "friendship," and classifying their benevolent deeds as "work" rather than charity. Both Johnston and Bacon, daughters of a Methodist minister, originally root their reform attitudes in Christian didacticism and benevolence. However, this changes over the course of their careers. Fisher points out how American reform literature in general demonstrated a "turning away from the sentimental benevolence of the past" as well as "decenter[ing] the church as a primary agent of social change" in favor of "institutional alliances with universities and new corporate philanthropies" and an increase of legislative process of reform, with industrialist perspectives (5–6). Johnston's own books, as with Bacon's experiences at the time, reflect a twenty-year shift from personally edifying Christian benevolence in charitable acts to professional progressive organizations focusing on the needs of recipients. The character Mary Ware accordingly demonstrates a shift from individual actions and dutiful, womanly benevolence as performed by Lloyd to a more systemically focused approach to combating poverty and improving conditions for the benefit of an entire community, city, or state.

CRITICAL RACE THEORY, BRIDGE TEXTS, AND COUNTERNARRATIVES

Critical race theory (CRT) is a powerful theoretical lens for reading the genre of reform literature to reveal layers of structural power as related to personal narrative. Developed to highlight structural oppressions in legal situations as well as healthcare in America and focusing on intersectional perspectives, CRT interrogates the locus of power in social systems and sees identities as socially constructed and contextual rather than biologically essential. Much like reform literature a century ago, CRT also demonstrates firm belief in "the power of representation to change public perception and subsequently social conditions translated into contests over who controlled the official narrative of marginalized groups" (L. R. Fisher 25). Narrative has not only imaginative power, but social and legal power as well, to "dislodge" people from their "normative universe" (Delgado and Stefancic 48); Richard Delgado and Jean Stefancic emphasize that in institutional contexts such as classrooms and courtrooms, "engaging stories can help us understand what life is like for others and invite the reader into a new and unfamiliar world," which can "help readers bridge the gap between their worlds and those of others" (48). This kind of counternarrative or counterstorytelling is defined in Daniel Solorzano and Tara J. Yosso's 2002 article "Critical Race Methodology: Counter-Storytelling as an Analytical Framework for Education Research" as "a method of telling the stories of those people whose experiences are not often told" (26). Counterstories, which Mary Ware, like Bacon, bring to court hearings and newspapers, challenge and destabilize assumptions of dominant narratives. Instead, counterstories emphasize those not often centered, including women, people of color, LGBTQ+ people, children, immigrants, poor people, and disabled people, prioritizing their voices and experiences.

In a 2018 exploration of ethnicity and disease, Chandra L. Ford and Collins O. Airhihenbuwa apply CRT to public health issues, including health inequality research. This kind of examination gives us means to query a subject's inclusion or exclusion in the narrative process, as well as their place and the storyteller's place in a story. It is not enough to ask, simply, *Whose stories are heard?* As Ford and Airhihenbuwa note, "Collective self-critiques can help us understand how our norms and conventions may unwittingly undermine efforts to achieve health equality" (230), and ask outright "Which structural factors are at play?" when examining the racial contexts of any health-related study in America (227). If CRT looks to build models for communication and interrogation, then Johnston's and Bacon's works provide historical points of interrogation to do so. Applying a lens like this to Johnston's and Bacon's works reveals America's reliance on constant, simplistic black-and-white, North-and-South, urban-and-rural binaries and how these dichotomies cause harm by erasing or obscuring intersections.

ERASURE: WHO IS LEFT OUT?

The obvious erasure in Johnston's books and Bacon's activism is of Black Americans. Blackness in Johnston's *Little Colonel* books, as I have examined elsewhere (see Sardella-Ayres), is always in a minstrel capacity; it is never included in any way but as a source of racist humor at the expense of Black people, specifically to reinforce whiteness and white girlhood as superior, all too common fictional tropes at the turn of the last century (see Bernstein's *Racial Innocence*). The texts are laden with the very racial hierarchies that CRT attempts to undo. Bacon's *Beauty for Ashes*, however, complicates the assumption that privileged or secondhand voices silence firsthand voices in ways that are uniformly harmful.

Unlike her sister's fiction, Bacon's memoir reveals some interactions with Black citizens that at least demonstrate shared humanity, values, and basic rights. Some of the Evansville women Bacon speaks with about neighborhood conditions are Black. Local neighborhoods are mixed racially. As Bacon first becomes aware of the complexities of poverty, health, and sanitation, she mentions a visit with "Aunt Lindy, an old coloured washwoman" who lives near one of the railroad stations in an alley neighborhood in the city (32). The two women share a deep concern for the lack of sanitary resources, the presence of liquor, and the effects on local children's health and living conditions. Bacon's interaction with Aunt Lindy is one of the initial experiences that prompts her local civic work to improve sanitation, after seeing how hard Aunt Lindy works to keep her home and self "spotless" even with "flakes of soot . . . falling like black snow, clouds of dust poured in from the street, and the slime of the alley ran to her very doorstep" (32). As the two women watch, a "shabby little girl" with "hair bleached a tan colour, matching her skin" carries an earthen pitcher to the saloon across the street, presumably to bring liquor back to her mother, a "meanly dressed white woman" with "a peculiar scar across her lowering face" whom Bacon recognizes as "a woman who had come begging to my door a few days before" (33). Aunt Lindy complains about "awful folks" in neighboring houses—white and, possibly, mixed-race—who frequent the saloon, and, for the first time, Bacon begins to question the assumptions she has made about the "evil" of the poor neighborhoods, seeing now the complicated systems that have caused these conditions and how others, including her daughters' schoolmates, have come to live in such homes. Bacon notes that "six families fought over one cistern" and "a cesspool reeked," "rats overran the place" and "people were sick in all the houses" (32). She was "amazed to see the snowy miracle [Aunt Lindy] had wrought, in such a place" when given her clean bundle of laundry, but wonders "what germs may be lurking in those folds" (33). Here, for the first time, Bacon makes the connections between sickness, filth, and conditions of poverty that are beyond the control of most of the individuals living there.

Critics have explored the links between racial stereotypes in America about cleanliness and disease, segregated cities and neighborhoods, and environmental racism. As Carl A. Zimring explores in *Clean and White: A History of Environmental Racism in the United States*, Black and nonwhite Americans, immigrants, and manual laborers have long been associated with disease and a lack of cleanliness. Zimring writes, "The rhetoric and imagery of hygiene became conflated with a racial order that made white people pure, and anyone who was not white [was] dirty" (89). White Americans' reactions to immigration and domestic migration included systems of oppressions and environmental racism such as the Ku Klux Klan, ghettos, and exclusion acts. With her newfound awareness, Bacon starts to realize how the physical conditions of dirt are beyond individuals' control. Aunt Lindy and the Black children Bacon sees are examples of cleanliness and hard work, but Bacon recognizes that they, too, are fighting a losing battle against the unsanitary conditions and inevitable disease of the neighborhood, thanks to structural oppression and environmental racism.

The local slum neighborhoods may be mixed in terms of racial demographics, as Bacon's interactions there demonstrate, but as Bacon begins her civic work in local tenements, she reveals why Black citizens are not included in most of her reforming. When discussing the demographics and needs of Evansville, including different immigrant groups, widows and widowers with children, the elderly, and the disabled, Bacon remarks, "We have a good sized negro population, also, but it is greatly to their credit that they look well after their own people, in sickness and in want. We rarely had a negro applicant for charity, so it happened that we did not realise until later how uniformly miserable and unsanitary were their dwellings" (53). A combination of intersectional erasures as well as assumptions about who needed and would ask for help in a community plays out in a Black-white racial binary. As with so many elements of social activism and progressive movements—and due to what were perceived as complimentary attributes, albeit still based on racist stereotypes—Black Americans' needs are invisible.

Bacon continues to reveal America's racial divisions when she discusses the moralities of newly arrived immigrants unable to establish homes: "We saw negroes and foreigners in the same house, for the latter do not understand our instinct of segregation" (278). She sees this as a "complex problem of the alien, living in a strange environment, mixed with native poor and negroes," which "too often undoes the home" because the family is not able to establish independence nor maintain what another reformer Bacon quotes calls "sturdy immigrant traits" that "would mean so much to our American citizenship" (278–79). This problematic racial essentialism is characteristic of the times but also reveals America's long-standing ideology that holds Black Americans and their needs apart, and, accordingly, ignores, dismisses, or leaves them unprotected, in part under the assumption that Black people will "look well after their own people" and don't want or need outside interference (Bacon 53). In both Johnston's and Bacon's texts, Black American experiences are, for the most part, rendered invisible or quickly dismissed.

While Black families in Bacon's community benefited from her general activism, even if they tell their own stories, no one is truly listening. That same obliviousness is part of Bacon's and Johnston's texts and should be interrogated as part of larger critical discourse about representation and invisibility. Bacon herself increasingly questions many of her assumptions the more she hears others' stories. For both Bacon and for her and Johnston's readers, scratching the surface of those assumptions reveals complicated systems of oppression that have kept power—as well as access to medical care, cleanliness, and good health—firmly in the control of America's white patriarchy. Just one example is the 1910 book-length Flexner Report, resulting in the standardization of American (and Canadian) medical education, which Barbara Ehrenreich and Deirdre English describe as "bias disguised as science" in *For Her Own Good: Two Centuries of the Experts' Advice to Women* (96).

The Flexner Report, "hailed by most medical historians as the most decisive turning point in American medical history" (English and Ehrenreich 96), was the result of long attempts to reform medical education and scientific medicine, but also instituted patriarchal regulations, diminishing Black and female roles in medical science. English and Ehrenreich write, "There were, according to Flexner, 'too many' doctors in the United States and they were too low class" (96). Furthermore, Flexner argued that "Few women doctors were needed . . . because of lack of 'any strong ungratified desire on the part of women to enter the profession.' (!)" (96, punctuation in original). As a result of Flexner's report, almost a hundred medical schools closed or merged in less than ten years, including all but three female medical colleges and two Black medical schools (97). Ehrenreich and English point out that this standardization resulted in medicine becoming even more elite, white, and male and suggest several alternative strategies for reform (98), revealing how poor people, nonwhite and Black people, immigrants, and women were consistently disenfranchised by American healthcare.

While Bacon could and did do many things, she, too, was limited by America's systemic oppressions, including how medicine and education continued to prioritize white, wealthy, and male citizens. Along with problems within marginalized communities, these standardizations also shaped what privileged women like Bacon could—and could not—see.

No single voice can tell every story.

DISPLACEMENT: WHO IS SILENCED?

It is crucial to explore the nuances of what stories are told, by whom, how, and to what effect. Storytelling plots in Johnston's earliest *Little Colonel* books demonstrate inherent problems and dangers when privileged people speak for the oppressed. More than once, Lloyd and her companions encounter disenfranchised children whose stories of abuse, illness, neglect, and poverty make other children (and often adults) aware for the first time of social injustices in their community. As in Bacon's writing, the conditions of poverty, dirt, and sickness are inextricably linked in the *Little Colonel* books, and the stories the disenfranchised children tell reflect intertwining cycles of starvation, illness, disease, injury, and lack of adult care. But the ways in which their personal histories are communicated in order to prompt action from other characters is critical. In response to the disturbing tales, Lloyd and her friends feel sympathy, but shift the focus of the storytelling from the disenfranchised children to themselves and their peers as storytellers for other children and their parents in the text, and ultimately, Johnston's child audience.

The plot of *The Two Little Knights of Kentucky* (1899) centers on the eponymous "knights," Lloyd's neighborhood friends Malcolm and Keith, rescuing a starving, abused orphan boy sick with "lung fever" who is traveling with an old tramp and pet bear and begging for handouts (22). The boy's own "pitiful" state should be enough to move the adults to action, but it isn't and hasn't been. Johnston highlights one of the main problems regarding social activism for children at the time: the book's narrator observes that "if Jonesy had been an attractive child" with "big, appealing eyes, he might have found his way more easily into people's hearts" (55). But since he is "a lean, snub-nosed little fellow, with a freckled face and neglected hair," then "no one would be moved, by any feeling save pity, to stoop and put affectionate arms around Jonesy. He was only a common little street gamin, as unlovely as he was unloved" (55). Even Jonesy's pet bear is treated more humanely.

Significantly, Jonesy never gets to tell his own story in the text. Instead, a man who saves Jonesy after a fire tells Jonesy's sad story to Malcolm and Keith. The boys then tell their aunt, father, and others about Jonesy, and the adults re-tell the details of Jonesy's poverty and abuse, but no real action to help Jonesy occurs until Keith himself becomes sick. Delirious with fever and near death, Keith begs his stricken parents to help Jonesy, which results in "the Jonesy Benefit" and the establishment of a local home for orphaned boys, the great "knightly" act in the book. This could have revealed the need for care on an institutional level, but, instead only reinforces the existing Christian charity ideology, which is almost always performative for the approval of other white Christians in the community; it frames Jonesy's appropriated narrative as charitable entertainment for the rich white Southerners and a vehicle for their own narratives.[1] Jonesy has been suffering, ill, and starving for years, but his circumstances do not matter as much as Keith's; *Keith's* dangerous fever is what moves the adults around them to real action.

Only well-to-do and socially prominent white people have the means to do anything to help, but they do so at the expense of Jonesy's agency. Jonesy might have power in his own version of his narrative, but the text denies him that. Several times, the text raises questions about Jonesy's place in relation to the other children and his own narrative, but nothing comes of it. The children appear to be aware of a class discrepancy at first, but then abandon this concern. After little Lloyd is rescued from a runaway handcart in the path of a train by the boys, including Jonesy, Lloyd notes, "Jonesy ought to be a knight, too" (96). The other children agree and propose a ceremony that very day. But if such a ceremony occurs, it is never spoken of nor shown, and Jonesy is never portrayed as a knight, unlike the attractive and appealing Malcolm and Keith. Emphatically, he does not share social standing with them, no matter how brave and noble his acts. In fact, in subsequent volumes of *Little Colonel* stories, the events of the book are no longer about Jonesy, but are instead referred to as "Gingah and the Beah," a story where Lloyd and the boys' Cousin Ginger are frightened by Jonesy's tamed bear at a Valentine party. The emphasis is the children's pseudo-royal roles in the community, with Malcolm and Keith (the "two little knights of Kentucky"), their quest to "right the wrongs of the world," and the token details of Lloyd's "Queen of Hearts" girlishness and attractiveness all framed in fairy-tale imagery. The overall effect is that Jonesy's agency and consciousness of his own experience is less important than ruling class children's, rendering Jonesy even more voiceless and disenfranchised. Jonesy is never mentioned again, even though there was supposedly an orphan home in Lloydsboro established for him and others and even though Lloyd and her friends encounter other children who might need such a facility.

Another example of this marginalizing is evident in Johnston's *The Little Colonel's Holidays* (1901), the first book after Betty Lloyd Lewis comes to live at the family home as Lloyd's foster sister. Betty is a gentle, sensitive orphan, a writer, and Mrs. Sherman's namesake goddaughter. After years of living in poverty as a de facto servant with distant relatives, Betty has been saved, Cinderella-like, by the wealthy Sherman family and nicknamed "little Tusitala," or "story-teller," after the Samoans' name for Robert Louis Stevenson. Now eleven years old, Lloyd goes with twelve-year-old Betty to visit her old home, the "Cuckoo's Nest," where the girls meet Molly.

Molly is a "wild" orphan girl who has been taken from an asylum and brought to the Cuckoo's Nest to do the housework in Betty's absence. Betty and the orphan girl Molly could not be more different, both in terms of how they progress through the stories and how they are textually represented. Despite their almost identical circumstances, Molly is portrayed as not only wild, but dangerous, a witch, and like a feral animal. Molly and Jonesy, both poor orphans, qualify as what Nancy Isenberg defines as "waste people" or surplus poor, eventually called "white trash"; they were assumed to be ignorant, vulgar, violent and dirty, and stigmatized for their ill health and their ostensible inability to be productive (xxvii). Molly has been discarded and ignored; like Jonesy, she has a missing sibling, a sister, another "throwaway" poor, sick child. At first, Molly asserts her own narrative and controls its access; the chapter is even titled "Molly's Story." When Lloyd and Betty see that Molly has hung on her "cheerless" bedroom wall a sad picture of a crying child, Molly confronts them "like an angry tigress" for spying, then bursts into tears at their intrusion on her privacy, claiming space, identity, property, and respect. But "Molly's Story" is delivered through the storyteller, Betty. After asserting her own position in relation to Molly ("I am an orphan, too, and maybe I can coax her to tell me, when she knows how sorry I am for her" [Johnston, *The Little Colonel's Holidays* 80]), Betty is the one who tells Lloyd the personal history Molly has told her off-stage, a biography of poverty, sickness, starvation, and abuse: Molly, her little sister Dot, and their family suffered after their father lost his job and were forced to move to a dirty city cottage. The family's suffering is due entirely to the fact that their father "took to getting drunk every Saturday night. He's going down-hill now, fast as a man can go" (81). Eventually, Molly is separated from Dot and sent to an orphan home. All of these details are related via Betty, "little Tusitala," the white, Christian storyteller. Betty begins Molly's story by telling Lloyd it is "just like a story in a book" (80). This may give Molly's story more weight *as a story*, but it is yet another way Molly's real suffering is diminished and romanticized by those in power. Betty's storytelling heightens the problems with appropriated narrative, especially since the text never depicts Molly communicating this information herself. Like Jonesy, Molly's own lived experiences are appropriated for others' storytelling.

From the beginning, many of Molly's personal details come from outside sources. Molly repeats things her grandmother has told her, which are delivered thirdhand when Betty re-tells Molly's story. This suggests the story is more effectively communicated through girls like Betty and Lloyd, the assumed good girls from the dominant class, than by Molly herself. Delgado and Stefancic suggest that one of CRT's antidotes for silencing is when "critical writers use counter-stories to challenge, displace, or mock" preconceived myths in legal discourse, "a valid destructive function" (48). In the *Little Colonel*, not only do most other usurped tales disenfranchise the characters experiencing sickness and poverty, but the stories are also rarely told, or countered, with any narrative to challenge preconceived myths. As demonstrated with Jonesy and Molly, the narratives don't go far enough to "provide a language to bridge the gaps in imagination and conception that gives rise to the differend" (Delgado and Stefancic 50–51). After all, the adults presented in the text are already well aware of poverty and illness and how they affect children; indeed, they know that there *are* poor, sick children in their own communities who need help, but they continually choose to ignore it. It is only when they have a personification of sickness and poverty made appealing by a more privileged child, and, even more, when the situation is amplified by privileged children's distress, that the adults respond with help. Long before they will be moved to productive action, they first must be shocked with "pity" for the suffering children; even then, it is only on a case-by-case basis, not a community or structural solution.

APPROPRIATION AND THE ABJECT: WHOSE STORIES MATTER?

The idea of who controls a narrative extends beyond storytelling to the artistic representation of that narrative. Notably, the identifying picture of Molly's lost little sister Dot is not an actual picture of the child herself, but rather, an illustration she has from an old *St. Nicholas* magazine. Johnston takes great pains to identify the picture, ostensibly prompting the book's readers to do what the children in the text do: search for it, look at it and feel moved by it. "It was the front page from an old Harpers Weekly [sic]. The date caught her eye first: December 25, 1897" (*The Little Colonel's Holidays* 76). The picture, captioned "A Caprice of Time," in which the viewer can "not see the face hidden in the tattered apron, which the disappointed little hands held up" (76), reveals that others' interpretations of the poor, sad, needy waif are more important than the personal experiences of children themselves.

This picture as a representation of Molly's story has a tremendous effect on all who see it. Johnston's text is specific about reactions each time another (white, middle- to upper-class, Christian, usually female) character encounters the illustration. These characters wallow in the misery of the child depicted, taking pains to explain exactly how affected they are by the depiction and what it makes them think. Lloyd "could not hear the sobs that she knew were shaking the thin little shoulders, but she felt the misery of the scene as forcibly as if the real child stood before her," and she compares this to her own life, because "if all the troubles and disappointments of her whole life could be put together, they would be as only a drop compared to the grief of the poor little creature in the picture" (Johnston, *The Little Colonel's Holidays* 76). Other children note "every detail of the shabby room," "the old broken stool . . . and her thin little arms," and one little girl sighs, "Her shoes are all worn out, too. I wish she had a pair of mine" (178). When Joyce sees the "forlorn little figure" she declares, "It makes me want to cry," and immediately asserts class- and wealth-based social responsibility: "If I were rich I'd go out and hunt for all the poor little children like this that I could find, and do something to make them happy" (102–3). The girls and women take masochistic, almost gothic pleasure as they immerse themselves in the morbid, painful details of Dot's misery and whip others up into a similar frenzy. This uncanny horror, framed in the safety of benevolence, also diminishes its corporeality by appropriating its voice: the firsthand accounts of experiences of poverty.

Appropriating others' stories in the presence of the abject allows the girls and women to stabilize their own identities as not-sick and not-poor, as well as their appropriate social roles as good Christian benefactors, fulfilling charitable duties. The only way to deal with the abject is to repurpose it into the symbolic, accomplished here through appropriated storytelling. Dot's plight has been personified, giving a picture of all other "poor little waifs in the world" for Lloyd and her friends, allowing them to literally picture the miseries of poverty and apply them to the related story Betty re-tells for them. Certainly Betty's telling of story and the associated illustration the girls find are able to travel further and affect more than Molly can do on her own. But by contextualizing it as such, the image silences and displaces the actual child, Molly.

Adult women in *The Little Colonel's Holidays*, too, fetishize the child in the illustration—again, not the actual Molly or Dot—and comment on how sad it makes them, using words like "misery," "pitiful" "poor creature," and "haunted." A New York woman (even though she lives in a city with poverty, tenement housing, and tens of thousands of such children living in abject conditions) responds to the picture with, "I thought such tales were made up by newspapers and magazines, just for something to write about" (Johnston 112). There is no indication that anyone has responded to Molly, in person, with such empathy or pathos until she had the image of little Dot to literally illustrate her own plight. Even when the girls vow to help Molly find Dot and to be her friend, it is from a place of reassurance, not the level of sorrow expressed when they look at the magazine drawing. The actual suffering child, Molly, who is dark and wild, cannot inspire such compassion the way a sentimental picture and second- or thirdhand story from a more appealing little girl can.

By the end of the book, the girls and women who have "rescued" the two abused sisters, Molly and Dot, essentially co-opt their story for their own moral purposes to illustrate lessons about charity and Christian spirit. Molly herself is silenced, reduced to a wordless, maternal, angelic figure sitting at her dying sister's bedside on Christmas night, while the well-to-do matron who has paid for their care whispers that Molly will be a fine nurse someday, sealing her fate instead of allowing Molly to vocalize it as her own desire. Even at Dot's funeral, Molly's own words are quoted by a neighbor lady to Lloyd, Betty, and friends. Molly herself does not speak directly, and, like Jonesy, is never mentioned in subsequent books.

In the earlier books of the *Little Colonel* series, the function of Jonesy's and Molly's stories is not to communicate the disenfranchised children's painful experiences from their own personal viewpoints, but to be circulated third- and fourth-hand among a privileged group of well-to-do white people with social connections. On the one hand, this is the group with the power to do something about the orphaned children's plights. But on the other hand, their firsthand voices and stories are lost, if they were ever present to begin with. The narrative becomes, for the rich white children, an almost masochistic and romantic tale to repeat for sentimental effect, reinforcing their own Christian goodness. This dichotomy exists outside the texts, as well: it was not poor children who could access books like the *Little Colonel* series easily. Rather, the presumed reader of the series was likely in a similar middle-class position to many of the books' secondary characters, readers who needed to be made to "see the misery of the world" via Johnston's series as the characters in the book do with the magazine illustration. Actual ill, poor children are removed from their own lived experiences and abilities to narrate them to others and are turned into object lessons for privileged children. In future books, Jonesy, Molly, and Dot are never mentioned again, as if their stories don't matter. Only the noble, charitable actions of the Little Colonel and her friends do. These acts in the first books of the *Little Colonel* series, mirrored by Johnston's readers' own clubs, fundraisers, and charity acts documented in multiple fan letters, amount to little more than benevolent playacting for the white Christian children involved, to be like Lloyd and Betty and other fictional characters in the books, not to empathize with Jonesy or Molly or Dot.

However, it is significant that Johnston included such stories in the *Little Colonel* books to draw her readers'—and their parents'—attention to social injustice, prioritizing children's abilities to enact social change. Johnston writes passionately in her 1929 autobiography of the powers of children in improving social conditions: "We could not go into their homes and say to their slovenly mothers: 'You must air your beds and sweep the corners of your rooms and keep your cooking vessels clean,' but these children can." (*The Land* 106). Not only are all of these ideas evident in the *Little Colonel* series, the books themselves function as a way of "going into their homes" and communicating social values. But this also reveals Johnston's own biases: that the "slovenly mothers" are the problem, rather than the systemic issues and approaches her own sister Bacon narrates over and over again, issues that finally make their way into the last book in the series almost twenty years later.

ACTIVISM: WHO IS EMPOWERED AND INCLUDED?

In the last *Little Colonel* book, social reformer and childhood "chatterbox" Mary Ware uses her established ability to tell stories to speak on behalf of those who are ignored by society and challenge structural oppressions. After her mother dies, eighteen-year-old Mary finds work as a private secretary for a wealthy politically active woman, which launches Mary into her own social reform work. As mentioned, this work is based on Johnston's sister's contemporaneous activism: most of the characters in the *Little Colonel* books are based on real people, and Mary Ware is influenced by Albion Fellows Bacon. So intrinsically linked are the two that Mary's counterstorytelling is often taken from Bacon's own letters and speeches at the time, and Bacon quotes *Mary Ware's Promised Land* in her 1914 memoir's conclusion.

In previous *Little Colonel* books, more than once, others fondly remark on something being told "as only little Mary Ware can" or quote things "little Mary Ware would say." One of Mary's characteristic traits is her forthrightness, described in American ideological terms: "Mary is as honest as the father of his country himself [George Washington].... I'll warn you now. She'll always tell exactly what she thinks" (Johnston, *The Little Colonel: Maid of Honor* 53–54). While one of her growing-up lessons involves Mary learning how to "curb her lively tongue," a common girls' *bildungsroman* lesson (Sardella-Ayres and Reese), Mary is never silenced or baited-and-switched into less-controversial subjects. In fact, as a social reformer, Mary successfully introduces controversial topics into stately social gatherings in Lloydsboro. From the beginning of the series, when Mary is only a secondary character, her impassioned storytelling or explanations furnish narratives for others. Even though she is not a fiction writer and poet like Betty, Mary nevertheless has power through her narrative ability.

Unlike Lloyd or even Betty, Mary has a fluid social position. With her links to the family in Lloydsboro, as well as her own struggles with poverty living in the Arizona desert, Mary occupies multiple spheres and crosses boundaries regularly. While Betty is wholly integrated into the genteel life of Lloydsboro, Mary can at once be a Wild West girl who speaks her mind as well as a young lady of Lloydsboro heritage, and she uses this fluctuating social position repeatedly. In terms of counterstorytelling and positionality, Mary's ability to tell someone else's story demonstrates that what are often assumed to be usurped narratives sometimes have a distinctly positive value: giving a voice to those who are ignored or erased by those in privileged positions.

Mary brings civic attention to a local tenement slum by "telling the story" of accidents, hazards, even deaths that have gone ignored thus far, and she does so at the behest and with the permission of the people for whom she speaks. The links between illness and unsanitary conditions are explicit:

> Mary turned to the girl on the musty mattress. It wasn't actual starvation which drew the skin so tightly over her cheek-bones; ... [it] was the

disease which had claimed a victim, sometimes several, from every family in turn who occupied the room, because it had never been properly disinfected. Not even the sunlight could get in to do its share towards making it fit for a human dwelling. (*Mary Ware's Promised Land* 211–12)

Unlike earlier books in the series, here, the tragic events and grim conditions are often first presented in the text to Mary by the people experiencing them before Mary repeats their stories to others, including a friend who is a newspaperman. When Mary re-tells these stories, it is not with a sense of wallowing in others' misfortune. Instead, Mary literally says what the marginalized poor cannot to the people at fault whom they cannot access, bringing about action.

Initially, Mary, like Bacon, is oblivious to others' realities: on her first visit to a slum neighborhood known as Diamond Row, she asks (as Bacon herself asked), "Why don't they leave here and go out to the country" where "they could at least have clean water, and clean grass to lie on. They'd be better off out under the trees than in that basement." One of the tenants, Mrs. Donegan, sharply corrects her assumptions by asking Mary, "Did you ever see a rat caught in a trap? . . . It can't help itself. It can't get out. No more can they. They can't even speak English" (Johnston, *Mary Ware's Promised Land* 213–14). Unlike earlier books, firsthand voices are represented and challenge the heroine's positionality. Furthermore, several firsthand voices explicitly ask her to use her privileges to help them, since their complaints to the landlord have gone unheeded thus far and will endanger them further. While wrapped in Johnston's familiar Christian savior rhetoric, Mary's approach is nevertheless different to that employed in earlier books in the series. She does not romanticize the tenements and their inhabitants, but rather is moved to furious action to hold those in power accountable. Instead of wallowing in masochistic pleasure, Mary works herself to exhaustion and collapse. When Mary finds a particular tenement owner's agent, she "told him it was not rents alone he was collecting, but blood-money, and that the owner of that tenement was as responsible for the forty deaths inside its walls as if he'd deliberately poisoned them. And I told him I'd make it my business from now on to see that the people knew the truth about him" (217).

When called upon to speak publicly about the slum conditions, "telling all she knows" like she had as a child, Mary tells the stories of the poor residents: a girl with two legs broken and internal injuries from rotted cellar stairs, a little boy killed on the same staircase, forty people, many children, dying of consumption in a single tenement in a decade due to "that basement room with the mould on the walls and the water seeping in from the adjoining cellar" (218). Her mentor has Mary tell "the same story" of the dangerous living conditions and residents' resulting sicknesses to groups in their community because "You can make them see it more plainly than I" (224), knowing few have listened to the firsthand voices, much less been "moved by pity" to help them. Mrs. Blythe, a local reporter, and the Diamond Row community themselves make use of Mary's abilities to effectively reach multiple audiences in ways that none of them can.

Most importantly, Mary fulfills a role that neither Lloyd nor any other girl in the series does: she questions and confronts the patriarchal, capitalist system that has caused the need for reform in the first place and singles out several local individuals as responsible. Mary addresses those in power both at meetings and individually, telling the stories of the sick and poor, yet told "so simply, so personally, that it was as if she had merely opened a door . . . and bidden them see for themselves the windowless rooms, the mouldy walls, the slimy yards" (Johnston, *Mary Ware's Promised Land* 268–69). Mary's journalist friend begins to cover the tenement problems and outs a corrupt landlord, and Mary's work results in the landlord's daughter—who has reaped the benefits of her father's ill-gotten wealth—publicly shaming her father, causing him to lose a city election as well as forcing reform on the tenements via public opinion. Moreover, she continues to question and confront once she moves to Lloydsboro and has contact with prominent politicians and wealthy members of Louisville society, even enlisting a Lexington judge to her cause. Mary is the only one able to move between groups and be wholly accepted by them, to perform authentically as herself, whether she is with Irish immigrants in an urban slum, social activists and journalists at a political meeting, or the social elite of Lloydsboro.[2] Mary is a direct reflection of Albion Fellows Bacon's own work in housing reform and child welfare in which counterstorytelling plays a crucial role. As documented by Bacon's memoir, and demonstrated by Mary's actions in *Mary Ware's Promised Land*, storytelling is employed as a conduit, bridging gaps and creating links. Bacon writes of speaking to others of her personal experiences working with local communities:

> I told them "A Tale of the Tenements," a true and simple story of life in the slums of our Indiana towns, and made it just as bare and sordid and miserable as I found it, in plain speech, for there was no need for eloquence. They could see . . . that not education, not culture, not music or art, not even home economics, could ever penetrate to those darkened places, where cleanliness was difficult, and sanitation was impossible. (264)

Bacon notes, too, that she can't always tell these stories in the same ways. She has to be a skilled storyteller, adjusting to audiences and situations: "To address a [state] legislative committee, I found, was very different from speaking before a missionary society, a charity organisation, or a civic club" (196). She writes that while sometimes it is effective to speak "with some of the fire that burned within me," other times she needs to be friendly and winsome. Still other times she must present the case "so clearly as to give the committee the whole situation, and nothing more was needed" (196–97). She sometimes must be "practical and business-like" in letters and meetings with "prominent men": "I remember checking myself in a description of the conditions of the poor, for fear I should verge on sentiment" (186). As Bacon works increasingly at the state level, it is always with awareness of her audiences and her purpose, as well as awareness of the people she is representing. Bacon writes that she speaks "for those who cannot employ their own advocate, and who need one most," "for these, who are always absent when they are maligned" (138–39), and Bacon finds herself "answering for the poor" because so many dismiss their firsthand voices (143–44).

Bacon does far more than present the stories—the counternarratives—of poor people, focusing on women, children, immigrants, and those in ill health. Like her fictional counterpart Mary Ware, she undertakes grueling labor at great personal cost: she develops trusted relationships with disadvantaged residents and, with their permission, acts as liaison; she writes "endless" personal letters (Bacon 180), seeks publicity to draw attention to the lack of clean water, light, and safe staircases (180), and confronts criminally negligent landlords. Bacon is also told by several of the white, male state leaders that these bills are more effective "if presented by some individual who is known to be working for the cause of humanity," who "has studied housing laws and housing conditions" and can "be present at the committee hearing" to "be the leader" (188–89). Accordingly, Mrs. Bacon, respected wife and mother of Evansville, Indiana, has access because of her privileges, and in her social role as a woman and a community member, Bacon makes connections and allies in valuable legislative positions. She learns how to navigate the legal system, when to work with the rules and when to challenge them, all the while repeating the stories of the people she has met.

Likewise, in the last *Little Colonel* book, Mary Ware learns how to manipulate patriarchal oppressions on behalf of those who are disenfranchised. When she thinks she must renounce marriage in order to "keep tryst" with duty, helping to pass a housing reform bill and continuing to work on improving conditions in tenement slums, it is not girlish hyperbole nor sentimental melodrama when she breaks her engagement, but instead, a difficult moral choice between duty and love. Part of Mary's triumph is that ultimately she does not have to renounce love in order to devote herself to housing reform work. Mary initially comes to the conclusion that she must give up marrying Phil after a church sermon "extolling sacrifice" by a young minister who "seemed to know no call of the flesh. It was all of the spirit," rhetoric rooted in Christian ideology (288). But Mary's mentor, Mrs. Blythe, subverts this patriarchal ideology, destabilizing Christian doctrine and the old Christian charity model, allowing Mary to see a way that she can have it all, can respond to the "call of the flesh" as well as the spirit. Mrs. Blythe clarifies that Mary will actually be more effective as a married woman because she will "show other girls that they don't have to be like nuns in order to help." Although it is not overtly presented as such, she articulates the ways in which she has manipulated or worked within the system to her advantage: "Because I have a home of my own, and a recognized social position, and am a happy wife and mother, people listen to me far more readily when I go to them with a plea for less fortunate homes and wives and mothers. Mrs. Philip Tremont will be able to accomplish even more than little Mary Ware" (Johnston, *Mary Ware's Promised Land* 295). While this seems anti-feminist a hundred years later, this also reflects Bacon's personal experiences, accessing certain social and legal spaces on behalf of the sick and disenfranchised because of her role as a trusted wife and woman of the community, consciously or unconsciously playing the system. Most crucial, this advice, from one woman to another, is privileged over the male-centric religious and social perspective. It is unlikely that Johnston's series can be seen as deliberately subverting patriarchy and religion; nevertheless, it undercuts it with its covert ideology.

A privileged woman speaking out on behalf of the sick and disenfranchised is not always usurpation, because this kind of labor is often impossible for many in the conditions of illness and poverty. When describing a failed attempt at passing their housing reform bill, Bacon writes of one of their legal allies confronting the rest of the Senate with the facts that she herself has been repeating in countless stories of the sick and poor: "'It is asked why there are not more here insisting upon this bill,' said Senator Halleck. 'Those who need the bill most cannot come. They are sick and weak, poor and ignorant, and they do not know how to protect themselves, and cannot afford to come'" (243–44). Over and over, Bacon demonstrates in real life what Mary does in fiction: often, those who are powerless need those with privilege to tell their stories for them to people they can't access themselves. Not every firsthand voice is able to tell their own stories in every situation. Accordingly, another way of framing Mary's and Bacon's portrayals of activism and storytelling is as what Leona W. Fisher calls "bridge texts" in historical children's fiction. These stories "provide links between two entities" to child readers, shifting them "from their unexamined ideological positions or cultural expectations to the 'new' or unfamiliar subject positions" in the books (L. W. Fisher 131). Fisher asserts that a successful bridge text "both destabilizes and complicates the child's sense of centrality in her universe and reaffirms the universality of such themes as courage, communication, and hope for the future" (134). This concept allows room to interrogate *Mary Ware's Promised Land*, and Mary's storytelling itself, as bridge narratives between sick, marginalized individuals and child readers who need to be made aware that these conditions exist.

Storytelling in the *Little Colonel* books and *Beauty for Ashes* reveals disadvantages of applying too-simplistic binaries about activism and narratives regarding social justice, especially in terms of intersectionality, social issues, and inequalities. In 1989, Patricia Hill Collins advocated that "we must shift our discourse away from" reductive "either/or dichotomous thinking" where "persons, things and ideas are conceptualized in terms of their opposites," and instead, we might view connections, view things occupying "both/and" identities and classifications (72–73). The approach of firsthand or own voices in storytelling has too often become an either-or binary in critical discourse. When receiving the Children's Literature Associations 2019 Phoenix Award in Indianapolis, speaking just blocks away from where Albion Fellows Bacon lobbied for sanitary living conditions and housing reform a century earlier, Christopher Myers shared his concern with social activism movements oversimplifying who has the right to tell a story and even silencing storytellers. He celebrated the valuable role of storytellers in communities and societies, and said, "I am not always comfortable with any philosophy that implies that we should only talk about ourselves, that the wings of our imaginations should be pinned, that storytellers are somehow useless to the project of witness. . . . We need not only those voices that can witness their own experiences, but can use the craft of storytelling to share across cultural gaps" (Myers). Michelle H. Martin uses the term "polyphonic" to describe research and teaching put in conversation with one another (220), where "voices that would normally speak only among themselves and only from the margins play a central role in parts of the discussion" (220). From theoretical as well as personal experience, I know that there are no answers or approaches that will satisfy everyone. There are just as many people who argue that those *with* privilege should be involved in the majority of the labor to address systemic oppression as there are people who advocate that those outside the disadvantaged group should not be involved in any way at all. However, I advocate that a polyphonic approach to confronting systemic oppression, bearing witness via storytelling and counterstorytelling in multiple mediums, is essential to give us a more complete picture of contemporary issues.

Bacon herself notes the practical advantages of polyphonic storytelling in her own meetings: "Here were mingled farmers' wives, women of wealth, women who worked for a living, college women, and women who had come into the clubs for the very purpose of getting the educational advantages they had been denied. Each one could teach the others out of her own experience, and their range was deep and wide" (262). Yet Bacon's and Johnston's books also demonstrate key silences, erasures, and misinformation and are more effective advocates for some people's health stories, especially white children, than others. As Bacon herself learned to do, it is possible to confront personal assumptions, misinformation, and structural oppressions in order to continually address issues without silencing those whose voices should be centered. Bacon acknowledges both hers and other women's privileges as well as their—our—responsibilities:

> "Sheltered"—that is what I was, and what thousands of other women are who have not seen life and who do not want to see it as it really is . . . that could be prevented and that they might help prevent. . . . And so sheltered women go on, sleep-walking, over trestles and dangerous places, sometimes with babies in their arms.
> And the ones who are not sheltered—! (22)

Bacon writes that her practical experiences "made clear to me the necessity of dealing with individuals" (51), and demonstrates repeatedly the ways in which different situations require a variety of active responses to empower those who are disadvantaged. Long before the disease-model of addiction became commonplace, Bacon's text debunks the idea that individuals—or their spouses—are to blame for alcohol consumption and addiction. She argues vehemently against those who claim poor, sick citizens are lazy or "shiftless," and writes "'Lazy'!" in astonishment, pointing out the systems of oppression in effect: "their mothers were overworked and under-nourished" and they, too "over-worked and under-fed, or have lost their efficiency through illness or exposure. And they breathe poisonous air . . . drink sewage-poisoned water" (139). She is enraged as privileged people condemn the poor as

> "having a pauper spirit," just as it would if a crowd mocked at a child for its weakness, or laughed at a lame man because he could not run or a blind man because he stumbled. The poor are lame, maimed, halt [sic], blind, in a way. They may not be defective enough to admit them to an asylum, but they are too defective, mentally and physically, to keep up in the race. (139)

Bacon recognizes lack of resources as well as responsibilities, and she repeatedly includes those most affected and their articulated needs and stories in the decision-making process and in her legislative work. Additionally, whether it is learning a job skill, providing a safe place for working girls and women to have lunches without sexual harassment, or fighting for a clean and sanitary water source for a tenement house, Bacon not only responds to each specific situation with individualized care, but is constantly questioning and changing her own perceptions. From her initial inclinations, so like her childhood habit of shutting her eyes and putting her fingers in her ears whenever something distresses her, Bacon not only moves toward acknowledging her privileges, but she actively uses them in service of others, all while centering the voices of those too sick and disenfranchised to speak for themselves.

Likewise, Mary Ware's social work is not the same charming, womanly, self-serving Christian charity that Lloyd and Betty have carried out in earlier books, but rather, a patriarchy-confronting challenge to the system that keeps poor people in perpetual ill health and a call for institutional reform. Mary demonstrates a more collaborative coalition between privileged girls with social obligation, the media, activists, and the disenfranchised people who need their help.

CONCLUSION

It is possible to argue that the *Little Colonel*'s female-dominated community functions as either a source of power or a repressed social stagnation. I suggest more nuanced answers are found in intersections of gender, race, class, health, and power that are too complicated for reductive binaries. Contextualizing Johnston's series with her sister's reform work and writings demonstrates the complexities of narrative and counternarrative as activism. Although the locus of power is still with white women of a certain class, Johnston's *Little Colonel* books and Bacon's *Beauty for Ashes* nevertheless offer progressive views of what it can mean to be a girl and a woman, as well as demonstrate ways in which women and children have real power to bring about social changes. In a few significant places, they are even authorities over men and patriarchal systems.

The texts resist tidy readings, and, even with problematic erasures, they demonstrate that children and young women can be trusted advocates, develop relationships, and act as points of contact for marginalized citizens, especially other children. Johnston's and Bacon's works are especially useful for demonstrating the effectiveness of using historical works to illuminate or illustrate contemporary structural oppressions both inside and outside of the text. Multiple stories do and must coexist. A polyphonic approach to confronting systemic oppression is essential. Johnston's and Bacon's collective work demonstrates the effectiveness of polyphonic storytelling and social activism as ways to use privilege and power to give voice to those who too often go unheard.

NOTES

1. Fan letters to Johnston often detail readers' own charity plays and events.
2. Of course, like everything else in Johnston's series, Black people and their needs are still perceived as separate and not included in Mary's reform work, either.

WORKS CITED

Bacon, Albion Fellows. *Beauty for Ashes*. Dodd, Mead, 1914.

Bell, Lee Anne. *Storytelling for Social Justice: Connecting Narrative and the Arts in Antiracist Teaching*. Routledge, 2019.

Bernstein, Robin. *Racial Innocence: Performing American Childhood from Slavery to Civil Rights*. New York UP, 2011.

Bishop, Rudine Sims. "Mirrors, Windows, and Sliding Glass Doors." *Perspectives*, vol. 6, no. 3, 1990, pp. ix–xi.

Collins, Patricia Hill. "Toward a New Vision: Race, Class, and Gender as Categories of Analysis and Connection." *Race, Sex and Class*, vol. 1, no. 1, 1993, pp. 25–45.

Delgado, Richard, and Jean Stefancic. *Critical Race Theory: An Introduction*. New York UP, 2012.

Ehrenreich, Barbara and Deirdre English. *For Her Own Good: Two Centuries of the Experts' Advice to Women*. Penguin, 2005.

Fisher, Laura R. *Reading for Reform: The Social Work of Literature in the Progressive Era*. U of Minnesota P, 2019.

Fisher, Leona W. "'Bridge' Texts: The Rhetoric of Persuasion in American Children's Realist and Historical Fiction." *Children's Literature Association Quarterly*, vol. 27, no. 3, 2002, pp. 129–35.

Ford, Chandra L., and Collins O. Airhihenbuwa. "Just What Is Critical Race Theory and What's It Doing in a Progressive Field like Public Health?" *Ethnicity and Disease*, vol. 8, suppl. 1, 2018, pp. 223–30.

Hamilton-Honey, Emily. *Turning the Pages of American Girlhood: The Evolution of Girls' Series Fiction, 1865–1930*. McFarland, 2013.

Isenberg, Nancy. *White Trash: The 400-Year Untold History of Class in America*. Penguin, 2016.

Johnston, Annie Fellows. *The Land of the Little Colonel*. L. C., 1929.

Johnston, Annie Fellows. (1895/1904). *The Little Colonel*. L. C. Page.

Johnston, Annie Fellows. *The Little Colonel at Boarding School*. L. C. Page, 1903.

Johnston, Annie Fellows. *The Little Colonel's Christmas Vacation*. L. C. Page, 1905.

Johnston, Annie Fellows. *The Little Colonel's Chum, Mary Ware*. L. C. Page, 1908.

Johnston, Annie Fellows. *The Little Colonel's Hero*. L. C. Page, 1902.

Johnston, Annie Fellows. *The Little Colonel's Holidays*. L. C. Page, 1901.

Johnston, Annie Fellows. *The Little Colonel's House Party*. L. C. Page, 1900.

Johnston, Annie Fellows. *The Little Colonel in Arizona*. L. C. Page, 1904.

Johnston, Annie Fellows. *The Little Colonel's Knight Comes Riding*. L. C. Page, 1907.

Johnston, Annie Fellows. *The Little Colonel: Maid of Honor*. L. C. Page, 1906.

Johnston, Annie Fellows. *Mary Ware in Texas*. L. C. Page, 1910.
Johnston, Annie Fellows. *Mary Ware's Promised Land*. L. C. Page, 1912.
Johnston, Annie Fellows. *The Two Little Knights of Kentucky*. L. C. Page, 1899.
Martin, Michelle H. "Saussure, Sex, and Socially Challenged Teens: A Polyphonic Analysis of Adolescent Fiction." *Children's Literature*, vol. 30, 2002, pp. 215–20.
Myers, Christopher. "Phoenix Picture Book Award Acceptance Speech." Children's Literature Association Conference, 16 June 2019, Indianapolis, IN.
Sardella-Ayres, Dawn. "Rewriting and Re-Whiting *The Little Colonel*: Racial Anxieties, Tomboyism, and Lloyd Sherman." *Children's Literature*, vol. 47, 2019, pp. 79–103.
Sardella-Ayres, Dawn, and Ashley Reese. "Where to From Here? Emerging Conversations on Girls' Literature and Girlhood." *Girlhood Studies*, vol. 3, no. 1, 2020, pp. 33–49.
Solorzano, Daniel, and Tara J. Yosso. "Critical Race Methodology: Counter-Storytelling as an Analytical Framework for Education Research." *Qualitative Inquiry*, vol. 8, no. 1, 2002, pp. 23–44.
Trites, Roberta Seelinger. *Twain, Alcott, and the Birth of the Adolescent Reform Novel*. U of Iowa P, 2007.
Zimring, Carl A. *Clean and White: A History of Environmental Racism in the United States*. New York UP, 2017.

Afterword

WOMEN OF COLOR HEALTH EQUITY COLLECTIVE EXECUTIVE BOARD DISCUSSION

Health Inequities and COVID-19

VANESSA E. MARTÍNEZ-RENUNCIO, DAYNA CAMPBELL, AND JENISE KATALINA

The Women of Color Health Equity Collective ("The Collective"), formerly known as MotherWoman, Inc., is a nonprofit grassroots, movement-building organization based in Springfield, Massachusetts (USA), and led by women of color engaged in community capacity building using a racial and social justice framework. The Collective works explicitly toward health equity and antiracism with a focus on women of color. Our work has gained even more urgency because of the COVID-19 pandemic's disproportionate impact on our communities, especially when looking at morbidity, mortality, and unemployment. We imagine a world without premature death, avoidable hospitalizations, racism, and disproportionately higher death rates in women and girls of color. We imagine a world where the disparities in maternal and infant mortality are not two to three times higher in women of color than their white counterparts. We imagine a world where little girls of color do not have to fear school suspension or expulsion because of the color of their skin. We believe that women of color are powerful and, when valued and supported, are more successful in all areas of their lives, thereby benefiting their children, families, and the larger communities. With a mission and vision so broad, we are tasked with increasing community capacity to support women and families of color in all aspects of daily life (Women of Color Health Equity Collective).

We are thrilled to contribute our insights on health equity to this afterword on *Healthcare in Children's Media*. As an organization committed to fostering health equity in communities, particularly among families of color, we're keenly interested in how children learn about COVID-19, health, and the healthcare system. Whether through books, social observations, or everyday conversations, we value the opportunity to shape these discussions. We extend our gratitude to the editors and writers for providing a platform for our leadership team to express ideas that often stem from our observations. This collaborative afterword, authored by three members of our team who are mothers of color and health equity advocates, aims to facilitate dialogue and share our experiences. While not all discussions directly relate to children's literature, they collectively inform our approach to educating children about health disparities in this field.

GRASSROOTS ORGANIZING

At the Collective, we see grassroots organizations and nonprofits as crucial in confronting historical oppression and narrowing health equity gaps for marginalized communities. These community-led agencies work to mitigate the flaws of our healthcare system under capitalism and white supremacy. Nonprofits often undertake tasks neglected by the government, providing ongoing community support while advocating for proper financial allocation to sustain our efforts.

Despite the important role of nonprofits, a challenge lies in leadership often being disconnected from the community, leading to dire consequences. Many operate with a "white savior complex," focusing on rescuing the "less fortunate" and offering short-term support with limited institutional impact. This model is incomplete for several reasons:

- It is missing a community needs assessment that is community centered and community driven.
- Providing a meal or two is not the same as providing an individual or a family with the necessary resources (e.g., skills, housing, transportation, environmental supports) to be able to have food on their table every day.
- Adaptability to community needs is critical and challenging, as it requires constant self-reflection at the individual and organizational level by engaging in hard questions and truly being willing to make internal changes to organizational structure.
- A better understanding of how nonprofits are rooted in white supremacy culture and the overall impact of interinstitutional structural harm is needed.

We must question the community service model of traditional nonprofit organizations completely in order to go beyond providing short-term community support and instead engaging in long-term institutional and societal change. Otherwise, organizations wishing to do good end up creating minimal sustainable positive change and, in fact, become part of the maintenance of harm in underserved communities.

The Collective challenges these frameworks in its approach to building community capacity. As an organization, we use an equity-empowered approach to governance that centers the voices and lived experiences of women and girls of color. Our consensus-driven decision-making model promotes collaborative thought and group empowerment. We model equity in our work through shared vision, resources, knowledge and skills, and responsibility. Our primary focus is on addressing the unique needs and root causes of inequitable outcomes. As previously mentioned, the Collective works to disrupt racism at the highest level, or what is referred to as *upstream*. This term specifically refers to the indirect and direct causes that lead to poor health status and outcomes. Located upstream are the systems and structures that promote and maintain white supremacy culture and lead marginalized populations *into the stream*. Given that nonprofits are tasked with addressing health outcomes that originate upstream with broader structural failures, the power we have is limited. That said, we can lead as change agents specifically in our communities, but we do have to be culturally humble in our role. Being culturally humble means that we self-reflect, ask questions, listen and learn, and work with (not over) our communities, knowing that we might make mistakes and need to repair relationships along the way. In our experiences, nonprofits can continue to help people while *in the stream* and at the same time work to *change the circumstances that have led the people to the stream*.

The Collective, and others like us, are working to close health equity gaps by increasing community capacity through training, consulting, coaching, advocacy, research, and engaging communities in working groups and dialogue-based focus groups. The very foundation of our work is the collective effort of people coming together for a cause—a movement.

Training and consulting remain at the forefront of our work. Specifically, our efforts to build community capacity involve working in partnership with local organizations to understand and be more accountable for their role in maintaining white supremacy culture, repair and rebuild relationships, and disrupt structural racism in policy and practice. We coach organizations around designing and implementing strategies to create a more equitable workplace and be better equipped to provide services using the lens of cultural humility. This work does not take a one-size-fits-all approach. In fact, we recognize that each organization has its own unique differences, so we tailor our scope of work to meet the specific needs. Along with this work, we engage in projects such as this afterword that provide a space for our voices to be heard.

Another of our efforts includes the writing of a book by our children on racial equity. This project, organized by one of our student interns, has engaged several of our children in thinking about racial equity and what this means to children of different ages. The outcome is a pictorial and verbal expression of what racial equity means, to kid readers from kid storytellers.

This racial equity work fits nicely into two genres of children's literature: formulaic issue books and problem novels. They allow for the multiple and varying understandings of real-world experiences and concerns that children are having although children's literature scholars tend to shy away from this genre. For example, when school re-opened during the pandemic, Board President Dayna's eight-year-old daughter attended a predominantly white school where mask wearing was optional. Dayna was adamant that her daughter wear her mask in public and school to protect herself. Her daughter agreed, but with many of the kids around her not wearing their masks in school, she felt awkward sometimes. The girl's friends all had differing opinions about COVID-19, mask wearing, and vaccinations, assumed to be from their parents. This situation could be represented in children's literature to show the varying ways that COVID-19 as an issue and mask mandates as a problem could be addressed by children. But how can they share their differing opinions and not put their friendships and classmate relationships in jeopardy? How do we teach our kids that we can respectfully disagree and open lines of communication and understanding, particularly when the issues intersect with race, class, and health?

REPRESENTATION MATTERS: DISRUPTING CURRENT SYSTEMS OF OPPRESSION

How do we raise children of color to be more empowered by who they are if there is not a substantial shift in how they are represented in children's literature? Our leadership team are all over forty years old and remember having significantly less availability of diverse representation of Black and brown people in the books we read as kids. The three of us who have children have done our best to provide a more diverse and accurate representation of different American communities. Representation is particularly important when thinking about mental health and well-being for marginalized people given our lived experiences with white supremacy. We are trying, as individuals and a collective team of moms of color, to use our *own* voices to tell our *own* stories to our children. Vanessa, our director of operations, a bilingual light-skinned Latina with a three-year-old daughter, finds that one of her greatest challenges is finding bilingual books that engage in the kinds of equity-focused

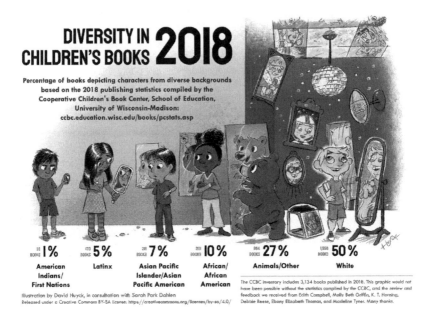

Figure 4.1. "Picture This: Diversity in Children's Literature 2018 Infographic." Image by Sarah Park Dahlen and David Huyck.

dialogue building for children. To address this, she uses diverse and radical books written in English, like *Antiracist Baby* by Ibram X. Kendi and *The Water Protectors* by Carole Lindstrom, as a way to engage in difficult conversations with her daughter about kindness, fairness, and equity in both languages. Then she finds bilingual or Spanish-only books about Latinx people, their holidays, their music, and other forms of visible culture to share the Spanish language and engage with her daughter about race and other forms of difference. This takes time, effort, and mental energy while living in a society that seemingly promotes love for diversity while also, contradictorily, pressuring assimilation.

While representation of marginalized communities has increased over time, the actual number of texts published with central characters of marginalized identities that are both accurately represented and of high quality continue to be disproportionately low. Sarah Park Dahlen, an associate professor of library and information science at the University of Illinois Urbana-Champaign, and illustrator David Huyck cocreate infographics tracking representation of people of color in children's books. From 2015 to 2018, they reported an increase in representation but also a continuing problem. For example, 14 percent of the children's books published in 2015 had people of color representation while 23 percent of the books published in 2018 had people of color representation, showing an increase in the quantity of books available with a nonwhite cast of characters. However, the 2018 infographic demonstrates how the representation is still flawed via the broken mirror elements (see figure 4.1). The numerical increase does not address other issues like quality of representation and range of representation or issues of global representation and other markets outside the United States.

One of the things that struck us the most in these infographics was that while white people's representation did significantly decrease (73 percent to 50 percent), representation for kids of color did not increase as significantly (14 percent to 23 percent). Where did the rest of the diverse representation go? Did it go into the number of animals and trucks being used as central characters? Instead of seeing a significant rise in diverse representation of people, the movement for equity seems to mean a move toward supposedly racially neutral animals and inanimate objects being anthropomorphized or humanized. This seems in line with the philosophy of color blindness, asking for us not to see color and therefore erase the differentiated lived experiences of people of color. On the issue of quality and accuracy of representation: How complex and radical would Helen Keller's story as a woman with disabilities be if we also learned about her socialist political actions and fighting for the working class?

We at the Collective believe that we are at a critical moment in children's literature when diverse representation of marginalized communities seems more accessible than ever before. We have an opportunity to capitalize on this timing while minds are open and wanting innovative and novel ideas to teach our youth about complex ideologies like antiracism, cultural humility, social justice, and so on. Using a new model for nonprofits, like that of the Collective as a framework for educating youth, we can prevent these kids from perpetuating the broken systems that lead people into the stream. But what does that look like in real life? First, adults must center children, their ideas, and their perspectives in order to better listen to children's needs and concerns. How might engaging with children before the writing process about the stories they want to see potentially shift the field of children's literature? Second, children's literature could take advantage of the opportunity to model a more realistic representation of *true* multiculturalism within a community. For example, children's authors and publishing companies could create and publish new books that show diverse friendships where the white-identifying kids do not outnumber the other groups. Or how about highlighting the friendship groups of children with disabilities without forcing them to exist within mainstream ideals? Or how about telling stories about the challenges children have in navigating adult terminology and understanding of racism and the difficulties parents have teaching racial equity and resilience in a world dictating sameness? In response, these books would then project less tokenism and include opportunities for children to learn and live by the tenets of cultural humility and antiracism.

CONCLUSION: THE FUTURE IS YOUNG

While we have seen a marked increase in representation of kids from marginalized backgrounds, including kids of color and kids with disabilities, one area that would benefit from exploration by children's literature authors and the publication industry as a whole is the representation of social movements and communities being led by groups of people instead of individuals. Think about what we know about the civil rights movement. For the majority of the United States, people know a few names of people and places but little else. How different might our understanding of the importance of Rosa Parks be to the larger civil rights movement if her dominant narrative included information about her being trained in nonviolent direct action and community organizing? What if we learned about the young black women that came before her, like fifteen-year-old Claudette Colvin of Montgomery, Alabama, who refused to give up her seat a mere nine months earlier than Rosa Parks? Just this semester, Spring 2024, Vanessa discussed the bus boycotts of the 1950s with her cultural anthropology college students, and none of them knew that Rosa had been trained in civil disobedience and direct action community organizing. Imagine if we taught history less as a series of names and dates and more as complex stories of inaction and action in the world?

Think about what we know about COVID-19 and the health equity issues that were made visible related to who was getting sick and dying more and whose communities were disproportionately without the vaccine. Looking at the available children's literature on COVID-19—like *My Hero Is You* by the Inter-Agency Standing Committee or *The Princess in Black and the Case of the Coronavirus* by Shannon Hale and Dean Hale—the focus has been on making sure kids understand the value of wearing masks, personal hygiene, and social distancing. And understandably so. But what is lacking from the stories for children about COVID-19 is the differing impacts it was having across the globe and in different racial and ethnic communities. Other stories that are missing involve the mental health impacts of isolation and even gratitude for *all* of our most vulnerable essential workers—janitors, grocery store workers, and agricultural workers along with our healthcare workers. Are these stories forthcoming? Will they be written in a nod to this experience years from now?

Children's literature often overlooks the impact of nonprofits, grassroots efforts, and collective action in shaping our world. Picture a book showcasing mutual aid programs filling gaps when governments fail, like during the

Texas winter storm of February 2021. Envision the narrative of a woman-of-color-led nonprofit emerging from racialized trauma, inspiring children with models of collaboration, innovation, and hope. Yet both children's and adult literature often focus on exceptional individuals, neglecting the power of collective action. As Margaret Mead said, "Never doubt that a small group of thoughtful committed citizens can change the world." We advocate for nonprofit and social movement leaders to spotlight health inequities, particularly in children's literature. By instilling in the next generation the belief in their capacity for change, we nurture future radical thinkers, community activists, healthcare professionals, and teachers who will begin early as change agents in their communities.

WORKS CITED

Hale, Shannon, and Dean Hale. *The Princess in Black and the Case of the Coronavirus*, Candlewick Press, 2020.

Huyck, David, and Sarah Park Dahlen. "Picture This: Diversity in Children's Books 2018 Infographic." Created in consultation with Edith Campbell, Molly Beth Griffin, K. T. Horning, Debbie Reese, Ebony Elizabeth Thomas, and Madeline Tyner, statistics compiled by the Cooperative Children's Book Center, School of Education, University of Wisconsin-Madison, *Reading Spark*, 19 June 2019, https://readingspark.wordpress.com/2019/06/19/picture-this-diversity-in-childrens-books-2018-infographic.

Huyck, David, et al. "Diversity in Children's Books 2015 Infographic." Statistics compiled by the Cooperative Children's Book Center, School of Education, University of Wisconsin-Madison, *Reading Spark*, 14 Sep. 2016, https://readingspark.wordpress.com/2016/09/14/picture-this-reflecting-diversity-in-childrens-book-publishing.

Inter-Agency Standing Committee. *My Hero Is You*. 2020, https://interagencystandingcommittee.org/iasc-reference-group-mental-health-and-psychosocial-support-emergency-settings/my-hero-you-storybook-children-covid-19.

Kendi, Ibram X. *Antiracist Baby*. Kokila, 2020.

Lindstrom, Carole. *The Water Protectors*. Roaring Brook Press, 2020.

Women of Color Health Equity Collective "Welcome Message." 2021, https://wochec.org/.

APPENDIX: FURTHER READING

DiAngelo, Robin, and Özlem Sensoy. "Getting Slammed: White Depictions of Race Discussions as Arenas of Violence." *Race Ethnicity and Education*, vol. 17, no. 1, 2014, pp. 103–28, https://doi.org/10.1080/13613324.2012.674023.

Kaiser Family Foundation. *KFF*. 2022, https://kff.org.

Liu, Sabrina R., and Sheila Modir. "The Outbreak That Was Always Here: Racial Trauma in the Context of COVID-19 and Implications for Mental Health Providers." *Psychological Trauma: Theory, Research, Practice, and Policy*, vol. 12, no. 5, 2020, pp. 439–42, https://doi.org/10.1037/tra0000784.

Los Angeles Nurse. "A Tale of Two Hospitals." *Medium*, 19 Mar. 2020, https://seiu121rn.medium.com/a-tale-of-two-hospitals-a91048057a52.

Mills, Charles W. "Global White Supremacy." *White Privilege: Essential Readings on the Other Side of Racism*, 3rd ed., edited by Paula S. Rothenberg, Worth, 2008, pp. 97–104.

Petersen, Emily E. "Racial/Ethnic Disparities in Pregnancy-Related Deaths—United States, 2007–2016." *Morbidity and Mortality Weekly Report*, vol. 68, no. 35, 2019, pp. 762–65. *CDC*, https://doi.org/10.15585/mmwr.mm6835a3.

Pitts, Andrea. "White Supremacy, Mass Incarceration, and Clinical Medicine: A Critical Analysis of U.S. Correctional Healthcare." *Radical Philosophy Review*, vol. 18, no. 2, 2015, pp. 267–85, https://doi.org/10.5840/radphilrev201412827.

Ratcliff, Kathryn Strother. *The Social Determinants of Health: Looking Upstream*. Polity Press, 2017.

Smith, Andrea. "Heteropatriarchy and the Three Pillars of White Supremacy: Rethinking Women of Color Organizing." *Transformations: Feminist Pathways to Global Change*, edited by Torry D. Dickinson and Robert K. Schaeffer, Routledge, 2015, pp. 66–73.

Washington, Harriet A. *Medical Apartheid: The Dark History of Medical Experimentation on Black Americans from Colonial Times to the Present*. Anchor, 2008.

Wheelis, Mark. "Biological Warfare before 1914." In *Biological and Toxin weapons: Research, Development and Use from the Middle Ages to 1945*, edited by Erhard Geissler, and John Ellis van Courtland Moon, Oxford UP, 1999, pp. 8–34.

ABOUT THE CONTRIBUTORS

Anna Bugajska, PhD, is an Associate Professor at the Ignatianum University in Cracow, where she is the head of the Language and Culture Studies Department and the Institute of Modern Languages. She collaborates closely with the General and Applied Ethics Department and gives classes on ethics, biopolitics, and utopianism. She is a member of the Utopian Studies Society–Europe and the City and Philosophy Association. She is the author of *Engineering Youth: An Evantropian Project in Young Adult Dystopias* (2019), as well as numerous articles on the ethical aspects of biotechnologies, as well as posthumanism and transhumanism.

Dayna Campbell is an assistant professor at American International College's School of Health Sciences and president of the Board of Directors and co-executive director of the Women of Color Health Equity Collective. She champions empowerment and resilience for women of color, families, and communities. With expertise in cultural humility and community-based research, Dayna trains future public health professionals and lectures on diversity, inclusion, and health disparities. Her research focuses on women's health, particularly reproductive health and pregnancy outcomes. Dayna holds graduate degrees from the Arnold School of Public Health, University of South Carolina.

Dallas Ducar (she/her), CEO of Transhealth, is a trailblazer in healthcare, focusing on transformative and affirming care. A faculty member at the University of Virginia School of Nursing, Columbia University, and the MGH Institute for Health Professions, Dallas is a Fellow of the American Academy of Nursing. Her leadership extends to roles such as co-chair of the Health Care Alliance and the Official Transition Team of the Attorney General of Massachussetts. She is deeply involved in health policy, advocating for equity and ethics. Dallas serves on several boards and actively advises on gender-affirming healthcare practices nationally.

Sudeshna Shome Ghosh is an editor and writer based in Bangalore. She has worked in the publishing industry for two decades at Penguin and Rupa, where she headed their children's publishing imprints. Presently, she is publisher of Talking Cub, the children's imprint of Speaking Tiger. She is also partner and co-librarian at Cosy Nook Library, a children's library in Bangalore.

Melanie Goss currently serves as an academic advisor and instructor at the University of North Carolina at Chapel Hill. She holds a PhD in English studies from Illinois State University. Her research interests in children's literature include representations of disability and neurodivergence in contemporary young adult texts.

Joseph Holloway achieved his doctorate from the University of Exeter in 2023 in English literature, specializing in critical disability studies. His research uses psychoanalysis and phenomenology to analyze nondisabled cultural representations of disability with a view to expose, explain, and resist the underlying ableism. He teaches at the University of Exeter and is the book review manager for *Literature and History* (SAGE). He is organizer of the Psychoanalysis for Critical Disability Studies network and reading group and can be followed on X via @EngTwiterature.

Jeremy Johnston (he/him) is an assistant professor of children's and young adult literature with the English Department at Illinois State University. His current research focuses on the intersections of adolescent mental health, gender, and neoliberal capitalism. His work has appeared in the *Children's Literature Association Quarterly*.

Manjushri Karthikeyan is a third-year undergraduate student studying neuroscience and human health at Emory University in Atlanta, Georgia. Outside of working as a research assistant for Dr. Valerie A. Ubbes, Manju currently works in addiction and biopsychology research, investigating the influences of prenatal substance exposure on developmental outcomes. She is passionate about bridging clinical discoveries with improved patient care, particularly through her research initiatives and scientific writing. Manju hopes to become a physician one day, continuing her passions to reform the future of health literacy and medical care.

Jenise Katalina is a healthy families resource specialist at the Children's Trust, a statewide agency focused on stopping child abuse in Massachusetts. She is the vice-resident of the Board of Directors and co-executive director for the Women of Color Health Equity Collective, a nonprofit organization based out of Western Mass dedicated to supporting the empowerment and resilience of women of color, families, and communities. Jenise is a licensed independent social worker and a certified trainer in trauma-focused models. She has studied the culturally humility framework and trains institutions striving to incorporate a culturally humble racial equity lens.

Sarah Layzell (they/she), PhD, is a writer and editor. Their research focuses on economics in children's literature and sports in children's literature. Sarah is a coeditor of *Song of the Land: Celebrating the Works of Mildred D. Taylor* (UPM, 2025) and the author of children's novel *Cottonopolis* (Northodox Press, 2024).

Naomi Lesley (she/her) is a professor of English at Holyoke Community College. She is the author of *Fictions of Integration*, an examination of children's literature about the legacies of school desegregation. Her previous research has focused on issues of race, education, and citizenship.

Anna Macdonald (she/they) is the Graphic Medicine project manager for Comics Youth CIC. She has worked at Comics Youth since 2019 and took on the management of the Graphic Medicine project in early 2020. It's such a fabulous project to work on, and they're so proud of the work Comics Youth have created together with the young people they support.

Vanessa E. Martínez-Renuncio, PhD, is a professor, leader, trainer, researcher, and advocate with over twenty years experience. She is a professor of anthropology and the community-based learning coordinator at Holyoke Community College. She is on the leadership team for the Women of Color Health Equity Collective. Vanessa is a trained cultural and medical anthropologist whose community-based research specializes in health equity and culturally responsive pedagogy. Vanessa received her bachelors of science from Columbus State University in sociology, her masters of arts in applied anthropology from Georgia State University and her PhD in anthropology from the University of Massachusetts, Amherst.

Nichole Mayweather-Banks (she/her) is a licensed clinical social worker (LCSW) in the state of Connecticut. She is the founder of Changing FACES Counseling and Wellness LLC, a Black, female, queer-owned therapy practice. Her work with gender-expansive clients helps enhance skills that encourage sustainable personal growth and coping with life transitions. She is an experienced lecturer and trainer on cultural humility and transgender homelessness. Nichole is a skilled community organizer and an AmerCorps VISTA alumni. She has supported several populations throughout her professional career to include early childhood, teen parents, mentoring, juvenile justice, and substance use.

Madison Miner (she/her) graduated from Miami University in Oxford, Ohio, in May 2023. Madison was a member of the University Honors College, and she completed her undergraduate degree with a major in public health, a co-major in pre-medical studies, and a minor in Spanish. During her time at Miami University, Madison worked as a HAWKS peer health educator and as a research assistant with Dr. Valerie Ubbes. In the summer of 2024, Madison will continue her education as a medical student attending Wake Forest University School of Medicine in Winston-Salem, North Carolina.

Dawn Sardella-Ayres received her PhD from the University of Cambridge in 2016, and has published on Alcott, Montgomery, Johnston, and Wilder. Her critical work explores girls' literature as a distinct genre, rooted in theories of genre as social action.

Farriba Schulz (she/her), PhD, is a senior lecturer in the Institute of Education at Humboldt-Universität zu Berlin and Universität Potsdam. Her research interest centers on construction of childhoods, (visual) literacy, inclusion with and in children's literature, and working collaboratively with schools, cultural institutions, and artists. She is a member of the advisory board of The Child and the Book, coeditor of *Political Changes and Transformations in Twentieth and Twenty-first Century Children's Literature* (2023), and since 2023, the Humboldt-Universität zu Berlin coordinator and academic lead in Seen and Heard: Young People's Voices and Freedom of Expression (https://seenandheardproject.eu/).

Carrie Spencer (she/her) is a PhD researcher taking a care ethics approach to mad mothers in contemporary young adult literature at the University of Cambridge. Her research focuses on relational values and principles as disruption, transgression, or positive alternative in young adult literature. Her published work has examined representations of the Anthropocene in speculative YA and offered a queer analysis of binary narrative structures in YA genre fiction (*International Journal of Young Adult Literature*).

Antje Tannen (she/her), PhD, is a nursing scientist, health scientist, and a senior lecturer in the Institute of Clinical Nursing Sciences at the Charité—Universitätmedizin Berlin, Germany. As medical instructor she teaches in a bachelor's program for nurses, with a focus on child and youth health. Current research fields are school health nursing, transition of young people into adult medicine, and family-centered care of families with preterm infants.

ABOUT THE CONTRIBUTORS

Valerie A. Ubbes is a professor emerita in the Department of Kinesiology, Nutrition, and Health at Miami University (Oxford, Ohio). Dr. Ubbes is a master certified health education specialist with a commitment to promoting the health education needs of children and youth through school-university-community partnerships. Her scholarship focuses on health literacy and skill-based health education. She was a co-writer of the National Health Education Standards (3rd ed.), released by the National Consensus on School Health Education in 2022. Her website, Digital Literacy Partnership at Miami University (https://dlp.lib.miamioh.edu), has an international reach to advance literacy, health, and technology on learning.

B.J. Woodstein has experienced hyperemesis gravidarum twice. She is an honorary professor in literature and translation at the University of East Anglia in England. She's also a writer, editor, Swedish-to-English translator, and consultant within equality, diversity, and inclusion. She is the author of a number of books, including *We're Here! A Practical Guide to Becoming an LGBTQ+ Parent*, *The Portrayal of Breastfeeding in Literature*, *Translation and Genre*; the editor of several books on literature; and the translator or writer of many other essays, articles, short stories, and other texts. Her most recent translations are Jenny Jägerfeld's *King Bro!* and Sara Stridsberg and Beatrice Alemagna's *We Go to the Park*. B.J. can be reached at bjwoodstein@gmail.com.

INDEX

Page references in *italics* indicate figures/tables.

Abani, Chris, 61
abjection, 68–69, 277–78
Abject Relations (Warin), 250
accessibility: of addiction treatment, 37–38, 43–44, 53; as barrier to healthcare, 8–9, 10–11, 12–13, 16n4; in *eBook for Oral Health Literacy©* curriculum, 173
Adamson, Heather, 169
addiction. *See* substance use disorder (SUD)
adulthood, in children's literature, 46–48, 49, 122–23. *See also* community networks
Aging and Self-Realization (Laceulle), 122
Airhihenbuwa, Collins O., 270
Albright, Kendra S., 7
Alcott, Louisa May, 268
Alder Hey Children's Hospital, 111, 112, 116
ALife. *See* artificial life (ALife)
Alkaf, Hanna, 257
All the Bright Places (Niven), 252
All the Days Past, All the Days to Come (Taylor), 3
allyship, importance of, 24, 29–30, 118
Alston, Ann, 69
Alston, Philip, 13
Alzheimer's disease. *See* dementia
American Academy of Pediatric Dentistry, 166, 183n6
American Academy of Pediatrics, 166, 179
American Dental Association, 166
American Medical Association, 165
American Psychiatric Foundation, 251

Angel Experiment (Patterson), 212–13
animals: in dementia care, 135–36; human-animal hybrid characters, 212–13; posthumans linked to, 210, 211; in *Teen Wolf*, 227; veterinary ethics, 214–17
animals as characters: and depictions of racial diversity, 154, 294–95, *294*; and health literacy, 182n2
anthropocentrism, 207, 209, 210, 211, 212, 215, 216
Applebaum, Noga, 208–9
appropriation, of narratives, 277–79
Archie's Grand Plan (Lowthian), 119
artificial life (ALife), 204–20; defined, 205; and ethics of care, 205–8; in juvenile fiction, 208–14; and veterinary ethics, 214–17
Art of Starving, The (Miller), 256
Asylum (Roux), 255–56
Attard twins, 60, 62–64
At the Dentist (Schuh), 178
Auf meinem Rücken wächst ein Garten (There Is a Garden Growing on My Back) (Unterholzner and Leitl), 130–32
Austin, LeAne, 148
Aveling, Helen A., 5

Bacon, Albion Fellows: *Beauty for Ashes*, 267, 271–72, 284; and housing reform, 266–67, 280, 282–83; and storytelling, 264, 280, 284, 285–87
Baltimore College of Dental Surgery, 165

INDEX

Barrie, J. M., 12
Beauty for Ashes (Bacon), 267, 271–72, 284
Becker, Saul, 144, 155
Belkin, Aaron, 88, 89, 102n2
Bell, Lee Anne, 264
Bend in Time, A (Vachharajani et al.), 199–203
Berlin, Isaiah, 218
Berridge, Virginia, 12
Bibby, Andrew, 144
bibliotherapy, 15; defined, 126, 152; picturebooks on dementia as, 121, 126; picturebooks on hyperemesis gravidarum as, 152. *See also* health literacy
bilingual books, 293–94
bioethics, 4, 11, 207
biotechnology. *See* artificial life (ALife)
Bishop, Rudine Sims, 264
Bitenc, Rebecca A., 122
Black Americans: and 1970s heroin crisis, 49–50; in Bacon's memoir, 271–73; in *The Hate U Give*, 44–45, 47, 50–51; in *A Hero Ain't Nothin' but a Sandwich*, 47–48, 49–50; in *Little Colonel* books, 270–71; in Taylor's series, 3
Black Lives Matter movement, 51
body ownership, and conjoinment, 66–67, 71–76, 79–80
book bans, 26–27
bookstores, 202
Braidotti, Rosa, 206, 220n4
Braun, Patricia A., 166
Bridges, Tristan, 88
bridge texts, 284–85
Bruner, Jerome, 132–33
Buffy the Vampire Slayer (television series), 233
Bugajska, Anna, 11, 15
buprenorphine, 39, 54n7
burden narratives, 120

Cadden, Mike, 59–60
Campbell, Dayna, 16
care ethics, 7–8; and artificial life, 205–8; development of, 225–26; four principles of, 232–33; and juvenile novel scholarship, 228–29. *See also* care ethics, in *Teen Wolf*
care ethics, in *Teen Wolf*, 225–43; and friendship groups, 232–37; and hospital policy, 237–42; and patient-practitioner relationship, 229–32
care relationships, in picturebooks on dementia, *128*, 129–30. *See also* child caregiving
Caring For Our Bodies book series, 178
censorship, 26–27, 39–40
Center for Disease Control (CDC, US), 10
Challenger Deep (Shusterman), 252, 260
Chamberlin, Jamie, 145
Changing FACES Counseling & Wellness, 21
Charity Mind, 13
child caregiving: in picturebooks on hyperemesis gravidarum, 141–42, 143–45, 146, 147–48, 149–50, 155; positive aspects of, 159n14; in US, 143
children: ability to enact social change, 279; writing and publishing by, 110, 119, 199–203, 293
Childress, Alice, 38
Chrisman, Alyssa, 6
chronic illness, 157
Chronic Youth (Elman), 249
Church, Imogen, 6
civil rights movement, teaching about, 296
Clare, Eli, 61, 66
Clark, Melinda B., 166
Clark, Rosalyn, 177, 178
Clean and White (Zimring), 271–72
clones, in Matt Alacrán duology, 208, 209–11
Colbert, Brandy, 42
collage, 130–31
Colledge, Paul, 145
Collins, Patricia Hill, 285
Comics Youth, 15; *Hospi-Tales* anthology, 112–16; and LGBTQIA+ youth, 117–19; Marginal Publishing House, 110; mission, 109; Pencil Pals program, 111–12, 116; projects, 110–12; and remote support, 116–17
community networks: and allyship, 24, 29–30, 118; and librarians promoting oral health literacy, 167–68, 178–80; in *Little Colonel* books and Bacon's work, 272, 274–75, 281–84, 287; in substance abuse recovery, 37, 38–39, 43–48; support groups, 31;

in Taylor's series, 3; twelve-step communities, 44; and Women of Color Health Equity Collective, 290–92, 296–97. *See also* Comics Youth

conjoinment, 59–82; Attard twins, 60, 62–64; and body ownership, 66–67, 79–80; decision making about, 76, 77–79; host/parasite trope, 61–67; "mapping" of, 71–74; "problematic" elements of, 67–71

Connell, R. W., 88

counternarratives, 122, 136–37, 265, 270

Counting Down with You (Bhuiyan), 257

COVID-19 pandemic, 3–4, 5; and bookstores, 202; children's literature on, 296; and Comics Youth, 116–17; Indian anthology of children's writing on, 199–203; and racial equity, 290, 293; and vaccinations, 293, 296

criminal justice system, and substance use, 37, 40–41

critical race theory (CRT), 269–70, 276

Crossan, Sarah. See *One* (Crossan)

Crow, Liz, 8–9, 40, 49

Crowe, Chris, 247

Crum, Anna-Maria, 145

cultural humility, 292

Cultural Variance Framework, 174

Dahlen, Sarah Park, 294

Daniel, Carolyn, 69

Darius the Great Is Not Okay (Khorram), 85–101; father figures in, 86, 92–94, 95–96, 99, 100; form of, 100; masculine silence and mental health in, 92–97, 101; masculine silence critiqued in, 97–101; masculinity's intersection with other identities in, 86–87; militaristic ideas in, 89; queerness in, 87, 89, 95, 98; racial othering in, 91, 93

Day in the Life of a Dentist, A (Adamson), 169

Dean, Caitlin, 145, 152

Delgado, Richard, 270, 276

del Real, Jose A., 43–44

dementia: prevalence of, 124; scholarship on, 121–22; stages of, 124–25; symptoms, 128, 130. *See also* picturebooks on dementia

dental clothing and equipment, in picturebooks on oral health, 169, 170, 177–78

dentistry, history of, 165. *See also* oral health literacy

dentists. *See* medical professionals

Dentists Help (Ready), 169

depression, 54n8; in *Darius the Great*, 92–93, 94, 97, 99; medication for, 42, 92–93; in picturebooks, 156–57

Der alte Schäfer (*The Old Shepherd*) (Elschner and Lauströer), 135–36

Desmond, Matthew, 46

Diagnostic and Statistical Manual of Mental Disorders (*DSM*), 32, 37, 247

Die neue Omi (*The New Grandmother*) (Steinkeller and Roher), 134

digestion, and conjoinment, 68–70, 73–74

disability: medical model of, 16n4, 40, 65–66; social model of, 16n4, 40. *See also* accessibility; conjoinment; disabled people

disability activism, 6, 48–49

disability studies, 8–9, 16n4

"disabled avenger" trope, 65

disabled people: inequalities faced by, 11, 12; parasite depiction of, 64–65; posthumans linked to, 210

Disabling Characters (Dunn), 8, 248

Diseased Brain and the Failing Mind, The (Zimmermann), 122

diversity: and counterstorytelling, 265; lacking in picturebooks on dementia, 136; lacking in picturebooks on hyperemesis gravidarum, 153–54; neurodiversity, 249, 261n4; in picturebooks on oral health, 169, 170, 176–77; and Women of Color Health Equity Collective, 293–96. *See also* gender

drag queen storytelling, 26–27

Dreger, Alice Domurat, 63, 80

Ducar, Dallas, 11, 14; interview with, 21–33

Duckels, Gabriel, 6

Dunn, Patricia, 8, 248

Dyksommar (*The Summer of Diving*) (Stridsberg), 156–57

eating disorders, 250–51, 253, 258–59

eBook for Oral Health Literacy© curriculum, 162, 171–73, 179, 181

economic justice, and gender, 25

Eder, Jens, 124
Ehrenreich, Barbara, 10, 91, 221n14, 273
elders: othering of, 122, 123; trans, 24
electronic texts, 162
Elman, Julie Passanante, 5, 249
Elschner, Géraldine, 135
emotions: and healthcare practice in *Teen Wolf*, 234–35, 242; and masculine silence, 85–86, 88–90, 92, 94, 96–99; in Matt Alacrán duology, 211, 217; in "sick-lit," 71
employment, 11, 64, 91
English, Deirdre, 10, 221n14, 273
environmental racism, 271–72
equity: and gender, 25; health equity, 10, 290–97; and oral health literacy, 173; racial equity, 290, 293
ethics: and artificial life, 205–8; nursing ethics, 206, 220n8; veterinary ethics, 214–17
Ethics in British Children's Literature (Sainsbury), 229
ethics of care. *See* care ethics
Evans, Ruth, 143, 144, 146, 155, 159n14

Falcus, Sarah, 8
Family in English Literature, The (Alston), 69
Fang (Patterson), 213
Farmer, Nancy. *See* Matt Alacrán duology (Farmer)
father figures: in *Darius the Great*, 86, 92–94, 95–96, 99, 100; in picturebooks on hyperemesis gravidarum, 142, 147, 150
First Fact book series, 169
firsthand voices, 281, 285. *See also* storytelling
first-person narration: in *Darius the Great*, 87, 100–101; in *A Hero Ain't Nothin' but a Sandwich*, 38; in *One*, 59–60
Fisher, Berenice, 233
Fisher, Laura R., 267–68, 269
Fisher, Leona W., 284
Fisher, Michael, 44
Flexner Report (1910), 273
food, and conjoinment, 68–70, 73–74
Ford, Chandra L., 270
For Her Own Good (Ehrenreich and English), 273
Forman, James, 49

free verse, 59–60
friendship: in *Darius the Great*, 86; in Matt Alacrán duology, 212; and racial equity, 293, 295; in reform literature, 267, 269; in *Teen Wolf*, 228, 232–37
Front Desk (Yang), 10

Gardner, Faith, 253
Gavigan, Karen W., 7
gender: and economic justice, 25; in picturebooks on dementia, 127, 129; in picturebooks on hyperemesis gravidarum, 146–48, 153–54; in *Teen Wolf*, 229–32. *See also* masculine silence; masculinity; trans youth
gender-affirming healthcare, 23–24
gender theory, 87–88
gene editing, 4. *See also* artificial life (ALife)
German picturebooks, dementia in. *See* picturebooks on dementia
Germany, 4; dementia healthcare in, 125–26; Federal Ministry for Family Affairs, Senior Citizens, Women and Youth, 120, 129
Get Well Soon (Halpern), 255
Ghosh, Sudeshna Shome, 15; interview with, 199–203
Girl on the Line (Gardner), 253
Goatly, Andrew, 248, 256
Goldstein, Joshua S., 88
Goss, Melanie, 4–5, 15, 60
Graphic Medicine, 112–16
graphic novels, 7
grassroots organizing, 291–92
Great Ormond Street Hospital (GOSH), 12
Green, John, 246
Grenier, Amanda, 122
grief: in *Darius the Great*, 87, 95–96; impact on children, 144; in *Little Colonel* books, 277–78; in *One*, 62; in writing by children on COVID-19 pandemic, 200–201
Griffiths, Rhiannon, 112
Gubar, Marah, 39, 47, 53n4, 122–23
Guthrie, Meredith, 5

Haddad, Vincent, 51, 53n4, 54n14
Halberstam, Jack, 61

INDEX

Hamilton-Honey, Emily, 268
Harris, Chapin A., 165
Harrison, Jennifer, 209
Hartung, Heike, 121
Harvey, David, 64
Hate U Give, The (Thomas), 38, 39–40, 44–45, 47, 50–51
Hayden, Horace H., 165
healthcare education, 15
healthcare systems: in Matt Alacrán duology, 210–12; in picturebooks on hyperemesis gravidarum, 142, 147; standardization of, 273; in UK, 12–13; upheavals in, 3–4; in US, 9–11; varieties of, 4–5
healthcare work, in *Teen Wolf*, 227. *See also* medical professionals
health equity, 10, 290–97
health literacy, 6, 15; types of, 175. *See also* bibliotherapy; oral health literacy
Health Literacy: A Prescription to End Confusion (Institute of Medicine), 174–75
Healthy People 2030 initiative (US), 171
hegemonic masculinity, 226
Hernandez, Elein, 214–15
Hero Ain't Nothin' but a Sandwich, A (Childress), 38–39, 40, 44, 47–48, 49–50
heroin crisis, 49–50
Higher Power of Lucky, The (Patron), 38, 39, 45–47, 52
HIV/AIDS, people with, 48–49, 70
Holloway, Joseph, 8, 13, 14
Home Home (Allen-Agostini), 257
hooks, bell, 92, 97
Horowitz, Alice M., 168
Hospi-Tales anthology, 111, 112–16
hospitals: Alder Hey, 111, 112, 116; GOSH, 12; in picturebooks on hyperemesis gravidarum, 147, 152; psychiatric, metaphors around, 254–56, 258–59; in *Teen Wolf*, 237–42
host/parasite trope, 60, 61–67
House of the Scorpion, The (Farmer), 209–10, 212, 215, 217
housing conditions, linked with illness, 271–72, 274, 280–82
How to Be an HG Hero! (Dean and Colledge): elements of, 145–46; gender roles in, 150, 154; medical professionals in, 153; mental health in, 151; overview, 149–50
Huppertz, Nikola, 130
Huyck, David, 294
hyperemesis gravidarum: authorial experience with, 142–43; defined, 141; prevalence of, 145. *See also* picturebooks on hyperemesis gravidarum

I Am Not Your Perfect Mexican Daughter (Sánchez), 42
Ibson, John, 90
illness: dementia, 121–22, 124–25, *128*, 130; hyperemesis gravidarum, 141, 142–43, 145; linked with unsanitary housing conditions, 271–72, 274, 280–81. *See also* COVID-19 pandemic; mental illness; substance use disorder (SUD)
Illness as Metaphor (Sontag), 249–50
immigrant identity, in *Darius the Great*, 91
immigrants, 272
incarceration, and heroin epidemic, 49–50
independence and autonomy, 8
India, effects of COVID-19 pandemic in, 199–203
individualism, and conjoinment, 67
industrialization, and ableism, 64
Institute of Medicine, 10, 174–75
insurance, 9–10, 53n2
intergenerational relationships, and dementia care, 123, 131, 134
intersectionality, importance of, 24–25
Islamophobia, 200
issue books, 156; on hyperemesis gravidarum, 141, 145, 152, 158; on racial equity, 293
Izpisúa Belmonte, Juan Carlos, 217

Jacques, Wesley, 7–8
Jennings, La Vinia Delois, 48, 54nn12–13
Jensen, Kelly, 85
Johnson, Mark, 248, 260
Johnston, Annie Fellows, on charitable work, 268–69. *See also Little Colonel* series (Johnston)
Johnston, Jeremy, 14
Johnston, John, 205

Jones, Eileen H., 152
Joosen, Vanessa, 121, 122–23
Jurecic, Ann, 249

Kale, Kavita Singh, 202
Karthikeyan, Manjushri, 7, 15
Katalina, Jenise, 16
Kavanagh, Amy, 64
Keen, Sam, 88
Keith, Lois, 8
Keller, Evelyn Fox, 249
Khorram, Adib. See *Darius the Great Is Not Okay* (Khorram)
Kimmel, Michael S., 88, 90, 91–92, 102n2
King, Shalinie, 174
Kiss of Broken Glass (Kuderick), 255, 256
Klever, Elsa, 130
Kristeva, Julia, 68
Kurtz, Linda Farris, 44

Laceulle, Hanne, 121, 122
Lacks, Henrietta, 11
Lakoff, George, 248, 260
Lauströer, Jonas, 135
Leitl, Leonora, 130
Lesley, Naomi, 9, 11, 14
Let's Get This ~~Straight~~ (Comics Youth), 118
Let the Circle Be Unbroken (Taylor), 3
LGBTQIA+ adults, 11, 28
LGBTQIA+ youth: and Comics Youth, 117–19; in *Darius the Great*, 87, 89, 95, 98; healthcare for, 14, 21–33
librarians as partners in literature-based dentistry, 163, 175–81; promoting oral health literacy in school-based health centers, 180–81; promoting oral health literacy in school libraries and classrooms, 180; promoting oral health literacy in the community, 178–80
Lilli und ihre vergessliche Oma (*Lilli and Her Forgetful Granny*) (Papp), 120, 135
linguistic relativity, 248–49
literacy, and literature-based dentistry, 175–76. See also oral health literacy
literature-based dentistry. See oral health literacy

Little and Lion (Colbert), 42
Little Colonel series (Johnston), 264–87; activism in, 279–87; appropriation in, 277–79; overview, 266; race in, 270–71; storytelling and silencing in, 273–76
Little Colonel's Holidays, The (Johnston), 275–76, 277–78
Liverpool, UK. See Comics Youth
Lorde, Audre, 67
Lord of Opium, The (Farmer), 210–11
Lowthian, Ray, 119
Lundberg, Sara, 156

Macdonald, Anna, 15; interview with, 109–19
Macy, Beth, 44, 48, 54n7
Mairs, Nancy, 70
Mama Has Hyperemesis Gravidarum (But Only for a While) (McCall and Crum): elements of, 145–46; gender roles in, 154; medical professionals in, 152; mental health in, 151; overview, 146–49
mapping, in *One*, 71–74
Marginal Leadership Programme, 110, 118–19
Marginal Publishing House, 110, 118
Martin, Michelle H., 285
Martínez-Renuncio, Vanessa E., 16
Mary Ware's Promised Land (Johnston), 266, 279–82, 283–84
masculine silence: in *Darius the Great*, 86–87, 89, 92–97, 98–101; defined, 86; historicizing in the US, 87–92
Masculinities (Connell), 88
masculinity: and mental health, 85–86, 92–97; multiplicity of, 88; in *Teen Wolf* film, 226–27, 230; in *Teen Wolf* series, 227, 229–30, 231–32, 242–43; and warrior archetype/militarism, 88–89, 90, 102n2. See also masculine silence
mask-wearing, 293
Massachusetts, shield law in, 23–24
Matt Alacrán duology (Farmer), 208, 209–12, 215–17
Maximum Ride series (Patterson), 208, 212–14, 215–17
Mayweather-Banks, Nichole, 11, 14; interview with, 21–33

McCall, Ashli, 145
McRuer, Robert, 64
medical ethics. *See* ethics
medical experimentation: and bioethics of artificial life, 204, 207, 209; in juvenile fiction, 212; and racial minorities, 11
medical history, 11, 16n6, 273
medicalization: of substance use disorder, 37, 40; of trans identity, 32–33
medical professionals: approaches to children's literature by, 6–7; diversity among, 177; in Matt Alacrán duology, 210–12, 219; in Maximum Ride series, 212–14, 219; partnerships between for oral health literacy, 162–63, 166, 167–75, 178–79, 181–82; in picturebooks on hyperemesis gravidarum, 147, 152–53; in picturebooks on mental health, 156. *See also* ethics
medication: for mental illness, 42, 92–93, 252–53; for substance use disorder, 37, 41, 42, 53, 54n7
Meine Omi, die Wörter und ich (*My Granny, the Words and Me*) (Huppertz and Klever), 130, 132–33
Memory of Light, The (Stork), 256, 258
mental health, 31; and masculine silence, 85–86, 92–97, 101; in picturebooks, 156–57; in picturebooks on hyperemesis gravidarum, 151–52; in UK, 13; in YA fiction, 85. *See also* mental illness
mental illness: defined, 247; as embodied, 257; obsessive-compulsive disorder (OCD), 6, 254, 257, 258–59; representations of, 6; schizophrenia, 42, 251, 260; stigma against medication for, 42; terminology of, 101n1. *See also* depression; mental illness, metaphors of
mental illness, metaphors of, 246–61; as animalistic, 257–58; comparison to physical illness, 251–53; and eating disorders, 250–51; as hurdle to clear vs. road to travel, 247; as invader, 253–54, 257
Messner, Kate, 53n2, 54n16
metaphors: around psychiatric healthcare, 254–56; defined, 248–49. *See also* mental illness, metaphors of

Metaphors We Live By (Lakoff and Johnson), 248
methadone, 39, 43–44, 54n16
Metzger, Lois, 253
Meyer, Abbye E., 8
militarism, and masculinity, 88–89, 90, 102n2, 102n8
Miner, Madison, 7, 15
misinformation, 30–31
Mitchell, David T., 249
Moran, Mary Jeanette, 7, 229
mortality, 70–71
Moskowitz, Hannah, 250
Mosse, George L., 88
Murphy, Patricia, 177
Muslims, 200
Myers, Christopher, 285

narrative pedagogy, 121, 126, 137. *See also* bibliotherapy
Narrative Prosthesis (Mitchell and Snyder), 249
National Alliance on Mental Illness (NAMI, US), 251
National Children's Dental Health Month (US), 180
National Culturally and Linguistically Appropriate Services (CLAS) Standards, 173
National Dementia Strategy (Germany), 120
National Health Education Standards (US), 164
National Health Literacy Month (US), 180
National Health Service (NHS, UK), 12
National Library of Medicine (US), 179
Nature (journal), 166
neoliberalism, 37, 41, 91, 103n10, 238
Ness, Patrick, 258–59
neurodiversity, 249, 261n4. *See also* mental illness
Nikolić, Marija, 174
nonprofits, challenges of, 291
Not Otherwise Specified (Moskowitz), 250, 259
nudging, 176
numeracy, 169

nurses: diversity among, 177; in Matt Alacrán duology, 210–11; in *Teen Wolf*, 229–32, 238–39, 240–42. *See also* medical professionals
nursing ethics, 206, 220n8
Nutbeam, Donald, 175

obsessive-compulsive disorder (OCD), 6, 254, 257, 258–59
Office of Minority Health (US), 173
One (Crossan), 59–82; Attard case recalled by, 60, 62–64; host/parasite trope in, 60, 61–67; individualism in, 60; "mapping" in, 60, 71–74; separation surgery in, 60, 62, 66, 76–79; verse form of, 59–60
online/remote support: and Comics Youth, 116–17; eBook for Oral Health Literacy© curriculum, 162, 171–73, 179, 181; telehealth, 23
opioid crisis, 43, 44
oral health: historical context of, 164–65; as key component of general health, 164–66; picturebooks on, 169–71; scholarship on, 165–66
oral health literacy, 162–95; and cultural variance, 174; defined, 163; eBook for Oral Health Literacy© curriculum, 171–73; factors influencing, 167–68, *168*; and interprofessional partnerships, 162–63, 166, 178–79; interprofessional partnerships in children's literature, 167–75; and librarians, 163, 175–81; and low-income needs, 173; thematic analysis of dental content, *169*
Our Community Helpers book series, 169
Owen, Gabrielle, 39, 45, 53n4
#OwnVoices, 265

Papp, Rika, 120, 135
Parks, Rosa, 296
Pascoe, C. J., 88
patient choice, 237–38, 242
Patron, Susan, 38, 39
Patterson, James. *See* Maximum Ride series (Patterson)
Pebble Plus Healthy Teeth book series, 178
Pencil Pals program, 111–12, 116

person-centered care: in dementia care, 125–26; and oral health literacy, 162; in picturebooks on dementia, *128–29*, 130, 137
Peter Pan (Barrie), 12
Philbin, Morgan M., 179
physicians. *See* medical professionals
picturebooks, 4; on oral health, 169–71; use of term, 158n1. *See also* picturebooks on dementia; picturebooks on hyperemesis gravidarum
picturebooks on dementia, 120–37; *Auf meinem Rücken wächst ein Garten*, 130–32; *Der alte Schäfer*, 135–36; *Die neue Omi*, 134; *Meine Omi, die Wörter und ich*, 130, 132–33; questions for evaluating, 127; table of, *127–29*
picturebooks on hyperemesis gravidarum, 141–58; children as heroes in, 149–50; children as protectors in, 146–49; elements of, 145–46; lack of diversity in, 153–54; lack of medical professionals in, 152–53; and mental health, 151–52; origins of, 145; positive elements of, 155
police, 39, 50–51
posthumanities. *See* artificial life (ALife)
power structures, in *Teen Wolf*, 229–32, 241–42
pregnancy, 67. *See also* hyperemesis gravidarum
privilege, in *Teen Wolf*, 236. *See also* Little Colonel series (Johnston)
Program, The, series (Young), 252–53
psychiatric healthcare, 261n1; metaphors around, 254–56, 258–59
public health, 7; and disability activism, 49; substance use in, 37
publishers: Marginal Publishing House, 110; self-publishing, 146, 156, 159n7; Talking Cub, 199–203
Puig de la Bellacasa, Maria, 206

queer relationships. *See* LGBTQIA+ youth

racial disparities, 10; in the healthcare workforce, 177. *See also* diversity; health equity
racial equity, 290, 293

racial othering: and animals as characters, 154; in *Darius the Great*, 91, 93; in Johnston's and Bacon's works, 270–73; in *Little Colonel* books, 270–71
Rafalovich, Adam, 44
Reach Out and Read, 179–80
Reading for a Healthy Smile© campaign, 173
"Reading for a Healthy Smile" project, *168*
Reading for Reform (Fisher), 267
Ready, Dee, 169
Reconsidering Dementia Narratives (Bitenc), 122
reform literature, 264–65, 267–69. See also *Little Colonel* series (Johnston)
reform movement, 266–67
rehabilitation programs: twelve-step approach to, 41; in YA novels, 38, 52
representation of marginalized communities, 293–96; and gender identity, 25–29; and *Little Colonel* series, 264–66
reproductive ethics, 216
reproductive healthcare, and shield laws, 23–24
responsibility, shared, and care ethics, 233–34, 235–36
Rest of Us Just Live Here, The (Ness), 258–59
Richmond, Kia Jane, 6, 85
Rigg, Khary, 43
Road to Memphis, The (Taylor), 3
Roher, Michael, 134
Rosenthal, Elisabeth, 10
Roswell (television series), 227–28
Roux, Madeleine, 255–56
Rudd, Rima E., 168
Rutherford, Jonathan, 90
Ryder, Amy, 6

sacrifice surgery. *See* separation surgery
Sáenz, Benjamin Alire, 54n8
Safe Spaces social action campaign, 117
Sainsbury, Lisa, 229
Sako, Katsura, 8
Sánchez, Erika, 42
sanitation/hygiene, 271–72, 280–82
Sapolsky, Robert, 11, 16n7, 43
Sardella-Ayres, Dawn, 11, 16

Saving the World and Other Extreme Sports (Patterson), 213
Savulescu, Julian, 216
schizophrenia, 42, 251, 260
School-Based Health Alliance, 180
school-based health centers, 180–81
schools: and COVID-19 lockdown, 199; mask-wearing in, 293; oral health education in, 164
Schuh, Mari, 178
Schulz, Farriba, 4, 8, 15
science fiction, 204. *See also* artificial life (ALife); *Teen Wolf* (television series)
Secret History of Las Vegas, The (Abani), 61
separation surgery, 60; of Attard twins, 62, 63–64; as disabling, 80–81; in *One*, 62, 66, 76–79
Shakespeare, Tom, 40, 48–49
Shelat, Jay, 45, 53n4
shield laws, 23–24
Shortman, Amanda, 152
Shusterman, Neal, 260
sick-lit genre, 5–6, 71
silence. *See* masculine silence
Skin (Vrettos), 256, 259
Skin and Bones (Shahan), 256
Smallville (television series), 227–28
Smith, Clint, 51
Smith, Penny, 170
smoking, 74–76
Snyder, Sharon L., 249
social capital, 43–44, 48
social media, 30–31
social role models, and oral health literacy, 176
social support structures. *See* community networks
SOGIEcon (Sexual Orientation, Gender Identity/Expression Conference), 32
Solorzano, Daniel, 270
Sontag, Susan, 121, 249–50
Spaces of Hope (Harvey), 64
Speaking Tiger Press, 15
Spencer, Carrie, 15
Star Trek (television series), 89
Stefancic, Jean, 270, 276

Steinkeller, Elisabeth, 134
Stork, Francisco X., 258
storytelling: as activism, 279–87; as appropriation, 277–79; as bridge narrative, 284–85; counternarratives, 122, 136–37, 265, 270; and displacement, 273–77
Storytelling for Social Justice (Bell), 264
stress, as risk factor for illnesses, 11, 23, 43, 46, 50–51
Stridsberg, Sara, 156
Substance Abuse and Mental Health Services Administration (US), 41, 42
substance use disorder (SUD), 37–53; criminalization of, 37, 40–41; in healthcare system, 37; medicalization of, 37; in public health system, 37; treatment in US, 40–43
suicide and suicidal ideation, 252–53, 261n5; in *Darius the Great*, 94, 97, 99, 101
surgery, of conjoined twins. *See* separation surgery
Surprising Power of a Good Dumpling, The (Chim), 257–58

Take Up Thy Bed and Walk (Keith), 8
Tannen, Antje, 4, 8, 15
Taylor, Mildred D., 3
Teen Wolf (1985 film), masculinity in, 226–27, 230
Teen Wolf (2011–2017 television series), 225–43; compared with other TV series, 227–28; friendship in, 228, 232; friendship/informal care in, 232–37; hospitals in, 237–42; masculinity in, 227, 229–30, 231–32, 242–43; patient-practitioner relationship in, 229–32
telehealth, 23
television. *See Teen Wolf*
therapy practices, Changing FACES Counseling & Wellness, 21
Thomas, Angie, 38, 39
Those Extraordinary Twins (Twain), 61
Tiwari, Tamanna, 174
tooth decay, 164
Transhealth (organization), 21–22, 32
trans youth: healthcare for, 14, 21–33; publications by and for, 118–19

Trick of the Light, A (Metzger), 253–54
"Trip To, A" book series, 170
Trip to the Dentist, A (Smith), 170
Trites, Roberta Seelinger, 7–8, 268
Tronto, Joan, 233
Turtles All the Way Down (Green), 246–47, 254
Twain, Mark, 61
twelve-step approach to rehabilitation, 41, 44, 45–46, 52
twins, conjoined. *See* conjoinment
Two Little Knights of Kentucky, The (Johnston), 274–75

Ubbes, Valerie A., 7, 15
United Kingdom, 4; nursing workforce in, 154; overview of healthcare in, 12–13; prevalence of hyperemesis gravidarum in, 145. *See also* Comics Youth
UN Convention on the Rights of the Child, 144
United States: child caregiving in, 143; federal initiative for oral health literacy, 171; historicizing masculine silence in, 87–92; militarism and masculinity in, 90, 102n2; nursing workforce in, 154; Office of Minority Health, 173; overview of healthcare in, 9–11, 16n5; prevalence of hyperemesis gravidarum in, 145; treatment of substance use disorder in, 40–43
Unterholzner, Birgit, 130

vaccinations, 293, 296
Valint, Alexandra, 5
verse novels, 59–60
veterinarians, 212–14, 227
veterinary ethics, 214–17, 218
Vidali, Amy, 258
vile bodies, 204, 209, 220n1. *See also* artificial life (ALife)
Visit to Community Helpers book series, 177
Visit to the Dentist's Office, A (Murphy), 177–78

wage gap, 25
Wahl, Otto F., 253

War and Gender (Goldstein), 88
Warin, Megan, 250
"waste people," 275–76
Weight of Our Sky, The (Alkaf), 257
We Need Diverse Books, 265
werewolves, and hegemonic masculinity, 226–27, 231. See also *Teen Wolf*
Where We Are and Where We Should Be (Comics Youth), 118
Why We Go to the Dentist (Clark), 178
Wickham, Anastasia, 249
Wicks, Stephen, 88, 102n8
Williams, Ian, 112
Wintergirls (Anderson), 252, 256
women: medical education for, 273; and reform movement, 265, 267–68; social roles in *Little Colonel* books, 283–84
Women of Color Health Equity Collective (WOCHEC), 10, 16, 290–97
Woodstein, B.J., 4, 13, 15
Words on Bathroom Walls (Walton), 255
writing as self-care and as caregiving, 200–201

Yang, Kelly, 10
Yosso, Tara J., 270
Young, Suzanne, 252
young adult (YA) fiction: media in, 256; mental health in, 85
youth. *See* children

Zimmermann, Martina, 122, 123
Zimring, Carl A., 271–72

Printed in the United States
by Baker & Taylor Publisher Services